Dialectic

A scholarly journal of thought leadership, education and practice in the discipline of visual communication design

Volume II, Issue I—Summer 2018

Peer review is facilitated under the responsibility of The AIGA DEC and *Dialectic's* Editorial Board and Producer.

Dialectic is a fully open access, biannual journal devoted to the critical examination of issues that affect design education, research, and inquiry into their effects on the practice of design. Michigan Publishing, the hub of scholarly publishing at the University of Michigan, publishes *Dialectic* on behalf of the AIGA (American Institute of Graphic Arts) Design Educators Community (DEC).

ISBN: 978-1-60785-510-1
http://dialectic.aiga.org is the URL for *Dialectic's* home page on the web.

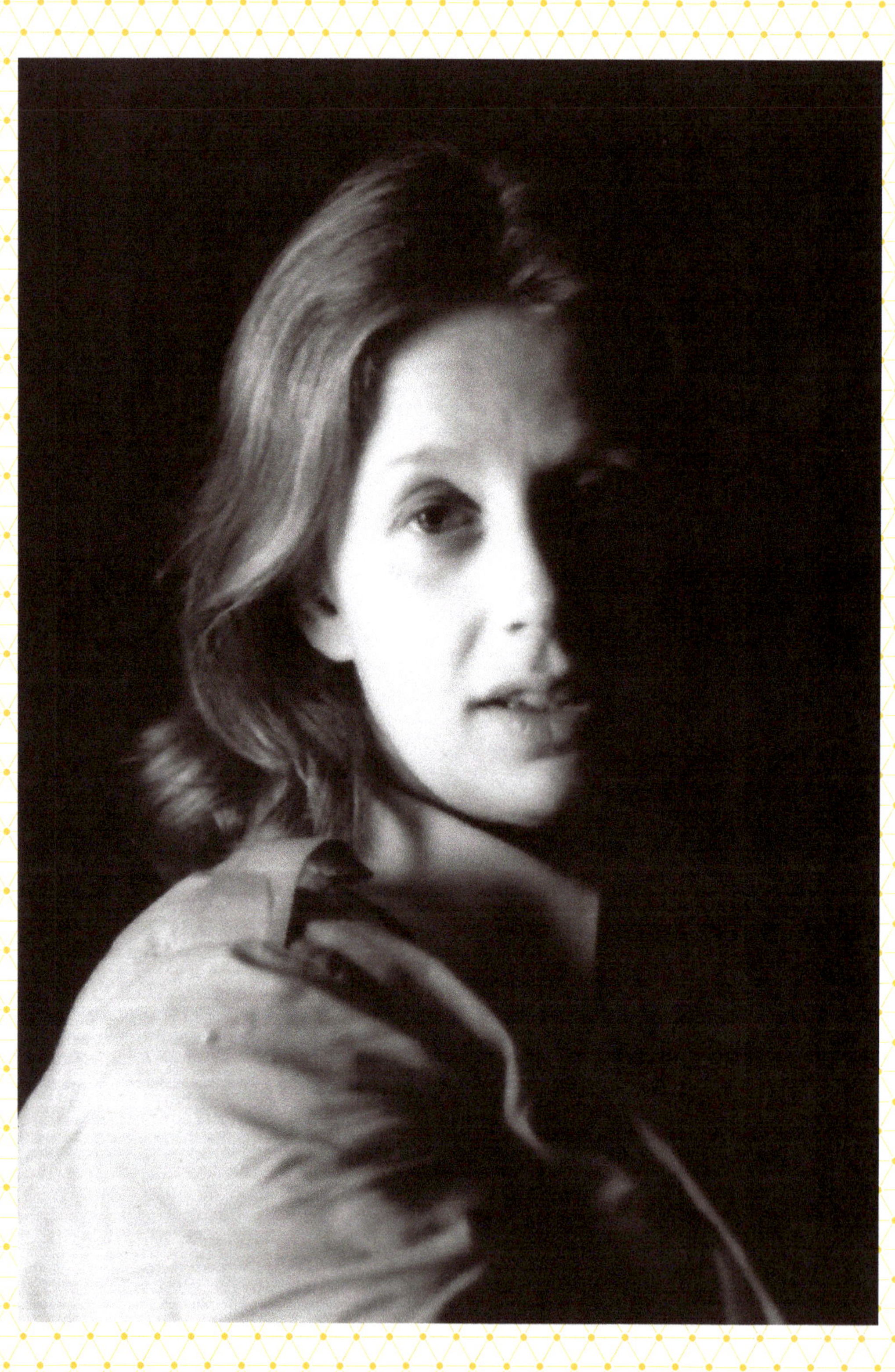

In Memoriam:

Joan Laura Secrest

May 25, 1938—March 10, 2018

Scholarly editor par excellence

Cherished member of Dialectic's internal editing team

"There's a special place in heaven AND *hell for editors—we don't merely straddle the divide so much as we're lashed to it. I'll be thanked and damned eternally for my critical efforts on behalf of all the authors I've worked with over the years..."*

"If I had a nickel for every college professor and senior research fellow who couldn't believe their precious scholarly prose needed critical, developmental editing, I'd have enough metal to build my very own goddamned aircraft carrier."

Contents

Dialectic Volume II, Issue I: Front Matter

Improvisation in the Design Classroom

NIDA ABDULLAH[1] AND DENISE GONZALES CRISP[2]

1. Michigan State University, USA
2. North Carolina State University, USA

SUGGESTED CITATION: Abdullah, N. & Gonzales Crisp, D. "Improvisation in the Design Classroom." *Dialectic,* 2.1 (2018): pgs. 10-17. DOI: http://dx.doi.org/10.3998/dialectic.14932326.0001.301

Abstract

This essay is a discourse on the value and benefits of utilizing improvisation, imbued with specific practices and rules, into design curricula as a means to:

- teach and model responsiveness within a given learning moment,
- facilitate students' interaction with the immediate social circumstances that contextualize a given design challenge, and
- prepare them to be ready for the uncertainties inherent in design processes.

The authors describe their version of an improvisational mindset, and present three classroom-based scenarios that demonstrate ways in which improvisational thinking can alter design processes to shift student mindsets from the all-too-common "I must solve this problem so that it answers a specific question" approach to "We should construct something together and see what it tells us."

> *"Designing, if it is to survive as an activity through which we transform our lives, on earth and beyond, has itself to be redesigned, continuously."*
>
> John Chris Jones, in *Designing Designing.* London, UK: Architecture Design and Technology Press (Longman Group UK Limited): 1991, pgs. xi–xii.

Improvisation in the Design Classroom

NIDA ABDULLAH & DENISE GONZALES CRISP

Our roles as designers have become undeniably complex, as media is now vastly accessible through almost infinitely rich technological means. Most of the information we consume and help construct is in constant flux, changing and evolving from one moment to the next. Preparing design students to actively participate in such dynamic, systemically complex circumstances, much less to positively influence them, calls for pedagogic approaches and methods that achieve two primary goals. First, they must ensure that students learn to engage in responsive, flexible thinking that allows them to adjust to the moment; second, they must help students become reflective enough to handle interactions within evolving sets of social circumstances, so that they are ever ready for uncertainty.

This type of pedagogical thinking is described in the book *A New Culture of Learning: Cultivating Imagination for a World of Constant Change,* where Douglas Thomas and John Seely Brown liken culture to the matter that scientists grow in petri dishes under controlled conditions. The scientist does not interfere with the process because the very point of the experiment is to allow the culture—constrained and affected by the medium and environment—to uninhibitedly reproduce, "and then see what happens." Unlike the view of culture that seeks stability and adapts to change when forced, this perspective views culture as responding to its surroundings organically rather than trying to alter the circumstances as a response after the fact. In other words, culture *thrives* on change, and integrates change "as one of its environmental variables," which creates further change as situations and the circumstances that affect them morph and evolve over time.[1]

Thomas and Seely Brown propose play as a strategy for embracing and adapting to change, rather than attempting to grow from it. Implicit in this perspective, in terms of how it can be effectively applied to formulating and operating design pedagogy, is the active participation of students and teachers in the discovery of viable and innovative design possibilities while regularly forestalling the more formulaic problem-to-solution equation. In improvisation, all concerned parties involved in a given scenario have agency—the freedom and expectation that anyone and everyone can affect how it evolves. All are engaged equally in the process. Judgement is suspended during the course of the exercise so that the gameplay can run its course organically.

---

1 Seely Brown, J., Thomas, D., *A New Culture of Learning: Cultivating the imagination for a world of constant change.* Charleston, SC, USA: CreateSpace Independent Publishing Platform, a DBA of On-Demand Publishing, LLC. 2011.

Improvisation as a Model for Play

As design educators, we (the authors) have written exercises and delivered workshops that promote and model such improvisational values in the studio classroom. When people improvise, they respond to immediate circumstances spontaneously rather than attempt to alter them. Improvising involves free association, logic, and no small amount of imagination. These exercises invoke group improv performances, wherein players collaboratively construct unpredictable narratives guided by a set of constraints, or rules of play.

Three practices characterize group improvisation: 1) everyone participates; 2) everyone contributes; 3) everyone applauds, for themselves and for everyone else in the room, for any reason, and throughout a session ("high-fives" abound).

Everyone Participates: A group of people, such as students and their teachers, collectively participate in improvisational construction, each bringing his or her personal experience, physicality, knowledge, inclinations, imagination, and aspirations to the *group* production. The thing, or "moment," under construction would be quite different if even only one person were not to participate. Everyone in the group can make a viable contribution bringing little other than their own free associations, immediate responses, and consequent ideas.

Everyone Contributes: Improv performances are built from what is said and acted out moment-to-moment, under the single principle "the only wrong answer is no answer." To say or do nothing would be to disengage with the most important goal of group improvisation: *together construct a thing that did not exist before.* Active involvement without fear of "doing it wrong" deters the tendency to have second-thoughts when making decisions (which are ultimately ephemeral). Hesitation delays the improvised scene and suspends the play. And because each person contributes to the formation of a scene, each has a stake in the results. Individual investment for the good of the whole tethers everyone to the goal.

Everyone Applauds: All people in the process of learning, whether amongst others or individually with a tutor, perhaps even alone, are vulnerable to feelings of insecurity and rejection, especially in a social environment. Even a teacher, who facilitates but one small part of the learning process, is vulnerable. Everyone involved is required to support each other in order to avoid hesitation or being "wrong," and must work together towards a shared goal. The realization that all participants share in this vulnerability simultaneously helps to create the supportive environment that effective improv requires. The nearly constant applause that is central to much of improv practice—appreciative and supportive feedback—indirectly acknowledges the vulnerability inherent in social creation and learning, and it encourages participants to take risks. Positive audible and visible responsiveness between all participants is a means of recognizing and confirming everyone's courage as they openly participate and contribute to the outcome. This type of exchange is essential to helping individuals engaged in challenging learning processes to first embrace the personal and social discomfort in which they are immersed during a given moment, and then use it to empower their ability to think inventively in ways that they were too inhibited to consider before.

These three practices foster organic and energetic responses to many different types and sets of circumstances, including sensory stimuli, implied and expressed concepts, and individuated actions and statements—each of which is always present on the improv stage (as it is in life).

Improv "rules of play" guide the unscripted performance, and these relatively simple rules are easy to follow. Our three rules of play align with the founder of *Improv LA* and "long form improv" master Keith Saltojanes' primary tenets, which state that the first rule of improvisation is to *"Listen."*[2] He teaches that one cannot respond to events occurring in a given moment if he or she is not paying attention. His second rule (more commonly considered the first rule of

2 Saltojanes, K. "Rules of Improv class lecture," *Improv LA*, May 15, 2011. Online. Available at: https://player.fm/series/improvla (Accessed June 11, 2017).

improv) is *"Say Yes...And."*[3] Players agree to agree with anything that other players state or perform, to accept statements and actions as true, and to add verbal details and physical deeds or gestures to whatever was initially stated or performed. Saltojanes' third rule is *"Support."*[4] It argues that all players must receive the actions and statements of others as *genius!* (Applause!) Saltojanes' fourth rule is *"Assume You Know:"*[5] if, in a given scene, one player points to a tiger in the room, the other players must accept the idea that there is in fact a tiger in the room and assume that they know why it is there, or how it got there, no questions asked. Other players are not supposed to respond with a query like "How'd that tiger get in here?" Rather, a player might respond with something like, "I see you left the front door open, *again*." With these and Saltojanes' other rules of play in mind (i.e. "mistakes are invitations"), the players begin the performance by responding to a prompt of some sort—a word ("oatmeal"), a location ("the moon"), or perhaps a phrase ("sailors cooking dinner").

Improvisation in the Design Classroom

Our endeavor to bring improvisation into studio courses is manifested in a number of exercises and workshops that we write and conduct in our courses as design educators.These improvisational experiments exploit aspects of the theatrical improv ethos to expand student thinking and reveal design options during the ideation, iteration, and refinement phases of the design process. We will now discuss three of the workshops we have developed and tested in our undergraduate studio courses that make use of improv, as well as offer additional approaches to design pedagogy.

The Improv Critique

The *Improv Critique* is a means of bringing a given sampling of student work out from under the constraints imposed upon it by students' often limited perceptions of the possibilities—an initial narrow range of conventional ideas. Our goal is to help students discover more surprising and engaging design. Improv critique begins by forming students into groups of four or five. We ask each student to submit something they're currently working on, such as a logo iteration, a series of page spreads, or an interface screen. One by one, each student in the group presents the work to be "critiqued" on a table or a wall (print media), or full screen on a large display monitor (screen media). We have learned that, to aid focus, the work being discussed should be isolated from other visual stimuli that might distract attention, although attending to this is not crucial to the success of the exercise.

Recall that one of Saltojanes' primary rules of improv is to *Listen* to what is said by those around. Because this exercise also includes a visual component (the work), we add the rule *"Look"* at the artifact under discussion. The critique begins as one person in the group offers a concrete statement about what he or she reads, perceives, or observes in the work. He or she might state, "It's a lonely sky," or "The red is smiling," or "It's an upside-down coffee cup." Because the exercise asks students to enter into a wholly imaginative space of play, everything that is said initially is in fact true in that moment. Another person in the group then responds (again, while also looking at the work) with *"Yes,* and...," and adds a new bit of information, such as "Yes, and the sky is lonely because it has no clouds;" "Yes, and the red is smiling like a Cheshire cat;" "Yes, and coffee is spilled all over the table." Because every addition becomes true upon utterance, statements are spoken in the present tense. Additionally, students who try to plan what they will say instead of listening to the previous statement and building on it find that their contributions do not fit into the flow of the emerging narrative.

The improv critique continues in this manner with each student speaking one after the other, around and around within the group. Meanwhile, the person whose work is being "critiqued" writes down what he or she hears. The round is complete when either time is up (usually between five and ten minutes, depending on the complexity of the piece), or the round yields at least a dozen or more "Yes, ands." Upon completion of the improv critique, everyone applauds

3 Ibid.
4 Ibid.
5 Ibid.

(Applause!) before the group moves on to critique the next person's work.

Improvisation requires free and immediate associations, individual interpretation, and timely and responsive reactions to advance the narrative. We have found that design students sometimes have a difficult time making direct and imaginative statements in this context. They often start by describing the thing they're looking at literally ("It's red and green," "It's making use of a classical typeface," and so on). We have found that we need to prompt students to move beyond simple formal descriptions, encouraging them to freely interpret what they see and respond to what has been said. Students also initially tend to employ common "design speak," prefacing statements with tropes such as "I think it looks like...," "It feels like...," or "It reminds me of...." Such deferrals direct focus away from the work being discussed and prevent students from engaging in an exchange rooted in the all-important *now.* Students also typically begin with "Yes, but...," which implies rejection rather than acceptance of what is offered. SO—"buts" are not allowed. Nor are "ifs." Only "Yes, and" can propel the critique into an unpredictable narrative.

Changing up the group members and running the exercise several times, perhaps with other artifacts that students are in the process of realizing, gives the students more material to work with and affords time for everyone to become comfortable with the practice in order to understand its potential for instigating lateral creative thinking.

The "I Wish..." Critique

The *"I Wish..." Critique* uses improv practices and rules to guide the iterative development of students' design work and help them expand the scope of their formal and conceptual ideas. This activity places students outside of project brief criteria (should these exist), and aims to interrupt both their self-imposed constraints, or those that have been inspired by language in the brief, or both. We have found that students who attempt to design work under these types of constraints can inhibit their own progress toward developing fresh (for them) ideas. As of this writing in January 2018, we have only tested this critique format at the point in the design process when a given project is nearing resolution, at least in the mind of the students who are anxious to complete a project.

To facilitate this type of critique, we separate students in the class into pairs, and then ask each student to present some part of his or her project for review by his or her partner. Paired students gather around a large piece of paper, such as butcher paper. Tracing paper, markers, scissors, adhesives, and other making materials are at the ready to facilitate quick ideation during the *"I Wish..." Critique.*

The pairs of students critique one student's work at a time. The student whose work is under review may take a brief minute or two to describe a particular aspect of or about his or her project, but long, drawn out defenses of the work are pointless in this exercise. The dialogue is prompted with the reviewer stating three "wishes" that he or she believes the work should fulfill in three successive rounds. The first of these wishes is practical: "I wish the letters were larger in scale." The second is arbitrary: "I wish the letters were reflective." The third is an absurd wish: "I wish the letters acted like kids jumping in a bounce house." In improv fashion, the student being critiqued cannot question or reject the reviewing student's wishes, but must accept them as points-of-fact that must be addressed. (Applause!) A student who express "wishes" likely has reasons for making particular wishes for a specific work, especially the practical one. However, the improv rule *"Assume You Know"* comes into play here, which means that the student whose work is under review accepts that the reasons and rationales that are guiding his or her partner's wishes are sound.

Once one student makes the first wish on behalf of his or her partner, both students set out to realize the wish through drawing, diagramming, illustrating, etc. using available materials. To visually manifest the wish, the partners build on each other's ideas in one or a series of connected visualizations. In this way, both students assume ownership of the work and together, enact the wish fulfillment with the butcher paper before them. Once a pair of students fulfills the three wishes for the first of their pair, they reverse roles and repeat the process for the second.

Following both the *"Improv"* and the *"I Wish..."* critiques, we ask students to quickly develop additional iterations, or to engage in further ideation, regarding a specific component of the project-in-progress (this sometimes occurs collaboratively, and other times occurs independently). Immediate return to the design allows students to apply to the work at hand concepts and ideas uncovered and/or invented during the critique, which effectively influences ensuing production. The visualized "wishes" serve as a document of the conversation as students proceed toward the final work. Students need not heed the wishes literally. Rather, the wishes and the ideas they spark are meant to encourage lateral thinking, to help students see their work in a fresh light and return to the full scope of the project with renewed energy.

The "OK, GO!" Workshop

The title of this workshop, *"OK, GO!"*, reflects its purpose: to jump-start ideation early in the students' design process with the aim of initiating concepts through visual exploration toward unforeseeable options. The first round of this workshop launches with two trigger questions: "What is it?" and "What is it not?"—the "it" being whatever students are working on to fulfill the parameters for a given project: a museum brand identity, for example. The students, teachers, and TAs (Teaching Assistants) who are participating in the workshop shout out anything that comes to mind that might be informed, at least in part, by their acquired knowledge about and lived experience with whatever is being designed. Someone then records the statements on a chalkboard or whiteboard: "It is free!;" "It is multifarious!;" "It is not silent;" "It is not scary." Everyone in the room is called upon to contribute at least one word in response to each of the two trigger questions. The words need not be the truest, nor the most exact or accurate, but, once they have been stated and recorded as concepts, they become "fact for the moment," as improv rules dictate.

A second round of this workshop invites all of the participants to add a descriptive association as a phrase to the first round of statements and words to render each more concrete. For example: "It is free!" might be amended by "...like *Harris Teeter*™ sugar cookies," or by "...like Wikipedia," or by "...like air." Any and all associations offered become valid and are written on the chalkboard or whiteboard. These phrases then serve as prompts for the ensuing "performance," which entails rapid image creation in a series of quick, five-minute rounds. Students sketch, draw, photograph, collage, construct, etc. using any media at hand and any digital software they have access to. In the first few rounds of these experiences, students create new images. In subsequent rounds, they build upon, add to, and/or manipulate selected images from previous rounds, applying the improv ethos of trying to add on to what has been posited previously as truths. These latter rounds are meant to evolve rather than to refine the images. Students end these processes by papering the walls of the classroom with all of the images they have produced. (Applause!) Together, the class identifies and discusses visual and conceptual patterns, triggers, and provocations as they affect and are affected by the project parameters.

In our experience, students, upon completing the *"OK, GO!"* workshops, begin the project with openness and concrete starting points. Students effectively triangulate their "improv" experiences and outcomes with their own hopes for the project, as well as with the project requirements. As creative individuals, design students naturally "put-two-and-two together" in order to make something that not only has not been made before, but that can also be considered *good.* When the whole class contributes to this goal together, the design work developed by each student with input from his or her peers is positively affected.

Picking up threads

The three exercises described in this article represent some of the many ways of introducing and then practicing the improvisational mindset into the design classroom. Improvisation is just one framework educators can use to teach students that uncertainty is an asset, and that responsiveness to change is an essential skill that enhances the design process. The beneficial outcomes of learning exercises like these, we speculate, make for more broad-minded design students who will carry such skills beyond the safe margins of the learning environment.

Pedagogical approaches using similar methods have been explored since at least the early 20th century. *Blueprint for Counter Education* was conceived by Maurice Stein and Larry Miller and designed by Marshall Heinrichs (1970), and included three, folded 45" × 37 ¼" posters plus a booklet entitled "Shooting Script." [6] The publication served as a syllabus of sorts for a program of courses offered beginning in 1971 at the *California Institute of the Arts* (formerly the *Chouinard Institute*) in its Department of Critical Studies.

The posters were originally designed to function as "a portable learning environment for a new process-based model of education, and a bibliography and checklist that map[s] patterns and relationships between radical thought and artistic practices—from the avant-gardes [sic] to postmodernism." Although anchored in the philosophies and theories of Herbert Marcuse and Marshall McLuhan, the posters presented students with a wide range of discussion points and potential trajectories of study. Selecting as a starting point a theorist, philosopher, or concept from one of the posters is akin to picking up a prompt to initiate an improv scene. In use, *Blueprint* inspired what were called "wanderings." Students embarked on explorations that were "predicated on individual perceptions, relationships among participants, text and visual pairings, and the immediate environment in time (physical contexts)." In a word, improvisation. The fact that *Blueprint* was re-printed in 2016 suggests renewed interest in pedagogical and curricular reform in the process of adapting to diverse cultures that thrive on change. [7]

Inserting improv practices and rules of play into design (or any) pedagogy teaches students to appreciate and accept that which can be expressed and that can occur "in the moment." They also learn that this type of acceptance precludes judgement in this process. Improv practices are, by definition, social and collaborative, and, if the ground is well-prepared, lead to fertile environments for learning and creativity. Improv rules help to encourage participation and elicit responsiveness in any momentary design scenario. These rules exemplify the value of expanding and adding to the ideas of others while maintaining a focus on the larger goal of generating appropriate and surprising design rather than on boosting individual performance. The lessons of improvisation, as well as the experience of improvising, help shift the design mindset from "I must solve this problem" to "We must construct something together and see what it tells us." [8]

Improv players are fond of prefacing performances with something along the lines of "This is the very first and very last time you will see this." What might happen if design educators were to attempt to guide their students through thinking and problem-solving processes wherein the principal ethos is exactly that? (Applause!)

References

Jones, J.C. *Designing Designing*. London, UK: Architecture Design and Technology Press (Longman Group UK Limited): 1991, pgs. xi–xii.

Saltojanes, K. "Rules of Improv class lecture," *Improv LA*, May 15, 2011. Online. Available at: https://player.fm/series/improvla (Accessed June 11, 2017).

Schnapp, J., Cronin, P., Michaels, A. *Blueprint for Counter Education, Expanded Reprint*. New York, NY, USA: Inventory Press, 2016.

Seely Brown, J., Thomas, D., A *New Culture of Learning: Culti-vating the imagination for a world of constant change. Charleston,* SC, USA: CreateSpace Independent Publishing Platform, a DBA of On-Demand Publishing, LLC. 2011. Online.

6 Stein, M, Miller, L., Heinrichs, M. *Blueprint for Counter Education*. New York, NY, USA: Doubleday, 1970.

7 Schnapp, J., Cronin, P., Michaels, A. *Blueprint for Counter Education, Expanded Reprint*. New York, NY, USA: Inventory Press, 2016.

8 Seely Brown, J., Thomas, D., *A New Culture of Learning: Cultivating the imagination for a world of constant change*. Charleston, SC, USA: CreateSpace Independent Publishing Platform, a DBA of On-Demand Publishing, LLC. 2011. Online. Available at: https://www.createspace.com/ (Accessed 2 April, 2018).

Available at: https://www.createspace.com/ (Accessed 2 April, 2018).

Stein, M, Miller, L., Heinrichs, M. *Blueprint for Counter Education.* New York, NY, USA: Doubleday, 1970.

Nida Abdullah is an Assistant Professor in the Department of Art, Art History and Design at Michigan State University. Prior to this appointment, she served as a Lecturer of Graphic Design at the Welch School of Art and Design in the College of Arts and Sciences at Georgia State University.

Her research explores communication and participation hierarchies in computer supported collaborative work (CSCW) processes and ad-hoc approaches as a model for design research, practice, and pedagogy. She has presented on *Designing the Participatory Design Experience* and contributed to *Respectful Design: Decolonization as an Urgent Imperative.* She has worked on projects with various cultural and educational institutions, including MASS MoCA, Project M and Winterhouse, SOMArts Cultural Center, the United Nations, UNOY, The Duke Center for Science Education, and the IEI Public Policy Institute. She holds a BGD and MGD from the College of Design at North Carolina State University.

Denise Gonzales Crisp is a graphic designer, writer, and professor of graphic design at North Carolina State University College of Design (since 2002), where she currently directs the graduate program. She holds an M.F.A. in graphic design from the California Institute of the Arts and a B.F.A. from Art Center College of Design.

She is author of *Graphic Design in Context: Typography* (Thames & Hudson, 2011). She has been invited to speak at numerous conferences, universities, and events—at TYPO Talks, ATypI (Association Typographique Internationale/the International Typography Association) in 2009 (Mexico City), the Walker Art Center (Minneapolis), GraficEurope (Berlin), RMIT (Melbourne), ArtCity (Calgary), among others. She has exhibited her work both nationally and internationally, and is published widely in design journals; among these are *Émigré, Metropolis, Print, Graphis, Eye, Items,* and *KAK.*

Gonzales Crisp was senior designer for the Art Center College of Design in Pasadena and principal of SuperStove!, a design studio focussed on designing "books for the cultural sector". She designed *Utopian Entrepreneur* by Brenda Laurel, part of the *Mediawork* pamphlet series for MIT Press, edited by Peter Lunenfeld on "the intersections of art, design, technology, and market culture."

Gonzales Crisp has taught graphic design at Art Center College of Design, CalArts, and the Otis Art Institute. She sits on the Executive Board of *Design Inquiry,* a non-profit educational organization devoted to researching design issues in intensive team-based gatherings, with (co-founder) Margo Halverson, (co-founder) Peter Hall, Emily Luce, Anita Cooney, Gabrielle Esperdy, Gail Swanlund, Joshua Singer, and Ben Van Dyke.

Dialectic Volume II, Issue I: Long-form Case Study Report

Envisioning Futures of Design Education: An Exploratory Workshop with Design Educators

SAPNA SINGH,[1] NICOLE LOTZ,[2] AND ELIZABETH B.-N. SANDERS[3]

1. The Ohio State University, Columbus, Ohio, USA
2. The Open University, Milton Keynes, UK
3. The Ohio State University, Columbus, Ohio, USA and MakeTools, USA

SUGGESTED CITATION: Singh, S., Lotz, N. & Sanders, E.B.-N. "Envisioning Futures of Design Education." *Dialectic,* 2.1 (2018): pgs. 19-46. DOI: http://dx.doi.org/10.3998/dialectic.14932326.0001.302

Abstract

The demand for innovation in the creative economy has seen the adoption and adaptation of design thinking and design methods into domains outside design, such as business management, education, healthcare, and engineering. Design thinking and methodologies are now considered useful for identifying, framing and solving complex, often wicked social, technological, economic and public policy problems. As the practice of design undergoes change, design education is also expected to adjust to prepare future designers to have dramatically different demands made upon their general abilities and bases of knowledge than have design career paths from years past. Future designers will have to develop skills and be able to construct and utilize knowledge that allows them to make meaningful contributions to collaborative efforts involving experts from disciplines outside design. Exactly how future designers should be prepared to do this has sparked a good deal of conjecture and debate in the professional and academic design communities.

This report proposes that the process of creating future scenarios that more broadly explore and expand the role, or *roles,* for design and designers in the world's increasingly interwoven and interdependent societies can help uncover core needs and envision framework(s) for design education. This approach informed the creation of a workshop [1] held at the Design Research Society conference in Brighton, UK in June of 2016, where six design educators shared four future scenarios that served as catalysts for conversations about the future of design education. Each scenario presented a specific future design education context. One scenario described the progression of design education as a core component of K-12 curricula; another scenario situated design at the core of a network of globally-linked local Universities; the third scenario highlighted the expanding role of designers over time; and the final scenario described a distance design education context that made learning relevant and "close" to an individual learner's areas of interest. Forty participants in teams of up to six were asked to collaboratively visualize a possible future vision of design education based on one of these four scenarios and supported by a toolkit consisting of a set of trigger cards (with images and text), along with markers, glue and flipcharts. The collaborative visions [2] that were jointly created as posters using the toolkit and then presented by the teams to all the workshop participants and facilitators are offered here as a case study. Although inspired by different scenarios, their collectively envisioned futures of what design education should facilitate displayed some key similarities. Some of those were:

- Future design education curricula will focus on developing collaborative approaches within which faculty and students are co-learners;
- These curricula will bring together ways of learning and knowing that stem from multiple disciplines; and
- Learning in and about the natural environment will be a key goal (the specifics of how that would be accomplished were not elaborated upon.)

In addition, the need for transdisciplinarity [3] was expressed across the collaborative visions created by each of the teams, but the manner that participants chose to express their ideas about this varied. Some envisioned that design would evolve by drawing on other disciplinary knowledge, and others envisioned that design would gradually integrate with other disciplines.

---

1 This workshop was attended by 40+ participants who formed six working groups.

2 Collaborative vision is defined here as a collectively developed and shared imaginative idea of the future that can then be used to guide a program of actions to realize the vision. The definition builds on what van der Helm defined as community vision (for more information about this, please reference p. 98 of Ruud van der Helm's article "The Vision Phenomenon: Towards a Theoretical Underpinning of Visions of the Future and the Process of Envisioning" in Volume 41, Issue 2 of *Futures Methodologies.*)

3 Transdisciplinarity refers to an approach that crosses and connects many disciplinary boundaries. It is especially relevant to identifying, framing and resolving complex and wicked problems that transcend the boundaries between two or more disciplines.

Envisioning Futures of Design Education:

An Exploratory Workshop with Design Educators

SAPNA SINGH, NICOLE LOTZ, & ELIZABETH B.-N. SANDERS

Introduction

Over the course of roughly the past 40 years, design practice and education across much of the world has been undergoing intensive changes to address shifts that have occurred as manufacturing economies have given way to service economies. Design processes have evolved from yielding mostly physical to digital products, and from a culture that celebrated "star designers" to cultures (plural) that celebrate co-designing with diverse design teams. [4,5] Design educators are faced with the challenge of keeping up with this rapid pace of change, as well as having to anticipate the kinds of future demands that design education experiences will have to meet. A crucial set of questions stem from this: what do design educators and administrators of design education need to know about where design education is heading in the next five to fifteen years and *why*? How can they participate in shaping the knowledge and understanding that will guide its evolution to affect positive change?

This paper argues that it is important to gain a long-term and visionary understanding of social, technological, economic, environmental and political factors impacting design practice and education to develop curricula for future design programs. Curricula for design courses are often developed in response to external events: national or institutional structural changes, growth opportunities in particular industry sectors, or advances in knowledge in a particular discipline. Considering the dynamic complexities of their operational contexts, educators and educational administrators have very little opportunity

4 Broadbent, J. & Cross, N. "Design Education in the Information Age." Journal of Engineering Design, 14.4 (2003): pgs. 439–446.

5 Buchanan, R. "The Problem of Character in Design Education: Liberal Arts and Professional Specialization." International Journal of Technology and Design Education, 11.1 (2001): pgs. 13–26.

to develop a long-term vision for the design discipline. Furthermore, techniques and tools that have been shown to guide effective and practical curriculum design in higher education are scarce.[6] A long-term view of the possible futures for design education would allow design educators and their administrators to be more agile planners and more flexible facilitators. It would give them a better understanding of where design as a discipline might be headed, help them to identify curricular needs for those future(s), and facilitate their role in leading and shaping curricular change. This conceptual approach was the foundation for planning and facilitating a visioning workshop on the "Future of Design Education" that was conducted at the Design Research Society (DRS2016) conference in Brighton, UK. The goal of the workshop was to explore possible futures for design education based within the context of different future scenarios which presented factors, conditions and situations that could influence design education.[7]

This paper presents the observations distilled from this visioning workshop, and its outcomes are articulated in the form of a case-study report. It begins with a brief description of the visioning method that was facilitated by the workshop leaders to help workshop participants engage in the process of generating ideas that could guide or affect curricular change in design education. The report continues by describing the activities that transpired within the workshop itself, the description of the possible future scenarios impacting design education and culminates with a discussion of the visualizations representing the visions of the workshop participants. In this context, *visions* are descriptions of some of the issues, examined singly or in related groups, that design curricula of the future will have to effectively address. The report concludes with a critical examination of these visions, and highlights key observations, similarities and variations.

About the DRS Conference and Visioning Workshop

The DRS *2016 Conference,* held in Brighton, UK in June 2016, was attended by over 200 members of the international design education and research community. The presence and willing participation of such a large group of people who are engaged and invested in trying to effectively facilitate design education made this event conducive to fostering several discussions about the future of design education, including those that transpired within our visioning workshop. This 90-minute workshop was attended by about 40 conference participants.

6 Broadbent, J. & Cross, N. "Design Education in the Information Age." Journal of Engineering Design, 14.4 (2003): pgs. 439-446.

7 Singh, S., Irwin, T., Sanders, E., Stappers, P. J., Lotz, N., & Bohemia, E. "The Future of Design Education." Workshop facilitated at the Design Research Society Conference, Brighton, UK, June 2016. Online. Available at: https://drs2016.squarespace.com/564/?rq=future (Accessed January, 19, 2017).

A discussion about the future, or particular aspects of it, required the use of a methodology that offered a framework and stimuli that could trigger constructive discussion. [8] The workshop facilitators chose the format of a participatory design activity using a generative design toolkit [9] to provide participants with the means to collaboratively visualize their ideas about what specific aspects of the future of design education might look like. This format facilitated gathering viewpoints from a large group in the limited time of 90 minutes.

8 Van der Helm, R. "The vision phenomenon: Towards a theoretical underpinning of visions of the future and the process of envisioning." Futures Methodologies, 41.2 (2009): pgs. 96–104.

9 Sanders, E. B.-N. and Stappers, P. J. Convivial Toolbox: Generative Research for the Front End of Design. Amsterdam, The Netherlands: BIS Publishers, 2012.

A Description of the Workshop Toolkit

The toolkit developed for the workshop included a set of trigger cards (some depicted images and others contained text; see Figure 1 for examples), along with large paper, markers and glue. The cards were sorted into five categories titled *People, Places, Roles, Skills and Statements.* These five categories were identified by the workshop facilitators as some of the key components to visualizing any future visions for design education. *People* and *Places* cards contained images; *People* cards depicted images of people—mostly individuals—and some others depicted groups. *Places* cards depicted images of different places—some indoors and some outdoors. *Roles, Skills* and *Statement* cards contained text. *Roles* and *Skills* cards contained one or two words (e.g., "Learner," "Making Sense"), supported by a brief description elaborating upon that "role" or "skill". The *Statements* cards contained short statements, such as, "Design can lead change." Content on the cards could be interpreted in many different ways, including some associated with education and/or design. An inclusive trigger set was created to ensure that diverse options for instigating ideas and thinking were presented in the images or the text, and that there was no single dominating theme that pervaded the subject matter inherent in these. The images of people depicted in the *People* cards represented diverse age groups, ethnicity, and genders; the visuals depicted in the *Places* cards represented diverse settings such as indoor spaces, outdoor places and abstract visualizations of environments. Additionally, the toolkit included *Wild Cards,* which were blank cards. Participants could use them to add words and sketches of their own choosing. Overall, the complete set of trigger cards contained content that was quite broadly constituted, yet it also connected to the main ideas that would be presented by the individuals who acted as catalysts/facilitators in each of the four future scenarios. The participants had the option to use all, some or none of the images and text from the toolkit to build a visual collage on a large sheet of paper that represented their ideas about the future of design education in the context of one of the presented future scenarios.

Workshop Participants

The 40+ people who participated in the workshop included design educators and students from academic institutions located in many different countries, including the Netherlands, Germany, Denmark, Sweden, Switzerland, the United Kingdom, Hong Kong, Australia, and the United States.

Workshop Facilitators

The six workshop facilitators were design educators from five different university-level, educational institutions who each possessed varying levels of design education experience and expertise. Three of the facilitators are the co-authors of this report. Sapna Singh is a design researcher, strategist and Lecturer at The Ohio State University in the US; Liz Sanders is a Design Research consultant and an Associate Professor of Design at The Ohio State University; Terry Irwin is the Head of the School of Design at Carnegie Mellon University in the US; Pieter Jan Stappers is a faculty member of Industrial Design Engineering at Delft University of Technology in The Netherlands; Nicole Lotz is a Lecturer at the Open University in the UK; Erik Bohemia is the Program Director in the Institute for Design Innovation at Loughborough University in the UK.

Workshop Outline

The 90-minute workshop was divided into the following three parts:

1. Presentation of future scenarios: The workshop began with a presentation of four future scenarios by the facilitators. The five-minute presentation that introduced each scenario concluded with one or more questions for participants to consider regarding the overarching concept of visioning the future of design education.
2. Participatory design activity: The workshop participants organized themselves into groups of five to seven members. All of those sitting at a given table typically formed a group. Each group chose to discuss one of the future scenarios and visualize some aspects of what the future of design education might be like in the context of that scenario. The groups discussed the scenario, browsed through the toolkit, selected cards that could communicate their ideas

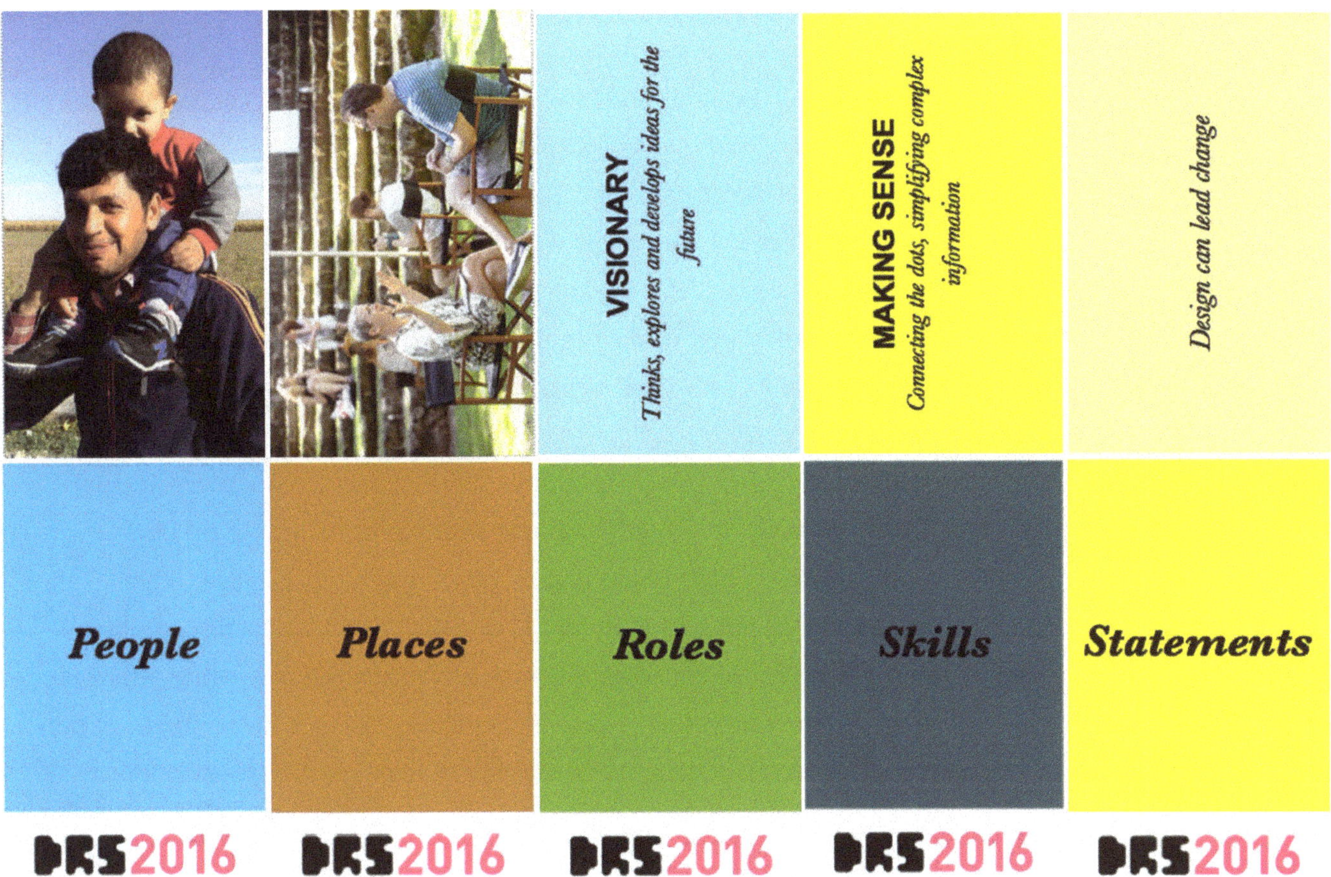

FIGURE 1: An example of trigger cards from the toolkit representing each of the five categories: *People, Places, Roles, Skills and Statements*. The cards were double-sided with the category names printed on one side and with an image or text printed on the other.

about how and why specific aspects regarding the future of design education might evolve or need to be addressed, and then used the cards to create a visual collage on a large (roughly 36" x 48") sheet of paper. They were also encouraged to add drawings and words of their own choosing to the collage.

3. Presentation of Visions: The workshop concluded with each group presenting their visions for the future of design education—as articulated in their collages—that highlighted the particular array of possibilities, concerns and contextual factors and issues that they felt could or should affect the future of design education. All of the presentations were audio and video-recorded so that the critical dialogues that occurred in and around them could be referenced to provide information and insights to future researchers.

Four Future Scenarios for Design Education

The four future scenarios presented by each of the facilitators or facilitation teams offered at least one provocative concept for addressing various aspects of the future of design education. Each facilitator or facilitation team articulated their distinct approaches and viewpoints that catalysed critical conversations across the group of workshop participants, and, eventually within each of the groups that were formed after the scenarios were presented. Each of the four future scenarios that were presented during our workshop are synopsized below:

Scenario #1: DRAW (Designing, Reading, Arithmetic and Writing)
Authored and presented by Liz Sanders and Sapna Singh

The DRAW (Designing, Reading, Arithmetic and Writing) scenario described a future where designing forms the core of a K–12 curriculum together with reading, arithmetic and writing (Figure 2). (K–12 is a term that, in many parts of the US and Canada, refers to primary/elementary, middle and high school education for children aged 5 to 18 years.) This curriculum has three stages:

- *a. Foundation in Grades K–3:* Students collaborate with their peers and family members to understand and develop concrete design knowledge, such as the process of developing a concept or idea and giving form to it. Students also develop foundational skills in empathy and collaboration. Teachers, designers and curriculum developers collaborate to develop toolkits for use in this effort. Children learn about designing through fun, hands-on experiences. They have classes, and workshops in making, repairing, reusing, and repurposing.
- *b. Exploration in Grades 4–7:* Students collaborate with local community members, including families in the neighborhood, businesses, and social and government organizations to tackle and design solutions that meet local community-based needs. The curriculum is project-based, and would bring together knowledge from multiple subject areas relevant to the context that surrounds a given project. Students learn about co-designing and develop toolkits to use in collaborative activities. Hacking (i.e., taking things apart to use the parts to make new things or facilitate better ways of doing things) is introduced in Grade 6.

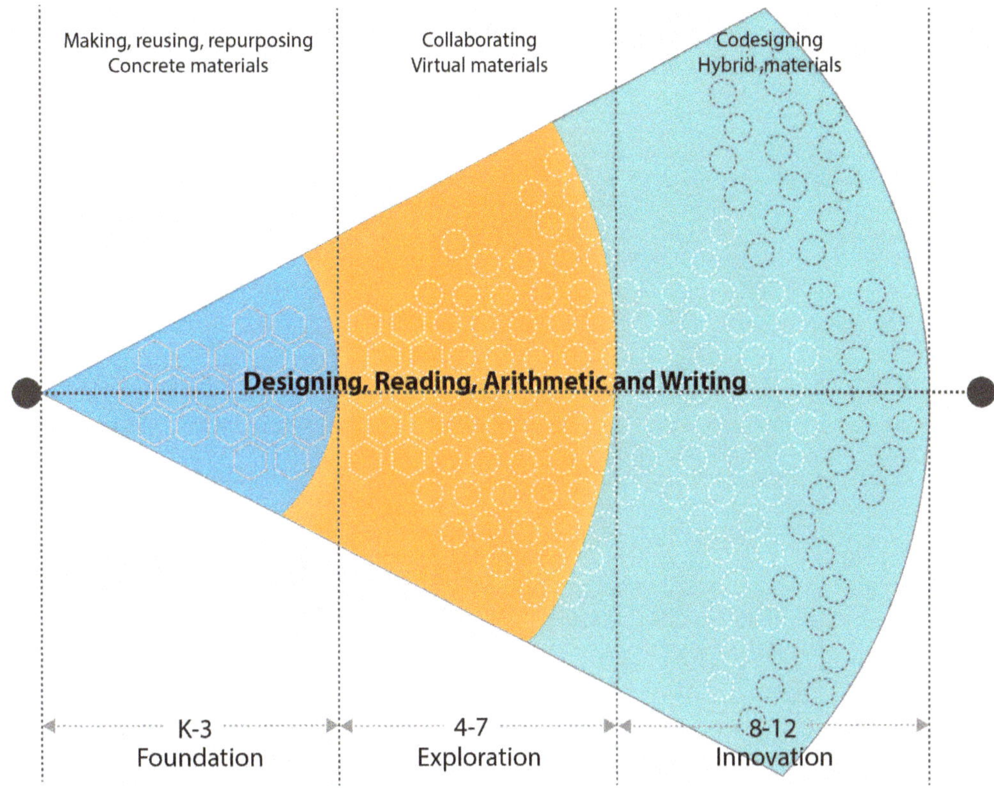

FIGURE 2: Graphic representation of the DRAW (Designing, Reading, Arithmetic and Writing) scenario for primary/elementary (grades K–3; five- to eight-year-old children), middle (grades 4–7; nine- to twelve-year-old children) and high school (grades 8–12; thirteen- to eighteen-year-old children) education.

c. ***Innovation in Grades 8–12:*** Students collaborate with social and public organizations to take on real world projects. They explore co-designing with community members across their region, their nation and internationally. Students develop their own co-design toolkits from hybrid (i.e., physical and digital) materials. They learn to effectively engage in the iterative processes of design by practicing it.

In this scenario, meaningful, sustained collaboration among teachers, families and the local community plays a significant role. In the DRAW scenario, the primary goal of K–12 education is to develop smart citizens who will be prepared to be agents of positive change. This scenario will require changes to be made in current assessment standards to place greater emphasis on multicultural, social and humanistic levels of achievement. The primary question was: *When designing forms the core of K-12 curricula, together with reading, writing and arithmetic, how will higher education in Design change?*

Scenario #2: The Cosmopolitan Localist
Authored and presented by Terry Irwin

The *Cosmopolitan Localist* scenario offered a framework for interdisciplinary education. This scenario is premised on the idea that, by 2030, a global network of Cosmopolitan Localist (CL) Universities would arise in which design will have evolved to be a core discipline on every campus (Figure 3). These universities will serve local and regional populations, and will be linked in their global exchange of knowledge and technology. In this new structure, academic disciplines will offer specialized learning and expertise that is embodied and applied in transdisciplinary collaboration that addresses *place-based problems.* Place-based problems are problems that are very specific to a location and require designing solutions that address its unique context. Faculty and students will 'toggle' between their home discipline and projects that have been undertaken within transdisciplinary labs to work on place-based projects and research. Faculty and students will often work in co-learning relationships in areas where deep expertise either does not yet exist or has been forgotten by 21st century societies. CL Universities will maintain close ties with local government/policy makers, social, political and environmental activists and entire communities, as well as a wide range of industry and non-profit partners.

The primary questions for the workshop participants to consider were: *What does a day-in-the-life of a CLU student look like? What are the core disciplines? What does it mean to be local? What does it mean to be cosmopolitan?*

The CL universities will have a common set of 'core' disciplines that are scaffolded by complementary disciplines representative of local/regional conditions, expertise, cultures and economy. Faculty and students will collaborate on projects, knowledge exchange, and best practices via technological interactions and physical exchanges. CL universities will provide spaces for students and faculty to participate in place-based community projects, take courses and conduct research (these form the "co-design labs" depicted at the center of Figure 3). CL students and faculty will visit traditional universities to make deeper dives into areas of knowledge or expertise that are embedded within a particular discipline or area of speciality. All CL students will take courses in two to four required 'gateway' disciplines, and design will be one of these. These courses will provide a practical and theoretical foundation for

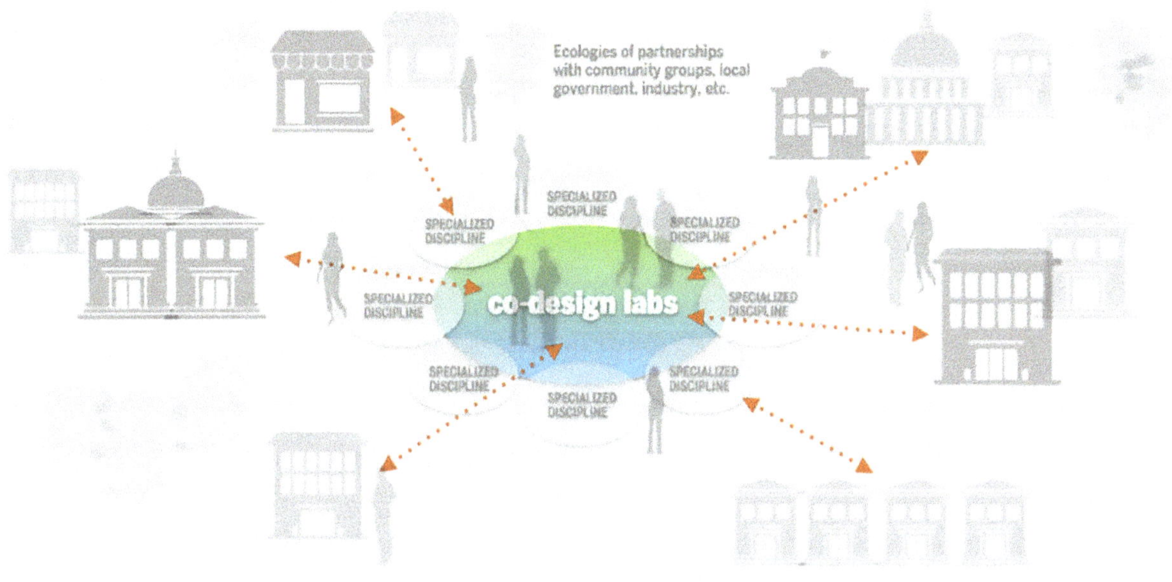

FIGURE 3: A graphical representation of the network of individuals, organizations and communities that are connected by co-design labs to Cosmopolitan Localist Universities.

place-based learning and problem-solving that emphasizes global awareness and responsibility. Students will customize degree pathways and spend about 75% of their time in transdisciplinary collaboration.

CL universities will be situated in areas where at least some indigenous flora/fauna remain so that the natural, place-based constraints and resources can inform solutions. Each CL University will be structured to help the students enrolled in it develop skills, knowledge and disciplines relevant to their particular eco-system. This is a cornerstone principle of place-based design. The University will transform into a catalyst for positive social and environmental change. Design and designers will play key roles in formulating and guiding this transformation.

Scenario #3: DesignX

Authored and presented by Pieter Jan Stappers

The *DesignX* scenario [10] highlights the expanding role of design and designers in modern societies around the world. Over the course of the last century, the primary intent of design has broadened from being a means to invent and distribute products to being a means to develop and effectively implement interfaces, interactions, experiences, services and now *complex systems*, where making a change involves contributions from many parties and actors.

10 Norman, D. & Stappers, P. J. "DesignX: Complex Sociotechnical Systems." She Ji: The Journal of Design, Economics, and Innovation, 1.2 (2015): pgs. 83–106.

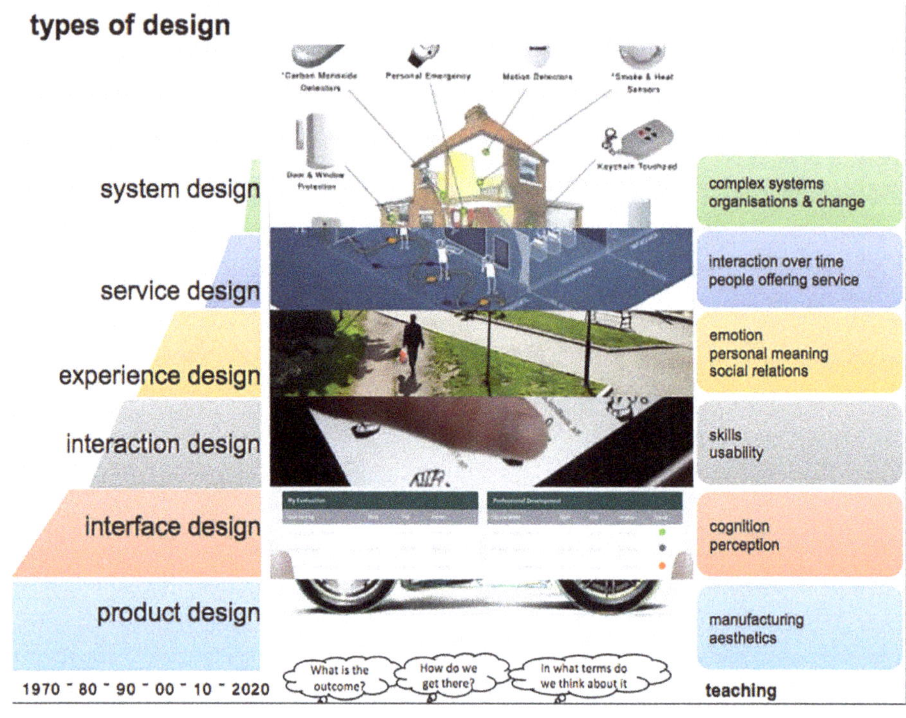

FIGURE 4: A visual representation of the progression of the types of design represented in the DesignX scenario, and what skills are taught at each level.

Examples of some of these complex systems are energy supply, healthcare services and mobility/transportation.

The change from domain-bound to purpose-driven design has led to designers' being involved in development efforts which surpass disciplines and domains. This expansion in what designers now "do" has positioned them to be involved in decision-making processes that shape public policy, affect socio-cultural and socio-economic agendas and activities, and inform thinking that impacts the functionality of civic and technological infrastructures. These newer activities of designing—identifying, framing and formulating new ways to address a wide variety of problematic situations through inventive and innovative practices—bind them together, especially when guided by a human-centered perspective. All those involved in efforts that endeavor to positively change complex systems will need to be able to operationalize design skills to varying degrees to effectively contribute to the development of these systems. These skills will include creativity, project management, communication, collaboration, empathy, prototyping and evaluation.

Partnerships will be formed around the systems of the domain of a given problematic situation, such as energy supply, healthcare services and mobility/transportation. For example, co-designing a new way to organize and effectively facilitate elder care across the community will require the constructive engagement of a broad cross-section of citizens, social and healthcare organizations, civil authorities, health insurance providers and designers. These collaborations are all integral to both the effective maintenance of the operation of this type of complex system as well as the exploration of new initiatives that could improve or replace it.

Cross-disciplinary development will bring together various disciplines, each with its own tools and materials, and each with its own ways of planning, doing and assessing. Models, materials, tools, and languages will need to be developed to connect and effectively manage the contributions of the different parties at the intersections, interfaces and overlaps that will occur between disciplines. The challenge in developing, implementing and effectively sustaining complex systems lies not in making a single predictable, perfect-forever solution, but in evolving solutions as they develop. This requires training that needs to take place *in vivo* (possibly in 'living labs'). This requires a sustained and high-level of involvement in the development of the system from various societal partners, as well as in the design activities that must occur to support that development. Each set of partners will need to be educated so that they acquire the requisite skills and understandings. By 2030, digital technologies will have matured to support large-scale information transfer, coordination of collaboration and consolidation of results. We will have developed ways to develop and prototypically test in vivo systems and services, and all involved (users, designers, managers) will be more able to easily shift between being part of running a given system to making smaller or larger changes within them. Making actual and possible changes visible to users, designers and managers, and synchronizing/harmonizing the actions of this diverse set of actors will be the main challenge.

In this scenario, the primary question posed to workshop participants was: *What design skills and understandings do 'all involved' need?*

Scenario #4: Distant-and-Yet-So-Close

Authored and presented by Nicole Lotz and Erik Bohemia

The "*Distant-and-Yet-So-Close*" scenario proposed that a key approach for effectively facilitating distance education in design in the near-future will be to make learning relevant and "close" to an individual learner's areas of interest as well as his or her physical location, and to be structured and delivered in a manner that helps him or her develop a feeling of belonging and responsibility.

Design students working in this scenario collaborate with a variety of stakeholders. They include, but are not limited to, learners studying in a wide variety of disciplines, as well as external stakeholders and experts from maker spaces, private companies, and public organizations such as "not-for-profits."

In this scenario, distance learners seeking to build knowledge and gain skills in design are advised and guided by a mix of artificial intelligence (AI), local expertise and online tutor groups. A 'closer to home' tutor such as a local design practitioner/teacher guides the design student throughout their learning journey. Individuals and communities of users utilize online-facilitated communications to assess and validate the outcomes of design processes, as well as design services and interactions that individual learners or groups of learners have created.

Additionally, planning and operating this scenario requires the maintenance of effective relations with the personnel who manage and operate local maker spaces, [a] community mending groups and workshops. Doing this effectively is central to distance learners' exposure to hands-on designing, and the iterative, heuristically informed processes that guide it. Local companies, ranging from corporations to start-ups and local shops and small businesses, offer limited services freely or at greatly reduced rates to the distance learners, and may also offer them apprenticeships, internships or limited opportunities to practice what they have learned. Distance learners also have opportunities to contribute to the realization of local community or government projects that have been formulated to design new services and interactions.

[a] *A "maker space" is an environment equipped with tools and people who know how to use them that operates as a center for engagement, learning, and activities that involve making and doing in a particular community.*

The *Distant-and-Yet-So-Close* scenario is guided by a project-based curriculum that facilitates a range of projects, which include designing objects, systems and services for individuals or groups living in "the real world," as well as abstract, theoretical or philosophically motivated assignments. Cooperative and collaborative curriculum components are derived from the distance learners' online social networks and local communities. A dynamic and intelligent curriculum (AI) suggests projects to the distance learner based on social, cultural, economic or even political relevance to him or her and proximity to his or her community. As distance learners gain more experience with design processes, they gain more autonomy to choose the content that constitutes their curriculum. By being integrated within online and offline communities that operate close to the distance learner's physical location, he or she will feel more responsible, and become more socially integrated and more adept at engaging in lifelong learning. Learning to design in close proximity to an individual or

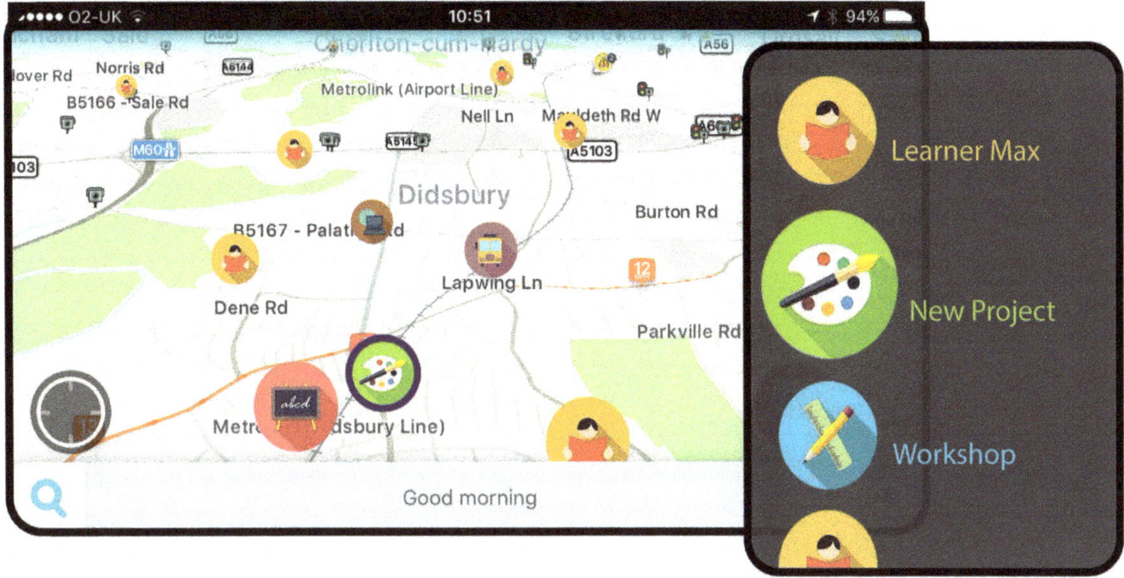

FIGURE 5: A collage of a new type of VLE—a Map-based app that depicts stakeholders, learners and workshops in physical proximity to a new project being created

group's communities of interest can promote the transformation of projects that were intended to merely satisfy a particular set of learning objectives into projects that become actualized and incorporated into the daily life of the community. Community integration and life-relevance are key to lifelong and self-directed design learning. Physical tools for prototyping and production are sourced from locally available maker spaces, local workshops, and local services (these include but are not limited to 2D and 3D printing).

The virtual tools used to facilitate design activities in this scenario are twofold: first, a central, map-based Virtual Learning Environment (VLE) (shown in Figure 5) connects learners and other stakeholders with objects, services and specific design applications that are acquired on demand. Second, distance design education will be orchestrated and facilitated virtually, but will still be anchored in physical spaces. With each new project, the VLE lists all live and past projects on a map.

The primary questions posed to workshop participants in context of this scenario were: *How do we accredit ubiquitous, lifelong distance learning in the future? If the educational institutions are calling for lifelong, ubiquitous learning, then do we still need traditional accreditation? Who will accredit learning and with what goal(s)? Which elements of learning will be assessed and accredited, and how will this occur?*

Future Visions for Design Education as Articulated by Participants in the Workshops

Workshop participants formed six groups, and each group chose one of the four scenarios to build upon their visions for the future of design education. Three groups selected the DRAW scenario, two groups selected the DesignX scenario, and one group focused on the Cosmopolitan Localist scenario as the context for their future visions. None of the groups chose to explore The Distant-and-Yet-So-Close scenario. For convenience, we refer to the groups in the descriptions that follow numerically as Groups 1 to 6. The summaries of the visions for the future of design education (henceforth referred to as "visions") presented by each group are described in the following sections. These were created based upon the authors' analysis of visual and audio recordings of each group's presentation of its vision, and the authors' interpretation of the visualizations that were created to communicate these.

Future visions based on the DRAW scenario

Groups 1, 3 and 5 developed their visions based on the DRAW scenario.

Group 1 (whose visualization is depicted in Figure 6) identified that design's being added to the core of the learning experiences that constitute K-12 education would cause greater emphasis to be placed on creative disciplines. First year students in undergraduate design will be more effectively prepared to use design knowledge and skills, while students entering disciplines outside design will be familiar with some aspects of design processes. Design learning will extend beyond classroom lecturing and the studio environment. This will result in students being able to collaborate with various constituent groups within their communities and explore the natural environment to improve less-than-desirable situations within and around them. The three wild cards (circled)—*more variety, complex thinking* and *global interest*—highlight the central ideas articulated in this visualization. Students will also need *more variety* regarding the types of learning experiences they are immersed in, and this will require options beyond classroom lecturing to be facilitated. Designing will involve introducing students to *complex thinking,* which will allow them to be braver, and to learn to experiment and take chances. Learners would need to think of design at a global scale, and learn to negotiate solutions that require collaboration, active listening and communication.

Group 3 (whose visualization is depicted in Figure 7) identified that K-12 students who are exposed to and immersed in design-based learning

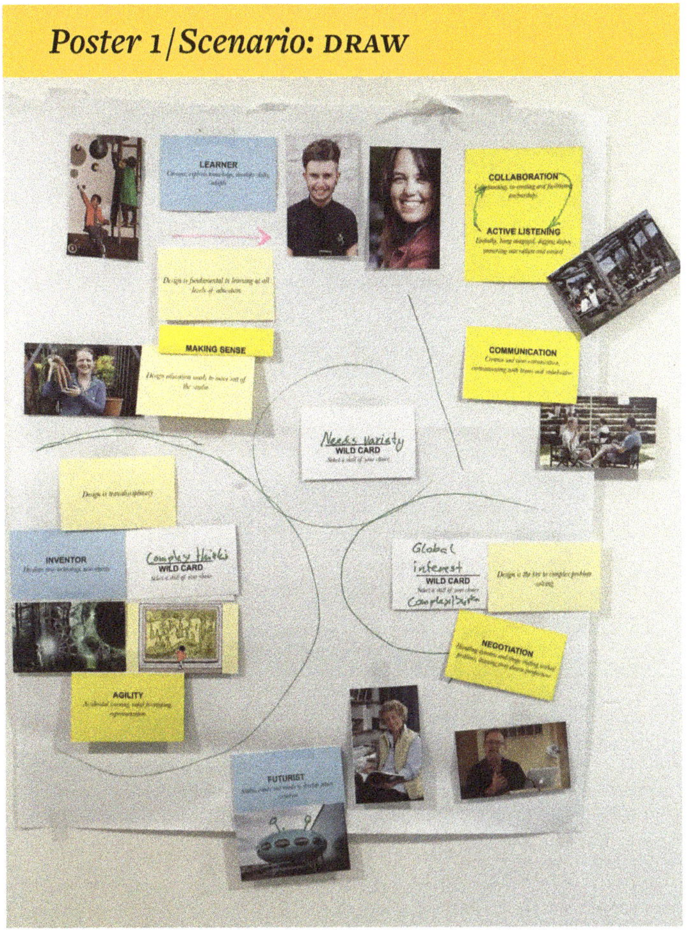

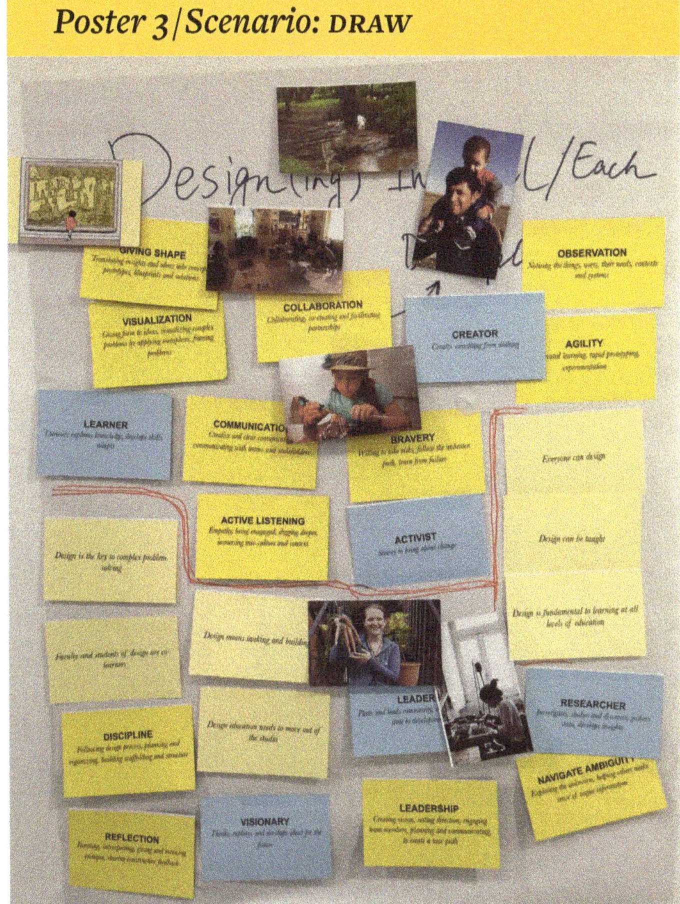

FIGURE 6 (L): Visualization for the *Future of Design Education* created by Group 1.

FIGURE 7 (R): Visualization for the *Future of Design Education* created by Group 3.

experiences will enter the university with a rich skill set in design, equipped with abilities to create, collaborate and observe with curiosity and a sense of activism. This is depicted in the visuals that occupy the upper half of the visualization. The group recognized that not everyone coming out of high school would become a professional designer. Design tools and methods will be integrated into many other disciplines. Students will pursue a Masters' degree or a PhD specializing in Design after earning an undergraduate degree in another discipline in addition to design. The lower half of this visualization highlights the outcomes of higher education captured through *Statements Cards* that characterize the transdisciplinary nature of design and *Roles Cards* that highlight leadership roles that students would be prepared to assume. Group 3 also contended that these students would be more well-prepared to use their experiences in higher education to become the kinds of social, civic and corporate leaders who would be able to anticipate and navigate ambiguous circumstances. Utilizing their knowledge of design skills and processes, students in every

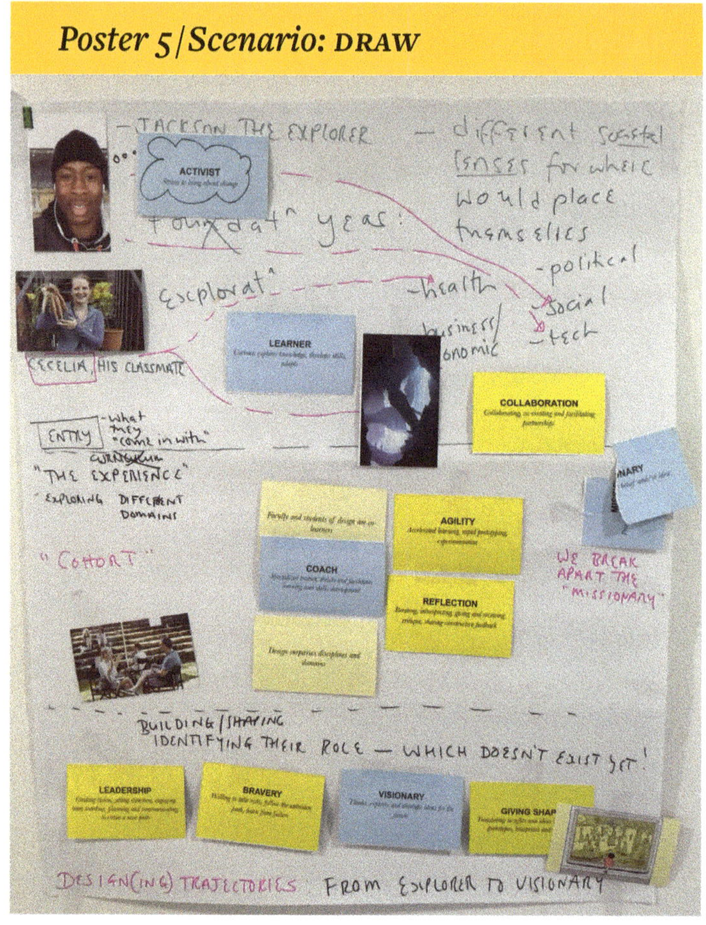

FIGURE 8: Visualization for the *Future of Design Education* created by Group 5.

discipline would be brave enough to identify, frame and tackle systems-level problems and/or soft and wicked problems.

Group 5 (whose visualization is depicted in Figure 8) identified that, in the DRAW scenario, K–12 students who have been educated to plan and operate design processes would enter the university as design literates who possess diverse skills, bases of knowledge, and interests. As a result, these students' career paths would not be linear or constrained within a rigid curriculum. The design program would be designed to be an immersive learning experience. In this type of learning context, faculty and students would be co-learners who work together to create experiences within which different types of knowledge and understandings could be discovered or constructed. For example, a student possessing design skills around health and alternative economics would explore learning by using different lenses such as political, health, and business economics in the foundation phase. Being educated in this way would also allow students to explore different disciplinary domains and would encourage them to become more broad-minded explorers of society. These learning experiences may conclude with students actively defining and shaping their particular social and cultural roles, which may not exist yet, in a society that will require people to be more nimble learners and thinkers. Towards the end of this type of design program, students enrolled in it will begin exploring what kinds of impacts—socially, technologically, economically, politically—they want to have on society, or some portion(s) of it, as a designers. This concept is depicted in the lower part of the visualization. The group represented the idea that "We break apart the missionary" in a torn *role card.* This type of design program will prepare design students to be brave leaders and visionaries who will need to be mobile, adaptable to changing situations and who can shape their own education.

Visions based on the DesignX scenario

Groups 4 and 6 developed their visions on the *DesignX* scenario.

Group 4 (whose visualization is depicted in Figure 9) presented the argument that, in the context of the DesignX scenario, all of the students enrolled in a design program need not learn "everything." They contended that most design students will embark on their respective learning experiences having formed their own ambitions or ideas about what they want to learn or want to become. The *Role Card* "learner" sits at the center of their visualization, from which radiate "arms" comprised of trigger cards depicting combinations of images and key words that together form descriptions of distinct learning personas. One of these personas describes Nina, a university student and futurist, with a horticultural background who is interested in exploring space agriculture. Since design surpasses boundaries imposed by disciplines and domains, and is structured to facilitate peer-to-peer learning, the students in the design class Nina is enrolled in will learn as much from each other as they would from their professors. This idea is highlighted by the heading for the poster that states: "We learn a lot—but not from you". In this visualization for the future, design students will learn *with* their Professors and Instructors—as co-learners—rather than *from* them.

Group 6 (whose visualization is depicted in Figure 10) focused on identifying key skills and roles required for design students to work towards. These are articulated in the "*Roles*" and "*Skills*" cards that flank each side of the column of visuals that appears in the center of their collage. The primary roles identified for future designers are *explorer, futurist, visionary, inventor* and

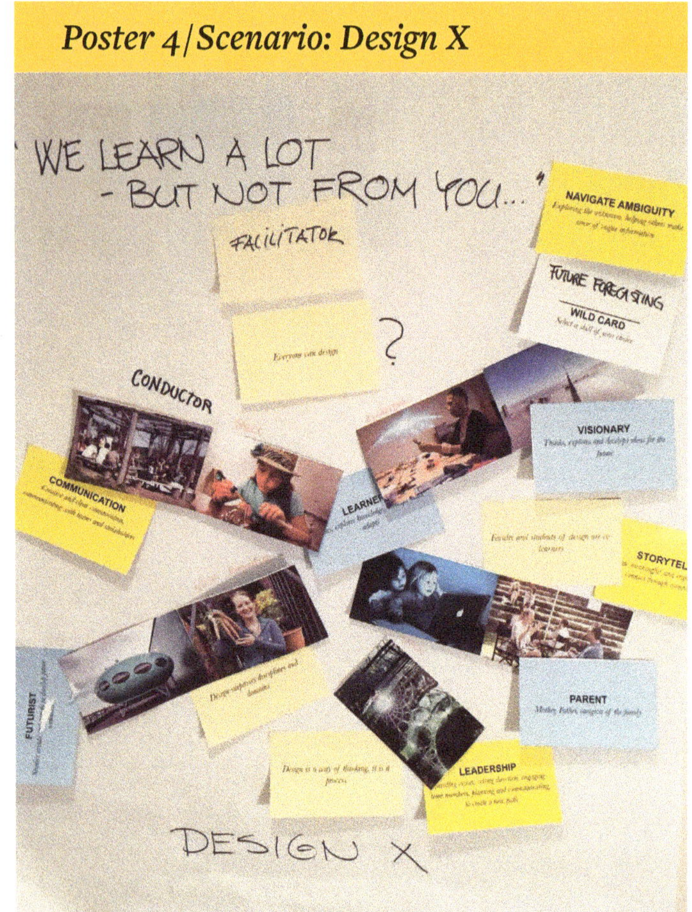

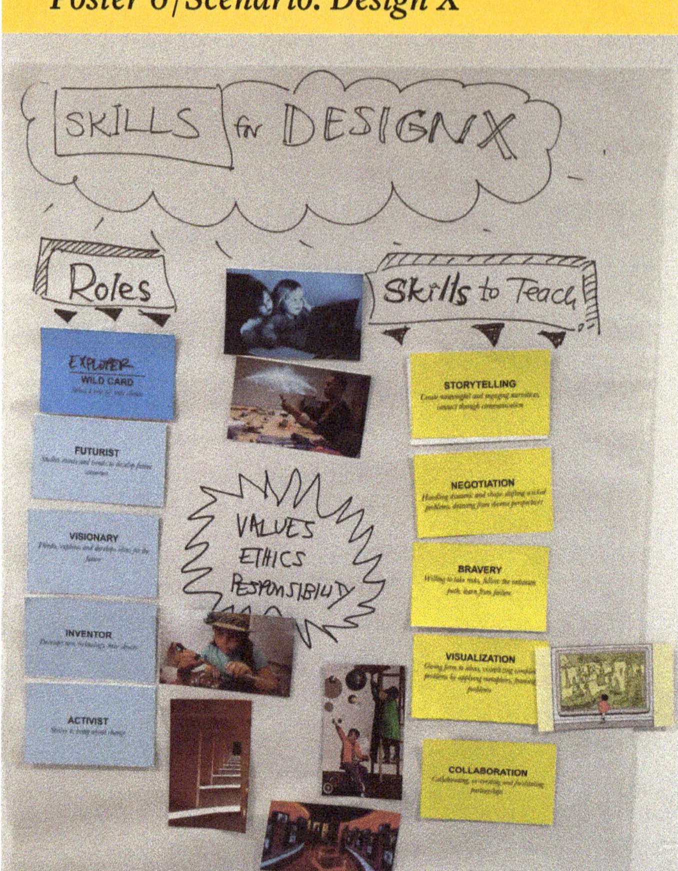

FIGURE 9 (L): Visualization for the *Future of Design Education* created by Group 4.

FIGURE 10 (R): Visualization for the *Future of Design Education* created by Group 6.

activist. The primary skills these designers would have to possess include *learning by doing, storytelling, negotiation, bravery, visualization* and *collaboration.*

The need for bravery is highly relevant to the *Explorer* role, which Group 6 identified on their visualization using their "Wild Card," that requires thinking in new ways. They also offered that behaving in the role of an *activist* means 1) actually having and then effectively articulating a point of view, and 2) considering diverse social and cultural value systems and ethical positions about topics such as intellectual property, privacy and inequality. Group 6 identified that "What makes the designers 'stand out' is their skill in storytelling...[and using this] to meaningfully engage with different types of people." The other key ability designers learning within this vision will cultivate effectively is *visualization,* which was described by the group as having the skill and knowledge necessary to create something that is visually and conceptually compelling enough to provoke conversation. The group emphasized that in this future scenario the considerations of values, ethics and responsibility

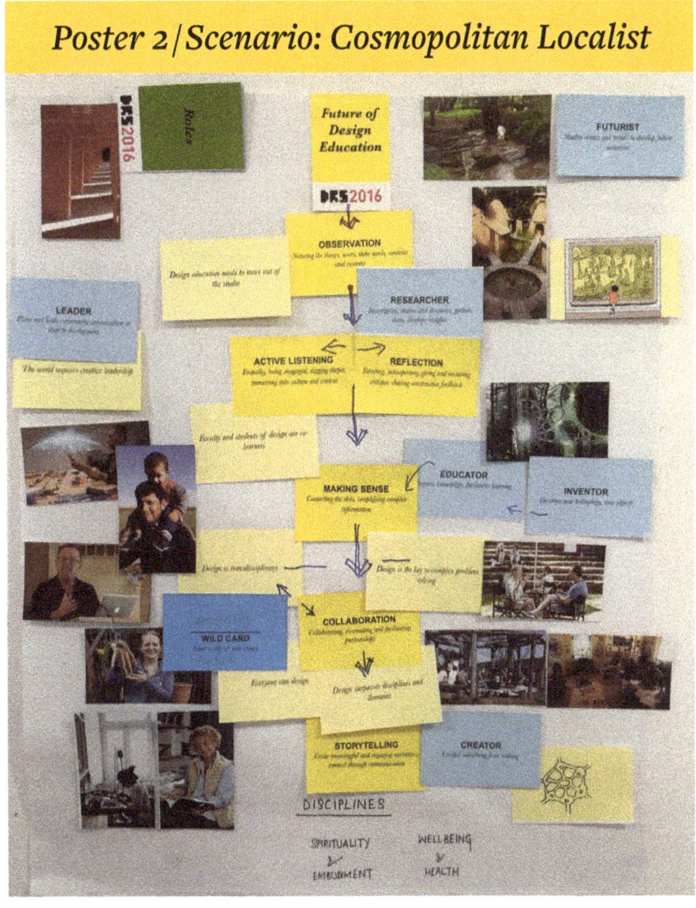

FIGURE 11: Visualization for the *Future of Design Education* created by Group 2.

would be central to design, placing these as text prominently in the middle of the poster. Additionally, the designers learning within this vision would need to develop skills of playfulness, experimentation and thinking at a global scale (this was not included in their visualization, but *was* emphasized in their verbal presentation).

Group 2 (whose visualization is depicted shown in Figure 11) developed their vision on the Cosmopolitan Localist scenario. In their vision, the future design student is on a path to discovery and respect for which environment is a core element. The learning spaces in this vision would be designed for reflection, spirituality, introspection, respect towards nature and learning to gain wisdom. Learning would not be separate from the students' other aspects of life. Family would play an important role in their everyday learning experiences. A typical day would follow the design process, which is represented along the middle spine of their visualization using the *Skills Cards* of *observation, active listening* and *reflection* leading to *sense making, collaboration* and *storytelling.*

This central spine highlighting skills is supported by visuals chosen from *People* and *Places Cards* placed on either side of it. In this scenario knowledge of the local environment and indigenous materials and practices would form the core of the curriculum. Topics such as well-being, health, nourishing and flourishing of communities will be a part of learning. Faculty and students would collaborate on projects as co-learners. Designing as a key to complex problem solving would be directed towards local community problems. The students attracted to this program would have more wisdom and experience behind them and would be interested in taking up leadership roles. This community of learners would be diverse in terms of age and experience.

Discussions About the Future Visions for Design Education

The discussions around the four future scenarios that were presented during this workshop yielded distinctly different concepts and areas of foci, although there were common concepts and themes that emerged across this spectrum, such as transdisciplinarity, and collaboration between designers and non-designers.

The six visualizations created by workshop participant groups revealed a surprising amount of overlap in their choices of *Roles, People, Skills, Places* and *Statement cards.* The common themes across the six visualizations for the future of design can be observed from cards from the toolkit that were most frequently selected (these are shown in Figure 12). Collaboration was the most used *Skill* card and was included in five out of six of the visualizations. The importance of co-learning is highlighted by the fact that the most frequently chosen Statement card—*Faculty and students of design are co-learners*—was chosen by four of the six groups. The most frequently used *Role* cards were *Learner, Inventor* and *Futurist,* which were included in four out of six posters. The image of a smiling woman showing off fresh produce was the most frequently chosen *People* card and was used by five out of six groups. The most frequently chosen *Place* card was an illustration showing a child attempting to enter a painting of a natural environment and was used by five out of six groups. An analysis of these most frequently chosen cards reveals that, at least in the minds of the participants in this workshop, the future of design education will be built on collaboration and co-learning. Additionally, design education in the future will not neglect study of and about how designers affect and are affected by the natural environment and will prepare design learners to act as futurists and inventors.

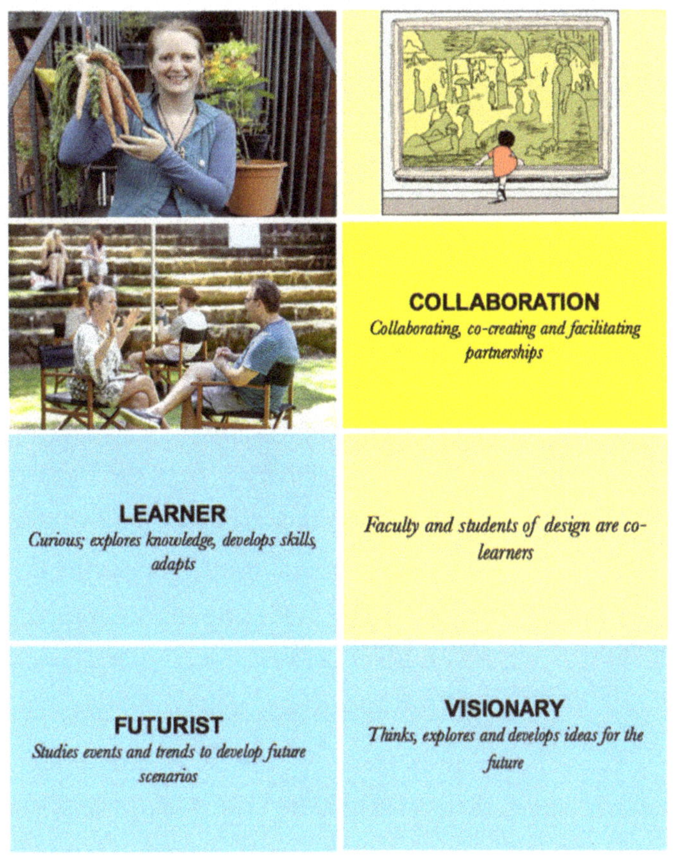

FIGURE 12: These were the most frequently selected cards from the toolkit.

Three groups highlighted that future designers would take on roles as visionaries and activists. Two groups created the *Explorer* role from a *Wild card. Communication* and *storytelling* were both described as important skills for future designers, as were *bravery, agility, negotiation* and *leadership.* Taken together, these indicate that future designers will have more opportunities to be proactive and to occupy positions of strength as their contributions to a broad array of social, economic and public policy initiatives evolve. The notion that design education needs to move beyond much of the current dogma that is guiding its planning and facilitation is supported by three of the six groups. These were articulated through following *Statement cards: "Design education needs to move out of the studio," "Everyone can design,"* and *"Design surpasses disciplines and domains."* The visuals representing natural environments were chosen by four of the six groups indicating that future learners will move into the natural environments for an immersive learning experience. The *People* cards chosen by half of the groups suggest that "thinking with your hands" by manipulating 3D objects, as well as tinkering and hacking are desirable activities for future designers to engage in.

Trigger cards that were not chosen at all were also noted. *People* cards that depicted men looking directly into the camera and communicating a sense of seriousness or authority were not chosen by any of the groups. These cards were passed over in favour of those that depicted women and small groups of people engaged in activities. Visuals that portrayed people moving through public spaces were also not selected. In one group's visualization, the *Missionary* role card was purposefully torn. The *Caregiver* role card was not included in any of the visualizations.

Statements (from the *Statements* cards) that were not chosen included: *"Design can lead change," "Effective and successful design requires collaboration," "Common physical space is required for design collaboration," "Design thinking is system thinking," "Prototyping is key to effective design process,"* and *"Design research is much more effective than scientific research."* Many of these exclusions may have occurred due to redundancies and/or overlap among Roles, Skills and Statement cards. Each of the six groups seemed to prefer using a single word, such as "collaboration", instead of a statement communicating a similar concept.

Despite some large overlaps between the six visualizations, differences can be found in the details of how the *Roles, Skills, People* and *Places* acted together. For example, Group 2 emphasized the need for collaboration between different age groups. The *Educator* role was only mentioned in the vision presented by Group 2. Group 4 considered that the *Parent* role is integrated in learning and envisioned the future designer as a *Conductor* and *Facilitator* of design activities and not necessarily as the primary creator. Group 3 utilized the Skill cards *Observation* and *Discipline.* Groups 3 and 6 were the only groups to use the Skill card *Visualization.* As indicated that while visual communication is a key skill for many contemporary designers, it might not be as central a piece of their future skill set. Whether future designers need to adhere to an established process (e.g., as was indicated by the deployment of the *Discipline* card) or deviate from this (e.g., as was indicated by the deployment of the *Bravery* card) was and is matter of debate.

The descriptions of how traditional disciplines might play a role in the future of design education became a matter of differentiation across the six groups as well. In some of their visions, new disciplines were created in addition to design (Group 2), or design learners were described as coming to design from a disciplinary background different from design (Group 4). In yet another vision, disciplines seem to disintegrate entirely (Group 1). These approaches point towards interdisciplinary and transdisciplinary curricula affecting the future of design education.

Differentiation of visions was also expressed throughout the array of visual layouts created by the six groups. All of the posters displayed a different configuration and pattern of arrangement of trigger cards. These were manifest as walls of cards, or groupings of cards that were arranged in linear order or radially or configured into zones or as clusters. Cards were organized to create opposition and tensions, or bridges between concepts; arrows and lines were drawn in three of the posters to emphasize specific relationships between cards. All of this indicates that the toolkit offers enormous flexibility as a participatory framework to help disparate individuals or groups engage in processes that challenge them to envision design futures.

Conclusions

The discussions and outcomes that emerged during the visioning workshop facilitated by the authors and their colleagues during the 2016 Design Research Society Conference highlight many commonly held values and views of design educators and their future visions for design education. These have been described in terms of how they might affect those living and working within the four future scenarios for design education described in this report.

Similarities across the six visions for the future of design education emphasized the need for a collaborative approach to teaching and learning about design that entails students and faculty learning *together*. Each of the visions also described ways for designers to play roles as brave explorers and activists.

The variations between the six visions also gave us a sense of how and why design education may branch out in the future. The most critical variation involves how design as a discipline is placed in relation to other disciplines. On one hand, design could be absorbed into everything we do, which would mean that it would be integrated into many other disciplines. On the other hand, design as a discipline could take the lead in solving complex global problems by integrating and applying knowledge from other disciplines.

Working within the context of a future scenario offered the workshop participants a different starting point to think about the future of design education, instead of starting from today's reality, which could have been a limiting factor. The toolkit provided workshop participant groups with elements that helped to provoke their particular type of storytelling, and gave them concrete people, environments and skills to think and talk about. The combination of 1) challenging each of the groups to work within one of the future scenarios along with 2) providing them with a sufficiently open-ended, diversely populated and generative design toolkit helped the workshop participants create visions for the future of design education that were not overly simplistic or superficial.

This case study reveals that an approach guided by visioning enabled design educators to demonstrate in-depth and differentiated understandings about where design education could be and (perhaps should be) heading in the future. A mixture of provocative future scenarios, positive visions for select aspects of the future of design education, and descriptions of desirable futures allowed the design educators who participated in this workshop to focus on articulating the design competencies that would need to be developed to tackle and deal with our global society's uncertain futures.

Acknowledgment

We would like to thank our workshop participants and collaborators for the DRS2016 workshop: Terry Irwin, Pieter Jan Stappers and Erik Bohemia. The concept of the visioning workshop was implemented successfully due to the collective efforts and contributions of all of the facilitators and participants.

References

AIGA Educators. "2016 Design Education Programming Recap," *AIGA Design Educators Community*, 10 January 2017. Online. Available at: https://educators.aiga.org/2016-design-education-conferences-recap/ (Accessed January, 19, 2017).

Broadbent, J. & Cross, N. "Design Education in the Information Age." *Journal of Engineering Design*, 14.4 (2003): pgs. 439–446.

Buchanan, R. "The Problem of Character in Design Education: Liberal Arts and Professional Specialization." *International Journal of Technology and Design Education*, 11.1 (2001): pgs. 13–26.

Currey, M. "D-School Futures," *Core77*, 6 June 2014. Online. Available at: http://www.core77.com/posts/27564/d-school-futures-scads-owen-foster-on-the-value-of-being-a-hybrid- designer-and-the-four-most-important-qualities-in-an-id-student-27564 (Accessed January, 19, 2017).

Kressy, M., "Why MIT's New Design Program Will Get Designers at the Table?,"

Core 77, 9 April 2015. Online. Available at: http://www.core77.com/posts/35588/Why-MITs-New-Design-Program-Will-Get-Designers-a-Seat-at-the-Table (Accessed January, 19, 2017).

Norman, D. & Klemmer, S., "State of Design: How Design Education Must Change." *Core77*, 14 March 2014. Online. Available at: http://www.linkedin.com/pulse/20140325102438-12181762-state-of-design-how-design-education-must- change (Accessed January, 19, 2017).

Norman, D. & Stappers, P. J. "DesignX: Complex Sociotechnical Systems." *She Ji: The Journal of Design, Economics, and Innovation*, 1.2 (2015): pgs. 83–106.

O'Neill, G. "Initiating Curriculum Revision: Exploring the Practices of Educational Developers." *International Journal for Academic Development*, 15.1 (2010): pgs.: 61–71.

Rodgers, P.A. & Bremner, C. "The Concept of the Design Discipline." *Dialectic*, 1.1 (2016): pgs. 19–38. doi: http://dx.doi.org/10.3998/dialectic.14932326.0001.104

Sanders, E. B.-N. and Stappers, P. J. *Convivial Toolbox: Generative Research for the Front End of Design*. Amsterdam, The Netherlands: BIS Publishers, 2012.

Singh, S., Irwin, T., Sanders, E., Stappers, P. J., Lotz, N., & Bohemia, E. "The Future of Design Education." Workshop facilitated at the Design Research Society Conference, Brighton, UK, June 2016. Online. Available at: https://drs2016.squarespace.com/564/?rq=future (Accessed January, 19, 2017).

Van der Helm, R. "The vision phenomenon: Towards a theoretical underpinning of visions of the future and the process of envisioning." *Futures Methodologies*, 41.2 (2009): pgs. 96–104.

Whitaker, B. "The Future of Design Education Post-Brexit," *CHEAD & APDIG*, 9 September 2016. Online. Available at: http://www.policyconnect.org.uk/events/chead-apdig-"-future-design-education-post-brexit" (Accessed January, 19, 2017).

Biographies

Sapna Singh is a design researcher, strategist and educator. She is a lecturer in the Design Department at The Ohio State University in Columbus, Ohio,

USA. As a design research consultant, she works on product development and service design for healthcare, consumer products, automobiles, retail environment, enterprise level applications and learning technology. Sapna has a multidisciplinary background with an undergraduate degree in architecture and graduate degrees in industrial design, education, business administration and design research. In 2016, Sapna completed her MFA research thesis at The Ohio State University that explored the future and value of graduate design education applying a multidisciplinary approach combining design research and organizational strategy. Her research interests are the future of design education, business strategy as a design problem and exploring design for learning.

Nicole Lotz is a Lecturer in Design at the Open University, UK. Before joining the OU, she was a Research Associate at the Hong Kong Polytechnic University and a professional Graphic/Web Designer at various design agencies in Hong Kong and Germany. She completed a Ph.D. in Cross-cultural Design at the Hong Kong Polytechnic University, and holds undergraduate and postgraduate degrees in Communication Design from Burg Giebichenstein, University of Art and Design in Halle, Germany.

Nicole is interested in design processes across the typical boundaries of domains, cultures and levels of expertise. She has studied co-located as well as distance designing across Europe, the USA, Africa and Southeast Asia. Outcomes of her research inform the development of learning designs, interactive tools and resources for co-located and distance designing and design education. Her work has affected the development of design skills and confidence in developing as well as developed countries.

Elizabeth B.-N. Sanders joined the Design Department at The Ohio State University in 2011 after working in industry as a design research consultant since 1981. She introduced many of the methods and tools being used today to drive and inspire design from a human-centered perspective and has practiced co-designing across all the design disciplines. Liz is also the founder of MakeTools, LLC where she works at the front end of many of the changes taking place today in design. Her academic research focuses on generative design research, collective creativity, and transdisciplinarity. She shares her experiences in human-centered design with clients, colleagues, and students around the world. Liz's goal is to bring participatory, human-centered design practices to the challenges we face for the future.

Dialectic Volume II, Issue I: Research Paper

Improving Science Students' Data Visualizations: A STEAM-Based Approach

KJ HEPWORTH[1] AND CHELSEA CANON[2]

1. Reynolds School of Journalism, University of Nevada, Reno, USA
2. Department of Geography, University of Nevada, Reno, USA

SUGGESTED CITATION: Hepworth, K.J., & Canon, C. "Improving Science Students' Data Visualizations: A STEAM-Based Approach." *Dialectic,* 2.1 (2018): pgs. 49-78. DOI: http://dx.doi.org/10.3998/dialectic.14932326.0001.303

Abstract

A course at the University of Nevada, Reno (UNR) teaches science students an interdisciplinary approach for designing data visualizations, in combination with big data computation and statistical analysis. This 15-week, undergraduate-level course, titled *"Computational Skills for Big Data: Analysis, Statistics, and Visualization,"* is co-taught by visual communication design, math, and physics faculty, and is an example of a pedagogy rooted in a STEAM[1]-based approach that combines instruction in art or design with instruction in science, technology, engineering or mathematics. This paper introduces the interdisciplinary data visualization typology that formed the basis of this course's visualization component: *data visualization for facilitating analysis* and *data visualization for sharing knowledge. Data visualization for facilitating analysis* is the use of visualization among an expert audience who are intimately familiar with the represented data, and *data visualization for sharing knowledge* is the use of visualization to represent data in a way that is intelligible to a non-expert audience. The authors argue that most of the extant data visualization education and science education literature can be classified as referring to one or the other of these types, and that this classification can help aid planning and facilitating instruction in data visualization (the design and use of graphical representations of data). This paper outlines the general structure of the course, and its data visualization components, in detail, and then provides an overview of how and why the course was assessed as it was, and finally reflects on its potential reproducibility. An analysis of work produced by students as the course progressed suggests that challenging STEM[2] undergraduate students to distinguish between *data visualization for facilitating analysis* and *data visualization for sharing knowledge* is a helpful typology to guide teaching data visualization. The paper also argues for greater collaboration between visual communication design faculty and STEM faculty in undergraduate courses, and posits that their collaborative efforts to teach data visualization is an effective way to do this.

1 Science, Technology, Engineering, Art (and design), and Math.

2 Science, Technology, Engineering, and Math. The origin of the acronym "STEM" has been attributed to Dr. Judith Ramaley, the former director of the education and human resources division of the U.S. National Science Foundation. She had originally coined the acronym "SMET" as she was working to help develop curricula that had the potential to enhance learning among science, mathematics, engineering and technology students around the country. She altered "SMET" to "STEM" to allow science and math to "serve as bookends for technology and engineering," and because she reportedly "didn't like the sound of [the] word [SMET]." Excerpted from Christenson, J. "Used Nationwide," Winona Daily News, 13 November, 2011. Online. Available at: http://www.winonadailynews.com/news/local/ramaley-coined-stem-term-now-used-nationwide/article_457afe3e-0db3-11e1-abe0-001cc4c03286.html (Accessed January 30, 2018).

RESEARCH PAPER

Improving Science Students' Data Visualizations:

A STEAM-Based Approach

KJ HEPWORTH & CHELSEA CANON

Introduction

Data visualization skills are crucial for science undergraduate students to effectively learn conceptual principles, analyze experimental data, and communicate experimental findings.[3,4,5,6] Despite the importance of the effective acquisition of data visualization skills being widely acknowledged in the science education literature, few STEM education scholars advocate for their students to receive explicit instruction on designing data visualizations using principles that are commonly recommended in visual communication design and data visualization literature.[7,8] The science education literature provides science educators with some awareness of why it is important for their students to acquire data visualization skills, but fails to provide them with a practical roadmap for how to teach these skills effectively, much less the bases of knowledge that inform them. At the University of Nevada, Reno (UNR), the expectation that science students will be able to produce data visualizations without any training in the design principles for doing so has frequently resulted in poor communication of scientific information in undergraduate student work, disadvantaging both students' comprehension of important scientific knowledge and their ability to develop the skills necessary to communicate this scientific knowledge effectively to those inside and outside their particular discipline.

In 2016-2017, an interdisciplinary course titled *"Computational Skills for Big Data: Analysis, Statistics, and Visualization"* was conceived by three

3 Crider, A. 2015. "Teaching Visual Literacy in the Astronomy Classroom." New Directions for Teaching and Learning, 141 (2015): pgs. 7-18.

4 Mathewson, J.H. "Visual-Spatial Thinking: An Aspect of Science Overlooked by Educators." Science Education, 83.1 (1999): pgs. 33-54.

5 Milner-Bolotin, M., and Nashon, S.M. "The Essence of Student Visual-spatial Literacy and Higher Order Thinking Skills in Undergraduate Biology." Protoplasma, 249. S1 (2012): pgs. 25-30.

6 Valle, M. "Visualization: A Cognition Amplifier." International Journal of Quantum Chemistry, 113.17 (2013): pgs. 2040-2052.

7 Trumbo, J. "Visual Literacy and Science Communication." Science Communication, 20.4 (1999): pgs. 409-425.

8 Vande Moere, A. and Purchase, H. "On the Role of Design in Information Visualization." Information Visualization, 10.4 (2011): pgs. 356-371.

faculty members. One had a background in visual communication design, another in mathematical statistics, and the third in atmospheric physics. Their primary goal was to address the need to improve students' capacities to design effectively communicative data visualizations of complex information. Secondarily, they sought to address a need for students to improve their understanding of how to work with open source, big data sets, as well as a need to improve their students' abilities to perform basic statistical analysis of the data that comprised these sets. The visual communication design faculty member assumed the responsibility for developing the details of the course pertinent to data visualization, while the faculty member with the background in mathematics assumed the responsibility for developing the details of the course pertinent to statistics, and the faculty member with the background in physics assumed the responsibility for developing the details of the course pertinent to numerical weather prediction and big data computation.

Big data computation is a methodological approach to engaging in analysis that relies on the automated cross-referencing of very large data sets. It is currently having a revolutionary effect on government, industry, and research in the humanities and sciences, and is consequently a methodological skill that is in very high demand. The qualities that lead data to be considered 'big' include the speed of its collection, the availability of real-time computational processing, low data accuracy, and its sheer volume compared with the data that was previously available in any given domain. [9,10]

This interdisciplinary teaching project intentionally introduced students to a "perceptual cognitive-based" approach to data visualization instruction, whereby principles of design are introduced for the purpose of improving clarity of communication within designed data visualizations. [11] This approach was chosen because the authors felt that it fit well pedagogically and conceptually with the statistical and computational instruction students received in the course. The authors note that many critical cultural, ethical, and rhetorical perspectives on data visualization instruction exist, and that these may be more appropriate when operationalized on behalf of a different cohort of students, or within the structure of a different course. Communication design researcher Meredith Davis observes that emphasis on utility in design does not negate acknowledgement or awareness of broader cultural contexts and meanings. [12]

Although the course was planned for all undergraduate first-year STEM pre-major students and will be offered to these students in the future, a small-scale pilot course was offered to physics seniors in the spring semester

9 Ali, S.M., Gupta, N., Nayak, G.K., Lenka, R.K. "Big data visualization: Tools and challenges." In: 2016 2nd International Conference on Contemporary Computing and Informatics. pgs. 656–660, 2016.

10 Mathewson, J.H. "Visual-Spatial Thinking: An Aspect of Science Overlooked by Educators." Science Education, 83.1 (1999): pgs. 33–54.

11 Milner-Bolotin, M., and Nashon, S.M. "The Essence of Student Visual-spatial Literacy and Higher Order Thinking Skills in Undergraduate Biology." Protoplasma, 249. S1 (2012): pgs. 25–30.

12 Valle, M. "Visualization: A Cognition Amplifier." International Journal of Quantum Chemistry, 113.17 (2013): pgs. 2040–2052.

of 2017 to test the effectiveness of the course planning. The pilot course used numerical weather prediction as the source of big data due to great industry demand for this skill; however, as this first-year course is taught in the future, it will make use of a wider range of big data sources. In order to highlight design educators' capacity to enhance science education through sharing a real-world example of effective interdisciplinary collaboration, this paper focuses on the visual communication design faculty member's work on developing and implementing the data visualization component of this pilot course. This focus demonstrates the possibilities for, and benefits of, visual communication design faculty collaborating with faculty members and other university personnel from disparate disciplines to improve pedagogical outcomes and cross-disciplinary practices, and it is hoped that this example will provide a useful roadmap for others.

This interdisciplinary course is an example of STEAM pedagogy, which integrates science, technology, engineering, and math (abbreviated to STEM) education with art or design (abbreviated into the 'A' in STEAM) education. Conceived by educator Georgette Yakman in 2006, STEAM pedagogy generally emphasizes thematic (rather than discipline-based) learning, so that students gain cross-disciplinary literacy in skills they are likely to apply in real-world scenarios.[13] In 2010, the Rhode Island School of Design advocated incorporating design into the STEAM education model, and widely promoted STEAM as a means for integrating design into many educational fields.[14,15] Other organizations and institutions have since also advocated for widespread adoption of STEAM-based education. These include the United Kingdom-based Design Council and the United States-based National Art Education Association, the STEAM Program at North Carolina State University, and the dSchool at Stanford University. The STEAM model has rapidly been incorporated into education, industry, research, and policy in many countries worldwide. However, visual communication design can be incorporated into STEAM-based pedagogy much more commonly than it is currently.

13 Yakman, G. "Recognizing the A in STEM Education." Middle Ground, August 2012.

14 Land, M.H. "Full STEAM Ahead: The Benefits of Integrating the Arts Into STEM." Procedia Computer Science, 20 (2013): pgs. 547–552.

15 Maeda, J. "STEM + Art = STEAM." The STEAM Journal, 1.1 (2013): pgs. 1–3.

Design for Analysis and Design for Sharing Knowledge

In physics education, as in broader science education and research, there are two main uses of data visualization: data visualization for facilitating analysis and data visualization for sharing knowledge.[16,17] Data visualization for facilitating analysis encompasses the production of visualization artifacts—charts, diagrams, maps, plots, and sketches—that provide overviews of complex data

16 Shoresh, N and Wong, B. "Points of View: Data Exploration." Nature Methods, 9.1 (2012): p. 5.

17 Trumbo, J. "Essay: Seeing Science." Science Communication, 21.4 (2000): pgs. 379–391.

that can be interpreted qualitatively through visual perception and pattern recognition skills for the purposes of exploring data, developing and testing hypotheses, and forming conclusions (see Figure 1a).[18,19,20] In terms of meeting the needs of a particular intended audience, data visualization for facilitating analysis is produced and used either individually or in groups that are limited to the people involved in any given experiment, research activity, or data collection event. Data visualization for facilitating analysis is of widespread interest in the science education literature, which focuses on how creating and learning to interpret data visualizations can enhance students' understanding of basic scientific concepts.[21,22,23,24] For example, biologists Jennifer Klug, Cayelan Carey and their colleagues emphasized data visualization for facilitating analysis in an ecology course module on lake ice. Students explored and graphed real-world, long-term monitoring data in spreadsheet software, visually assessed the results, and then applied linear regression to understand change over time.[25] Chemist Lisa Gentile and her colleagues took a similar approach in designing a unit on diffusion, asking students to compare data visualizations representing transmission via different mechanisms and to qualitatively examine those visualizations for evidence of how the mechanism affects transmission.[26] Learning scientists Douglas Gordin and Roy Pea describe another instance of data visualization for facilitating analysis using spatial data, that involved students in an undergraduate class on atmosphere and climate performing arithmetic operations on data layers to produce a visual representation of different rates of change.[27]

The other main use of data visualization—data visualization for sharing knowledge—encompasses those visualizations that are designed and distributed for the purpose of communicating research findings beyond the individual or group directly involved in a research activity. Although this can make use of the same forms (charts, maps etc.), it is distinguished from data visualization for facilitating analysis by *purpose, intended audience,* and *intentional persuasiveness.* There are several sub-groups within data visualization for sharing knowledge: visualization for sharing detailed knowledge, visualization for sharing summary knowledge, and visualization for intentionally evoking emotive responses (persuasion and/or storytelling). Visualization for sharing detailed knowledge is the production of visualizations with the intention to communicate detailed scientific findings to any audience that has not participated in the particular experiment or event (see Figure 1b). This includes detailed diagrams, charts, and maps such as those used as figures in academic journals, as well as physical and virtual three-dimensional renderings of scientific phenomena, as used for teaching purposes. Visualization for sharing summary knowledge is the production of highly simplified diagrams, charts, and maps for the purpose of

18 Gordin, D.N. and Pea, R.D. "Prospects for Scientific Visualization as an Educational Technology." The Journal of the Learning Sciences, 4.3 (1995): pgs. 249-279.

19 Johnson, C., Moorhead, M., Munzner, T., Pfister, H., Rheingans, P., and Yoo, T.S. NIH-NSF Visualization Research Challenges Report. IEEE Computer Society, 2006.

20 Valle, M. "Visualization: A Cognition Amplifier." International Journal of Quantum Chemistry, 113.17 (2013): pgs. 2040-2052.

21 Ellwein, A.L., Hartley, L.M., Donovan, S., Billick, I. "Using Rich Context and Data Exploration to Improve Engagement with Climate Data and Data Literacy: Bringing a Field Station into the College Classroom." Journal of Geoscience Education 62, (2014): pgs. 578-586.

22 Gilbert, J.K. "Visualization: An Emergent Field of Practice and Enquiry in Science Education." In Visualization: Theory and Practice in Science Education, edited by J.K. Gilbert, M. Reiner, and M. Nakhleh, pgs. 3-24.

23 Reiner, M. "Sensory Cues, Visualization and Physics Learning." International Journal of Science Education, 31.3 (2009): pgs. 343-364.

24 Zhang, Z.H. and Linn, M.C. "Can Generating Representations Enhance Learning with Dynamic Visualizations?" Journal of Research in Science Teaching, 48.10 (2011): pgs. 1177-1198.

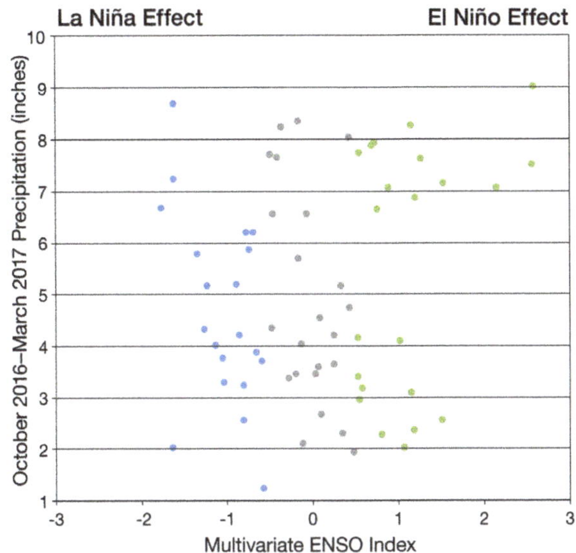

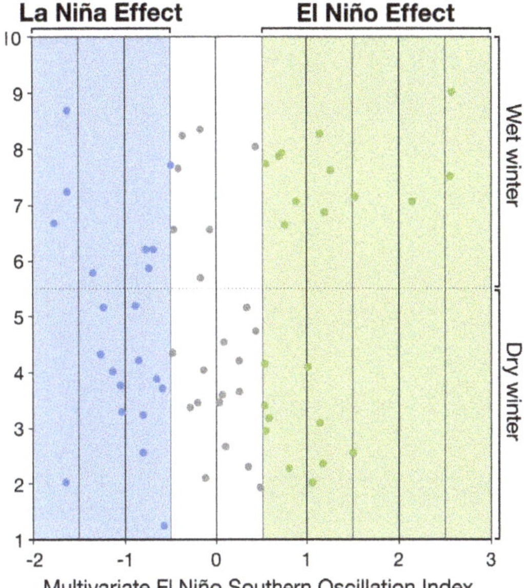

FIGURE 1: Examples of two types of data visualization identified in the literature, designed using principles taught in the visualization module: color use, legibility, and visual hierarchy. Figure 1a (left) "a visualization for facilitating analysis"—depicts a scatter plot as typically designed by scientists for data analysis. Figure 1b (right) "a visualization for sharing knowledge"—depicts an annotated scatter plot as it would be depicted on a scientific poster, representing the same data. Data source: Nevada State Climate Office, 2017.

communicating general conceptual awareness of scientific findings. [28] Summary knowledge visualization formats include overview figures, visual abstracts, and scientific posters produced for educational purposes. Visualization for intentionally emotive purposes is the production of visualizations with the intention of altering the emotional state of their audiences, often in order to alter their beliefs or behaviors (see Figure 1d). [29] This is a far larger category than the previous two, and includes infographics, graphic re-enactments and reconstructions, and visualizations used in advertising, entertainment, journalism, and propaganda activities. [30,31] Figure 2 shows the proximity of various visualization purposes to the original experiment or data collection event. This figure also indicates an increase in the intentional persuasiveness of each of the represented levels of data visualization. With that stated, it should be noted that various scholars acknowledge that all data visualizations are inherently persuasive. [32,33,34]

These categorizations in the data visualization literature, data visualization for facilitating analysis and data visualization for sharing knowledge,

25 Klug, J.L., Carey, C.C., Richardson, D.C., and Gougis, R.D. "Analysis of High-Frequency and Long Term Data in Undergraduate Ecology Classes Improves Quantitative Literacy." Ecosphere, 8.3 (2017): pgs. 1-3.

26 Gentile, L., Caudill, L., Fetea, M., Hill, A., Hoke, K., Lawson, B., Ovidiu Lipan, et al. "Challenging Disciplinary Boundaries in the First Year: A New Introductory Integrated Science Course for STEM Majors." Journal of College Science Teaching, 41.5 (2012): pgs. 44-50.

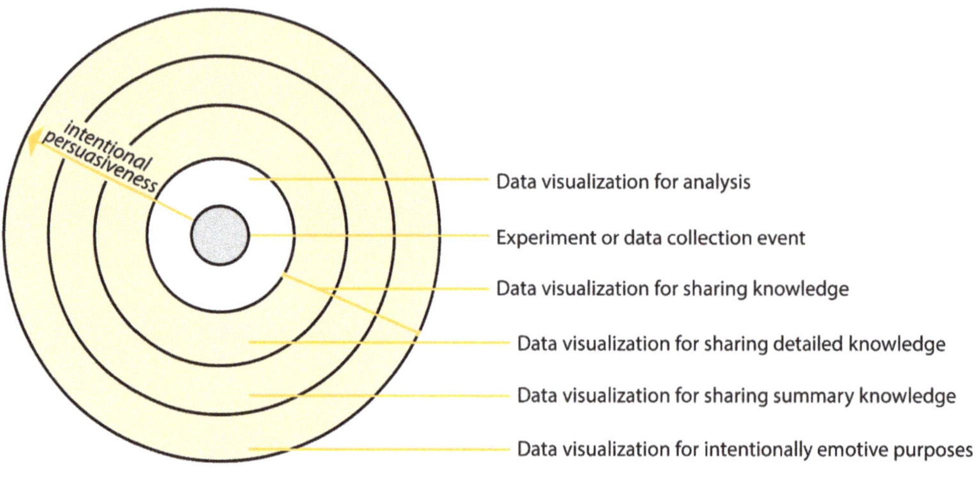

FIGURE 2: Proximity of the various types of visualization identified in the data visualization literature to the original experiment or data collection event. The further a visualization is located from the original experiment or data collection event, the more *intentionally persuasive* it tends to be.

27 Gordin, D.N. and Pea, R.D. "Prospects for Scientific Visualization as an Educational Technology." The Journal of the Learning Sciences, 4.3 (1995): pgs. 249–279.

28 Krause, K. "A Framework for Visual Communication at Nature." Public Understanding of Science, 26.1 (2017): pgs. 15–24.

29 Sheppard, S.R.J. "Landscape Visualisation and Climate Change: The Potential for Influencing Perceptions and Behaviour." Environmental Science & Policy, 8.6 (2005): pgs. 637–654.

30 Dur, B.I.U. "Data Visualization and Infographics In Visual Communication Design Education at The Age of Information." Journal of Arts and Humanities, 3.5 (2014): pgs. 39–50.

31 Segel, E., and Heer, J. "Narrative Visualization: Telling Stories with Data." IEEE Transactions on Visualization and Computer Graphics, 16.6 (2010): pgs. 1139–1148.

form the basis of the visualization component of the first-year course described in this discourse. STEM students are required to create both types of data visualizations in their undergraduate work, and, as such, need training on how to differentiate between and apply the two types. For example, if a student is trying to discover a pattern in data they have collected, they rely on data visualization to guide their analysis. On the other hand, if they have already identified an important pattern or structure, and want to communicate their findings, they turn to techniques appropriate to data visualization for sharing knowledge. Understanding the difference between the two types of data visualizations is treated as the first step to developing effective toolsets for creating them. The required fields of knowledge for teaching students to design effective data visualizations are outlined below.

Teaching Students to Design Data Visualizations for Analysis and Data Visualizations for Sharing Knowledge

Design of these two modalities of data visualization requires some overlapping skills. Data visualization for both analysis and for sharing knowledge requires designing a given example of each of these variants in a way that renders it understandable within the limits of human experience. In turn, this requires the accommodation of human sensing and behavior, information processing, and visual conventions. Human sensing considerations for data visualization include cultivating understanding about how people receive and process input through their bodily sensations and movement. There is an increasing body of work on the important roles that sensory experience play in the facilitation of learning.[35,36,37] These studies suggest that while input from all senses can theoretically influence how effectively a given data visualization can be interpreted, the predominant sensory factors that affect interpretation are aesthetic (relating to their visual nature) and, increasingly, haptic considerations (in the case of interactive visualizations). For example, if a particular data visualization uses multiple colors to communicate some of its essential meaning, and those colors are difficult to distinguish from each other visually, the visualization will be difficult to interpret.[38]

Information processing considerations that affect visualization include the cultivation of understandings regarding how people synthesize sensory experience into conceptual knowledge. These factors relate to cognitive information processing and storage through processes such as *chunking, dual coding,* and *serial position effects.*[39,40] For example, it is important to present only five or fewer groups of information (as delineated either by color, shape, shading or saturation, or position) in any one visualization, because this is the maximum number of 'chunks' of information that humans can comfortably process at one time.[41] Visual convention considerations for visualization include the repeated uses of visual elements—composition, color, line, shape and type—in a way that ensures the perception of a consistent, readily understood visual hierarchy, that allows them to be easily understood as specific types. For example, a student's drawing or plot of a bar chart can only be easily understood as a bar chart if it contains the visual conventions that are commonly associated with a bar chart. These include a series of solid vertical or horizontal color bars aligned along a solid black axis line, a title or labels indicating what the bars represent, and numerical indicators of what quantities the bars represent.[a] Visual conventions are effective due to their adherence to expected forms: if a viewer is able to identify elements of a data visualization and their purpose based on his or her familiarity with other similar images, the data visualization is more likely to communicate its message successfully.[42,43]

Data visualization for sharing knowledge requires greater skill and the ability to draw from a wider base of knowledge, because it must account for and address additional contextual considerations. To be effective, data visualization for sharing knowledge requires consideration of the aforementioned factors relevant to the facilitation of visualization for facilitating analysis, as well as awareness of and designing to accommodate a specific audience's biases and belief systems. Additionally, the socio-cultural context within which the

32 Blair, J.A. "The Rhetoric of Visual Arguments." In: Defining Visual Rhetorics, edited by C.A. Hill & M.H. Helmers, pgs. 41–62.

33 Kinross, R., "The Rhetoric of Neutrality." In: Design Discourse: History, Theory, Criticism, edited by V. Margolin, pgs. 197–218.

34 Kostelnick, C. "The Visual Rhetoric of Data Displays: The Conundrum of Clarity." IEEE Transactions on Professional Communication. 50.4, (2007): pgs. 280–294.

35 Psotka, J. "Educational Games and Virtual Reality as Disruptive Technologies." Educational Technology & Society, 16.2 (2013): pgs. 69–80.

36 Reiner, M. "Seeing Through Touch: The Role of Haptic Information in Visualization." In Visualization: Theory and Practice in Science Education, edited by J.K. Gilbert, M. Reiner, and M. Nakhleh, pgs. 73–84.

37 Reiner, M. "Sensory Cues, Visualization and Physics Learning." International Journal of Science Education, 31.3 (2009): pgs. 343–364.

[a] *These visual conventions, while widely accepted, have sometimes been challenged by prominent data visualization scholars. Notably, Edward Tufte suggests axis lines are not always necessary. However, we consider such removal of key design elements "advanced moves" that are best utilized by expert practitioners only, and do not recommend them for the majority of practitioners or data visualization use cases.*

visualization will be interpreted must be considered, as well as its intended purpose, or call to action, or evocation of emotion (or both) that the visualization has been designed to fulfill. To be effective, almost any given visualization requires the consideration of a broad array of factors that affect audience perception, logical interpretation, and emotional response. These include but are not limited to analysis and assessment of: demographics, psychographics, literacy, culturally rooted mindsets, socioeconomic class, and visual trends. While it would be ideal to consider all of these areas when attempting to design almost every data visualization for sharing knowledge, it is important for practical reasons—mostly related to being able to create these in limited amounts of time—to focus on only a few of them.

The key considerations regarding audiences when designing data visualization for sharing knowledge are *interest*, *expertise*, and *cognitive level*. When considered together, these factors provide a clear indication of the level of attention and cognitive effort audience members are likely, or able, to expend to effectively interpret the information they have been presented with. Designing to account for the relative level or interest, or attention span, a specific audience might have in a given subject or presentation, and accounting for the relative amount of cognitive effort they will have to expend to glean meaning from it, is a key tenet of user experience design. This discipline is rooted in attempting to ensure that the tasks required of a given individual in a particular context of use are not more than he or she can reasonably achieve given his or her attention span, level of education, cognitive abilities, socio-cultural beliefs, and sociopolitical and socioeconomic factors.[44,45] The qualities that make a particular line chart (see figure 3) effective for interested adults with average cognitive function for their age and expert knowledge of the subject matter on offer are quite different from the qualities that would make a line chart effective for middle school-aged children who have no prior interest in or exposure to that subject matter. Charts that endeavor to present essentially the same information to both of these audiences may depict some of the same data, but essential meaning can be visually communicated to the former group using much more complex means than the latter, and still remain intelligible to its audience. If a line chart designed for experts in a given type of scientific inquiry were presented unaltered in a scientific textbook aimed at first-year university students, it would likely be ineffective. To increase this line chart's intelligibility to these students, it would ideally be simplified visually, and perhaps include a greater amount of visual or textual annotation to help them

38 Wong, B. "Points of View: Color Coding." Nature Methods, 7.8 (2010): p. 573.

39 Lidwell, W., Holden, K., and Butler, J. Universal Principles of Design. Beverly, MA, USA: Rockport Publishers, Inc., 2003.

40 Meirelles, I. Design for Information. Beverly, MA, USA: Rockport, 2013.

41 Benson, N., Collin, C., Grand, V., Lazyan, M., Ginsburg, J., and Weeks, M. "George Armitage Miller: Cognitive Psychology." In The Psychology Book: Big Ideas Simply Explained, pgs. 170–173.

42 Krause, K. "A Framework for Visual Communication at Nature." Public Understanding of Science, 26.1 (2017): pgs. 15–24.

43 Wong, B. "Points of View: The Design Process." Nature Methods, 8.12 (2011): p. 987.

44 Krug, S. Don't Make Me Think: A Common Sense Approach to Web Usability. Berkeley, CA, USA: New Riders, 2006.

45 Rodríguez Estrada, F.C. and Davis, L.S. "Improving Visual Communi-cation of Science Through the Incorporation of Graphic Design Theories and Practices Into Science Communication." Science Communication 37.1 (2015): pgs. 140-148.

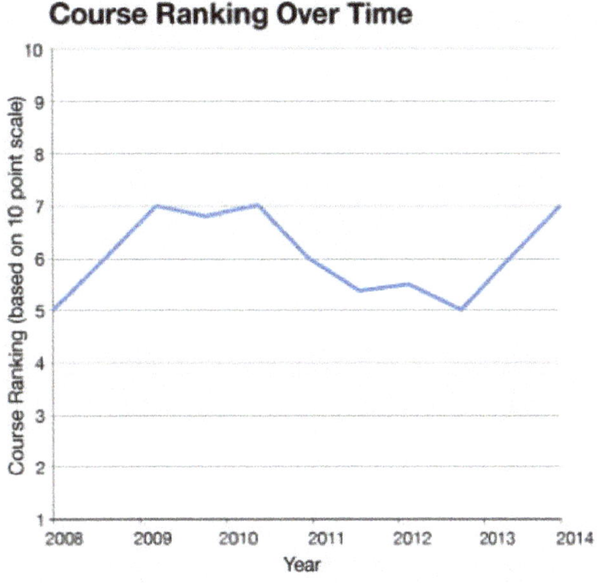

FIGURE 3: A line chart, also sometimes referred to a "fever chart."

connect the represented data with concepts that are better explained or further emphasized in the additional annotation.

When designing data visualizations for sharing knowledge, it is also critically important to consider and account for the effects that *context* will have on a given audience's ability to effectively interpret (and act on) meaning. The audience considerations discussed above focus on analyzing and assessing the individual characteristics of specific audiences or audience members. In this discourse, context refers to the way that location, situation, medium, and sociocultural, sociopolitical, and socioeconomic considerations affect presentation and interpretation of a data visualization, and it determines the likelihood that an audience can interpret a data visualization. Legibility, a term that refers to how clearly a given data visualization can be read by someone who is not visually impaired, is context dependent. For example, research posters are typically read from a distance of 4 feet away or greater, so charts that appear on posters need to be designed so that all of the type they make use of is clearly visible at this distance. In contrast, academic papers are typically read at a distance of 2 feet away or closer, on a printed page, or often on the screen of a digital device that affords the audience the possibility of zooming in to the figure, so that it may be viewed in closer detail. Therefore, in order to be legible *in context*, a chart for an academic paper can contain type at a much smaller type size than that which appears on a poster, without any loss of contextual legibility.[46]

46 Davis, M. Graphic Design Theory. London, UK: Thames & Hudson, 2012.

47 Mathewson, J.H. "Visual-Spatial Thinking: An Aspect of Science Overlooked by Educators." Science Education, 83.1 (1999): pgs. 33–54.

48 Gilbert, J.K. "Visualization: An Emergent Field of Practice and Enquiry in Science Education." In Visualization: Theory and Practice in Science Education, edited by J.K. Gilbert, M. Reiner, and M. Nakhleh, pgs. 3–24.

Science classes do not allow time to study each of the knowledge areas that contribute to effective data visualization in detail, if at all. The most practicable way to instill these considerations is to operate a two-part approach. The first of these involves providing students with a wide variety of examples of well-designed data visualizations (in the specific area they are learning about, whether that is data visualization for facilitating analysis, or one of the kinds of data visualization for sharing knowledge). The second involves presenting these examples in tandem with hands-on data visualization activities, and to have an instructor who possesses at least basic knowledge of the formal principles that guide effective layout design guide these activities. He or she can then point out the various formal factors (i.e., effective color use, the importance of legibility, and clear visual hierarchy) that make each data visualization effective as teachable moments arise.[47] Unfortunately, very few science educators are trained in visualization, and there is little awareness among science educators or in the science education scholarship that such specialist expertise exists in the field of visual communication design.[48] Visual communication design educators' expertise in data visualization holds promise for enhancing science instruction, and helping students to produce more effective data visualizations. However, this potential can only be realized if more visual communication design educators participate more fully in interdisciplinary teaching practices, especially in those that involve reaching across disciplinary boundaries into the sciences.

Computational Skills for Big Data: Analysis, Statistics, and Visualization

The educators who developed and implemented this course recognized that visualization instruction, along with big data and statistical analysis skills within STEM education at UNR, could be improved by introducing some basic, formal principles of layout and typography. The visual communication design faculty member and the physics faculty member informally discussed ways to remedy these pedagogical shortcomings, and settled on a grant-funded, interdisciplinary, co-taught course as the most viable solution. This approach was decided upon after careful analysis of the multiple knowledge disciplines such a course would need to draw from, and recognition that significantly more resources were necessary for such a course than is usually available for development and teaching of courses at UNR. An interdisciplinary course addressing the three pedagogical needs described in the previous sections of this article

[b] *The NASA Nevada Space Grant Consortium has a mission to develop Nevada's college and pre-college curricular and informal STEM education projects. This proposal was funded because the proposed course clearly fulfilled this mission. There are NASA Space Grant Consortium's based in most states that offer similar programs.*

was planned, and a curriculum development grant was awarded from the NASA Nevada Space Grant Consortium [b] to fund the pilot course. Typically, co-teaching is dissuaded at UNR due to the pressure to have faculty teach as many students as possible , but the teaching team felt that co-teaching was required to address this complex mix of pedagogical needs. Also, the scholarly literature indicated that this type of interdisciplinary approach is usually necessary to effectively address the needs of students enrolled in a STEAM course. [49,50]

Conceiving, planning, and teaching the pilot course involved more complex teaching arrangements than is typical of a course at UNR. The learning goals for this course, as well as its funding arrangements, and co-teaching logistics described in this article are outlined below. Additionally, this section of this piece provides a description of the course materials used, with heavy emphasis on the manner in which visual communication design instruction was facilitated; a detailed articulation of these appears in the visualization modules that occur on pages 56-58. While this course was intended for first-year STEM students and will be offered to them in the future, the pilot course described here was offered only to fourth-year students majoring in physics (due to logistical constraints). First-year STEM students were targeted in the course design because similar statistical and data visualization skills are required in each of the individual disciplines that constitute STEM at UNR, and teaching them to first-year students in an interdisciplinary course reduces the perception that certain techniques pertinent to data visualization might only be applicable with the confines of certain disciplines. [51]

49 Land, M.H. "Full STEAM Ahead: The Benefits of Integrating the Arts Into STEM." Procedia Computer Science, 20 (2013): pgs. 547–552.

50 Yakman, G. "Recognizing the A in STEM Education." Middle Ground, August 2012.

51 Gentile, L., Caudill, L., Fetea, M., Hill, A., Hoke, K., Lawson, B., Ovidiu Lipan, et al. "Challenging Disciplinary Boundaries in the First Year: A New Introductory Integrated Science Course for STEM Majors." Journal of College Science Teaching, 41.5 (2012): pgs. 44–50.

52 Crider, A. 2015. "Teaching Visual Literacy in the Astronomy Classroom." New Directions for Teaching and Learning, 141 (2015): pgs. 7–18.

53 Vande Moere, A. and Purchase, H. "On the Role of Design in Information Visualization." Information Visualization, 10.4 (2011): pgs. 356–371.

Pedagogical Goals

As described in the previous section, this course was created and implemented to address several gaps in undergraduate students' knowledge and skills, particularly those involving big data computation, statistical analysis, and data visualization skills. These gaps in student knowledge have appeared over roughly the past decade as university coursework has not kept pace with the increasingly heavy reliance on big data analysis in the arenas of government, industry, and research. [52,53] As such, the overarching aim of this course was to improve students' preparedness for upper-level (i.e., third- and fourth-year undergraduate) big data courses and, ultimately, readiness for careers in these three arenas that now require big data processing and analysis. This course was planned to address this overarching aim by articulating and achieving the pedagogical goal of strengthening students' big data computation, statistical analysis, and data visualization skills. As well as helping students improve their skills in each of the three targeted areas, this course was designed to help students attain an additional pedagogical goal related specifically to addressing the data visualization skills gap: that students would learn the difference between data visualization for facilitating analysis and data visualization for sharing knowledge.

Pedagogical context and demographics of the course

The total enrollment for the pilot course—a fourth-year undergraduate STEM course in physics that was taught in the spring of 2017—during which data visualization content was introduced was four. Each student brought a different set of skills to the course based on his or her previous academic preparation, but none of them had prior exposure to visual communication design principles. Each of these students were fourth-year undergraduates who were majoring in atmospheric sciences, but who were minoring in different areas, including mathematics and creative writing. One student was a double major in atmospheric sciences and secondary education. The course met once per week for 2.5 hours, and the students were expected to complete the majority of their assignments during this span of time; 40% of their workload, including the data visualization component, was assigned to be completed outside of class time. The big data component of the course was completed in the first eight weeks of the semester, and included parameterizing and running a numerical weather prediction model, navigating directories and files in a Linux computing environment, and executing tasks in a high-performance computing environment. The statistical analysis component of the course was taught in remainder of the classes, during which students learned to apply hypothesis testing, distribution fitting, and goodness-of-fit techniques to the data generated in the first half of the course.[c] The data visualization course materials were delivered online in the last half (seven weeks) of the semester. This provided the students with timely support for the chart creation that was a required aspect of their statistical analysis.

[c] *For people unfamiliar with these terms, a brief definition follows. Hypothesis testing: a method of statistical inference. Distribution fitting: fitting a probability distribution to data containing repeated measurement of a variable phenomenon. Goodness-of-fit techniques: determining whether sample data can be considered within a given specified distribution.*

An overview of data visualization instruction

The online data visualization materials that were taught during the final portion of the semester were taught to the students in three modules of one to four-week duration that consisted of readings, examples of visualizations, weekly activities, and a discussion board on which students were expected to submit completed activities weekly. These online materials were supported by an in-class review of activities, frequent email communication between students and the instructors, and one-on-one meetings between students and the visual communication design faculty member outside of class time. In the first module, *Introduction to Design for Visualization*, students spent one week learning about the course's interdisciplinary approach to data visualization, including being introduced to the discipline of visual communication design. They were also given an overview of the requirements, structure, and activities of the visualization segment of the course. In the four-week-long second module, *Visualization for Analysis*, the students were introduced to three visual communication design principles that are essential for effective data visualizations—effective color usage, legibility, and visual hierarchy—and were introduced to standard visual conventions of three fundamental chart types: bar charts, line charts, and scatter plots. In each of the first three weeks of this module, students were introduced to one visual communication design principle, and given a data visualization activity in which they had to demonstrate effective use of that particular principle. In the final week of this module, students applied the principles and visual conventions they learned during the previous three weeks to a data visualization for facilitating analysis activity using data they collected themselves [d], and choosing from one of the three chart types covered in the data visualization component of the course. Bar charts, line charts, and scatter plots were chosen for the visualization for facilitating analysis activities because they are so commonly used in basic statistical analysis.

[d] *Students collected data in the first component of the course, during their immersion in the numerical weather prediction activity.*

In the third and final module, *Visualization for Sharing Knowledge*, students learned about the intended audience, academic context, and purpose of visual abstracts, after which they completed an activity that involved working with a *visual abstract*. Visual abstracts are a relatively new kind of data visualization for sharing knowledge that presents an extremely simplified, visual overview of a research paper's main argument, typically without headings, and with as few labels as possible. When they are used to support scholarly pieces published in academic journals, visual abstracts appear between the paper's title and its written abstract. In the last few years, many scientific publishers have started requesting visual abstracts—also referred to as graphical abstracts or overview figures—in their submission guidelines for academic papers; in some instances it is listed as preferred, but inclusion of visual abstracts is becoming an increasingly compulsory requirement. Visual abstracts were chosen as the specific type of data visualization for sharing knowledge activity due to their widespread usage across a broad spectrum of disciplines, combined with a general lack of easily accessible, clear instruction regarding how best to design them.

All of the data visualization instruction that occurred during the final portion of the semester was scaffolded, so that each week's coursework progressively built on and incorporated what the students had learned the previous week. *Scaffolding* is a term frequently used in educational literature to refer to the practice of providing educational resources in a step-by-step manner in which later materials and activities build on materials and activities presented previously. This technique is crucial to the process of teaching subject matter related to data visualization because it arranges learning materials and activities so that learned concepts build progressively upon one another, which affords opportunities for students to gain integrated understandings of given subject materials by the end of a course. [54,55] All of the materials used to help facilitate these instructional processes were also designed to provide maximum support for students as they engaged in work on their final project, a 3,000 word academic paper reporting the findings of their big data computational modeling and statistical analysis. As such, the scaffolded approach extended beyond the data visualization component of the course, so that students continued to implement newly acquired statistical and big data skills as they learned about data visualization techniques. This scaffolding technique has been identified by other authors teaching similar courses as a key way to balance and synthesize interdisciplinary content while encouraging active learning for the students. [56,57]

Each week as the course progressed, students watched a short video made by the visual communication design faculty member that contained an overview of the essential concepts and activities that would be emphasized that week. Additionally, they read one relatively brief reading on a specific visual communication design principle, such as legibility and color when relevant, viewed examples of data visualizations, and completed one data visualization activity. The data visualization activities taught skills cumulatively: for example, the first data visualization activity required the students to design a line chart, bar chart, or scatter plot that had a high level of legibility, while the second week required them to produce a chart with a high level of legibility *and* an appropriate use of color. Students produced their data visualizations for analysis (as part of the second module) in R, a widely used open-source statistical analysis tool, thereby incorporating visual communication design

54 Marshall, J.A., Castillo, A.J., Cardenas, M.B. "The Effect of Modeling and Visualization Resources on Student Understanding of Physical Hydrology." Journal of Geoscience Education, 63.2 (2015): pgs. 127-139.

55 Mercer-Mapstone, L.D., Kuchel, L.J. "Integrating Communication Skills into Undergraduate Science Degrees: A Practical and Evidence-Based Approach." Teaching & Learning Inquiry, 4.2 (2016): pgs. 1-14.

56 Ellwein, A.L., Hartley, L.M., Donovan, S., and Billick, I. "Using Rich Context and Data Exploration to Improve Engagement with Climate Data and Data Literacy: Bringing a Field Station into the College Classroom." Journal of Geoscience Education, 62.4 (2014): pgs. 578-586.

57 Langen, T.A., Mourad, T., Grant, B.W., Gram, W.K., Abraham, B.J., Fernandez, D.S., Carroll, M., Nuding, A., Balch, J.K., Rodriguez, J., and Hampton, S.E. "Using Large Public Datasets in the Undergraduate Ecology Classroom." Frontiers in Ecology and the Environment, 12.6 (2014): pgs. 362-363.

```
####
#### Activity 1: Change the position of the legend
#### (options are: none, top, bottom, right)
####

kh_theme=theme_bw()+
  theme_bw(base_family='quadraat_serif', base_size=13) +
  theme(panel.grid.major=element_line(color = '#E5E5E5'),
        panel.grid.minor=element_line(color = '#E5E5E5',
linetype = 'dotted'),
        panel.border=element_blank(),
        # Adds white space around chart and labels
        plot.margin=unit(c(8,12,8,8),"mm"),
        # Formats the caption
        plot.caption=element_text(face='italic',
color='#666666'),
        # Creates an L shaped line for axes
        axis.line=element_line(),
        # Makes most text black
        text=element_text(color='black'),
        # Makes axis tick labels black
        axis.text = element_text(color='black'),
        # Changes title size and font weight to bold
        plot.title = element_text(face='bold', size=26,
           # Adds a little space between title and chart
           margin=margin(0,0,10,0)),
        #
        # Step 1: Change the position of the legend
        #
```

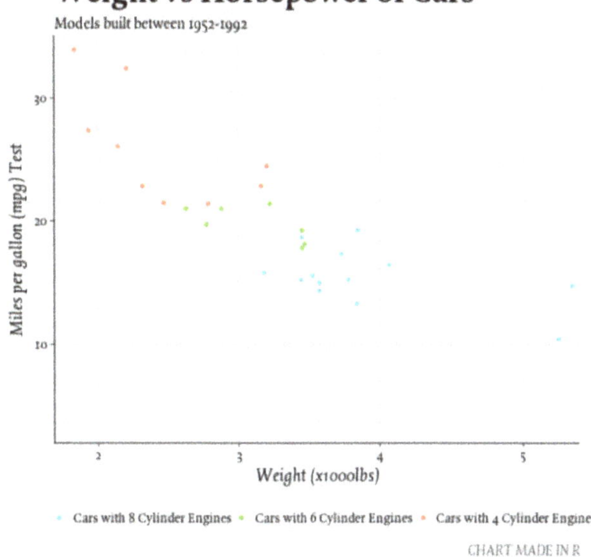

FIGURE 4: A visualization activity provided to students. Figure 4a (left) shows the code students were provided with, containing instructions and identifying variables to change. Figure 4b (right) shows the chart that the code produces when run in R.

practices into a common scientific workflow. Integrating design of data visualizations into familiar processes in this way is recommended in much of the scholarly literature (and consequently this is why using programs more commonly used in visual communication design schools, such as the Adobe suite, were avoided).[58] In the data visualization activities, students were provided with R code that generated a particular chart, with certain variables identified that they needed to change to practice that week's design activity. This approach was deemed more appropriate than having students write all the R code themselves, due to the complexity of writing it, and the relatively short time students had to complete their visualization modules. Figure 4 shows a typical data visualization activity provided to students on the left (Figure 4a) with the resultant visualization output on the right (Figure 4b).

To produce their visual abstracts (data visualizations for sharing knowledge, designed in the third module), students used online visualization software called *Plotly* (https://plot.ly/). This software provides its users with a simple WYSYWIG user interface for adjusting data visualizations made with R code, and was deemed to be more appropriate than R for creating the simplified design work typically depicted in visual abstracts. The software had an

58 Peterlin, P. "Data Analysis and Graphing in an Introductory Physics Laboratory: Spreadsheet versus Statistics Suite." European Journal of Physics, 31.4 (2010): pgs. 919–931.

additional benefit of enabling the production of both static and interactive versions of charts. Interactive effects of *Plotly* charts include hover effects indicating numerical markers at any data point in the chart and responsive chart re-sizing. Students used images created from *Plotly* in their major assignment, which consisted of a final paper and final presentation. The final paper was formatted and structured in a style appropriate for submission to a peer-reviewed physics journal, and the presentation was prepared to standard appropriate in a physics conference. In the final paper, static images from plot.ly were used as visual abstracts, while final presentations demonstrated the interactive elements in final presentations.

Measurement of Course Effectiveness

Effectiveness of the pilot course was measured in two ways: assessment of students' data visualization work as it was implemented in their final projects, and pre- and post-knowledge surveys administered to evaluate the effectiveness of the course's three subject areas, working with big data sets, statistical analysis, and data visualization. Visual assessment of students' data visualizations was chosen as a measure of effectiveness because skills acquisition (or lack thereof) was clearly demonstrated in the students' abilities to realize the effective visualization of complex data in the physical work they produce in response to the assigned coursework they were given. [59] Pre- and post-knowledge surveys based on course content were chosen because they are a common measure of skills acquisition in science education research. [60,61,62] Students' data visualization work throughout the various learning modules that constituted the bulk of the coursework and that was submitted as part of their final projects was assessed for evidence of high levels of legibility and a clearly discernable visual hierarchy. Legibility was determined be of a high level if paper figures could be comfortably read by an expert audience with a normal range of vision at the extreme end of the contexts in which they were presented. For the final paper, this was determined by on screen viewing at 100% magnification and at a distance of three feet away. For the final presentation, this was determined from an audience member's view of a presentation screen 30 feet away. Students accomplishment in understanding and executing data visualization for facilitating analysis was assessed through their module 2 visualization activity submissions. The visual abstracts produced in module 3 were assessed for the improvement of skills and increasing understanding of data visualization for sharing knowledge. During these assessments, two questions were asked in

59 Reiner, M. "Sensory Cues, Visualization and Physics Learning." International Journal of Science Education, 31.3 (2009): pgs. 343–364.

60 Kohnle, A., Douglass, M., Edwards, T.J., Gillies, A.D., Hooley, C.A., Sinclair, B.D. "Developing and evaluating animations for teaching quantum mechanics concepts." European Journal of Physics, 31.6 (2010): pgs. 1441–1455.

61 Hill, M., Sharma, M.D., Johnston, H. "How online learning modules can improve the representational fluency and conceptual understanding of university physics students." European Journal of Physics, 36.4 (2015): pgs. 1–20.

62 Marshall, J.A., Castillo, A.J., Cardenas, M.B. "The Effect of Modeling and Visualization Resources on Student Understanding of Physical Hydrology." Journal of Geoscience Education, 63.2 (2015): pgs. 127–139.

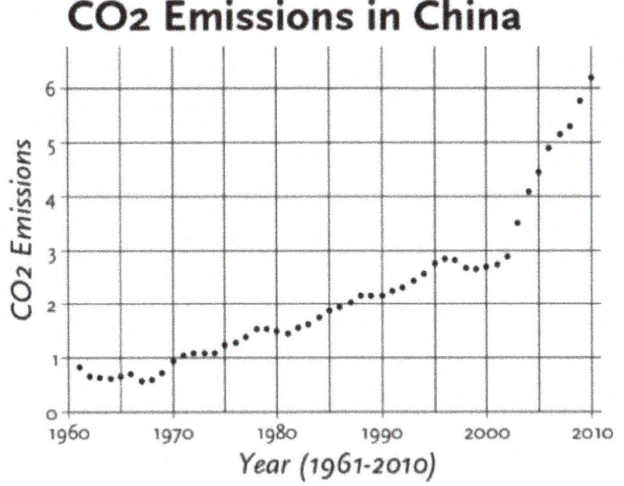

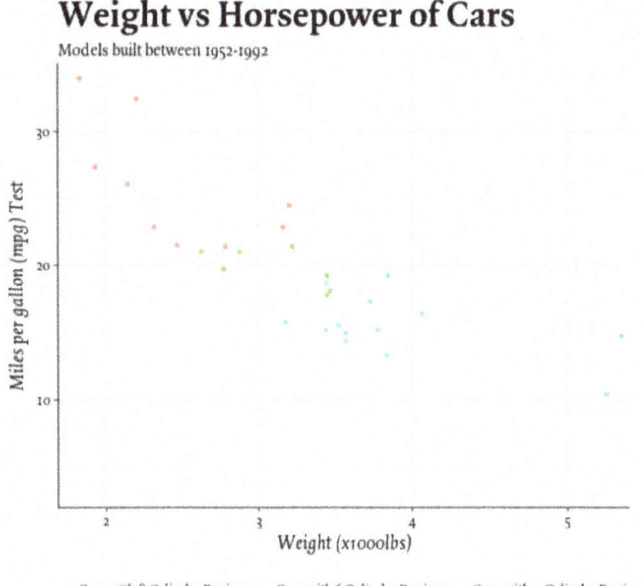

FIGURE 5: Student 1's visualization sample work. Figure 5a (left) is the first visualization exercise submission, where focus on legibility was required. Figure 5b (right) is one of the last visualization exercise submissions, where legibility, appropriate color use, and visual hierarchy were required.

relation to all of the students' data visualizations. First: is all text in the data visualizations clearly legible? Second: do the data visualizations embody a clear usage of the visual principles that yield an effective visual hierarchy? An additional question was asked of the visual abstracts: are the visualizations for sharing knowledge easy for their particular audiences to understand? The pre- and post-knowledge surveys were based on the evidence-based, customizable UC-Berkeley Course Evaluation Questions (http://teaching.berkeley.edu/course-evaluations-question-bank). The pre- and post-knowledge surveys instructed students to rank their own experience with big data skills, statistical methods, and visualization skills on the first day and the last day of the classes respectively. The post-course knowledge survey also assessed students' views of their newly acquired skills for creating effective visualizations. Answers to the questions were presented in qualitative form on a Likert scale, ranging from "not well at all" to "extremely well."

Overall, student work demonstrated progressive improvements in their application of color, configuration of typography, and establishment of visual hierarchy, resulting in the majority of the figures and visual abstracts that appeared in their final papers being significantly clearer in their communication of research findings than they had been in their early visualization

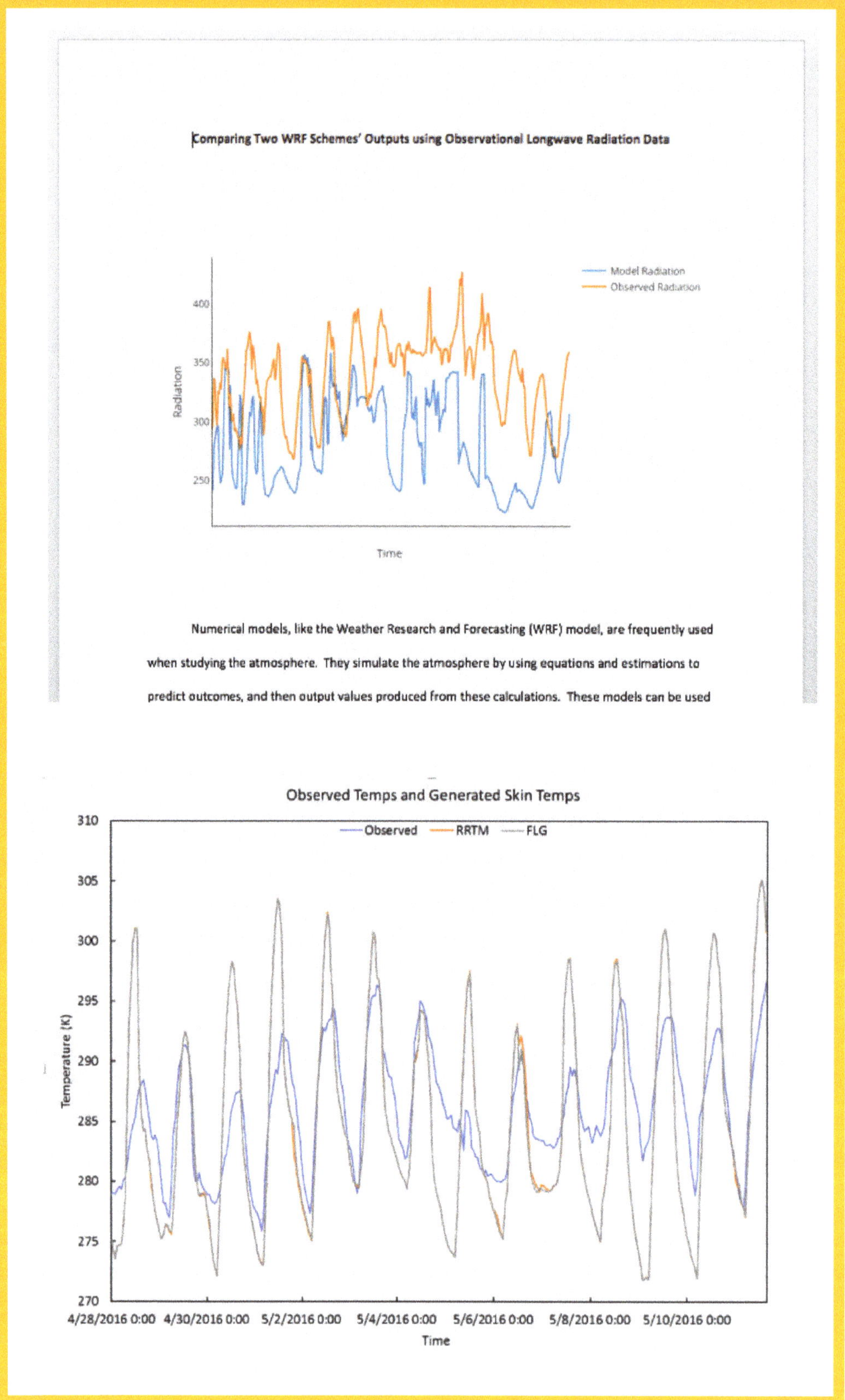

FIGURE 6: Student 2's data visualization for sharing knowledge and data visualization for facilitating analysis work. Figure 6a (top) shows the visual abstract 'in situ' as it appears in the student's paper. Figure 6b (bottom) shows a figure from the main text of the student's paper. Note that Figure 6a contains less numerical and textual details and thicker line weights in the lines representing data, resulting in an overall simplified appearance preferable for a visualization for sharing knowledge.

exercises. Figure 5 shows a typical example of progression of visualization skills in terms of the implementation of visual communication design principles. In the first chart (Figure 5a), the student practiced implementing legibility, while in the second chart (Figure 5b), the student practiced implementing legibility in combination with effective color use and visual hierarchy. Three out of four of the students demonstrated his or her ability to effectively make use of all of the visual communication design principles they learned throughout the data visualization module in the visualizations that appeared in their final papers, while one student did not. One student effectively used legibility throughout his/her final paper, but demonstrated an inconsistent use of appropriate and effective color and the establishment of visual hierarchy.

In their final papers, two of the four students demonstrated clear understanding of the difference between data visualization for sharing knowledge and data visualization for facilitating analysis in their differing design decisions evident in their visual abstracts and figures in their final papers. Figure 6 demonstrates effective student understanding of the different design decisions required of a visual abstract (Figure 6a) and a figure in an academic paper (Figure 6b). Two of the students in the class demonstrated partial understanding of the distinction between data visualization for sharing knowledge and data visualization for facilitating analysis.

In the pre- and post- course evaluation questions relating to data visualization skills, students reflected that their skills had improved on several measures (see Table 1). These reflections were collected as self-assessed measures–students were given five reply options, and for Table 1 these were converted to numerical measures 1–5 on a Likert scale. Collectively, their scores demonstrated an increase in their confidence with creating data visualizations for analysis and for sharing knowledge. The questions about data visualization for facilitating analysis and for sharing knowledge listed in Table 1 are phrased slightly differently than they are referred to in this paper in order to communicate to students in the most clear and simple language. Students also felt greater confidence after the course than before it in their understanding of legibility and visual hierarchy.

Pedagogical Reflections

According to student self-assessment that was later shared with the instructors, the pilot course was successful in its aim of improving the industry and research relevance of their skill sets specifically related to visualization of big

Question	*Pre-Test Mean*	*Post-test Mean*	*Change*
How well can you currently create data visualizations to interpret data?	2.25	3	0.75
How well can you currently create data visualizations to communicate findings?	2.25	2.75	0.5
How well do you understand the role of legibility when creating visualizations?	3.25	4	0.75
How well do you understand the role of visual hierarchy in creating data visualizations?	2.25	3.25	1

TABLE 1: Class collective pre- and post-test results for visualization component of the pilot course, demonstrating improvements in students' confidence on all measures.

data. Upon completion of the course, students identified that the material covered was relevant to their future intended careers. This interdisciplinary STEAM collaboration is a replicable model that has great promise for providing a much needed skill set to students at UNR and beyond. The success of the pilot course depended upon securing external funding, as the funding allowed important resources to be provided, and these resources made the course effective for students, and viable for all participating educators. These resources included font licenses, postgraduate researcher assistant salary for teaching purposes, graduate student assistant salary to assist in conducting pedagogical research about the course, and supercomputer processing time. The grant also allowed some instructors to receive teaching stipends that made teaching in this course as an overload viable. The grant also brought managerial support for the course, since externally funded projects are welcomed at the university.

On reflection, future iterations of this course could be strengthened by incorporating reflective discussion of data visualizations by instructors and students after each assignment to encourage deeper understanding of learned design principles. Future iterations of this course could also be strengthened by allowing for reflective time among instructors, in which new negotiated understandings of the benefits of cross-disciplinary collaboration could emerge. Before embarking on this project, the teaching team did not fully appreciate that co-teaching is a specific teaching skill, let alone the fact that each instructor had yet to master that skill. Co-teaching—the practice of multiple teachers providing instruction in the same class—can enrich a learning environment by imbuing it with multiple teacher perspectives, but it does require prior preparation on the part of instructors specific to co-teaching. Several miscommunications between instructors arose throughout the semester, sometimes resulting in contradictory information being shared with students, and other times making re-direction of student assignments necessary. The experience of the course could have been made richer for students if all the instructors who worked together to facilitate it had familiarized themselves with the foundational skills of co-teaching and committed to closer collaboration throughout semester.[63,64] This interdisciplinary STEAM collaboration is a replicable model that has great promise for providing a much-needed base of knowledge and skill set to students at UNR and other university and academy settings. If this model is used more broadly, it will be important to test its effectiveness in different university-level contexts and adjust the model according to the needs and learning styles of local students, and the curricula within which they are taught.

63 Lester, J.N. and Evans, K.R. "Instructors' Experiences of Collaboratively Teaching: Building Something Bigger." International Journal of Teaching and Learning in Higher Education, 20.3 (2009): pgs. 373-382.

64 McDonald, A. "In Between: Challenging the Role of Graphic Design by Situating It in a Collaborative, Interdisciplinary Class." In Design Studies: Theory and Research in Graphic Design, edited by A. Bennett, New York, NY, USA: Princeton Architectural Press, pgs. 354–69.

Conclusion

In the pilot course *"Computational Skills for Big Data: Analysis, Statistics, and Visualization,"* the use of data visualization for facilitating analysis and data visualization for sharing knowledge proved to be effective for teaching non-design students foundational principles of data visualization from a visual communication design perspective. Over the course of a 15-week semester, students' data visualization skills improved, as demonstrated by improvement in their design of charts and a marked increase in their levels of confidence regarding their visualization skills. The authors are aware that it is possible that data visualization activities strengthened students' data literacy and statistical analysis skills, one limitation of the course evaluation is that we did not test for this outcome. This is an opportunity for further evaluation in a future study. The broader benefits of introducing undergraduates to big data skills in combination with visual communication design principles for visualizations include clearer communication of scientific findings across disciplines and improved career prospects for students. Due to the success of this pilot course, the ongoing course of the same name has been submitted for inclusion in UNR curriculum and is currently under review. This fruitful course was made possible due to the combination of external funding and collaboration between visual communication design and STEM faculty. Visual communication design faculty have the capacity to effect transformative pedagogical change to the degree they are willing to engage in external grant seeking and interdisciplinary pedagogical collaboration.

Funding Statement

This project was funded in part by a Higher Education Curriculum Development sub-award from the Nevada NASA Space Grant Consortium: Award #NNX15AI02H.

References

Ali, S.M., Gupta, N., Nayak, G.K., Lenka, R.K. "Big data visualization: Tools and challenges." *In: 2016 2nd International Conference on Contemporary Computing and Informatics*. pgs. 656–660, 2016. Online. Available at: https://doi.org/10.1109/IC3I.2016.7918044 (Accessed July 1, 2017).

Benson, N., Collin, C., Grand, V., Lazyan, M., Ginsburg, J., and Weeks, M. "George Armitage Miller: Cognitive Psychology." In *The Psychology Book: Big Ideas Simply Explained*, pgs. 170–73. New York, NY, USA: DK Publishing, 2012.

Blair, J.A. "The Rhetoric of Visual Arguments." In: *Defining Visual Rhetorics*, edited by C.A. Hill & M.H. Helmers, Routledge, London, pgs. 41–62. London, UK: Routledge, 2004.

Kinross, R. "The Rhetoric of Neutrality." In: *Design Discourse: History, Theory, Criticism*, edited by V. Margolin, pgs. 197–218. Chicago, US: University of Chicago Press, 1989.

Crider, A. 2015. "Teaching Visual Literacy in the Astronomy Classroom." *New Directions for Teaching and Learning*, 141 (2015): pgs. 7–18. Online.

Available at: http://onlinelibrary.wiley.com/doi/10.1002/tl.20118/abstract (Accessed June 2, 2017).

Davis, M. *Graphic Design Theory.* London, UK: Thames & Hudson, 2012.

Dur, B.I.U. "Data Visualization and Infographics In Visual Communication Design Education at The Age of Information." *Journal of Arts and Humanities,* 3.5 (2014): pgs. 39–50. Online. Available at: http://thearts-journal.org/index.php/site/article/view/460 (Accessed June 2, 2017).

Ekbia, H., Mattioli, M., Kouper, I., Arave, G., Ghazinejad, A., Bowman, T., Suri, V.R., Tsou, A., Weingart, S., Sugimoto, C.R., 2015. "Big data, bigger dilemmas: A critical review." *Journal of the Association for Information Science and Technology,* 66.8 (2015): pgs. 1523–1545. Online. Available at: https://doi.org/10.1002/asi.23294 (Accessed July 2, 2017).

Ellwein, A.L., Hartley, L.M., Donovan, S., and Billick, I. "Using Rich Context and Data Exploration to Improve Engagement with Climate Data and Data Literacy: Bringing a Field Station into the College Classroom." *Journal of Geoscience Education,* 62.4 (2014): pgs. 578–86. Online. Available at: http://nagt-jge.org/doi/abs/10.5408/13-034 (Accessed July 17, 2017).

Gentile, L., Caudill, L., Fetea, M., Hill, A., Hoke, K., Lawson, B., Ovidiu Lipan, et al. "Challenging Disciplinary Boundaries in the First Year: A New Introductory Integrated Science Course for STEM Majors." *Journal of College Science Teaching,* 41.5 (2012): pgs. 44–50. Online. Available at: https://facultystaff.richmond.edu/~dszajda/research/papers/challenging_disciplinary_ boundaries.pdf (Accessed June 2, 2017).

Gilbert, J.K. "Visualization: An Emergent Field of Practice and Enquiry in Science Education." In *Visualization: Theory and Practice in Science Education,* edited by J.K. Gilbert, M. Reiner, and M. Nakhleh, pgs. 3–24. Dordrecht, Netherlands: Springer Netherlands, 2008.

Gordin, D.N. and Pea, R.D. "Prospects for Scientific Visualization as an Educational Technology." *The Journal of the Learning Sciences,* 4.3 (1995): pgs. 249–79. Online. Available at: https://telearn.archives-ouvertes.fr/hal-00190593/document (Accessed June 1, 2017).

Hill, M., Sharma, M.D., Johnston, H. "How online learning modules can improve the representational fluency and conceptual understanding of university physics students." *European Journal of Physics,* 36.4 (2015): pgs. 1–20. Online. Available at: https://doi.org/10.1088/0143-0807/36/4/045019 (Accessed July 1, 2017).

Johnson, C., Moorhead, M., Munzner, T., Pfister, H., Rheingans, P., and Yoo, T.S. *NIH-NSF Visualization Research Challenges Report.* IEEE Computer Society, 2006. Available at: http://nrs.harvard.edu/urn-3:HUL.InstRepos:4138744 (Accessed July 17, 2017).

Klug, J.L., Carey, C.C., Richardson, D.C., and Gougis, R.D.. "Analysis of High-Frequency and Long-Term Data in Undergraduate Ecology Classes Improves Quantitative Literacy." *Ecosphere,* 8.3 (2017): pgs. 1–13. Online. Available at: http://onlinelibrary.wiley.com/doi/10.1002/ecs2.1733/full (Accessed July 17, 2017).

Kohnle, A., Douglass, M., Edwards, T.J., Gillies, A.D., Hooley, C.A., Sinclair, B.D. "Developing and evaluating animations for teaching quantum mechanics concepts." *European Journal of Physics,* 31.6 (2010): pgs. 1441–1455. Online. Available at: https://doi.org/10.1088/0143-0807/31/6/010 (Accessed July 17, 2017).

Kostelnick, C. "The Visual Rhetoric of Data Displays: The Conundrum of Clarity." *IEEE Transactions on Professional Communication,* 50.4 (2007): pgs. 280–294. Online. Available at: https://doi.org/10.1109/TPC.2007.908725 (Accessed July 10, 2017).

Krause, K. "A Framework for Visual Communication at Nature." *Public Understanding of Science,* 26.1 (2017): pgs. 15–24. Online. Available at: http://journals.sagepub.com/doi/abs/ 10.1177/0963662516640966 (Accessed June 2, 2017).

Krug, S. *Don't Make Me Think: A Common Sense Approach to Web Usability.* Berkeley, CA, USA: New Riders, 2006.

Land, M.H. "Full STEAM Ahead: The Benefits of Integrating the Arts Into STEM." *Procedia Computer Science,* 20 (2013): pgs. 547–52. Online. Available at: http://www.sciencedirect.com/science/ article/pii/S1877050913011174 (Accessed July 12, 2017).

Langen, T.A., Mourad, T., Grant, B.W., Gram, W.K., Abraham, B.J., Fernandez, D.S., Carroll, M., Nuding, A., Balch, J.K., Rodriguez, J., and Hampton, S.E. "Using Large Public Datasets in the Undergraduate Ecology Classroom." *Frontiers in Ecology and the Environment,* 12.6 (2014): pgs. 362–63. Online. Available at: http://onlinelibrary.wiley.com/doi/10.1890/1540-9295-12.6.362/abstract (Accessed July 17, 2017).

Lester, J.N. and Evans, K.R. "Instructors' Experiences of Collaboratively Teaching: Building Something Bigger." *International Journal of Teaching and Learning in Higher Education,* 20.3 (2009): pgs. 373–82. Online.

Available at: http://files.eric.ed.gov/fulltext/EJ869322.pdf (Accessed July 12, 2017).

Lidwell, W., Holden, K., and Butler, J. *Universal Principles of Design.* Beverly, Massachusetts, USA: Rockport Publishers, Inc., 2003.

Maeda, J. "STEM + Art = STEAM." *The STEAM Journal,* 1.1 (2013): Article 34. Online. Available at: http://scholarship.claremont.edu/steam/vol1/iss1/34/ (Accessed July 12, 2017).

Marshall, J.A., Castillo, A.J., Cardenas, M.B. "The Effect of Modeling and Visualization Resources on Student Understanding of Physical Hydrology." *Journal of Geoscience Education,* 63.2, (2015): pgs. 127-139. Online. Available at: https://doi.org/10.5408/14-057.1 (Accessed June 2, 2017).

Mathewson, J.H. "Visual-Spatial Thinking: An Aspect of Science Overlooked by Educators." *Science Education,* 83.1 (1999): pgs. 33–54. Online. Available at: http://onlinelibrary.wiley.com/doi/ 10.1002/(SICI)1098-237X(199901)83:1%3C33::AID-SCE2%3E3.0.CO;2-Z/abstract (Accessed June 1, 2017).

McDonald, A. "In Between: Challenging the Role of Graphic Design by Situating It in a Collaborative, Interdisciplinary Class." In *Design Studies: Theory and Research in Graphic Design,* edited by A. Bennett, pgs. 354–69. New York, NY, USA: Princeton Architectural Press, 2006.

Meirelles, I. Design for Information. Beverly, MA, USA: Rockport, 2013.

Mercer-Mapstone, L.D., Kuchel, L.J. "Integrating Communication Skills into Undergraduate Science Degrees: A Practical and Evidence-Based Approach." *Teaching & Learning Inquiry,* 4.2 (2016): pgs. 1-14. Online. Available at: https://doi.org/10.20343/teachlearninqu.4.2.11(Accessed June 3, 2017).

Milner-Bolotin, M., and Nashon, S.M. "The Essence of Student Visual–spatial Literacy and Higher Order Thinking Skills in Undergraduate Biology." *Protoplasma,* 249.S1 (2012): pgs. 25–30. Online. Available at: https://link.springer.com/article/10.1007%2Fs00709-011-0346-6 (Accessed June 2, 2017).

Peterlin, P. "Data Analysis and Graphing in an Introductory Physics Laboratory: Spreadsheet versus Statistics Suite." *European Journal of Physics,* 31.4 (2010): pgs. 919–931. Online. Available at: http://iopscience.iop.org/article/10.1088/0143-0807/31/4/021/meta (Accessed June 1, 2017).

Psotka, J. "Educational Games and Virtual Reality as Disruptive Technologies." In *Educational Technology & Society,* 16.2 (2013): pgs. 69–80. Online.

Available at: http://www.ifets. info/journals/16_2/7.pdf (Accessed May 18, 2017).

Reiner, M. "Seeing Through Touch: The Role of Haptic Information in Visualization." In *Visualization: Theory and Practice in Science Education*, edited by J.K. Gilbert, M. Reiner, and M. Nakhleh, pgs. 73–84. Dordrecht, Netherlands: Springer Netherlands, 2008.

Reiner, M. "Sensory Cues, Visualization and Physics Learning." *International Journal of Science Education*, 31.3 (2009): pgs. 343–64. Online. Avaiable at: http://www.tandfonline.com /doi/abs/10.1080/09500690802595789 (Accessed June 1, 2017).

Rodríguez Estrada, F.C. and Davis, L.S. "Improving Visual Communication of Science Through the Incorporation of Graphic Design Theories and Practices Into Science Communication." *Science Communication*, 37.1 (2015): pgs. 140–48. Online. Available at: http://journals.sagepub.com / doi/abs/10.1177/1075547014562914 (Accessed June 2, 2017).

Segel, E., and Heer, J. "Narrative Visualization: Telling Stories with Data." *IEEE Transactions on Visualization and Computer Graphics*, 16.6 (2010): pgs. 1139–48. Online. Available at: http://vis.stanford.edu/papers/narrative (Accessed June 16, 2017).

Sheppard, S.R.J. "Landscape Visualisation and Climate Change: The Potential for Influencing Perceptions and Behaviour." *Environmental Science & Policy*, 8.6 (2005): pgs. 637–54. Online. Available at: http://www.sciencedirect.com/science/article/pii/S1462901105001188 (Accessed June 1, 2017).

Shoresh, N and Wong, B. "Points of View: Data Exploration." *Nature Methods*, 9.1 (2012): pg. 5. Online. Available at: http://www.nature.com/nmeth/journal/v9/n1/full/nmeth.1829.html (Accessed June 17, 2017).

Trumbo, J. "Visual Literacy and Science Communication." *Science Communication*, 20.4 (1999): pgs. 409–25. Online. Available at: http://journals.sagepub.com/doi/abs/10.1177/ 1075547099020004004 (Accessed June 2, 2017).

Trumbo, J. "Essay: Seeing Science." *Science Communication*, 21.4 (2000): pgs. 379–91. Online. Available at: http://journals.sagepub.com/doi/abs/10.1177/1075547000021004004 (Accessed June 1, 2017).

Valle, M. "Visualization: A Cognition Amplifier." *International Journal of Quantum Chemistry*, 113.17 (2013): pgs. 2040–52. Online. Available at: http://

onlinelibrary.wiley.com/doi/ 10.1002/qua.24480/abstract (Accessed June 2, 2017).

Vande Moere, A. and Purchase, H. "On the Role of Design in Information Visualization." *Information Visualization*, 10.4 (2011): pgs. 356–71. Online. Available at: http://journals.sagepub.com/ doi/abs/10.1177/1473871611415996 (Accessed June 2, 2017).

Wong, B. "Points of View: Color Coding." *Nature Methods*, 7.8 (2010): pg. 573. Online. Available at: http://www.nature.com/nmeth/journal/v7/n8/full/nmeth0810-573.html (Accessed July 16, 2017).

Wong, B. "Points of View: The Design Process." *Nature Methods*, 8.12 (2011): pg. 987. Online. Available at: https://www.nature.com/nmeth/journal/v8/n12/full/nmeth.1783.html (Accessed June 17, 2017).

Yakman, G. "Recognizing the A in STEM Education." *Middle Ground*, August 2012. Online. Available at: https://steamedu.com/recognizing-the-a-in-stem-education/ (Accessed July 13, 2017).

Zhang, Z.H. and Linn, M.C. "Can Generating Representations Enhance Learning with Dynamic Visualizations?" *Journal of Research in Science Teaching*, 48.10 (2011): pgs. 1177–98. Online. Available at: http://onlinelibrary.wiley.com/doi/10.1002/tea.20443/abstract (Accessed June 2, 2017).

Biographies

Katherine Hepworth is a communication design practitioner-researcher currently working as an Assistant Professor of Visual Journalism at the University of Nevada, Reno. Her research interests center around how communication design artifacts mediate power relationships, with a particular focus on the power implications of data visualization across disciplines. This research focus has led her to formulate and operate current projects on ethical data visualization in the digital humanities, efficacy and ethics in big data visualization, and pedagogical research on improving educational strategies related to visualization in the sciences. Dr Hepworth also has a broad research interest in improving communication effectiveness in higher education. In her research, teaching, and professional practice, Dr. Hepworth takes a human-centered approach to communication design, prioritizing the cultivation of broader understandings of and about people's lived experience of communication design artifacts.

Chelsea Canon is a Ph.D. student in Geography at the University of Nevada, Reno. Her research identifies key factors influencing the formation of collaboration and communication networks linking climate scientists to other researchers in physical science, social science, and the humanities, as well as to resource managers and stakeholders. Her goal is to provide actionable information about how to initiate, grow and sustain these networks. Prior to studying science communication, Ms. Canon received a B.A. in Spanish and Spanish American Studies from Mills College in Oakland, California. Her M.S. in Geography, also from the University of Nevada, Reno, used material culture artifacts to consider and contest a commonly-accepted narrative about Nevada's mining history. This interdisciplinary background informs her current research interests.

Dialectic Volume II, Issue I: Theoretical Speculation

Employing Rhetorical Theory in Design Education Practice

SUSANNA KELLY ENGBERS[1]

1. Kendall College of Art and Design, Ferris State University, Grand Rapids, Michigan, USA

SUGGESTED CITATION: Engbers, S.K. "Rhetorical Theory in Design Education Practice." *Dialectic,* 2.1 (2018): pgs. 81-95. DOI: http://dx.doi.org/10.3998/dialectic.14932326.0001.304

Abstract

Intersections between the disciplines of rhetoric and design, though well-articulated by scholars in those areas, generally remain more in the realm of theory than practice. This article presents a strategy for integrating rhetorical theory into the university-level classroom to support the processes of student designers (particularly those in visual communications, interaction design, and user experience design). Practice in the art of rhetoric will help such students to both analyze visual, verbal, and material texts (i.e., anything from products to posters to persuasive essays to front porches) as species of discourse and create more successful texts themselves. One fundamental tool to advance students' work in design (as well as in writing and other communicative arts) is the *rhetorical triangle;* it provides students with a developed, systematic theory and corresponding lines of inquiry to help them achieve their most rhetorically savvy, intelligent work. In addition, an understanding of the rhetorical triangle illuminates one of the most vital intersections between design and the humanities.

Employing Rhetorical Theory in Design Education Practice

SUSANNA KELLY ENGBERS

Introduction

For this issue of *Dialectic*, which invites conversation of "issues operating at the intersection of design and the humanities," I offer a discussion of rhetoric. Knowledge of principles and practices from this ancient humanistic discipline can help students—especially those in the areas visual communications, interaction design, and user experience design—use rhetoric's systematic approach when analyzing the work of others and when creating their own work. Although scholars such as Richard Buchanan, David Kaufer, Brian Butler, and others have analyzed at length the relationship between rhetoric and design, such connections are often constructed more for use by the researcher-scholar in the field and less for use by the instructor and student in the classroom. To address this deficiency, I offer here some practical strategies to help design students understand and effectively employ key rhetorical theories and concepts in their study and practice.

Rhetoric's Theoretical Connections with Design

In contemporary popular usage, the word *rhetoric* often carries pejorative connotations—"hate rhetoric," "empty rhetoric," "mere rhetoric"—yet over its long history the term has generally been defined more favorably. For example, Aristotle described it as "the faculty of discovering in any particular case all of the available means of persuasion." Other Classical rhetoricians presented various alternatives: for example, focusing on the character of the speaker (for

1 Foss, S., Foss, K., & Trapp, R. Contemporary Perspectives on Rhetoric, 2nd ed. Prospect Heights, IL, USA: Waveland Press, 1985, p. 14.

2 Kaufer, D., & Butler, B. Rhetoric and the Arts of Design. Mahway, NJ, USA: Erlbaum, 1996, p. 18.

3 Corbett, E. & Connors, R. Classical Rhetoric for the Modern Student, 4th ed. New York, NY, USA: Oxford UP, 1999, p. 1.

4 Buchanan, R. "Declaration by Design: Rhetoric, Argument, and Demonstration in Design Practice." Design Issues, 2.1 (1985): p. 108.

it was, of course, initially only an oral art), Quintilian defined rhetoric as the "good man speaking well." Cicero presented rhetoric as "speech designed to persuade." Modern scholars have offered other definitions such as "an action human beings perform when they use symbols for the purpose of communicating with one another."[1] In *Rhetoric and the Arts of Design,* David Kaufer and Brian Butler put forth an uncommon but provocative definition, maintaining that rhetoric is "the control of events for an audience."[2] Edward Corbett and Robert Connors' definition is perhaps the most direct and intelligible for a modern audience: "the art or the discipline that deals with the use of discourse...to inform or persuade or motivate an audience."[3] "Discourse" may refer not only to spoken and written communication but also to visual, material, and hybrid forms—everything from campaign speeches to newspaper editorials, websites, clothing, film documentaries, architecture, and other designed objects. And like designed objects, spaces, systems, communities, and experiences, rhetorical texts are almost developed and deployed in light of those who will listen to, read, view, and/or interact with them. Given its age as a discipline, rhetoric may *seem* less relevant than more modern methods of inquiry, but the categories of rhetorical analysis provide an adaptable, productive system for students to use in analyzing and creating all manner of communicative texts.

To be sure, the potential for fertile practical connections between the disciplines of rhetoric and design has been articulated in the theoretical scholarship. For example, Richard Buchanan has argued that rhetoric is the *architectonic* art for all design. Buchanan explains that rhetoric is the "art that organize[s] the efforts of [the design arts] giving order and purpose to production."[4] He points to rhetoricians' abilities to invent, organize, and present not just words but also material objects to audiences. He notes that traditionally, a rhetorical argument involved a speaker who was "seek[ing] to provide the audience with the reasons for adopting a new attitude or taking a new course of action." He adds that:

> "with the rise of technology in the twentieth century, the remarkable power of man-made objects to accomplish something very similar has been discovered. By presenting an audience of potential users with a new product—whether as simple as a plow or a new form of hybrid seed corn, or as complex as an electric light bulb or a computer—designers have directly influenced the actions of individuals and

communities, changed attitudes and values, and shaped society in surprisingly fundamental ways."[5]

In other words, when we sit in hotel rooms that interior designers or architects have created, use the bath products industrial designers or consumer product developers have invented, and work at the tables furniture designers have designed, we are shaped in similar ways—and perhaps even more strongly—as we are shaped by the verbal arguments we encounter. He suggests that "the designer, instead of simply making an object or thing, is actually creating a persuasive argument that comes to life whenever a user considers or uses a product as a means to some end."[6] In *Rhetoric and the Arts of Design,* Kaufer and Butler share Buchanan's goal of relating design and rhetoric more closely, yet they focus more strictly on the idea of designing with words rather than looking more widely at multimodal rhetoric, as Buchanan does. Kaufer and Butler seek to re-present a theory of rhetoric as design and to understand rhetoric as a "type of productive knowledge." As such, they argue for rhetoric as a "member in full of the family of design arts," akin to architecture and engineering, similar because of their complexity, pragmatic objectives, and contingency, to cite just a few parallels.[7] And in her more recent article on design rhetoric, Annina Schneller points out that the rhetoricity of designed visual objects—as opposed to written texts—is frequently difficult to discern, partly because visual "language" is almost always more implicit than explicitly expressed verbal language:

> "While there is an explicit content to any normal uttered sentence, the 'content' of an armchair or lemon squeezer is of a rather implicit nature. What is more, spoken and written language usually have a linear and temporal structure, which is why rhetorical effects can be created by contrasting, stressing, or repeating linguistic elements over time. The 'reading' process of designed objects is guided to a lesser extent than that of a printed text. Designed things mostly generate effects of contrast, stress, or repetition within the spatial arrangement of a formal whole present at one time."[8]

As Schneller points out, given their tendency toward the indirect rather than the direct, discerning the rhetorical qualities of designed objects is hardly a straightforward exercise. In addition to Buchanan, Schneller, Kaufer and Butler,

5 Ibid, p. 93.

6 Buchanan, R. "Declaration by Design: Rhetoric, Argument, and Demonstration in Design Practice." Design Issues, 2.1 (1985): p. 96.

7 Kaufer, D., & Butler, B. Rhetoric and the Arts of Design. Mahway, NJ, USA: Erlbaum, 1996, p. xvi.

8 Schneller, A. "Design Rhetoric: Studying the Effects of Designed Objects." Nature and Culture, 10.3 (2015), p. 335.

scholars in graphic design have contributed to a greater appreciation for the rhetorical nature of design. In *Graphic Design as Communication,* for example, Malcolm Barnard examines the constructions and communication of meaning through graphic design, using rhetoric as one among many critical lenses. [9] And, in *Graphic Design Theory,* Meredith Davis presents various communication models from the school of communications theory, noting their underappreciated role in the creation and critique of designed objects and texts. [10] Despite the fact, however, that the *theoretical* connections between rhetoric and design are clear to these and many other faculty and scholars whose work is rooted in these respective areas, effectively operationalizing the *practical* connections between them often proves elusive for design faculty and students.

Developing an awareness of texts—written, oral, visual, material, and hybrid—as being fundamentally communicative poses a challenge for students in rhetoric and design studio classes alike. As a faculty member with a background in rhetoric and composition teaching at a college of art and design, I have long been curious about how to exploit the potentially rich connections between the humanities and art/design in my own classroom and across the college. I began my own education about the teaching and learning going on in the studio classrooms at my college of art and design by turning to my faculty colleagues in these areas. I asked a dozen of them to write about how they invited their students to analyze their designs as rhetorical texts—i.e., as texts that respond to the exigencies of the particular situations for which they were created. When I studied the language of the responses, I noticed that three concepts recurred far more than others—namely the ideas of branding, reaching the client/user, and working on a problem/solution. For example, regarding branding, an interior design faculty member noted that, among the projects she taught in her undergraduate classrooms in a given academic year, her "hospitality project and office environment project" best illustrated an emphasis on transmitting the brand messaging of a specific company. She noted that the design must "work in conjunction with its 'mission' and communicate the goals/ethics/business practices of the company—creative/open/sleek/fun/cool, etc." She pointed to examples of the physical design of Google's or Apple's office spaces that "embody the philosophies" of those companies. Regarding the focus that is often placed on understanding the goals and social or economic biases of a particular user or audience in graphic design, a faculty member from this area said: "We talk about [how] communication design must be 'user-centered' to be effective, because design

9 Barnard, M. Graphic Design and Communication. London, UK: Routledge, 2005.

10 Davis, M. Graphic Design Theory. New York, NY, USA: Thames & Hudson, 2012.

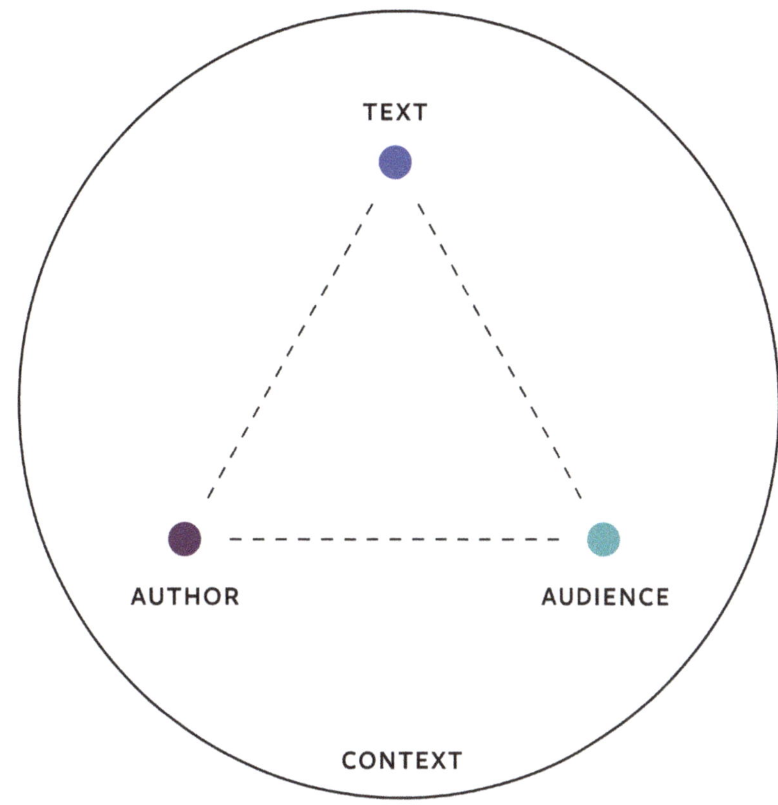

FIGURE 1: The Rhetorical Triangle

for the sake of design and not people is just art." And on the idea of problem/solution, one industrial design faculty member put it this way: "At its core, the design process is focused on identifying a problem and creating a solution." I recognize that there is a wide body of scholarship in and around all of these areas that add necessary nuance and sophistication to these fundamental ideas that guide how design processes are framed and taught, particularly at the undergraduate level. My faculty colleagues' responses to my fairly casual question elicited appropriately casual responses, but what became most compelling to me as I continued to pose this question was the way in which the comments I received quickly resolved themselves into three basic, practical categories of *text*, *sender*, and *audience*, which are quite familiar to those of us who teach rhetoric and writing.

The Rhetorical Triangle

In the fields of rhetoric and writing, we refer to those three basic categories as the main elements of the "rhetorical triangle," a term coined by James

11 Kinneavy, J. A Theory of Discourse: The Aims of Discourse. Englewood Cliffs, NJ, USA: Prentice Hall, 1971.

12 Davis, M. Graphic Design Theory. New York, NY, USA: Thames & Hudson, 2012, pgs. 14–31.

Kinneavy, well-known rhetorician and author of *A Theory of Discourse* (1971) among other works. [11] Kinneavy developed an image (similar to the one presented here) that could be used as a visual metaphor for a rhetorical (or "communication") situation.

This model presents the relationship between writer, audience, and text, as well as the surrounding context. It points to the ways in which writer, audience, and text (or creator, viewer/user, and object, to recast these in terms more appropriate to the analysis of visual and/or material objects and their relative effects) necessarily affect one another and guide how and why a given object is created and interpreted as it is. For example, a speech on gun control (a text) is necessarily different (either in its creation or its interpretation) when given to gun owners than when presented to peace activists (audience). And a monument designed by Maya Lin (a well-known writer/creator), for example, for a specific situation or occasion also "reads" differently to viewers than one designed by a designer or an artist freshly graduated from college and, as such, who is unknown to the design or the art world. It is an image that now appears commonly in many texts on the study of composition and rhetoric; students in writing and speech classes at both the high school and university levels would likely see this image reproduced quite frequently. Examples of such visual models abound, but some of the most notable include the Shannon-Weaver 1949 Mathematical Model, which is a linear model that depicts a message coming from an information source and going to an encoder, a channel, a decoder, and then a destination; Schramm's 1954 Model of Communication, which is a circular model that also maps a message from an encoder to a decoder; and structural linguist Roman Jakobson's 1960 model of interpersonal verbal communication, which considers the context, contact, addresser, and addressee of a message in an inter-connected manner. These models are well-known to many scholars in visual communication and interaction design. In *Graphic Design Theory,* for example, Meredith Davis outlines a number of these models, noting their centrality for theorists and practitioners in these areas of design. [12] The specific strategies that I outline below, all of which are based on the rhetorical triangle, can help instructors make them even *more* central, and *more* useful, in the education of design students studying to enter these professional disciplines.

Though certainly not the most detailed of the models, the rhetorical triangle is imbued with an elegant simplicity, making it well-suited for students to recall and deploy; further, it corresponds neatly to Aristotle's artistic appeals of *ethos, pathos,* and *logos.* Aristotle, and the many rhetoricians who would pattern themselves after him, focused on *persuasive* discourse, which he maintained was affected through three kinds of "proofs" (*pistis*): ethical (appeals to the sender's character); pathetic (appeals to audience's emotions); and logical (appeals to reason). Aristotle referred to these proofs as "artistic," highlighting the idea that they could be generated via the productive art of rhetoric, unlike the "inartistic" or "extrinsic" proofs (e.g., expert or witness testimony, statistics, and the like) that were simply *gathered* and deployed by the sender/speaker, and not generated, or "invented," through rhetoric. Through the careful generation and deployment of appropriate appeals, the rhetorician stood a greater chance of getting his audience to assent to his line of argument. It is wholly fitting that the appeals dubbed "artistic" are those that so nicely bridge the gap between the humanities and *artful* discipline of design.

Practical Strategies to Bridge the Gap

The feedback that I received from the design faculty I questioned in the Art and Design College within which I teach indicated that they emphasize teaching the principal aspects of the traditional rhetorical triangle: namely, (1) a focus on developing or understanding the branding (image, personae, etc.) of the organization being served (ethos), (2) a focus on understanding clients' and users' feelings (pathos), and (3) a concern for ensuring that clients understand the logical advantages associated with the product/design itself (logos). They tended, however, not to implement these appeals in their respective classrooms in a *systematic* way. Equipping students with a basic system gives them a valuable, easily recalled tool to use as their educational experiences progress. In the design classroom, an awareness of the intersection between design and rhetoric might chiefly be useful in two ways. First, as a means to methodically probe the ways in which communication operates implicitly, and second, as a means to encourage students to look past the immediate effects that a given designed artifact or system appears to have on them as its maker, so that they can examine the medium- and long-term effects that these artifacts or systems might invite or facilitate among a broad cross section of audiences or users in various contexts.

I would stop short of urging an investigation such as that which Schneller undertakes in her study of "design rhetoric," which partly seeks to determine design *rules.* Using a "triangulation of researchers" to "eliminate individual bias in effect ascription" (p. 341), Schneller attempts to, as she puts it, "pin down" the effects of various formal design elements (e.g., color, font, size) on a universal audience (e.g., "The color black will produce these specific feelings and associations in audiences.") (p. 345).[13] This kind of investigation is bound to end—as Schneller's does—in a failure of certainty. It recalls the use of "handbooks" of rhetoric that circulated in ancient Greece—documents that, in part, offered hard-and-fast strategies for engaging in good speaking, and listed both figures of speech and longer, more strictly structured speeches for students to memorize. Such systems simply do not account for the complexities integral to most systems of information delivery. In *Classical Rhetoric and its Christian and Secular Traditions,* George Kennedy notes that such "technical rhetoric" concentrated on the speech at the expense any concern for audience or sender.[14] It is not that this kind of technical, even mechanical, approach cannot be helpful. Certainly, appreciating basic conventions and connotations of verbal and/or visual "grammar" is useful, and imitation is one important form of learning (through habit and repeated practice, we acquire wisdom and deftness of approach), but the rule-bound approach would not seem to be useful as the *primary* method for learning that would equip students to deal with the inevitable complexities involved in any communicative enterprise.

Instead, I suggest that the art of rhetoric—and specifically the scheme of the triangle—offers both a full, systematic theory and corresponding lines of inquiry for designers to consider as they develop their projects. Those questions might revolve around the three categories of proof—those related to sender, audience, and text (i.e., ethos, pathos and logos). The three categories—especially when embodied in triangular form—are simple and easy for students to remember as a touchstone, though as they deepen their understanding of the three types of proof, the analysis—and resulting designed projects—should become quite nuanced and complex. To be clear, I am not suggesting that such a process is unknown among design faculty and students, only that it could be used more widely, perhaps especially to consider the role of the *sender,* the element that is the most subtle and easy to overlook, especially for novice practitioners.[a] Aristotle himself maintained that—in practice—the ethical appeal was the most persuasive. Thus, at the most basic level, students can simply be taught to be mindful of the three main components of any text: sender, audience, and text. At the next level, students can operationalize a set of standard questions they utilize to help them critically interrogate each component. For example:

13 Schneller, A. "Design Rhetoric: Studying the Effects of Designed Objects." Nature and Culture, 10.3 (2015): pgs. 333-356.

14 Kennedy, G. Classical Rhetoric and its Christian and Secular Tradition 2nd ed. Chapel Hill, NC, USA: U of North Carolina P, 1999, p. 14.

[a] *See Engbers,* S. "Branded: The Sister Arts of Rhetoric and Design." Art, Design, and Communication in Higher Education, 12.2 (2013), pgs. 149-158.

Re: the sender: Who are all the "senders" of this text? (e.g., in the case of the design of a hotel lobby, the sender might be the hotel company, the designer, and/or the city in which the hotel is located, etc.) How do the identities of those senders appear in this text? In what ways might those identities be at odds with one another and/or support one another? What improvements might be made in light of the answers to these questions?

Re: the audience: who are all the "users" of this text? What range of emotional and intellectual responses might this text invite in them? (It should be pointed out that this is a different question than analyzing the emotions that might be expressed by and/or through the text; for example, a man looking confident in an advertisement might actually invite opposing feelings—e.g., of intimidation or inadequacy—in its viewers.) How might those responses be shaped by the exigencies of time and other contextual factors? Are there more or less appropriate ways to design this text with those exigencies in mind?

Re: the text: What are the formal properties of the designed text (e.g., its layout, font, proportions, etc.)? How do the visual and verbal elements work to support the logic of the text? What other formal elements might add to the text's effectiveness?

Beyond this array of questions lies even greater possibilities for complex yet potentially fruitful inquiry, chiefly as it relates to investigations of the *text,* via logical appeals, and the *sender,* via ethical appeals. Analyses that address the audience's or users' roles seem to be the most well-traveled terrain for design students, who are accustomed to those kinds of investigations through coursework in, for example, the application of color theory or user-experience design. Rhetoricians would note the similarities that such investigations bear to pathetic, or emotional, analyses. Additionally, as a means to indicate the value of employing the lenses of the other two artistic appeals—logos and ethos—I will briefly describe two specific examples of these kinds of focused analyses.

Take, for example, the case of a hypothetical print advertisement for a toothpaste: with it, students may consider the various species of *logical* proof. The ad might include explicit verbal logic, such as Brand X, "brightens your teeth more effectively than leading competitors," and "it kills 98% of bacteria" and so on. The ad might, as well, include explicit visual logic—perhaps an image of a smiling woman with brilliant white teeth or a close-up of the product itself with its layers of "bacteria-fighting" agents made visible in some overt way. More subtly, though, students might observe implicit verbal logic—perhaps words with militaristic connotations (e.g., *fight, depend, guard against, defeat,* etc.) that imply, rather than directly support, the ad's argument. And, similarly, the ad might include images that suggest support rather than provide or facilitate it directly. Perhaps the ad includes recurring images of small shields to underline the theme of "defense." Or maybe the ad's use of a thick, bold typeface implies the fortified, sturdy nature of the product. That kind of investigation of logic—visual and verbal, explicit and implicit—can deepen and extend students' ability to invent and refine successful designs of all kinds that operate as fundamentally logical arguments, especially since they are not often conceived of as such.

With regard to ethical appeals—i.e., those focused on the sender—it is useful to get a bit more deeply into the details of the Aristotelean concept of ethos, which includes three components (of which one, two, or all three may be present): namely, the ways in which the sender conveys to the audience a sense of *phronesis* (prudence), *arête* (virtue), and/or *eunoia* (goodwill). *Phronesis* refers to the audience's impression of the sender as a person/institution of "practical wisdom"—perhaps authority, power, experience, savvy or some combination thereof. *Arête* might be better translated now as "likeability" or "relatability"—the audience's belief that the sender is like them—or admirable in some way. Finally, *eunoia* is the audience's feeling that the sender expresses care for them. In this case, I will use an actual example from the built environment: the well-known Apple Store on Fifth Avenue in Manhattan.

Designed by the architecture firm Bohlin, Cywinski, Jackson, the store opened in 2006, and as of 2017, the building began major renovations that, as of this writing in March of 2018, have yet to be revealed.[15] The relatively small glass structure that *has* been present in this location for the past decade, however, is notably different from the tall, "traditional" buildings around it. When applying the questions prompted by utilizing the rhetorical triangle, one might theorize that the "sender" (i.e., Apple) expresses a certain power, authority, even *chutzpah* as a company with the means, first, to be located in such a prestigious spot—on Fifth Avenue, just steps away from Central Park—and on a space where it does not even appear as if there should be room for a building (and, in fact, the bulk of the retail space they operate in that

15 Anuta, J. "Apple is as savvy about real estate as it is tech: Why is Apple dismantling its glass cube? Because it can," Crain's New York Business, 26 April 2017. Online. Available at: http://www.crainsnewyork.com/article/20170426/REAL_ESTATE/170429922/why-is-apple-dismantling-its-cube-because-the-company-has-the-clout-to-be-a-player-in-retail-and-command-lower-rents (Accessed May 11, 2018).

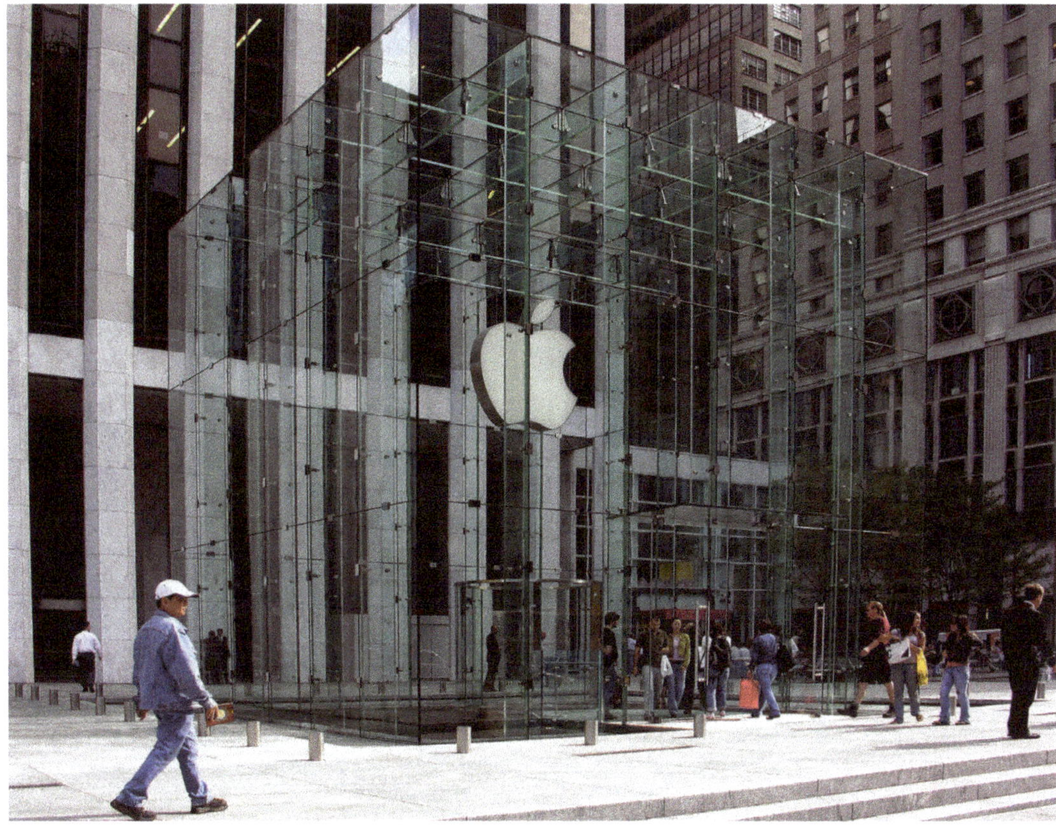

FIGURE 2: By Fletcher6 (Own work) [CC BY-SA 3.0 (https://creativecommons.org/licenses/by-sa/3.0) or GFDL (http://www.gnu.org/copyleft/fdl.html)], via Wikimedia Commons.

location is subterranean). The building as text appears bold enough to bend the rules of zoning and conventions of design for its own purposes. Additionally, the building's transparency allows it to suggest a certain degree of compassion and care, given that its walls often seem to fade away, allowing, at some angles, the trees of Central Park, the blue sky, or the people on the other side of the building to be as apparent as much as, or more than, its walls. In this way, Apple as the sender may be seen to be deferential, a listener, a humble presence. The building's ethos suggests a sender that is simultaneously powerful (an aspect of *phronesis*) and humble (*arête*). Such design choices help to shape the rhetoric of the space so that it appears as an attractive, successful site for potential customers.

Conclusion

The rhetorical triangle provides the basis for an elegantly simple, yet still rigorous and systematic, process to support designers' analytical and creative practices. Equipping student designers with a scheme of concepts and associated questions—grounded in a strong understanding of a specific theory—gives them a clear path toward thoughtful, rhetorically savvy work. An associated benefit of this process of inquiry is students' greater appreciation for designed objects as fundamentally *communicative* and, accordingly, quite *similar* to their written texts. Familiarity with such a process is also useful for faculty hoping to build stronger bridges between students' studio and humanities coursework. In my own case, mining the intersection between design and rhetoric has helped me teach writing concepts. For example, when I urge writing students to attend to audience (which involves accounting for their current base of knowledge, their preferences, their likely objections, their aspirations), I often point out the ways in which a designer has to take similar exigencies into consideration, whether dealing with readers, viewers, users, or some combination. Similarly, as I encourage students to consider the frequently-overlooked aspect of building their own character through language (i.e., their *ethos*), if I connect ethos (without making it merely equivalent) to the concept of "branding," they are more likely to see its relevance and importance. [b] This kind of rhetorical practice has the power to inform both students' design work and their overall habits of writing and communication that are so necessary to the formation of adaptable and articulate citizen designers.

[b] *See Engbers,* S. "Branded: The Sister Arts of Rhetoric and Design." Art, Design, and Communication in Higher Education, 12.2 (2013): pgs. 149–158.

References

Anuta, J. "Apple is as savvy about real estate as it is tech: Why is Apple dismantling its glass cube? Because it can," *Crain's New York Business,* 26 April 2017. Online. Available at: http://www.crainsnewyork.com/article/20170426/REAL_ESTATE/170429922/why-is-apple-dismantling-its-cube-because-the-company-has-the-clout-to-be-a-player-in-retail-and-command-lower-rents (Accessed May 11, 2018).

Barnard, M. *Graphic Design and Communication.* London, UK: Routledge, 2005.

Buchanan, R. "Declaration by Design: Rhetoric, Argument, and Demonstration in Design Practice." *Design Issues,* 2.1 (1985): pgs. 4–22.

Corbett, E. & Connors R. *Classical Rhetoric for the Modern Student,* 4th ed. New York, NY, USA: Oxford UP, 1999.

Davis, M. *Graphic Design Theory.* New York, NY, USA: Thames & Hudson, 2012.

Engbers, S. "Branded: The Sister Arts of Rhetoric and Design." *Art, Design & Communication in Higher Education,* 12.2 (2013): pgs. 149–158.

Foss, S., Foss, K & Trapp, R. *Contemporary Perspectives on Rhetoric,* 2nd ed. Prospect Heights, IL, USA: Waveland Press, 1985.

Kaufer, D. S. & Butler, B. *Rhetoric and the Arts and Design.* New York, NY, USA: Routledge, 2013.

Kennedy, G. *Classical Rhetoric and its Christian and Secular Tradition from Ancient to Modern Times,* 2nd ed. Chapel Hill, NC, USA: University of North Carolina Press, 1999.

Kinneavy, J. *A Theory of Discourse: The Aims of Discourse.* Englewood Cliffs, NJ, USA: Prentice Hall, 1971.

Schneller, A. "Design Rhetoric: Studying the Effects of Designed Objects." *Nature and Culture,* 10.3 (2015): pgs. 333–356.

Biography

Susanna Kelly Engbers, Ph.D., is Professor of English at Kendall College of Art and Design of Ferris State University. She teaches courses in rhetoric, writing, and literature, and her research focuses on the visual and verbal rhetorical strategies of nineteenth-century American suffragists, narrative theory and design, and the intersections of visual rhetoric and design. Her work has been published in *American Catholic Studies, Rhetoric Society Quarterly; the College English Association Forum;* and *Art, Design, and Communication in Higher Education.*

Dialectic Volume II, Issue I: Visual Essay

Portraits of Obama: Media, Fidelity, and the 44th President

KAREEM COLLIE[1]

1. Director of Design and Creativity at the Sontag Center for Collaborative Creativity and Clinical Professor of Visual Communication Design at the Claremont Colleges.

SUGGESTED CITATION: Collie, K. "Portraits of Obama: Media, Fidelity, and the 44th President." *Dialectic,* 2.1 (2018): pgs. 97-128. DOI: http://dx.doi.org/10.3998/dialectic.14932326.0001.305

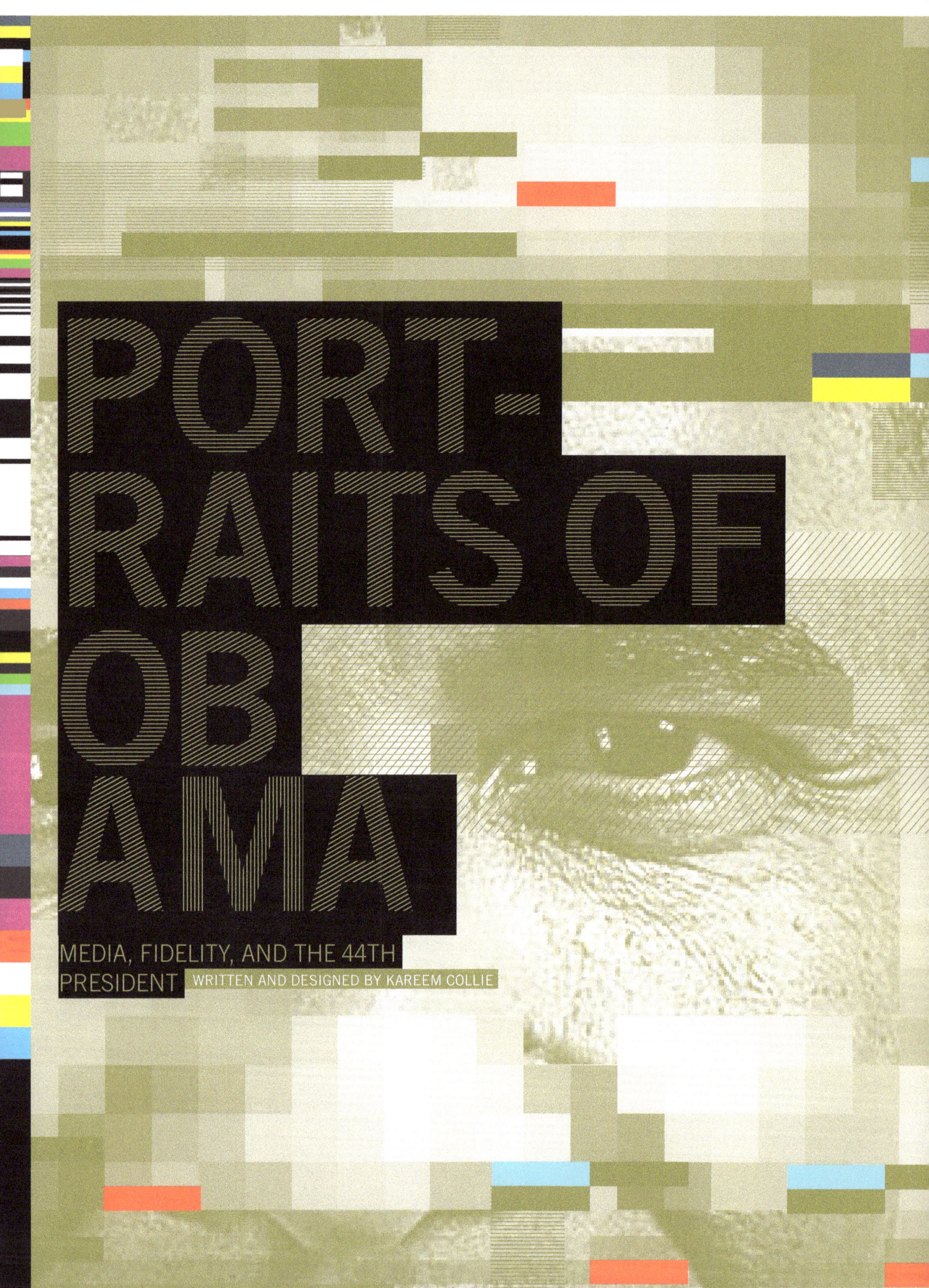
PORT-
RAITS OF
OB
AMA
MEDIA, FIDELITY, AND THE 44TH
PRESIDENT
WRITTEN AND DESIGNED BY KAREEM COLLIE

"THE MOST INTERESTING KIND OF PORTRAITURE IS THAT WHICH ARISES SPONTANEOUSLY IN PEOPLE'S MINDS"[1]

In the wake of the first radio broadcasts nearly a century ago, writer, intellectual and political journalist Walter Lippmann published *Public Opinion*, a book that criticized the functions and dysfunctions of Western democratic government. It closely analyzed the media's role in shaping reality—or the public's perception of it—and the resulting effect this was having on aspects of our democracy. *Public Opinion* shed light on many of the woes, ills and opportunities that the mass media of the time either created or catalyzed to shape public opinion and behavior.

Lippmann's primary concern was the fidelity of media— a measure of the quality and faithfulness of the news reported—and public perception of what's real and objectively presented. In his burgeoning information age of the 1920s, which saw a rapid proliferation of newspapers, radio broadcasts and moving pictures across the U.S. and other industrialized nations, the portrait which arises spontaneously in people's minds[2] began to obscure the perception of what was actually happening in the world beyond one's day-to-day experiences. In *Public Opinion*, Lippmann demonstrated the complexity of a democratic public informed largely by assumptions, contradictions, biases, and overgeneralized stereotypes endeavoring to mediate a world that had quickly become amplified by a new media landscape.

The following visual essay—"Portraits of Obama: Media, Fidelity and The 44th President"—explores the question of fidelity and some of the key issues that surround it in our 21st Century media landscape, where the picture is ubiquitous and the meanings now layered in a given media message have achieved greater levels of complexity than at any time in human history. By using the media's portrayal of President Obama during his first few years in office as a case study, I hope to re-examine Lippmann's primary ideas, and those of select other media critics and analysts, to illuminate both the news media's and the audience's diversifying and ever more intertwined roles in our current 24/7 media-moderated reality.

---

1. Lippmann, W. *Public Opinion*. New York, NY, USA: Harcourt, Brace and Co., 1922; p. 4.

2. Ibid.

INSIDE

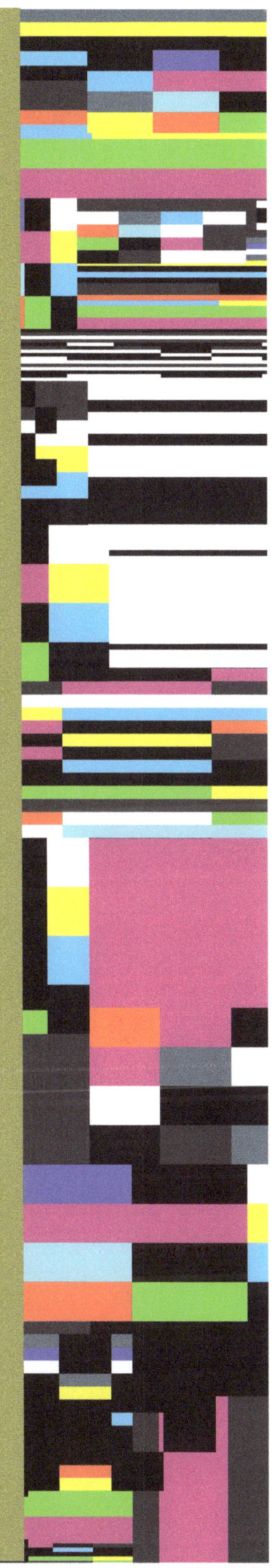

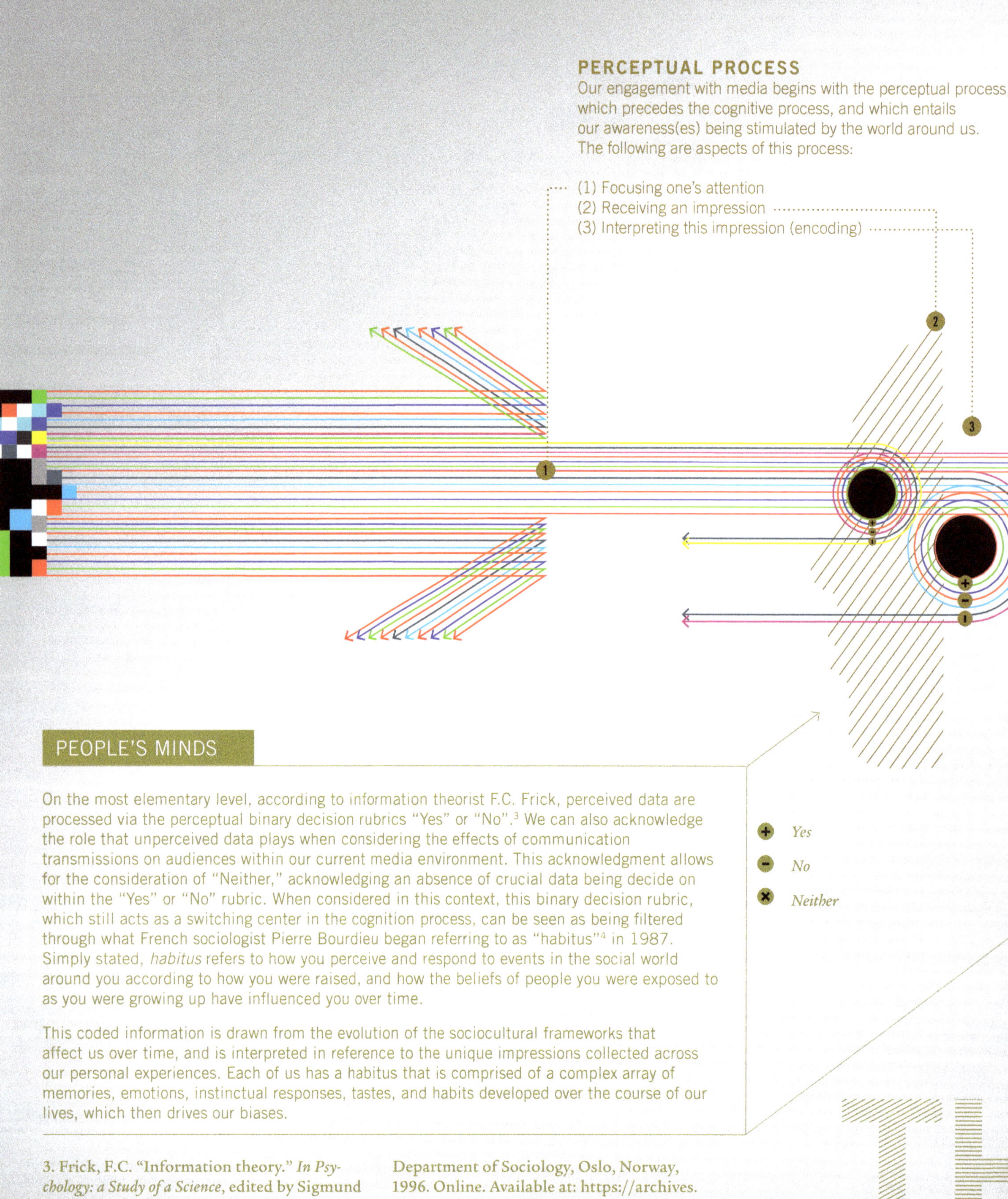

PERCEPTUAL PROCESS

Our engagement with media begins with the perceptual process, which precedes the cognitive process, and which entails our awareness(es) being stimulated by the world around us. The following are aspects of this process:

(1) Focusing one's attention
(2) Receiving an impression
(3) Interpreting this impression (encoding)

PEOPLE'S MINDS

On the most elementary level, according to information theorist F.C. Frick, perceived data are processed via the perceptual binary decision rubrics "Yes" or "No".[3] We can also acknowledge the role that unperceived data plays when considering the effects of communication transmissions on audiences within our current media environment. This acknowledgment allows for the consideration of "Neither," acknowledging an absence of crucial data being decide on within the "Yes" or "No" rubric. When considered in this context, this binary decision rubric, which still acts as a switching center in the cognition process, can be seen as being filtered through what French sociologist Pierre Bourdieu began referring to as "habitus"[4] in 1987. Simply stated, *habitus* refers to how you perceive and respond to events in the social world around you according to how you were raised, and how the beliefs of people you were exposed to as you were growing up have influenced you over time.

This coded information is drawn from the evolution of the sociocultural frameworks that affect us over time, and is interpreted in reference to the unique impressions collected across our personal experiences. Each of us has a habitus that is comprised of a complex array of memories, emotions, instinctual responses, tastes, and habits developed over the course of our lives, which then drives our biases.

3. Frick, F.C. "Information theory." *In Psychology: a Study of a Science*, edited by Sigmund Koch, pgs. 611–636. New York, NY, USA: McGraw-Hill, 1959

4. Bourdieu, P. "Vilhelm Aubert memorial lecture: Physical Space, Social Space and Habitus." Presented at The University of Oslo & Institute for Social Research; Oslo: Department of Sociology, Oslo, Norway, 1996. Online. Available at: https://archives.library.illinois.edu/erec/University%20Archives/2401001/Production_website/pages/StewardingExcellence/Physical%20Space,%20Social%20Space%20and%20Habitus.pdf (Accessed March 23, 2018).

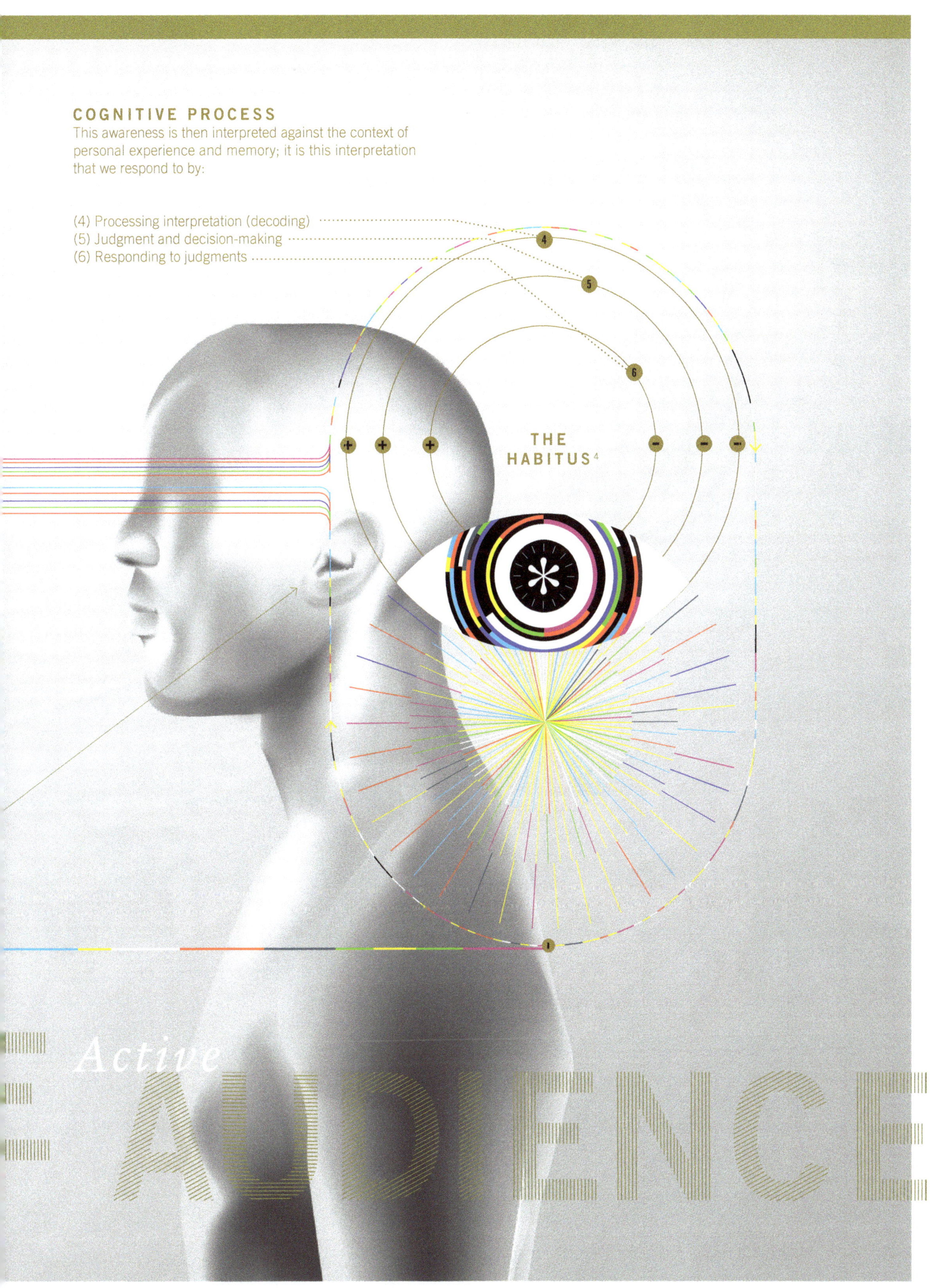
COGNITIVE PROCESS
This awareness is then interpreted against the context of personal experience and memory; it is this interpretation that we respond to by:
(4) Processing interpretation (decoding)
(5) Judgment and decision-making
(6) Responding to judgments
4
5
6
THE HABITUS4
Active
AUDIENCE

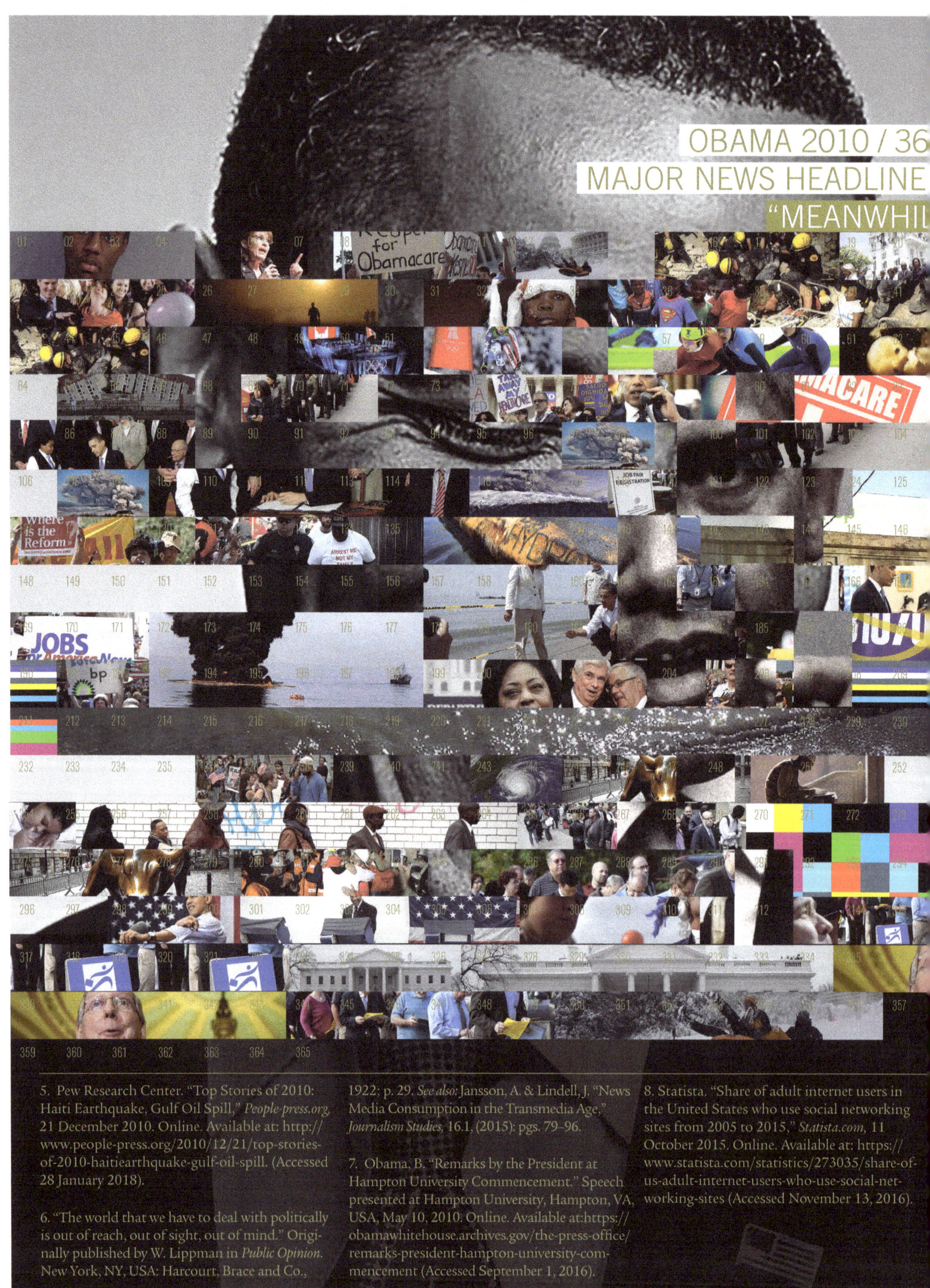

5. Pew Research Center. “Top Stories of 2010: Haiti Earthquake, Gulf Oil Spill,” *People-press.org*, 21 December 2010. Online. Available at: http://www.people-press.org/2010/12/21/top-stories-of-2010-haitiearthquake-gulf-oil-spill. (Accessed 28 January 2018).

6. “The world that we have to deal with politically is out of reach, out of sight, out of mind.” Originally published by W. Lippman in *Public Opinion*. New York, NY, USA: Harcourt, Brace and Co., 1922: p. 29. *See also*: Jansson, A. & Lindell, J. “News Media Consumption in the Transmedia Age,” *Journalism Studies*, 16.1, (2015): pgs. 79–96.

7. Obama, B. “Remarks by the President at Hampton University Commencement.” Speech presented at Hampton University, Hampton, VA, USA, May 10, 2010. Online. Available at:https://obamawhitehouse.archives.gov/the-press-office/remarks-president-hampton-university-commencement (Accessed September 1, 2016).

8. Statista. “Share of adult internet users in the United States who use social networking sites from 2005 to 2015,” *Statista.com*, 11 October 2015. Online. Available at: https://www.statista.com/statistics/273035/share-of-us-adult-internet-users-who-use-social-networking-sites (Accessed November 13, 2016).

NA 24/7

OU'RE COMING OF AGE...

MEDIA ENVIRON-MENT"[7]

This is our world—a jumbled mesh of pictures, peoples, problems, debates, delights, devastations, redactions, distractions, reds, greens, blues, blacks and whites, pixels and bytes, gyrating around the sound bites of a world too complex for the simple narrative tropes espoused in 72-point type on the front page of our daily newspapers or in 140 high-resolution alphanumeric characters tweeting at you from the cloud... "click here."

From this cacophony, we are challenged to produce a viable portrait of a world stable enough for us to grasp the complex narrative of and about Barack Hussain Obama II, the 44th president of the United States. Added to this challenge is the difficulty inherent in attempting to contextualize his agenda and policies with any meaningful depth or breadth. The question of fidelity, is and of itself, stands in high definition contrast against the noise.[6]

a's 2008 campaign for Hope and Change took place in the midst of a media revolution, and by 2010 there had been a worldwide sea change dia communication.[8]

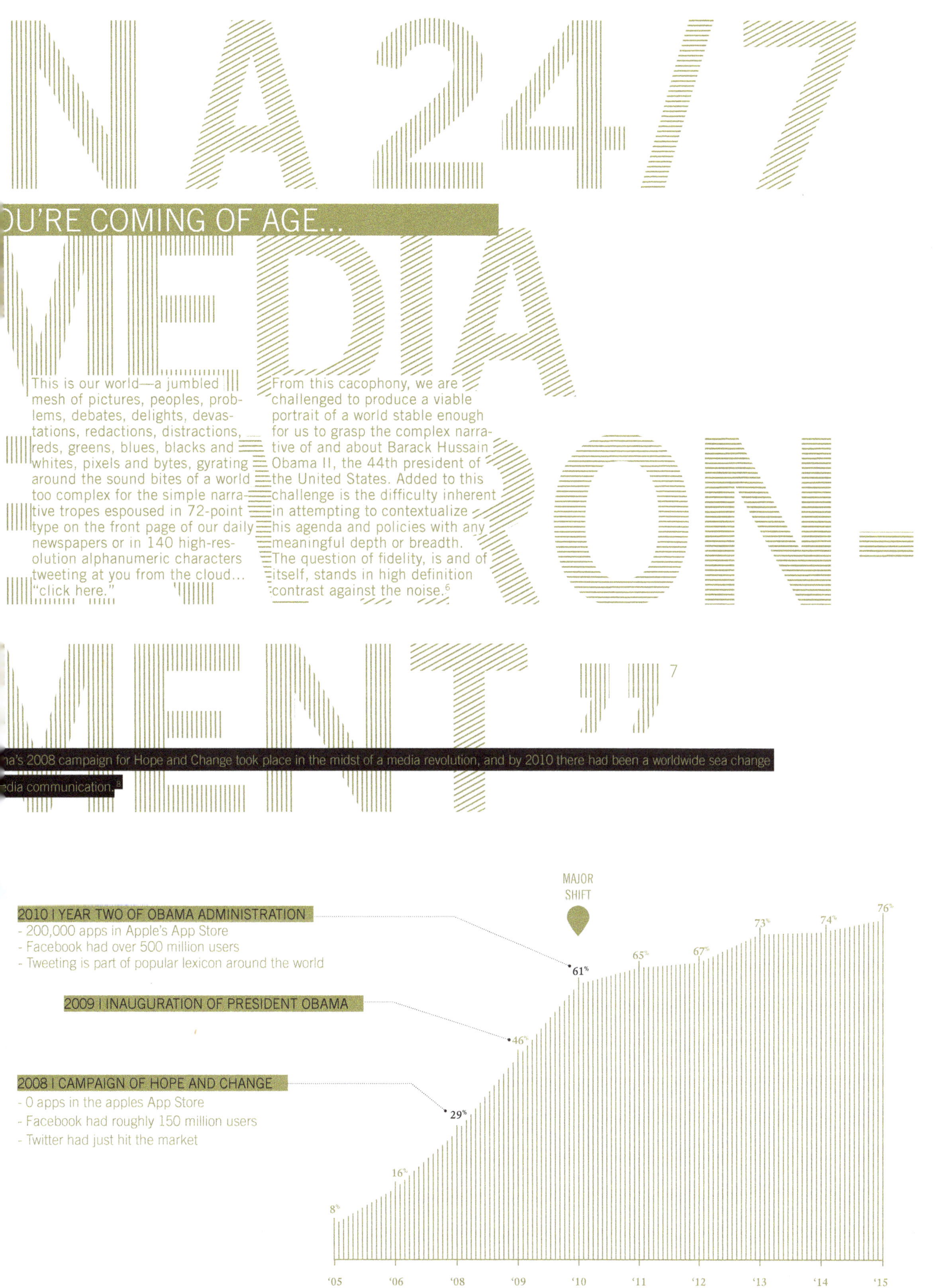

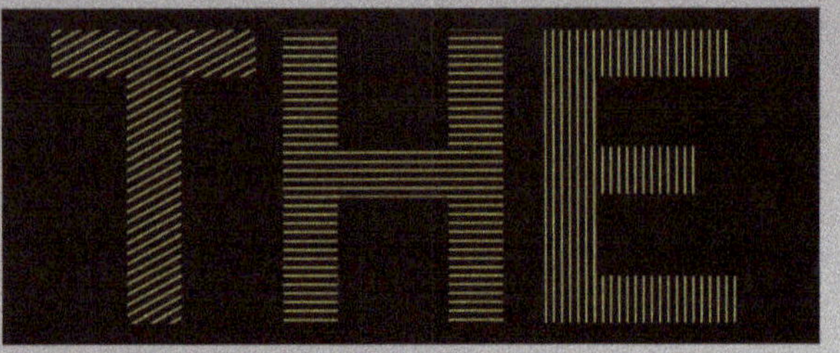

STEREOTYPES

The term stereotype,[9] coined by Lippmann, references the way in which we reduce the complexity of our hyper-mediated world to discrete symbols, icons, and indexes—or, rather, *signs*—so that we may make sense of it. These reductive interpretations, often presented to us as news, trigger our "Yes" or "No" rubric and often then fuel a semi-informed response.

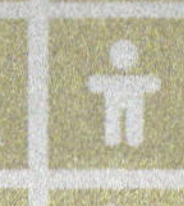

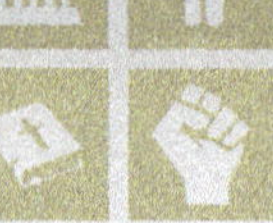

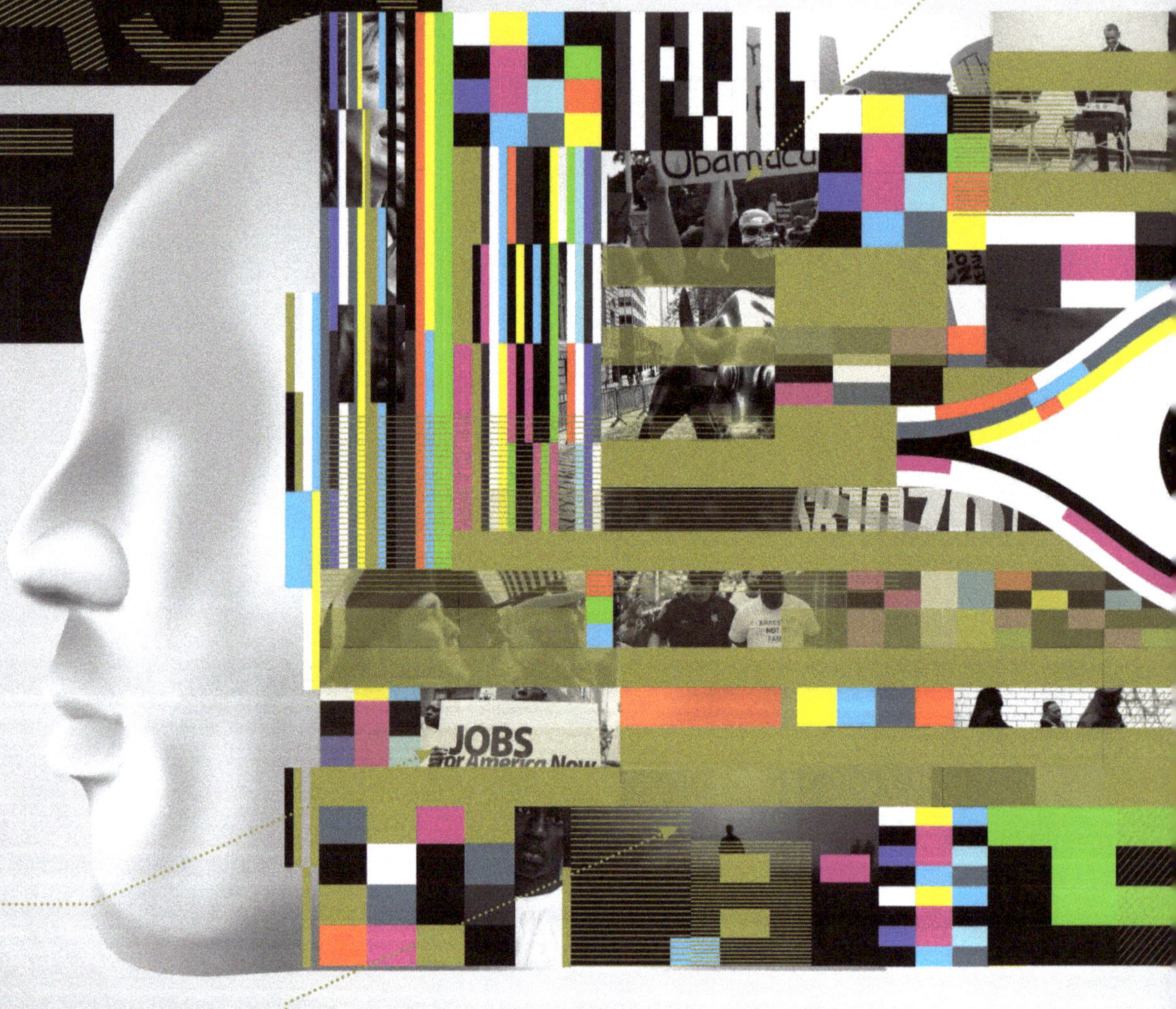

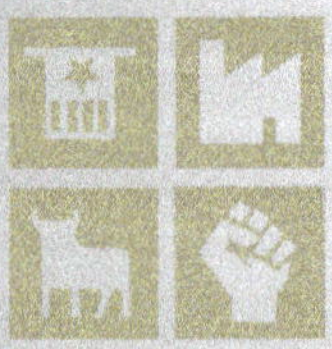

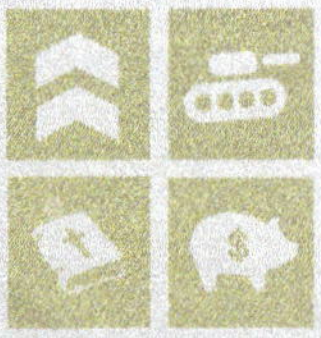

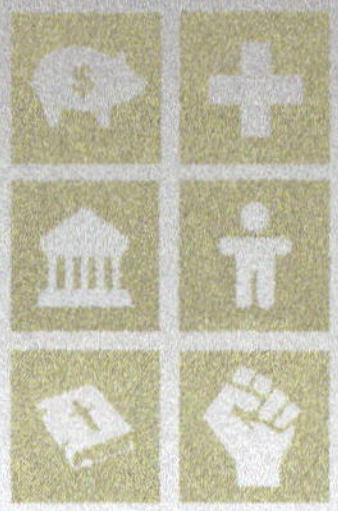

9. Lippmann, W. *Public Opinion*, pgs. 79-158.

10. Hall, S. "Encoding/Decoding." In Kellner, M. G. *Media and Cultural Studies: Keyworks*. Malden, MA, USA: Blackwell Publishing Ltd., 1973/2006; pgs. 163-173

11. Ibid.

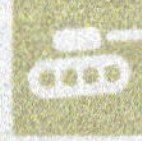

The mass of pictures in our heads shift fluidly in meaning against the ocean of unique experiences we each use to frame our engagement with the mediated world. To some extent, the media is our world, and we each use our individual library of icons, symbols, and indexes to navigate and find stability within a vast and dynamic sea of information.

In his essay, "Encoding and Decoding", Stuart Hall[10] illuminates this idea, arguing that no televisual message has a universal meaning. Each is tethered to dominant (preferred) cultural codes, and must be decoded by the audience. Hall states that the potential interpretation of each code is driven not by the intended meaning of the message, but instead by whatever social, cultural, economic and political belief systems contextualize and guide how a given audience, or reader, decodes the encoded message.

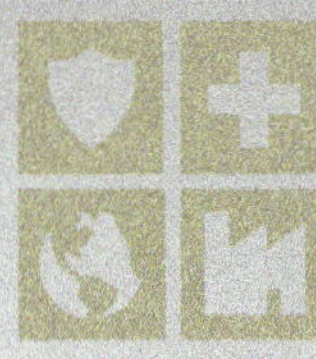

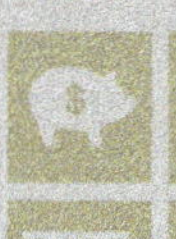

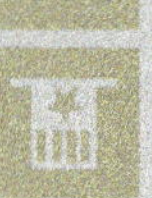

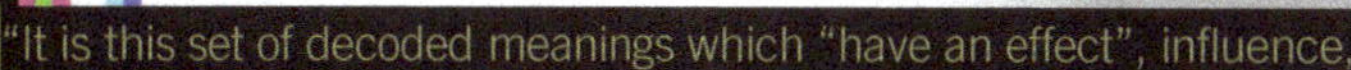

"It is this set of decoded meanings which "have an effect", influence, entertain, instruct or persuade, with very complex perceptual, cognitive, emotional, ideological or behavioral consequences."[11]

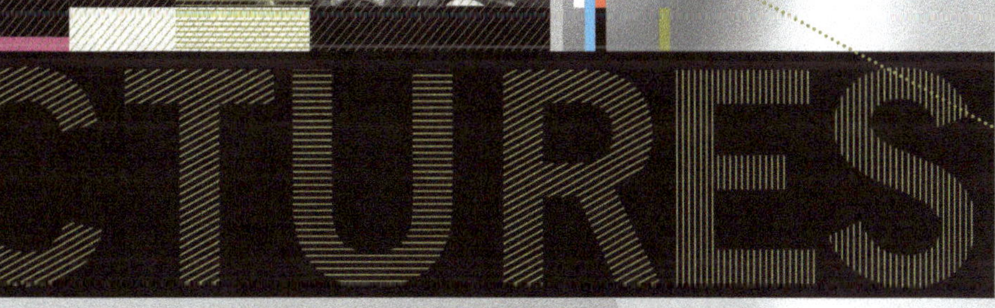

PICTURES IN OUR HEADS

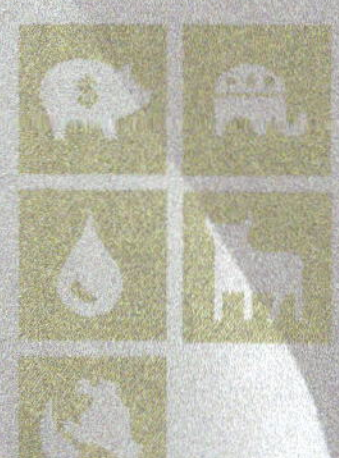

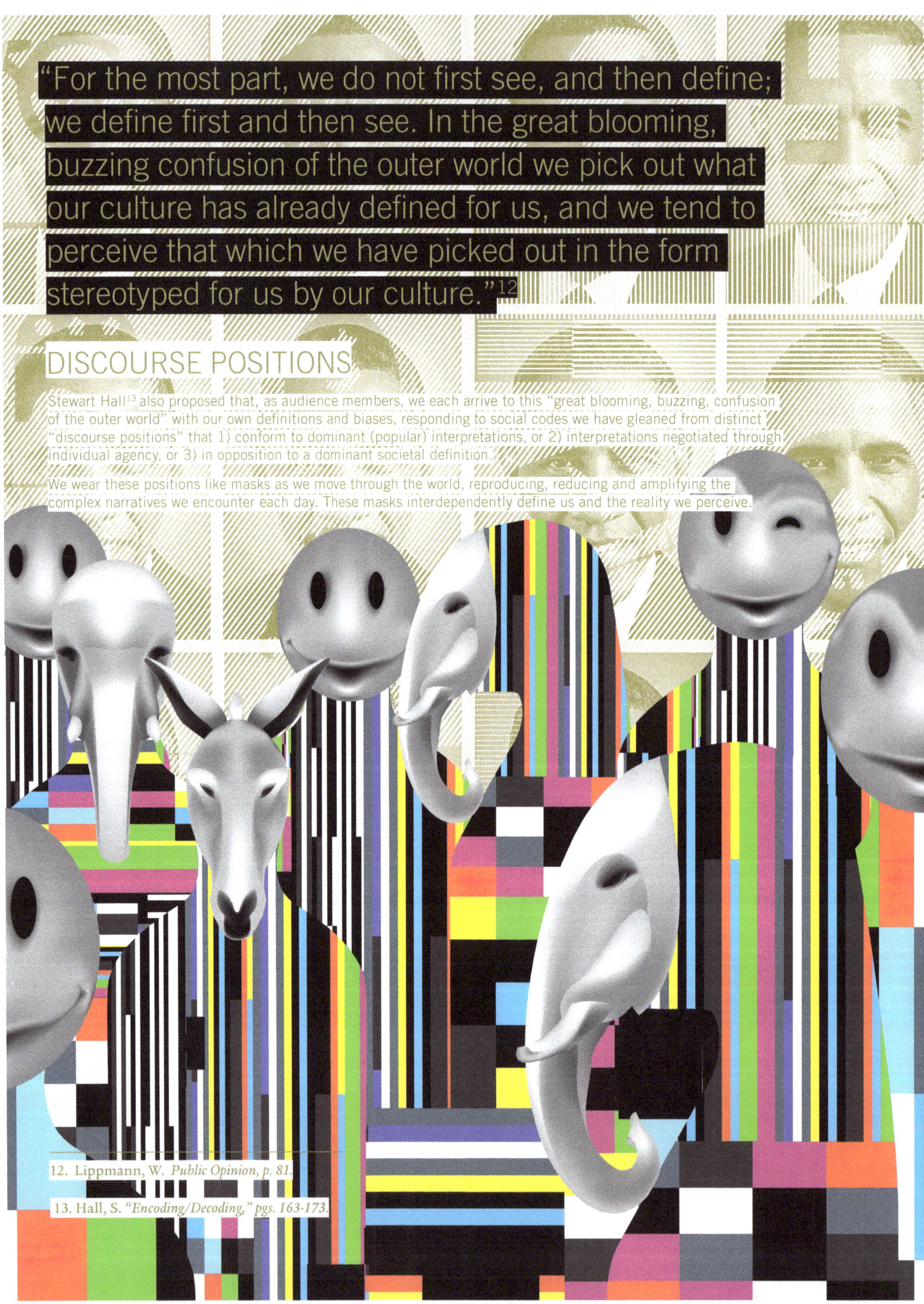

"For the most part, we do not first see, and then define; we define first and then see. In the great blooming, buzzing confusion of the outer world we pick out what our culture has already defined for us, and we tend to perceive that which we have picked out in the form stereotyped for us by our culture."[12]

DISCOURSE POSITIONS

Stewart Hall[13] also proposed that, as audience members, we each arrive to this "great blooming, buzzing, confusion of the outer world" with our own definitions and biases, responding to social codes we have gleaned from distinct "discourse positions" that 1) conform to dominant (popular) interpretations, or 2) interpretations negotiated through individual agency, or 3) in opposition to a dominant societal definition.

We wear these positions like masks as we move through the world, reproducing, reducing and amplifying the complex narratives we encounter each day. These masks interdependently define us and the reality we perceive.

12. Lippmann, W. *Public Opinion, p. 81.*

13. Hall, S. *"Encoding/Decoding," pgs. 163-173.*

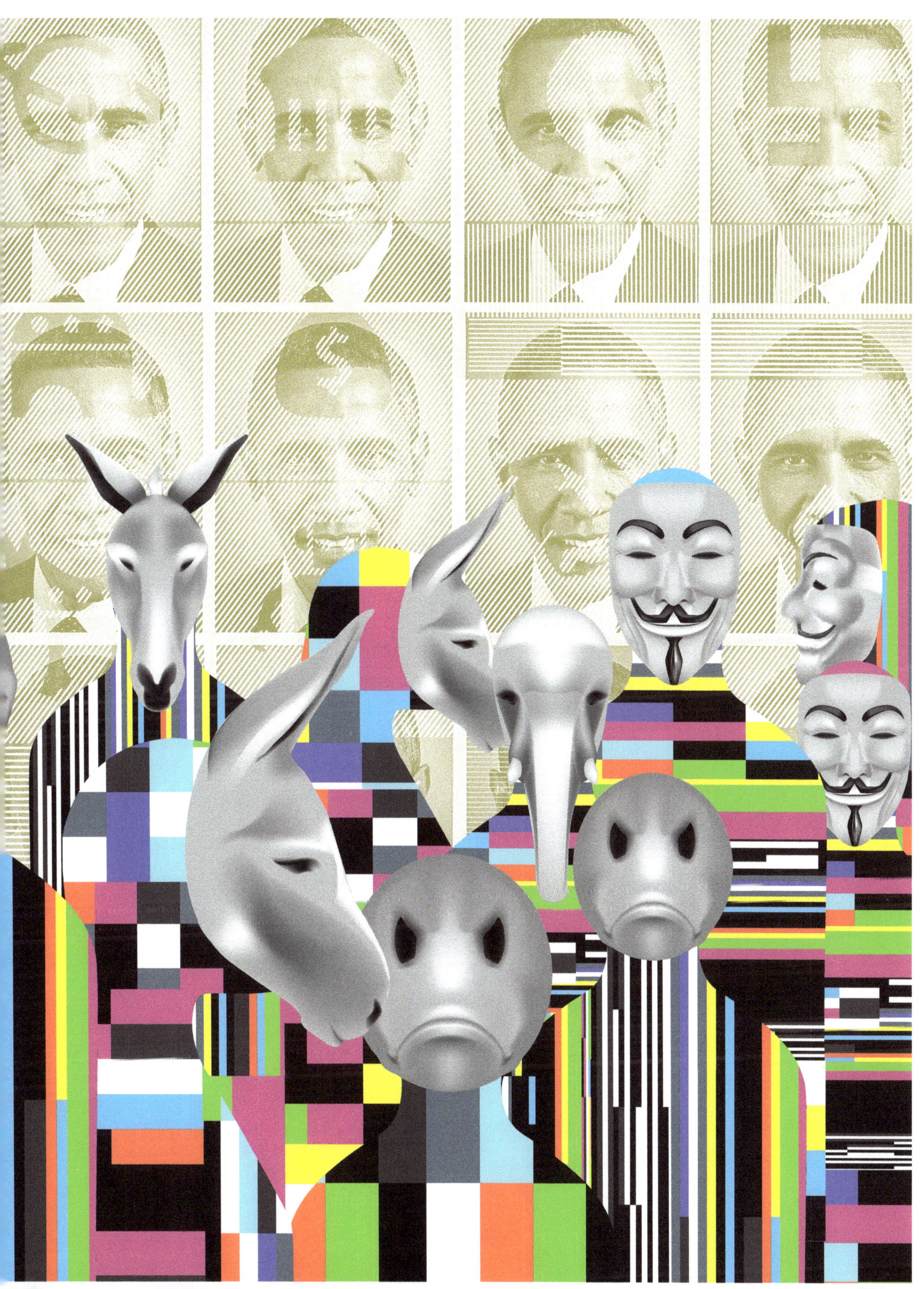

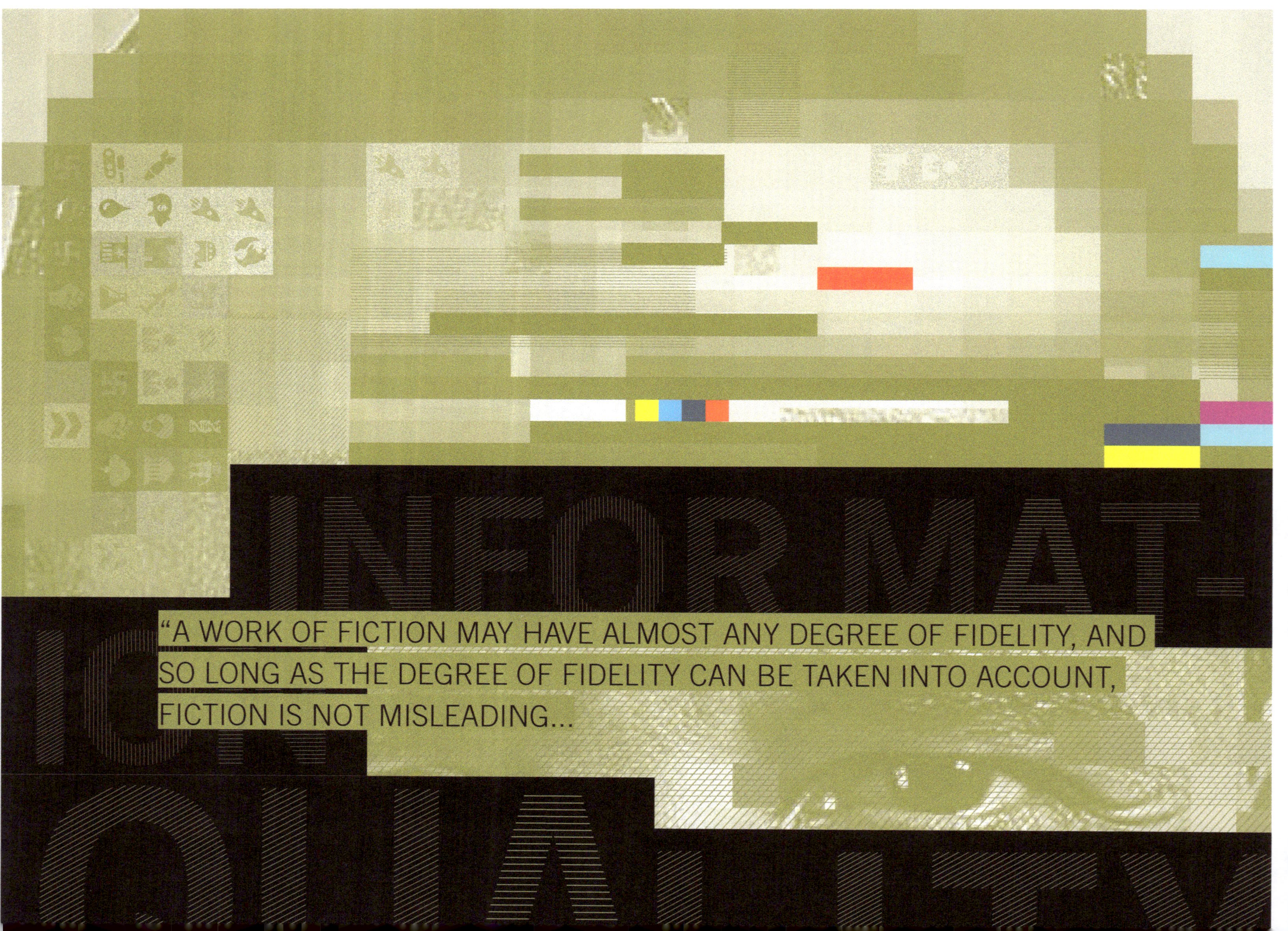
INFORMAT-
“A WORK OF FICTION MAY HAVE ALMOST ANY DEGREE OF FIDELITY, AND
SO LONG AS THE DEGREE OF FIDELITY CAN BE TAKEN INTO ACCOUNT,
FICTION IS NOT MISLEADING...

IN FACT, HUMAN CULTURE IS VERY LARGELY THE SELECTION, THE REARRANGEMENT, THE TRACING OF PATTERNS UPON, AND THE STYLIZING OF... "THE RANDOM IRRADIATIONS AND RESETTLEMENTS OF OUR IDEAS." [14]

THE QUESTION BECOMES: WHO CREATES THE FRAMES THROUGH WHICH YOU PERCEIVE?

On Mother's Day in 2010 in Hampton, Virginia, blue skies received the 44th President of the United States of America at Hampton University, one of the country's leading historically black colleges and universities.While attempting to stymie the full embrace of a knowing grin, President Obama stood at the commencement podium looking out over a sea of black and brown faces. The students sat victorious, having conquered the hurdles that imperiled the long pilgrimage towards the cap and gown.

Obama's commencement address acknowledged their arduous journey, their potential, and of course, the field of obstacles—cultural, social, global, economic, political, and/or self-imposed—that will continue to lay before them as their lives progress.

Overall, the speech was congratulatory and pointed and imbued with the message that, "Education can fortify you"[15] against the challenges of today. Obama fumbled a couple of words, embroiled by passion, and, here and there, that grin seemed to extend to its extremities.

It was a good day. However, for those of us not not present under that pristine blue sky, on that day, our only means of experiencing this event is through fragments of media images, sound bites, and headlines. Given this context, an essential question becomes: Who creates the frame through which we perceive the speech? Were the individuals and organizations reporting the event even there? What masks were they wearing? What is the nature and quality of the frame through which they perceive the world? Is it complete, accurate, and relevant, and who gets to decide if it is?[16]

---

14. Lippmann, *Public Opinion*, p. 16.

15. Obama, B. "President Obama at Hampton University." *The Obama White House.* YouTube. 9 May, 2010. 21:59. Available at: https://youtu.be/Hwg636C-Qnrc (Accessed 10 September 2016).

16. McQuail, D. et al. "Objectivity and its Measurement." *McQuail's Mass Communication Theory 6th edition.* London, UK: SAGE Publications Ltd., 2010; pgs. 355-359.

INFORMAT-ION

THE FICTION OF A "COMPLETE" PICTURE:

A Content Analysis of Obama's 2010 Hampton University Commencement Speech

1 Selection is a process of elimination–the constant choices we each must make between "this" or "that." It is a bracketing of a datum gleaned from the data. It is where we rest our eyes and give focus and shape to a piece of the world; how defined this shape, how refined this focus, is a question of completeness.

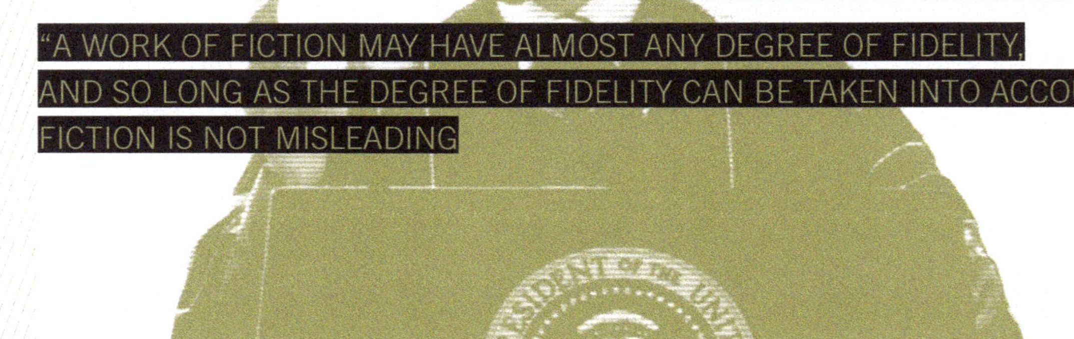

"A WORK OF FICTION MAY HAVE ALMOST ANY DEGREE OF FIDELITY, AND SO LONG AS THE DEGREE OF FIDELITY CAN BE TAKEN INTO ACCOUNT, FICTION IS NOT MISLEADING

HAMPTON UNIVERSITY COMMENCEMENT SPEECH MAY 10TH 2010	83° F	MESSAGE FOCUS*: Education and Education Reform	DOMINANT THEMES: Education can fortify you... Refusing to be denied Education...means emancipation	TOP 5 WORDS USED You x 66 Our x 33 Your x 19 Education x 15 Hampton x 15	TOTAL WORD COUNT: 2514 TOTAL BYTES: 14531

GREETINGS

~~Thank you. Thank you very much. Thank you. Thank you, Hampton. Thank you, Class of 2010. Please, everybody, please have a seat.~~

~~(I love you!— Audeince Memeber) That's why I'm here. I love you guys. Good morning, everybody. Good morning.~~

The Commencement Celebration landed on Mother's Day 2010

~~To all the ▬ As somebody who is surrounded by women in the White House grew up surrounded by women, let me take a moment just to say thank you for all that you put up with each and every day. We are so grateful to you, and it is fitting to have such a beautiful day when we celebrate all our mothers. Thank you to Hampton for allowing me to share this special occasion -- to all the dignitaries who are here, the trustees, the alumni, parents, grandparents, aunts, uncles, cousins -- that's a cousin over there.~~

HAMPTON

~~Now, before we get started, I just want to say, I'm excited the Battle of the Real H.U. will be taking place in Washington this year. You know I am not going to pick sides. But my understanding is it's been 13 years since the Pirates lost. As one Hampton alum on my staff put it, the last time Howard beat Hampton, The Fugees were still together.~~

~~Well, let me also say a word about President Harvey, a man who bleeds Hampton blue. In a single generation, Hampton has transformed from a small black college into a world-class research institution. And that transformation has come through the efforts of many people, but it has come through President Harvey's efforts, in particular, and I want to commend him for his outstand-~~

EDUCATION FORTIFIES

~~ers the skills of an industrializing nation. At the close of World War II, we made it possible for returning GIs to attend college, building and broadening our great middle class. At the Cold War's dawn, we set up Area Studies Centers on our campuses to prepare graduates to understand and address the global threats of a nuclear age.~~

CHALLENGES OF A CHANGING WORLD

~~▬ And Hampton, that has never been more true than it is today. This class is graduating at a time of great difficulty for America and for the world. You're entering a job market, in an era of heightened international competition, with an economy that's still rebounding from the worst crisis since the Great Depression. You're accepting your degrees as America still wages two wars -- wars that many in your generation have been fighting.~~

24/7 MEDIA

~~And meanwhile,~~ *you're coming of age in a 24/7 media environment that bombards us with all kinds of content and exposes us to all kinds of arguments, some of which don't always rank that high on the truth meter. And with iPods and iPads; and Xboxes and PlayStations -- none of which I know how to work information becomes a distraction, a diversion, a form of entertainment, rather than a tool of empowerment, rather than the means of emancipation. So all of this is not only putting* ~~*new pressure on our country and on our democracy.*~~

~~Class of 2010, this is a period of breathtaking change, like few others in our history. We can't stop these changes, but we can channel them, we can shape them, we can adapt to them.~~ ▬

CHALLENGES

~~But I have to say, Class of 2010, all of you have a separate responsibility. To be role models for your brothers and sisters. To be mentors in your communities. And, when the time comes, to pass that sense of an education's value down to your children, a sense of personal responsibility and self-respect. To pass down a work ethic and an intrinsic sense of excellence that made it possible for you to be here today.~~

~~So, allowing you to compete in the global economy is the first way your education can prepare you. But it can also prepare you as citizens. With so many voices clamoring for attention on blogs, and on cable, on talk radio, it can be difficult, at times, to sift through it all; to know what to believe, to figure out who's telling the truth and who's not. Let's face it, even some of the craziest claims can quickly gain traction. I've had some experience in that regard.~~

~~Fortunately, you will be well positioned to navigate this terrain. Your education has honed your research abilities, sharpened your analytical powers, given you a context for understanding the world. Those skills will come in handy.~~

~~But the goal was always to teach you something more. Over the past four years, you've argued both sides of a debate. You've read novels and histories that take different cuts at life.~~

~~(Amen!— Audeince Memeber)~~

~~You've discovered -- see, I got a little "Amen" there, somebody you've discovered interests you didn't know you had. You've made friends who didn't grow up the~~

HAMPTON NORMAL

~~The success of their experiment, they understood, depended on the participation of its people -- the participation of Americans like all of you. The participation of all those who have ever sought to perfect our union.~~

~~I had a great honor of delivering a tribute to one of those Americans last week, an American named~~ ▬

~~And as you probably know, Dr. Height passed away the other week at the age of 98. One of the speakers at this memorial was her nephew who was 88. And I said that's a sign of a full life when your nephew is 88. Dr. Height had been on the firing line for every fight from lynching to desegregation to the battle for health care reform. She was with Eleanor Roosevelt and she was with Michelle Obama. She lived a singular life; one of the giants upon whose shoulders I stand. But she started out just like you, understanding that to make something of herself, she needed a college degree.~~

~~So, she applied to Barnard College -- and she got in. Except, when she showed up, they discovered she wasn't white as they had believed. And they had already given their two slots for African Americans to other individuals. Those slots, two, had already been filled. But Dr. Height was not discouraged. She was not deterred. She stood up, straight-backed, and with Barnard's acceptance letter in hand, she marched down to New York University, and said, "Let me in." And she was admitted right away.~~

~~I want all of you to think about this, Class of 2010, because you've gone through some hardships, undoubtedly, in arriving to where you are today. There~~

HAMPTON NORMAL

have met for generations, not far from where it all began, near that old oak tree off Emancipation Drive. I know my University 101. There, beneath its branches, by what was then a Union garrison, about 20 students gathered on September 17th, 1861. Taught by a free citizen, in defiance of Virginia law, the students were escaped slaves from nearby plantations, who had fled to the fort seeking asylum.

And after the war's end, a retired Union general sought to enshrine that legacy of learning. So with a collection from church groups, Civil War veterans, and a choir that toured Europe, Hampton Normal and Agricultural Institute was founded here, by the Chesapeake — a home by the sea.

Now, that story is no doubt familiar to many of you. But it's worth reflecting on why it happened; why so many people went to such trouble to found Hampton and all our Historically Black Colleges and Universities. The founders of these institutions knew, of course, that inequality would persist long into the future. They were not naive. They recognized that barriers in our laws, and in our hearts, wouldn't vanish overnight.

EDU FORTIFIES

But they also recognized the larger truth; a distinctly American truth. They recognized, Class of 2010, that the right education might allow those barriers to be overcome; might allow our God-given potential to be fulfilled. They recognized, as once put it, that "education...means emancipation." They recognized that education is how America and its people might fulfill our promise. That recognition, that truth — that an , to meet any test — is reflected, again and again, throughout our history.

EDUCATION CAN FORTIFY YOU *

In the midst of civil war, we set aside land grants for schools like Hampton to teach farmers and

CHALLENGES

In the 19th century, folks could get by with a few basic skills, whether they learned them in a school like Hampton, or picked them up along the way. As long as you were willing to work, for much of the 20th century, a high school diploma was a ticket into a solid middle class life. That is no longer the case.

Jobs today often require at least a bachelor's degree, and that degree is even more important in tough times like these. In fact, the unemployment rate for folks who've never gone to college is over twice as high as for folks with a college degree or more.

Now, the good news is you're already ahead of the curve. All those checks you or your parents wrote to Hampton will pay off. You're in a strong position to outcompete workers around the world. But I don't have to tell you that too many folks back home aren't as well prepared. Too many young people, just like you, are not as well prepared. By any number of different yardsticks, African Americans are being outperformed by their white classmates, as are Hispanic Americans. Students in well-off areas are outperforming students in poorer rural or urban communities, no matter what skin color.

Globally, it's not even close. In 8th grade science and math, for example, American students are ranked about 10th overall compared to top-performing countries. But African Americans are ranked behind more than 20 nations, lower than nearly every other developed country.

So all of us have a responsibility, as Americans, to change this; to offer every single child in this country an education that will make them competitive in our knowledge economy. That is our obligation as a nation.

been opened, it's up to you to keep them that way. It will be up to you to open minds that remain closed that you meet along the way. That, after all, is the elemental test of any democracy: whether people with differing points of view can learn from each other, and work with each other, and find a way forward together.

And I'd add one further observation. Just as More and more, America's economic preeminence, our ability to outcompete other countries, will be shaped not just in our boardrooms, not just on our factory floors, but in our classrooms, and our schools, at universities like Hampton. It will be determined by how well all of us, and especially our parents, educate our sons and daughters.

What's at stake is more than our ability to outcompete other nations. It's our ability to make democracy work in our own nation. Now, years after he left office, decades after he penned the Declaration of Independence, sat down, a few hours' drive from here, in Monticello, and wrote a letter to a longtime legislator, urging him to do more on education. And Jefferson gave one principal reason — the one, perhaps, he found most compelling. "If a nation expects to be ignorant and free," he wrote, "it expects what never was and never will be."

What Jefferson recognized, like the rest of that gifted founding generation, was that in the long run, their improbable experiment — called America — wouldn't work if its citizens were uninformed, if its citizens were apathetic, if its citizens checked out, and left democracy who those — to those who didn't have the best interests of all the people at heart. It could only work if each of us stayed informed and engaged; if we held our government accountable; if we fulfilled the obligations of citizenship.

FORTIFY AMERICA

Refusing to be denied her dignity. Refusing to be denied her place in America, her piece of America's promise. Refusing to let any barriers of injustice or ignorance or inequality or unfairness stand in her way. That refusal to accept a lesser fate; that insistence on a better life, that, ultimately, is the secret not only of African American survival and success, it has been the secret of America's survival and success.

So, yes, an to meet the tests of our economy, the tests of our citizenship, and the tests of our times. But what ultimately makes us American, quintessentially American, is something that can't be taught — a stubborn insistence on pursuing our dreams.

It's the same insistence that led a band of patriots to overthrow an empire. That fired the passions of union troops to free the slaves and union veterans to found schools like Hampton. That led foot-soldiers the same age as you to brave fire-hoses on the streets of Birmingham and billy clubs on a bridge in Selma. That led generation after generation of Americans to toil away, quietly, your parents and grandparents and great-grandparents and great-great grandparents, without complaint, in the hopes of a better life for their children and grandchildren.

That is what makes us who we are. A dream of brighter days ahead, a faith in things not seen, a belief that here, in this country, we are the authors of our own destiny. That is what Hampton is all about. And it now falls to you, the Class of 2010, to write the next great chapter in America's story; to meet the tests of your own time; to take up the ongoing work of fulfillin[g] promise. I'm looking forward to wat[ching]

Thank you, God bless you, and may United States of America.

IN FACT, HUMAN CULTURE IS VERY LARGELY THE (1) SELECTION,

QUALITY

Analyzing & Measuring the Fidelity of Reporting

"EDUCATION CAN FORTIFY YOU"...

... was the message of the commencement speech. A collage of desperate facts, historical and current events, anecdotes and statistics were strung together into a narrative of empowerment, prudence and encouragement; A portrait of a world with structure, rhyme, reason, and purpose... a way forward.

FREDERICK DOUGLASS
(born Frederick Augustus Washington Bailey, c. February 1818 – February 20, 1895) was an African-American social reformer, abolitionist, orator, writer, and statesman. After escaping from slavery in Maryland, he became a national leader of the abolitionist movement from Massachusetts and New York, gaining note for his dazzling oratory and incisive antislavery writings. – Wikipedia*

** This and the following two Wikipedia references reference contemporary media's role in the attempt to create a complete body of knowledge, and rather than representing an accurate historical account reference the rabbit hole one can find themselves in within that attempt)*

THOMAS JEFFERSON
(April 13 [O.S. April 2] 1743 – July 4, 1826) was an American Founding Father who was principal author of the Declaration of Independence (1776). He was elected the second Vice President of the United States (1797–1801), serving under John Adams and in 1800 was elected third President (1801–09). Jefferson was a proponent of democracy, republicanism, and individual rights... – Wikipedia

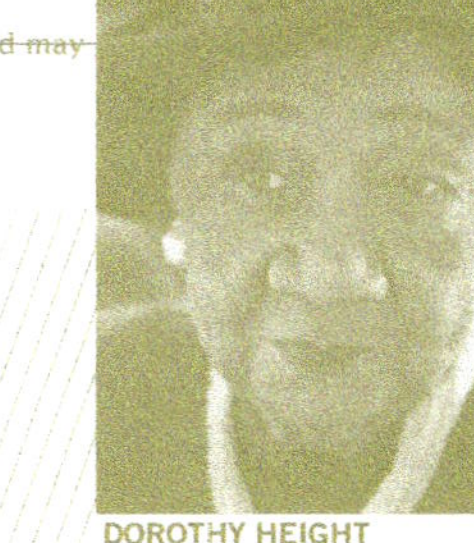

DOROTHY HEIGHT
(March 24, 1912 – April 20, 2010) an American administrator and educator, was a civil rights and women's rights activist specifically focused on the issues of African-American women, including unemployment, illiteracy, and voter awareness. She was the president of the National Council of Negro Women for forty years and was awarded the Presidential Medal of Freedom in 1994 and the congressional Congressional Gold Medal in 2004. – Wikipedia

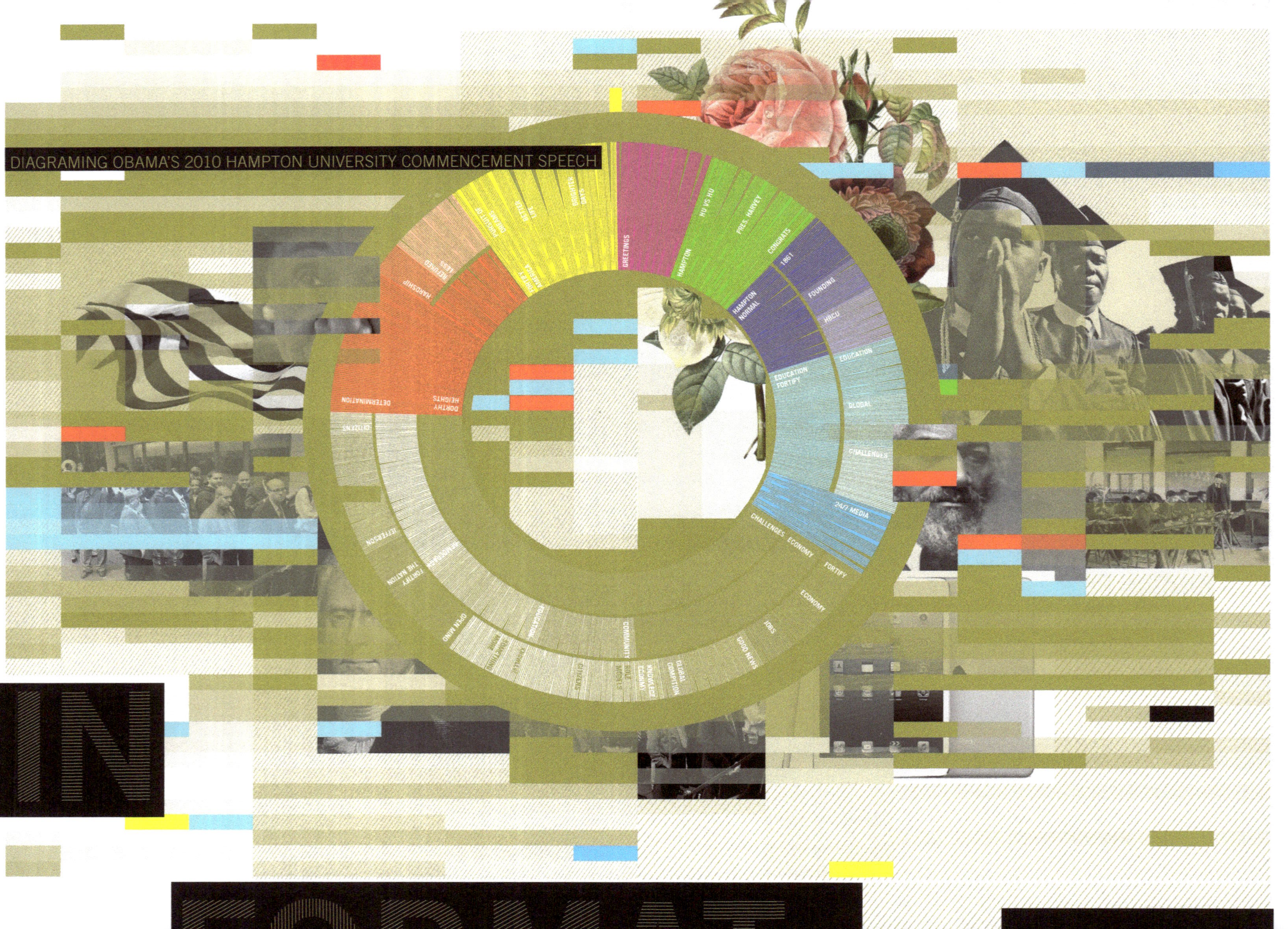

DIAGRAMING OBAMA'S 2010 HAMPTON UNIVERSITY COMMENCEMENT SPEECH
GREETINGS
HAMPTON
HU VS HU
PRES. HARVEY
CONGRATS
1861
HAMPTON NORMAL
FOUNDING
HBCU
EDUCATION FORTIFY
EDUCATION
GLOBAL
CHALLENGES
24/7 MEDIA
CHALLENGES
ECONOMY
FORTIFY
ECONOMY
JOBS
GOOD NEWS
GLOBAL COMPITION
KNOWLEGE ECONOMY
ROLE MODELS
COMMUNITY
CITIZENS
EDUCATION
OPEN MIND
FORTIFY THE NATION
JEFFERSON
CITIZENS
DETERMINATION
DORTHY HEIGHTS
HARDSHIP
BRIGHTER DAYS
IN

QUALITY

THE DATA OF A DATUM:
The Accuracy Of Reporting And The Rearrangement Of Context

(2) THE REARRANGEMENT, THE TRACING OF PATTERNS UPON, AND THE STYLIZING OF...

2 For the most part, the brilliant blue skies, radiant faces, and pointed message about challenge and triumph were left out of reports and summaries of Obama's speech in the news media. Several media outlets seemed to miss the point of his speech altogether, instead fixating on a comment Obama made about using his iPad in a segment of the speech that offered little insight regarding the speech's overall content and intended message.

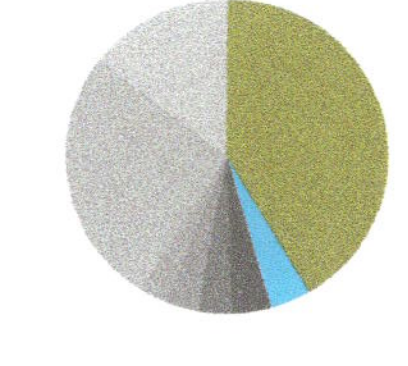
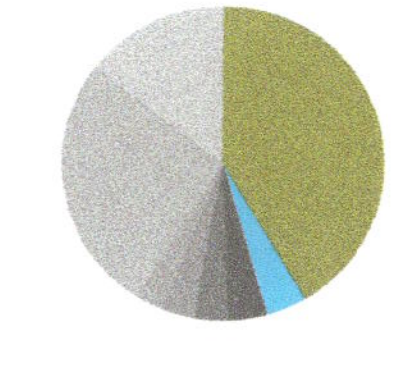
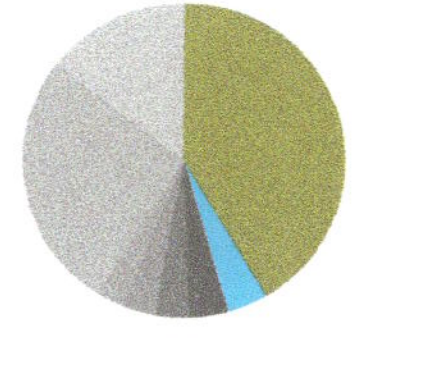
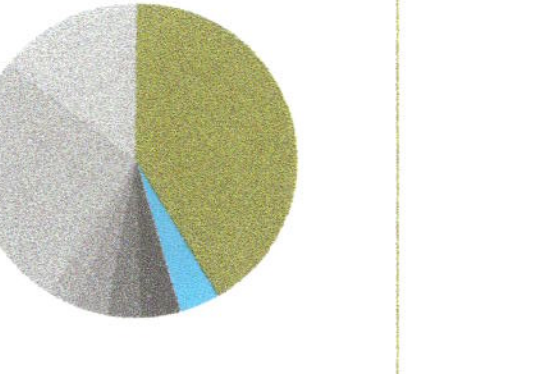
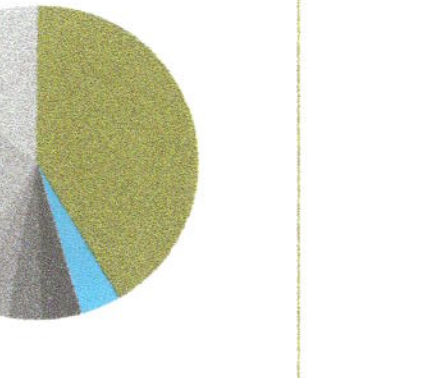

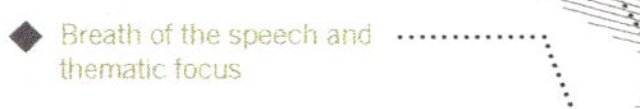
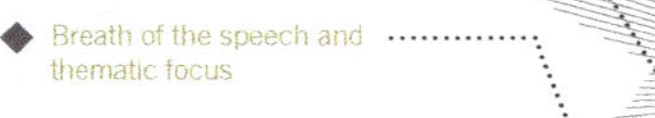

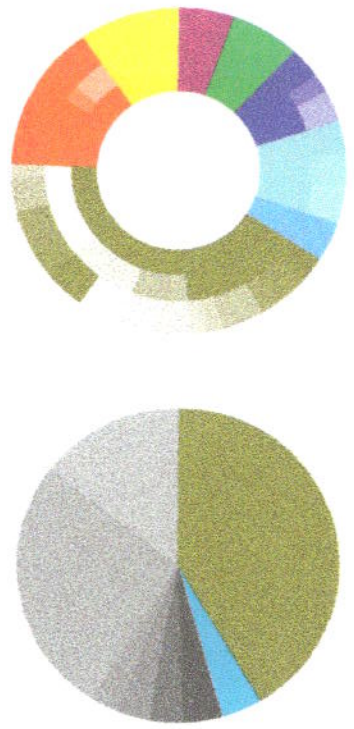

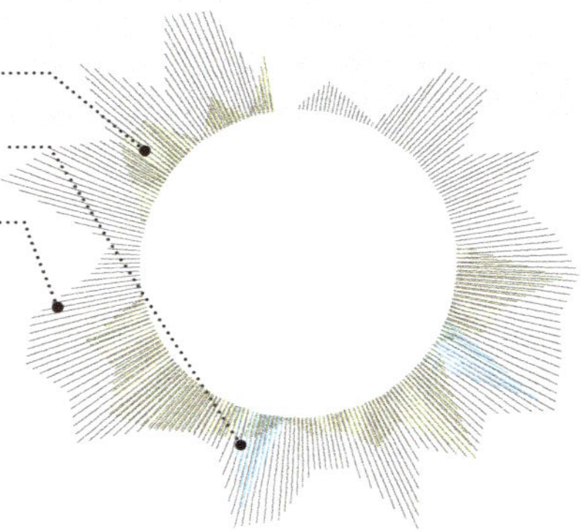

A selection process reframes and disassociates codes and their meanings from the "Complete" context of obama's message. The resultant variability of meaning and codes across news media:

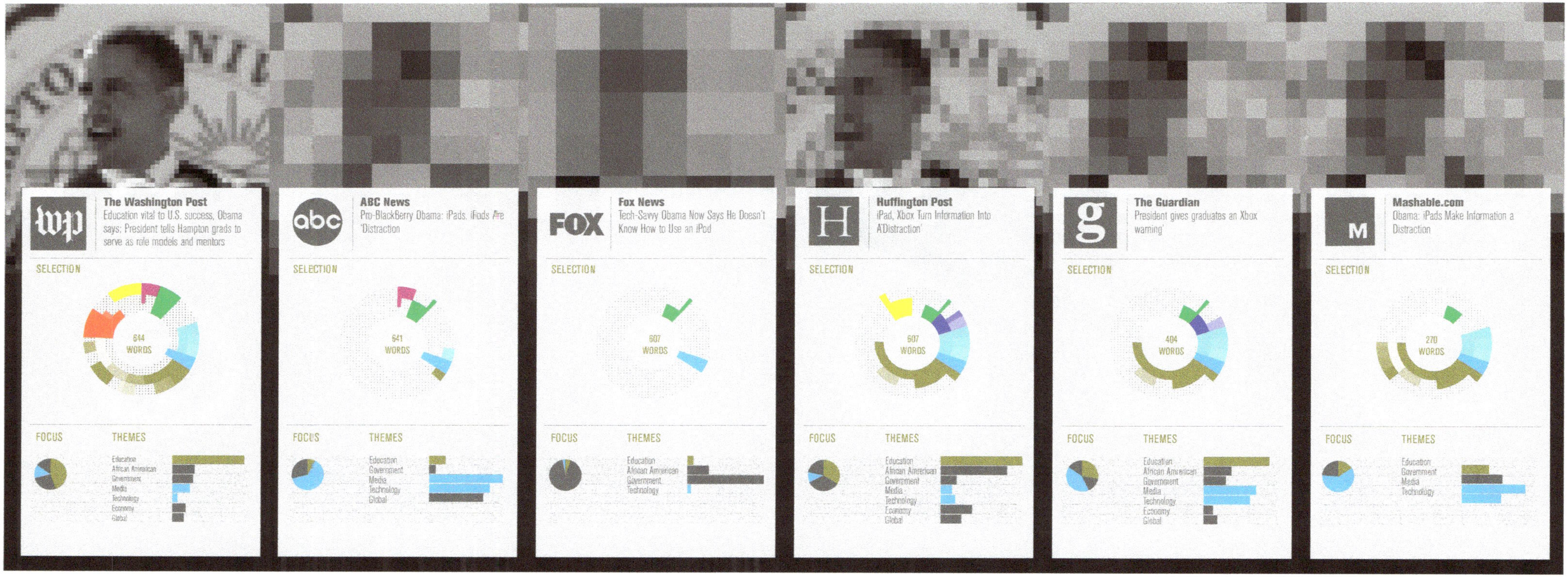

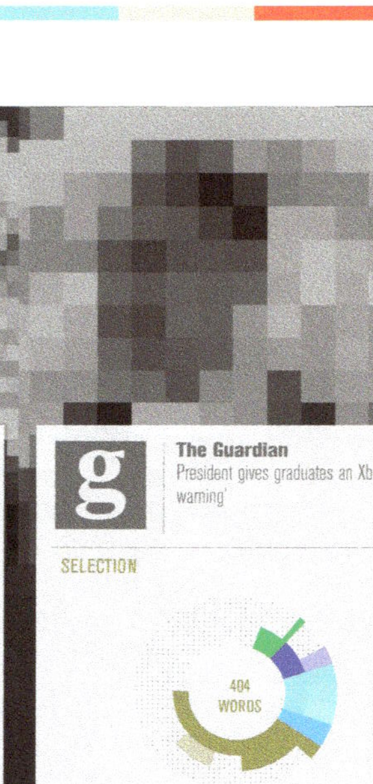
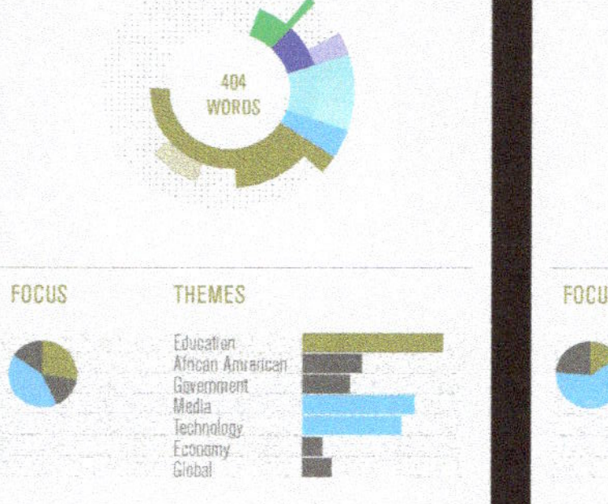

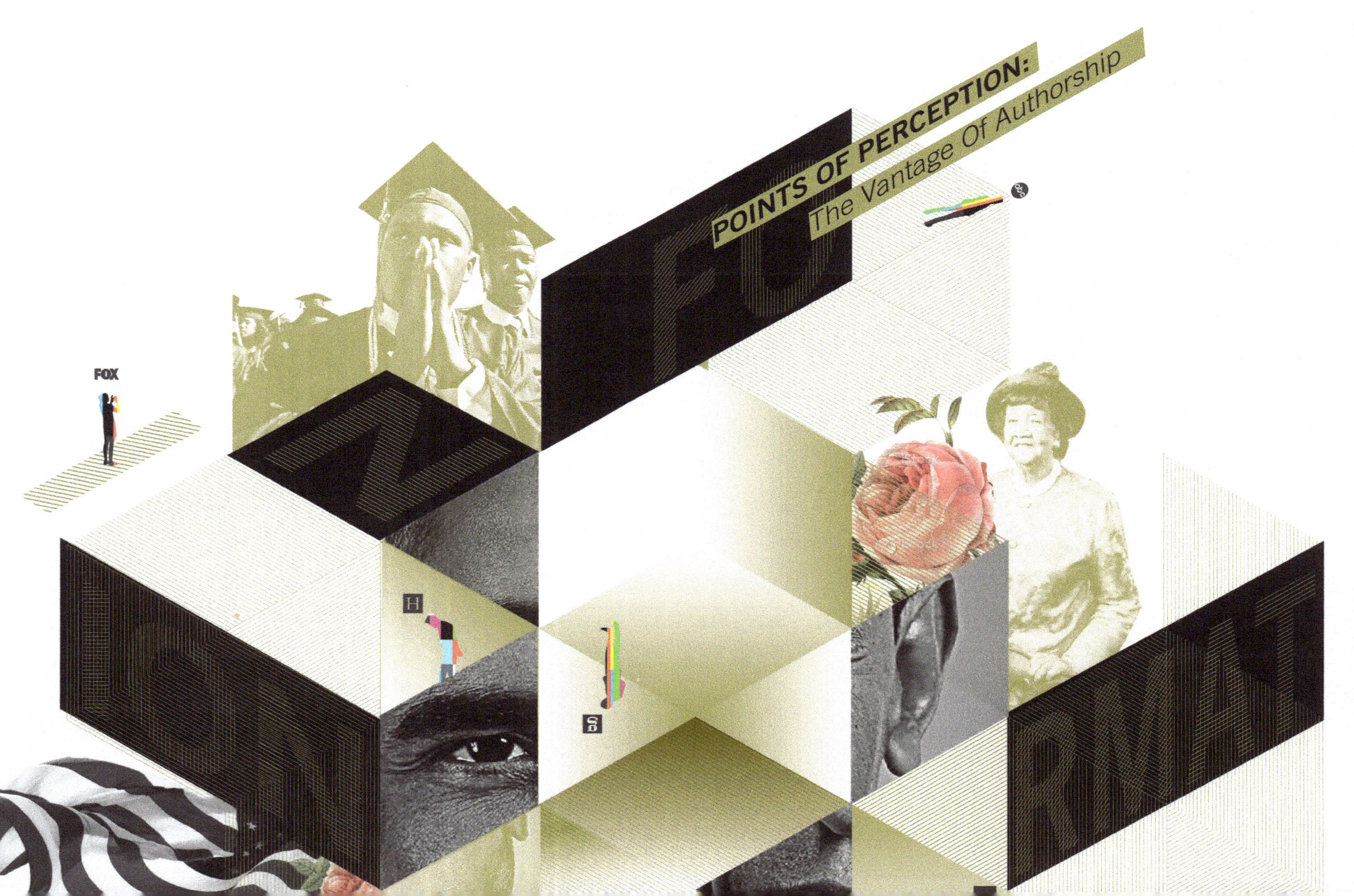
POINTS OF PERCEPTION:
The Vantage Of Authorship
FOX

(3) "THE RANDOM IRRADIATIONS AND RESETTLEMENTS OF OUR IDEAS."

3 Meaning is constructed at the point that a message is perceived. The random irradiations and resettlements of our ideas participate in the construction of this meaning.

Our physical proximity to a message, as well as our general knowledge and experience, all contribute to the obtuse nature of our reception of the world around us. The way we perceive things commands the way we make meaning out of what is being received.

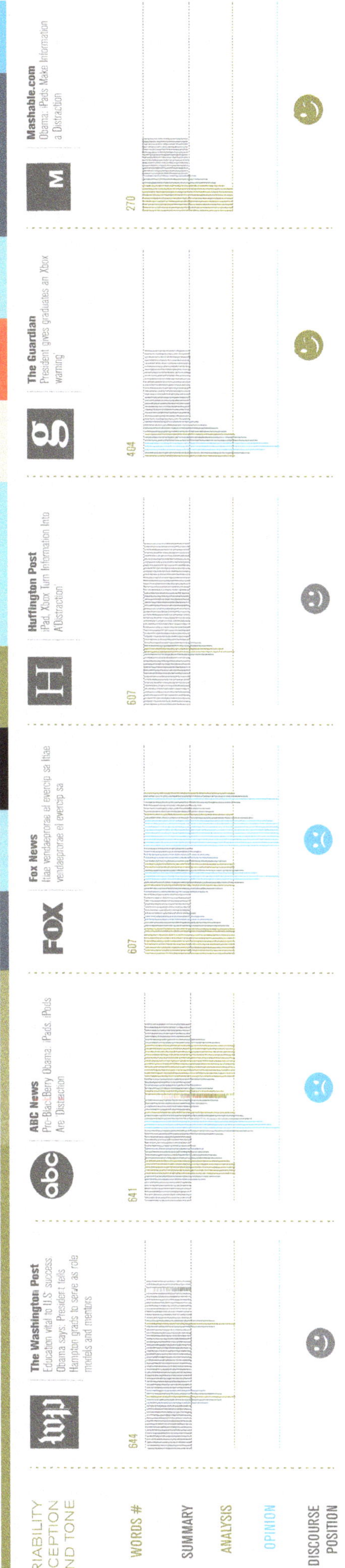

"WITH SO MANY VOICES CLAMOURING FOR ATTENTION ON BLOGS, AND ON CABLE, ON TALK RADIO, IT CAN BE DIFFICULT, AT TIMES, TO SIFT THROUGH IT ALL; TO KNOW WHAT TO BELIEVE; TO FIGURE OUT WHO'S TELLING THE TRUTH AND WHO'S NOT."[17]

In this increasingly technologically connected world, information-cum-understanding collected through media channels becomes our connection to a massive virtual neighborhood of diverse cultures, languages, and beliefs. In this virtual reality, the complexity of human engagement and the distance between people become more and more irrelevant, while the day-to-day effect the media we consume has on us emotionally, culturally, socially, and politically grows greater.

Despite the variable nature of a datum our dependence on the information we collect from mass media is crucial to our understanding of the world[18]. We can see this need and dependence in the increased volume of media consumed t

17. Obama, "Remarks by the President at Hampton University Commencement."

18. Livingstone, S. "The changing nature of audiences: from the mass audience to the interactive media user." *In Companion to Media Studies. Blackwell companions in cultural studies (6)*, edited by A. Valdivia, pgs. 337–359. Oxford, UK: Blackwell Publishing, 2003.

19. Short, J. *How Much Media? 2013: Report on American Consumers.* California: Institute for Communications Technology Management, Marshall School of Business, University of Southern California, Los Angeles, CA, USA, 2013. Available at: http://www.marshall.usc.edu/faculty/centers/ctm/research/how-much-media (Accessed September 10, 2016).

Average media consumption per day of Adults in America

12HRS 5MINS[19]

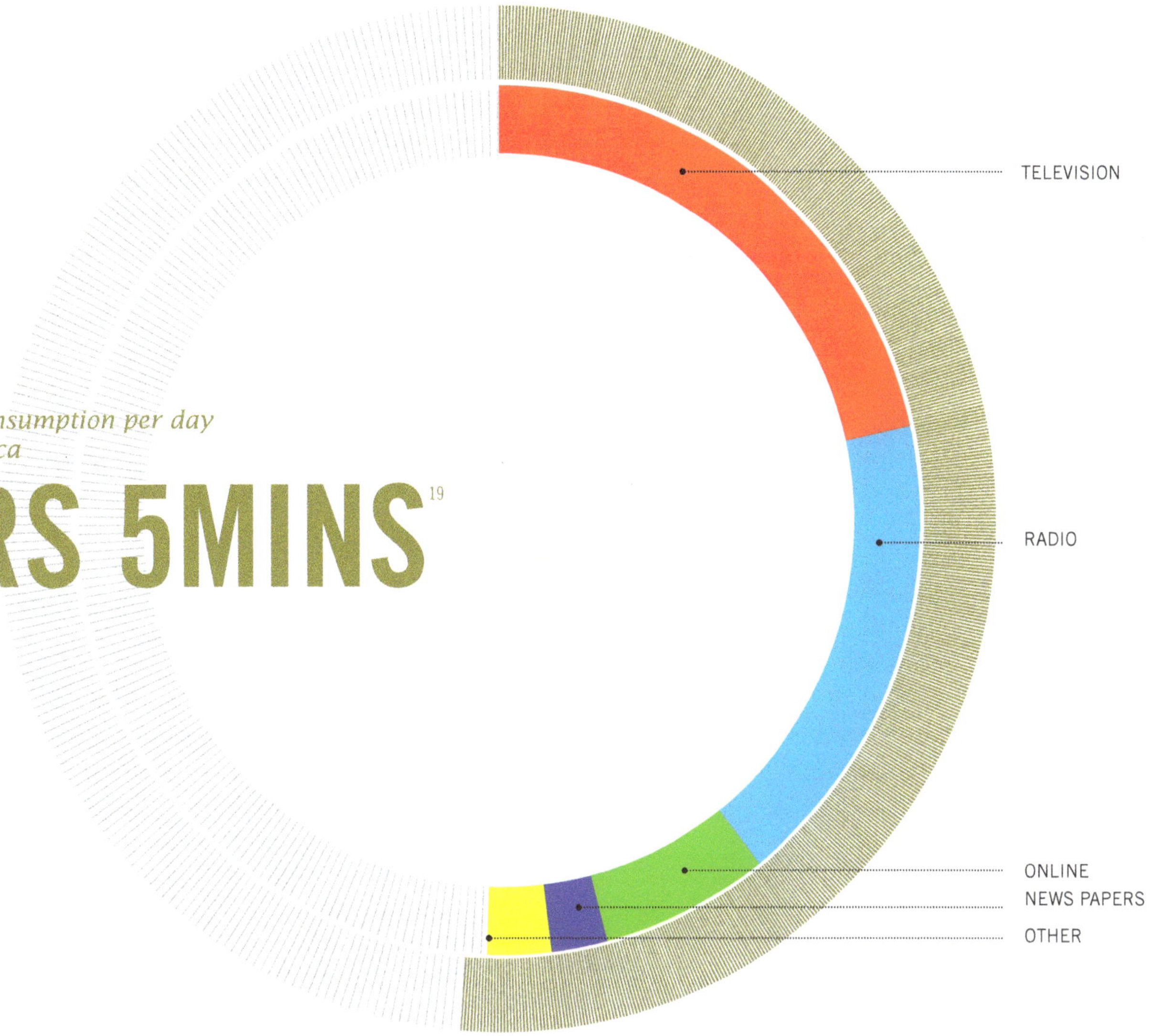

TELEVISION

RADIO

ONLINE

NEWS PAPERS

OTHER

2/3 OF OUR WAKING HOURS ARE SPENT CONSUMING MEDIA

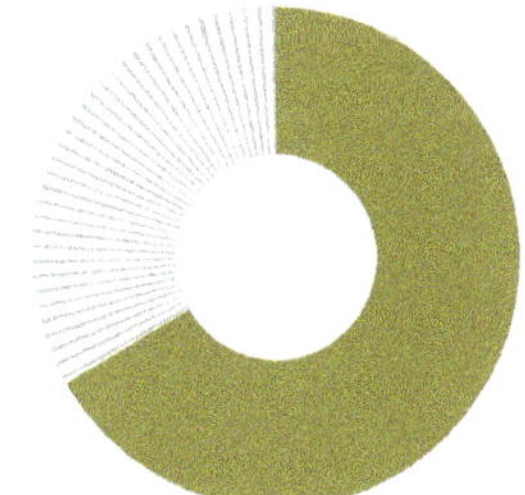

In 2012, The average American on an average day received

63GB

OF MEDIA DATA

OR

8 DVDs

OR

12,946 Bibles

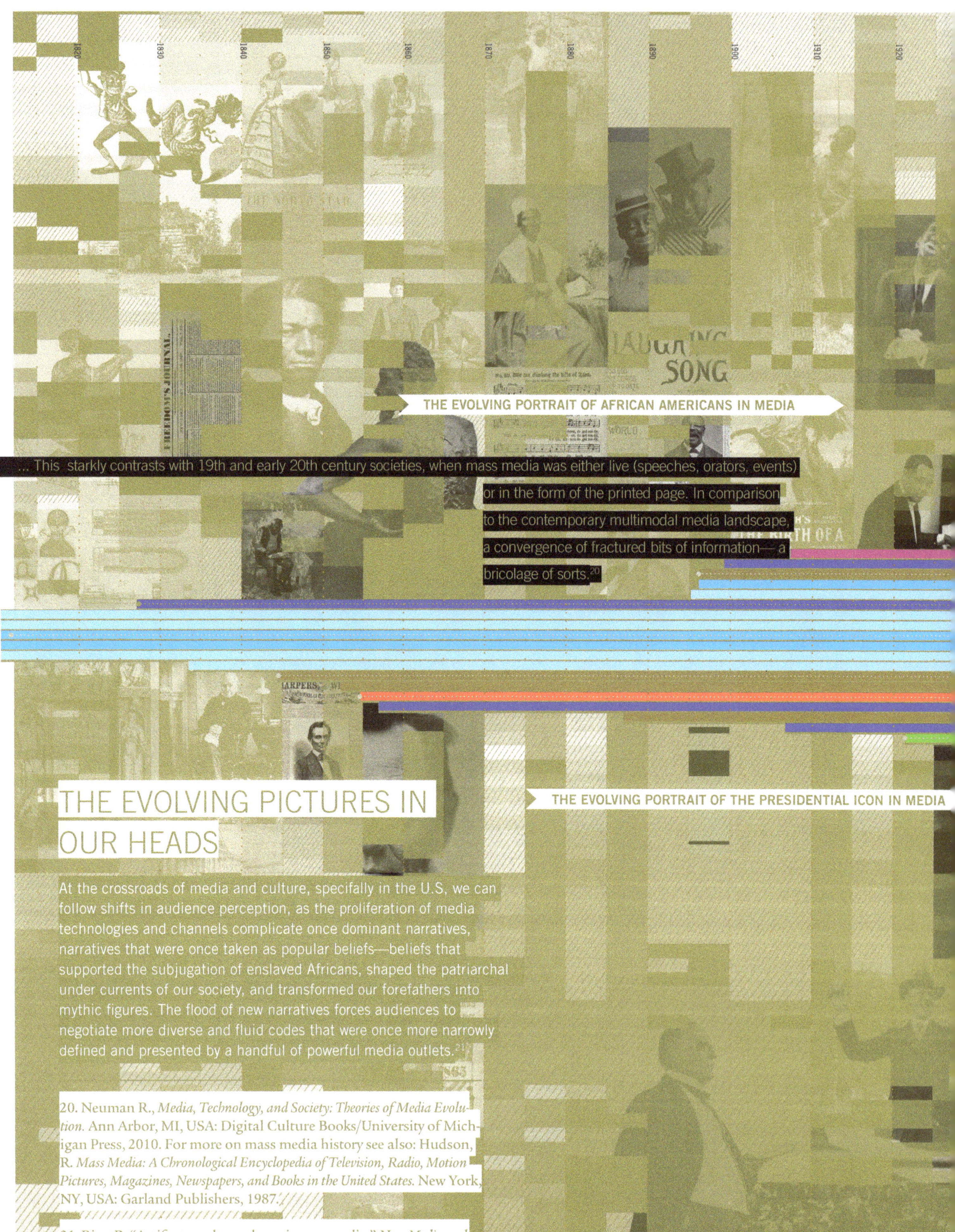

... This starkly contrasts with 19th and early 20th century societies, when mass media was either live (speeches, orators, events) or in the form of the printed page. In comparison to the contemporary multimodal media landscape, a convergence of fractured bits of information— a bricolage of sorts.[20]

THE EVOLVING PICTURES IN OUR HEADS

At the crossroads of media and culture, specifally in the U.S, we can follow shifts in audience perception, as the proliferation of media technologies and channels complicate once dominant narratives, narratives that were once taken as popular beliefs—beliefs that supported the subjugation of enslaved Africans, shaped the patriarchal under currents of our society, and transformed our forefathers into mythic figures. The flood of new narratives forces audiences to negotiate more diverse and fluid codes that were once more narrowly defined and presented by a handful of powerful media outlets.[21]

20. Neuman R., *Media, Technology, and Society: Theories of Media Evolution.* Ann Arbor, MI, USA: Digital Culture Books/University of Michigan Press, 2010. For more on mass media history see also: Hudson, R. *Mass Media: A Chronological Encyclopedia of Television, Radio, Motion Pictures, Magazines, Newspapers, and Books in the United States.* New York, NY, USA: Garland Publishers, 1987.

21. Rice, R. "Artifacts and paradoxes in new media." *New Media and Society, 1.1,* (April 1999): pgs. 24–32.

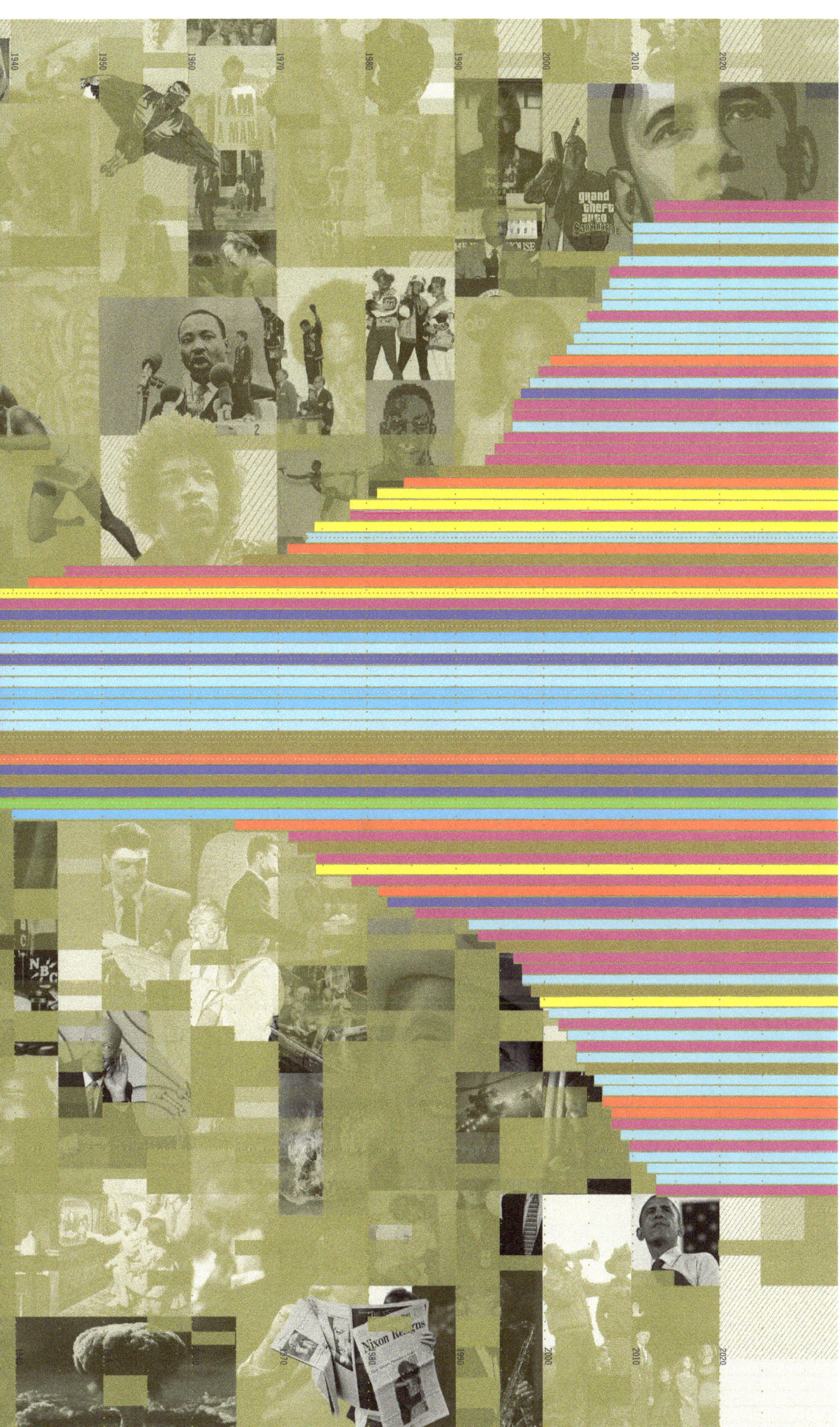

FORMS OF MEDIA DISTRIBUTION

(A Cross-section)

CLOUD STORAGE
IPAD IS INTRODUCED
SPOTIFY
TUMBLR
IPHONE
KHAN ACADEMY
GOOGLE LIBRARY
YOU TUBE LAUNCHED
FACEBOOK
DIGG
VIRTUAL WORLDS
LINKEDIN
MEETUP
TRIPADVISOR
MP3 PLAYERS
NETFLIX LAUNCHES
FREE WEB-BASED EMAIL
DIGITAL CAMERAS
SEARCH ENGINE
MATCH.COM
PORTABLE DOC FORMAT
APPLE RELEASES QUICKTIME
WWW GOES PUBLIC
LAPTOP COMPUTER
COMMERCIAL EMAIL
COMPACT DISC
VHS-VIDEOCASSETTES
CABLE TELEVIOSN
FLOPPY DISC
COMMERCIAL VCR
ARPANET EMAIL
VIDEOCASSETTE
MODERN FAX MACHINES
DIGITAL COMPUTER
AUDIOTAPES
TV TRANSMISSION
TABULATING MACHINE
MOVING PICTURE
TELEPHONE
TYPEWRITTER
POSTCARDS
PHOTOGRAPHY
NEW SHEETS
EUROPEAN PRINTING
PRINTING (INTRO)
FIRST ETCHINGS
ENCYCLOPIDIA
PUBLIC LIBRARY
TELEGRAPH TRANSMISSION
TELEFAX
PHONOGRAPH
FILM CAMERA
WIRELESS
MOVIE THEATRES
RADIO BROADCAST
XEROX COPIERS
AUDIOCASSETTES
DOD'S ARPANET
VIDEOPHONE
ATARI RELEASES PONG
HBO VIA SATELLITE
PORTABLE COMPUTER
SONY WALKMAN
ELECTRONIC CAMERA/CAMCORDER
GRAPHICAL USER INTERFACE
INSTANT MESSAGER
VIRUTAL ENVIRONMENTS
FIRST SMART PHONE
NETSCAPE 1.0
AMAZON.COM LAUNCHES
WIKI
SMART PHONES
DVDS
NAPSTER
RSS INTRODUCED
WIKIPEDIA
IPOD
FRIENDSTER
CAMERA PHONE
SKYPE
FLICKR
PODCAST
PANDORA RADIO
GOOGLE MAPS
TWITTER
KINDLE LAUNCHES
SOUNDCLOUD
KICKSTARTER
INSTAGRAM
DIGITAL PUBLIC LIBRARY

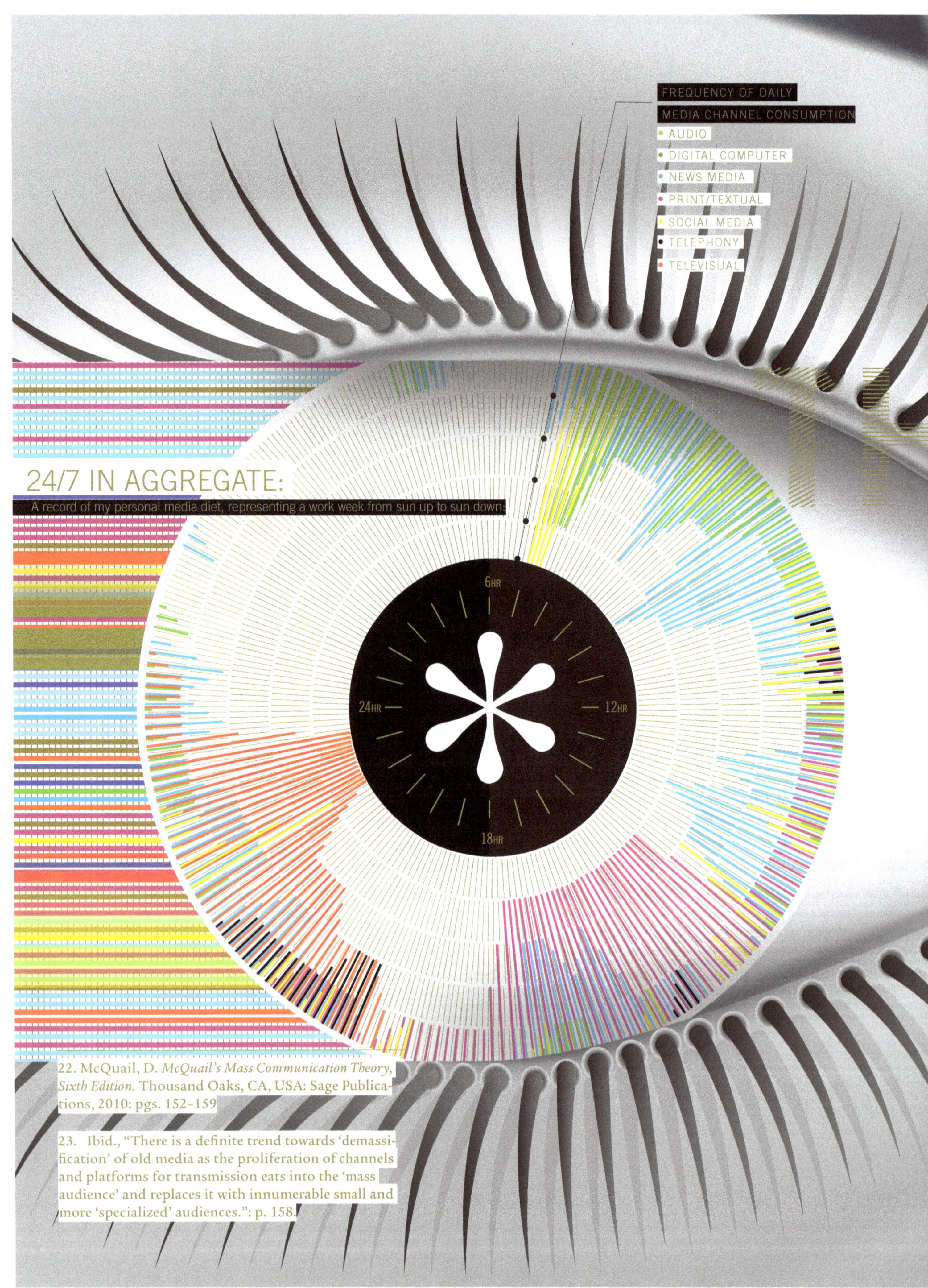

22. McQuail, D. *McQuail's Mass Communication Theory, Sixth Edition.* Thousand Oaks, CA, USA: Sage Publications, 2010: pgs. 152–159

23. Ibid., "There is a definite trend towards 'demassification' of old media as the proliferation of channels and platforms for transmission eats into the 'mass audience' and replaces it with innumerable small and more 'specialized' audiences.": p. 158.

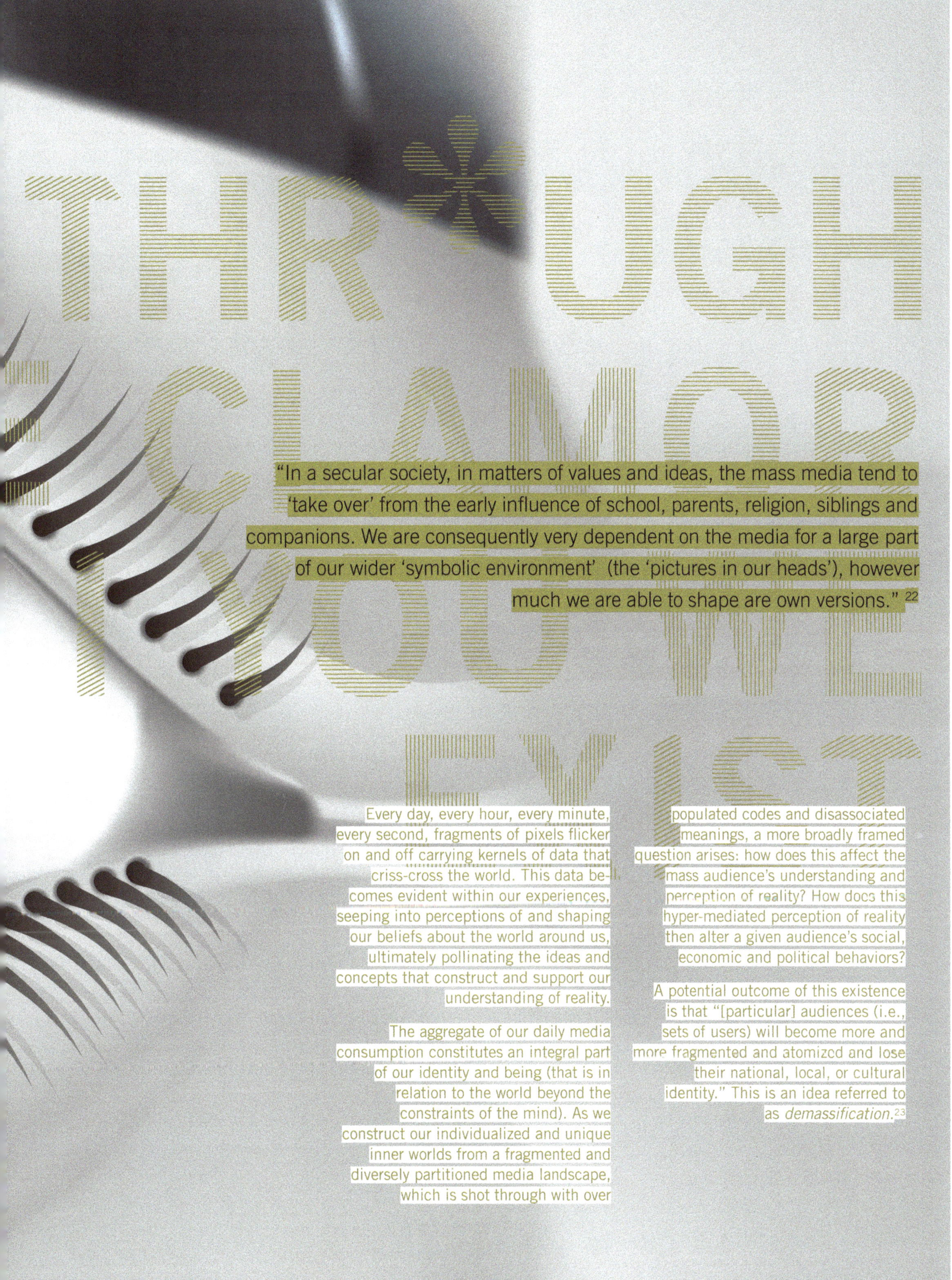

"In a secular society, in matters of values and ideas, the mass media tend to 'take over' from the early influence of school, parents, religion, siblings and companions. We are consequently very dependent on the media for a large part of our wider 'symbolic environment' (the 'pictures in our heads'), however much we are able to shape are own versions." [22]

Every day, every hour, every minute, every second, fragments of pixels flicker on and off carrying kernels of data that criss-cross the world. This data becomes evident within our experiences, seeping into perceptions of and shaping our beliefs about the world around us, ultimately pollinating the ideas and concepts that construct and support our understanding of reality.

The aggregate of our daily media consumption constitutes an integral part of our identity and being (that is in relation to the world beyond the constraints of the mind). As we construct our individualized and unique inner worlds from a fragmented and diversely partitioned media landscape, which is shot through with over populated codes and disassociated meanings, a more broadly framed question arises: how does this affect the mass audience's understanding and perception of reality? How does this hyper-mediated perception of reality then alter a given audience's social, economic and political behaviors?

A potential outcome of this existence is that "[particular] audiences (i.e., sets of users) will become more and more fragmented and atomized and lose their national, local, or cultural identity." This is an idea referred to as *demassification*.[23]

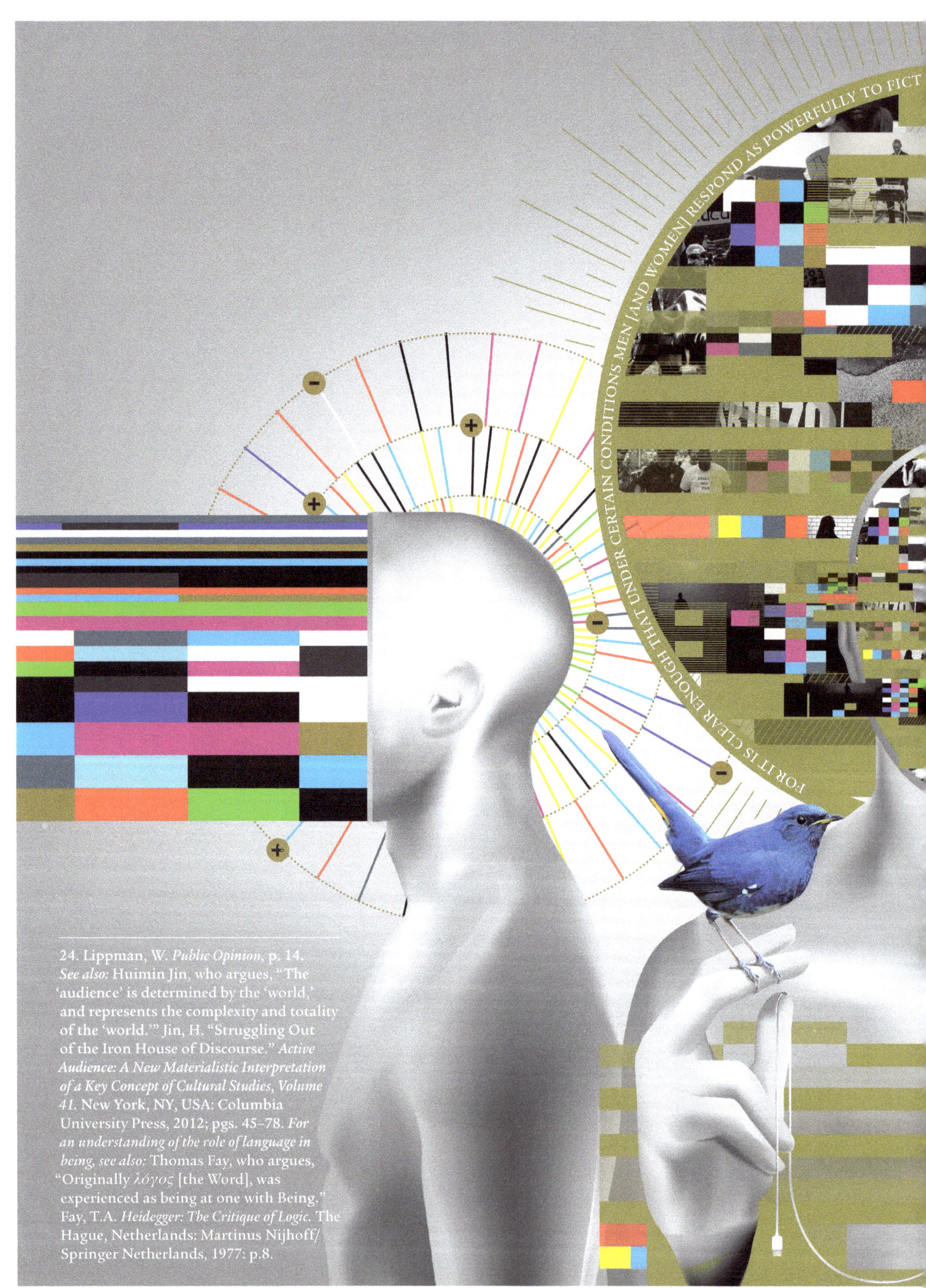

24. Lippman, W. *Public Opinion*, p. 14. *See also:* Huimin Jin, who argues, "The 'audience' is determined by the 'world,' and represents the complexity and totality of the 'world.'" Jin, H. "Struggling Out of the Iron House of Discourse." *Active Audience: A New Materialistic Interpretation of a Key Concept of Cultural Studies, Volume 41.* New York, NY, USA: Columbia University Press, 2012; pgs. 45–78. *For an understanding of the role of language in being, see also:* Thomas Fay, who argues, "Originally *λόγος* [the Word], was experienced as being at one with Being." Fay, T.A. *Heidegger: The Critique of Logic.* The Hague, Netherlands: Martinus Nijhoff/ Springer Netherlands, 1977: p.8.

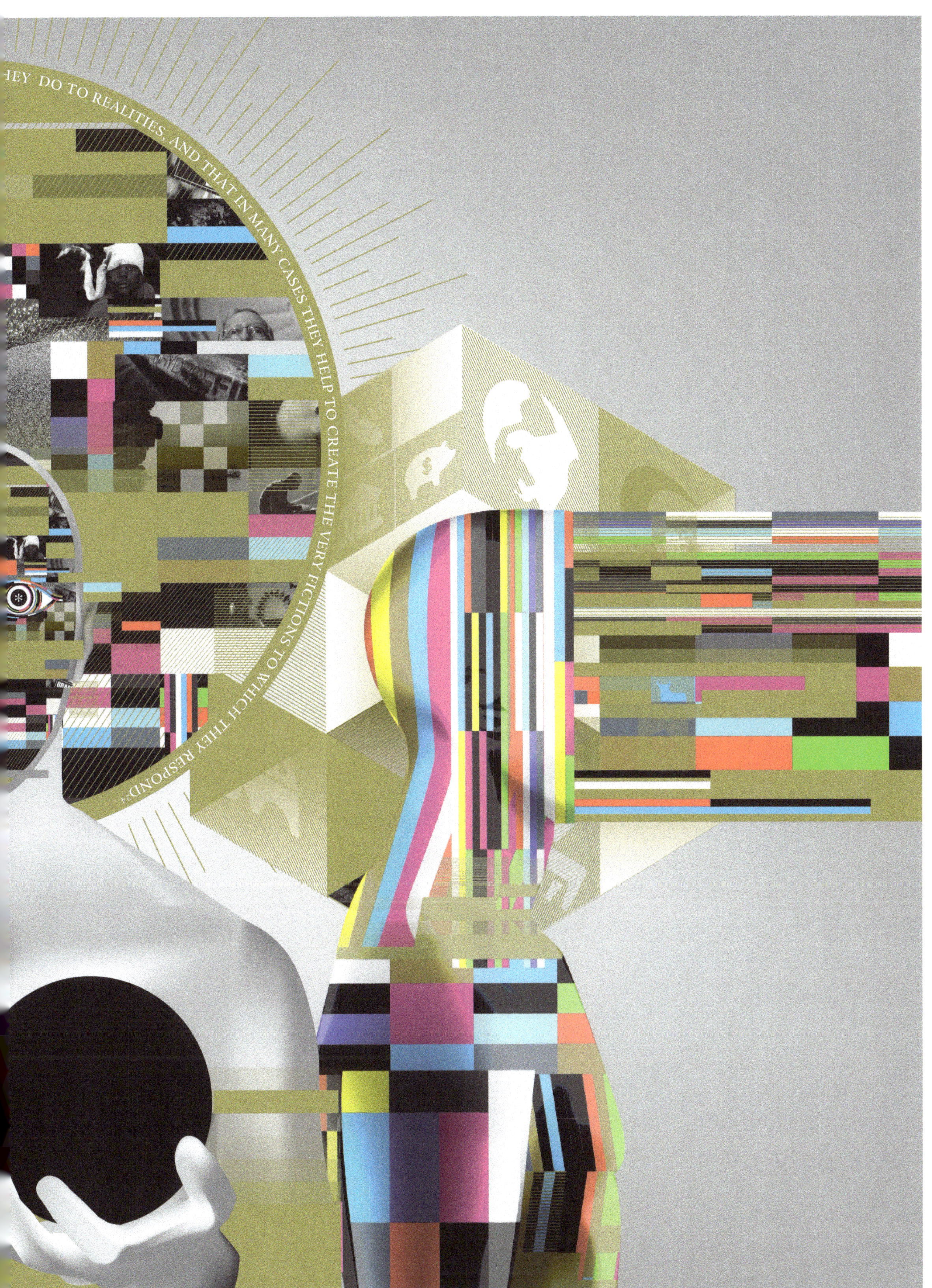
HEY DO TO REALITIES, AND THAT IN MANY CASES THEY HELP TO CREATE THE VERY FICTIONS TO WHICH THEY RESPOND[24]

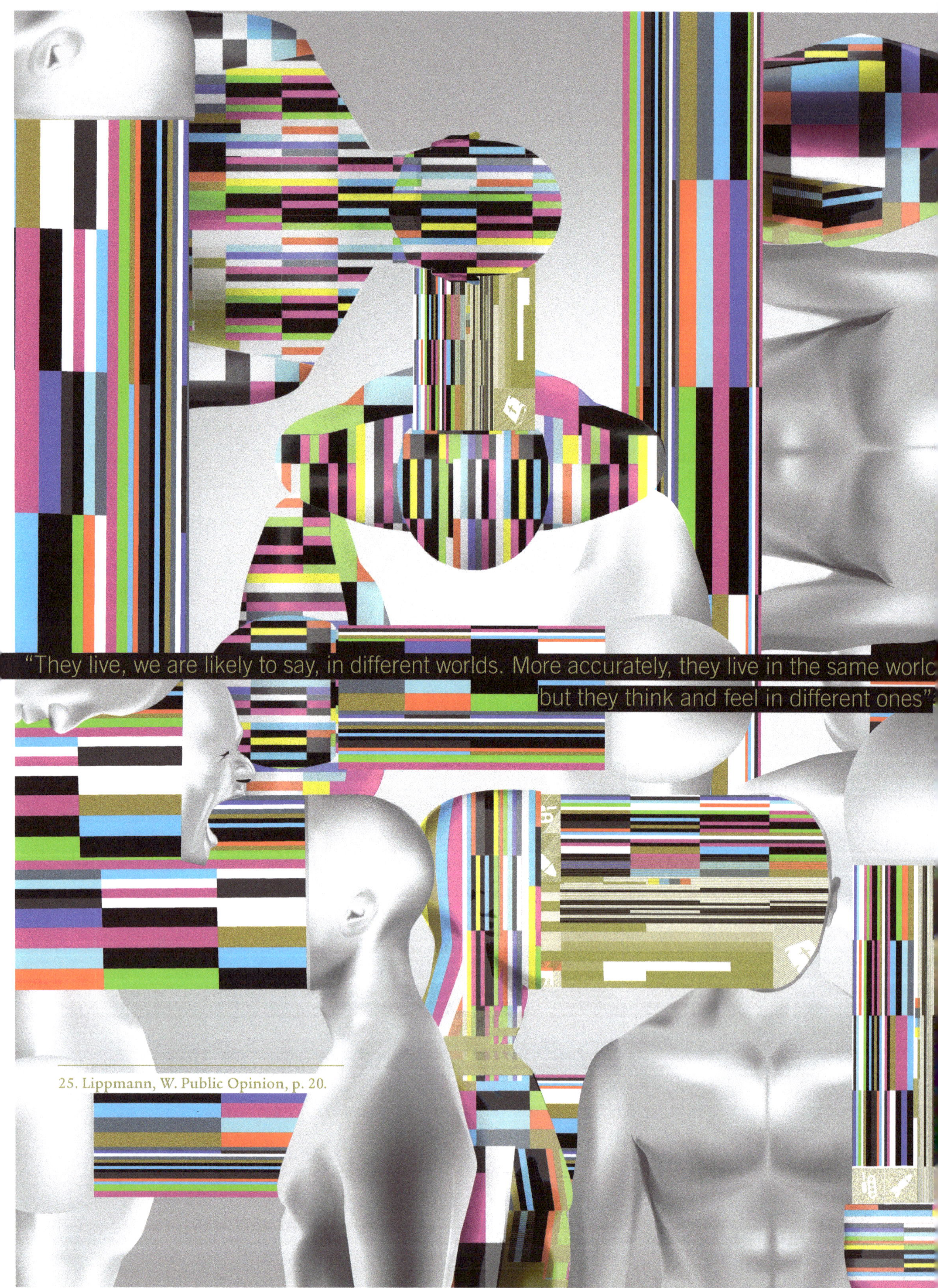

25. Lippmann, W. Public Opinion, p. 20.

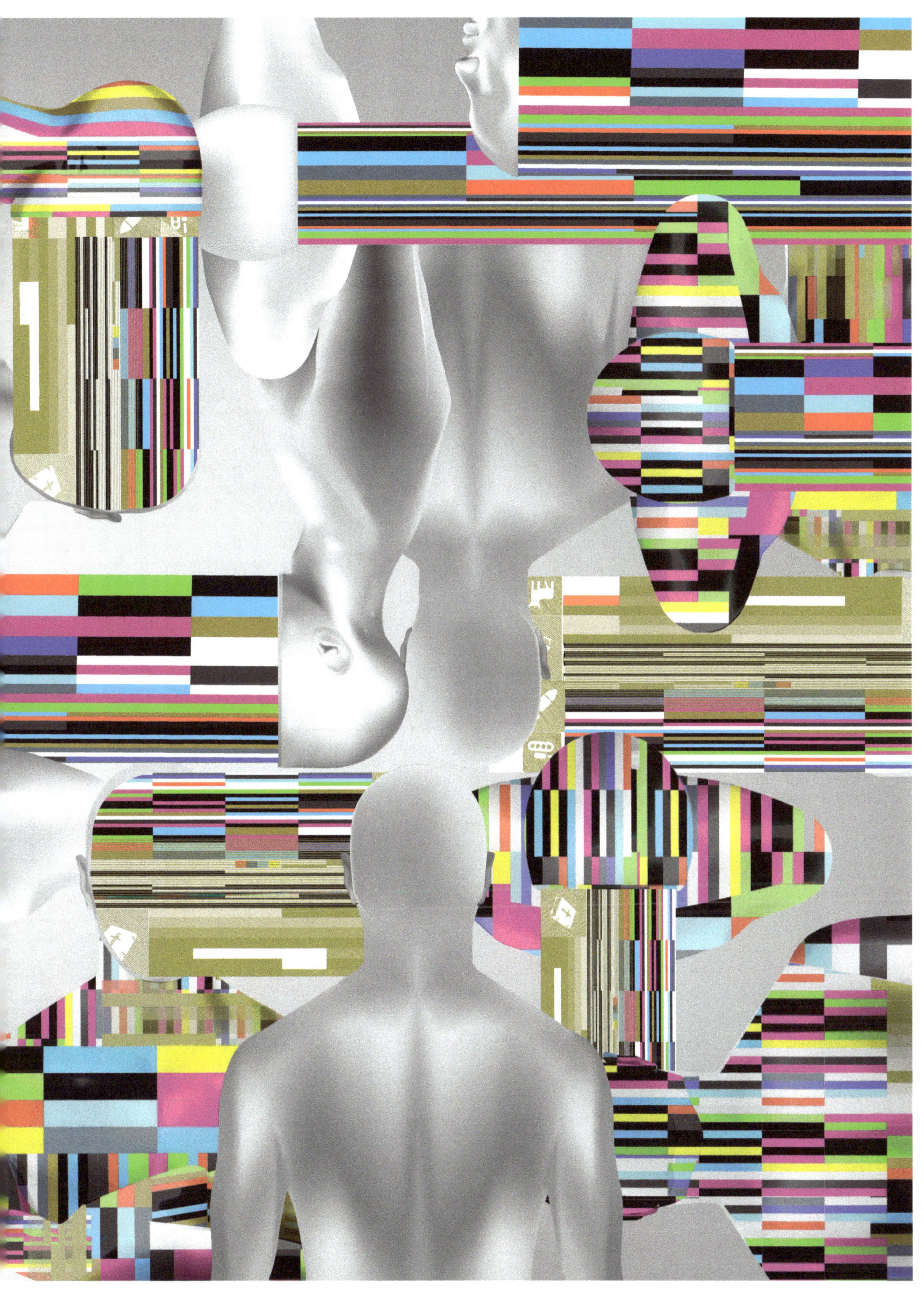

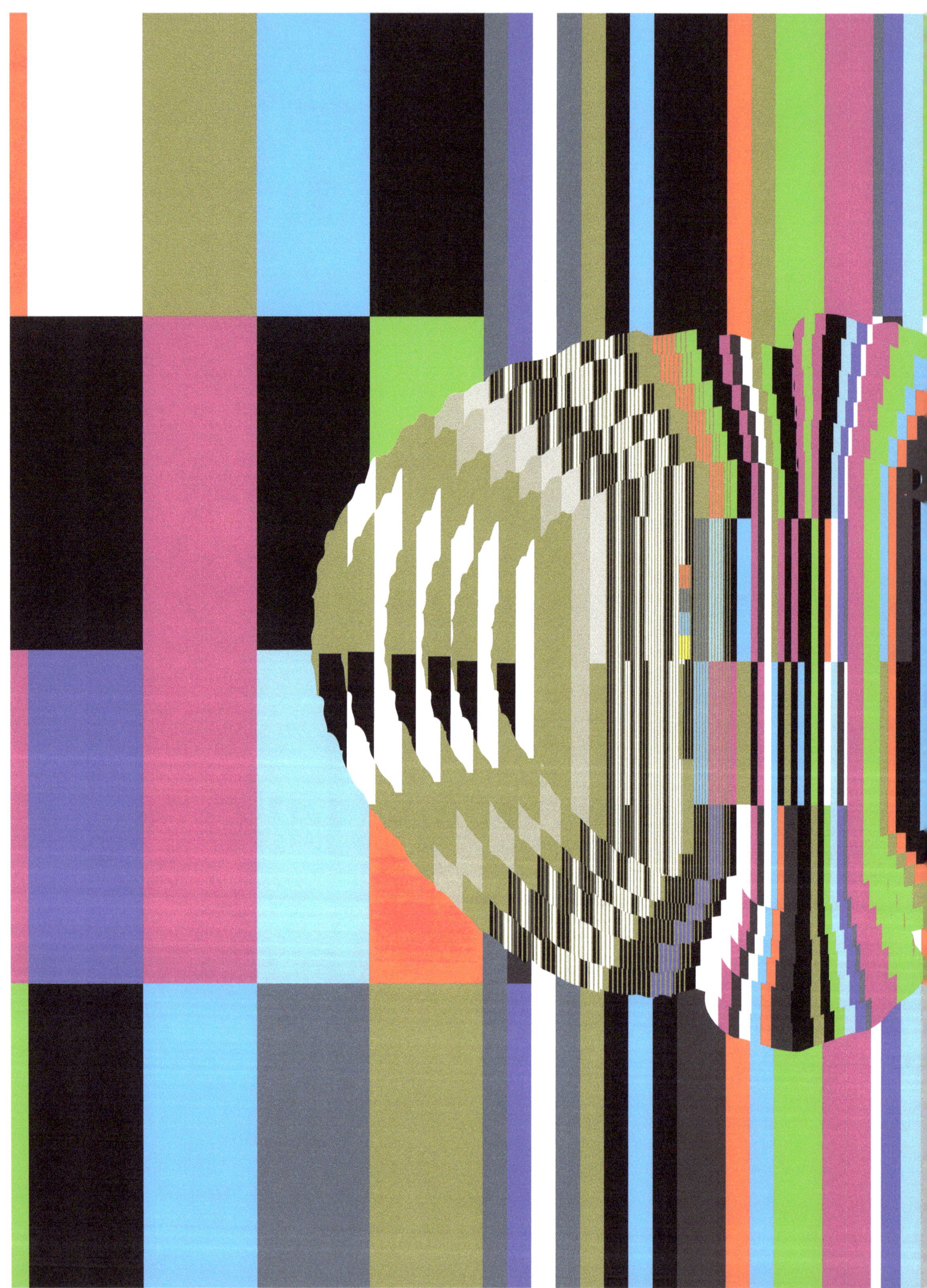

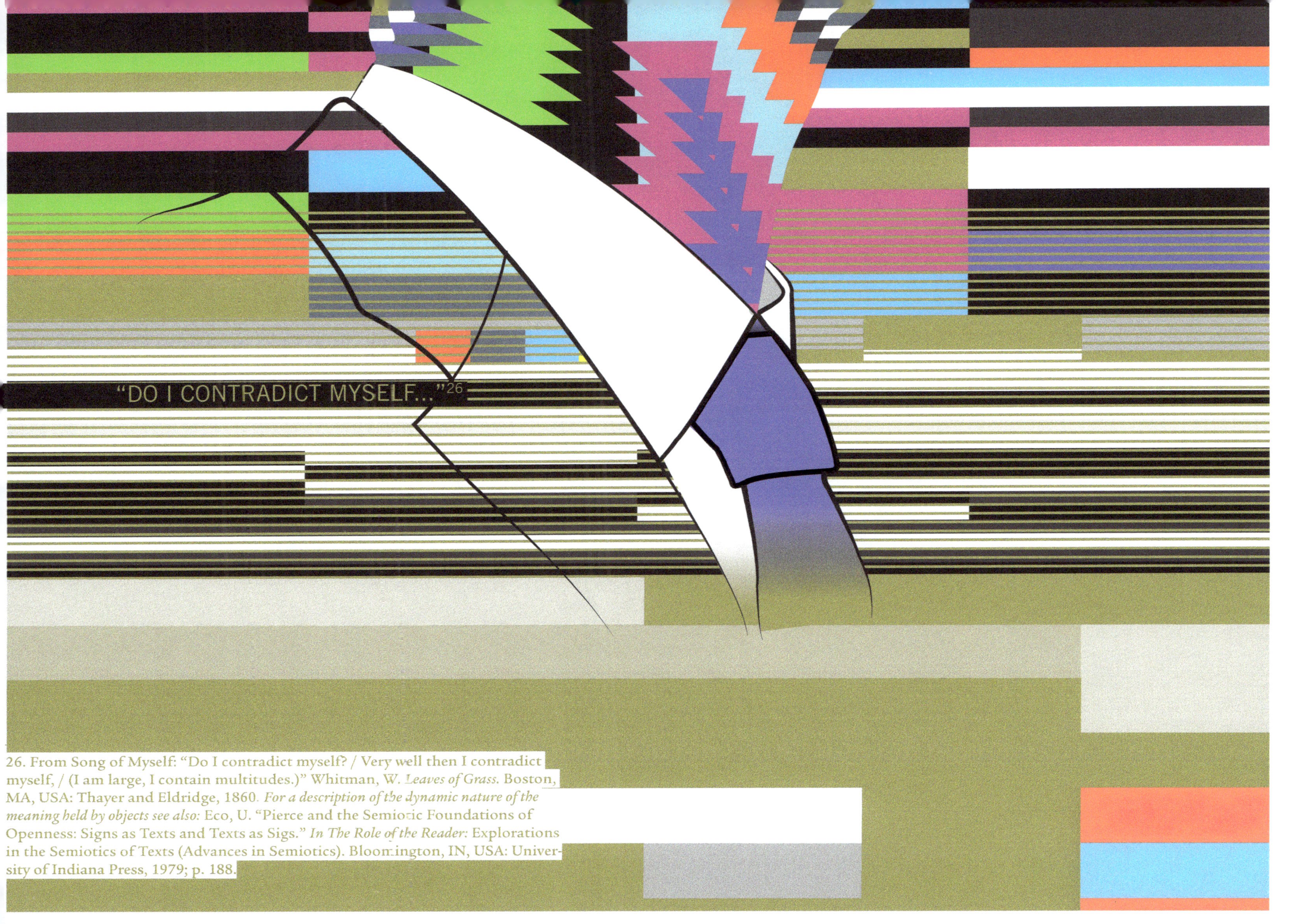

"DO I CONTRADICT MYSELF..."[26]

26. From Song of Myself: "Do I contradict myself? / Very well then I contradict myself, / (I am large, I contain multitudes.)" Whitman, W. *Leaves of Grass*. Boston, MA, USA: Thayer and Eldridge, 1860. *For a description of the dynamic nature of the meaning held by objects see also:* Eco, U. "Pierce and the Semiotic Foundations of Openness: Signs as Texts and Texts as Sigs." *In The Role of the Reader:* Explorations in the Semiotics of Texts (Advances in Semiotics). Bloomington, IN, USA: University of Indiana Press, 1979; p. 188.

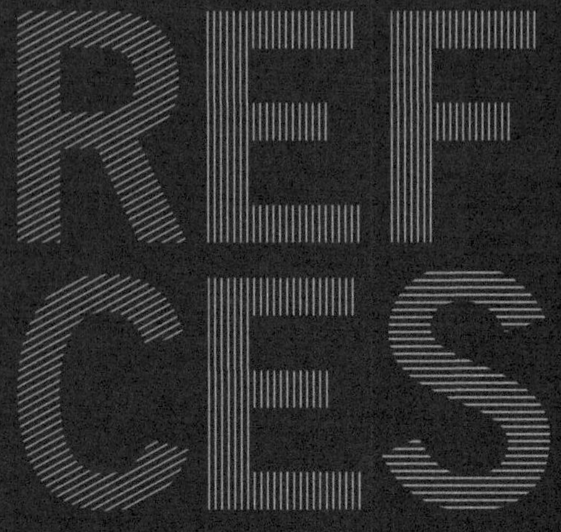

- al., McQuail_et. *McQuail's Mass Communication Theory 6th edition*. London: SAGE Publications Ltd, 2010.
- Bourdieu, Pierre. *Physical Space, Social Space and Habitus*. Oslo: Department of Sociology, University of Oslo & Institute for Social Research, 1996.
- Bruner, Jerome. "The Narrative Construction of Reality." *Critical Inquiry* (The University of Chicago Press) 18, no. 1 (1991): 1-21.
- Eco, Umberto. *The Role of the Reader*. Indian: University of Indiana Press, 1979.
- Fay, Thomas A. *Heidegger: The Critique of Logic*. The Hague: Martinus Nijhoff, 1977.
- Frick, F.C. "Information Theory." *In Psychology: A study of a Science*, by Sigmund Koch, 611-36. New York: McGraw-Hill, 1959.
- Goffman, E. Frame *Analysis: an Essay on the Organization of Experience*. Harper and Row, 1974.
- Hall, Stuart. "Encoding/Decoding." *In Media and Cultural Studies: Keyworks*, by Meenakshi Gigi Durham and Douglas M. Kellner, 163-173. Malden, MA: Blackwell Publishing Ltd, 1973/2006.
- Hudson, Robert V. *Mass Media : A Chronological Encyclopedia of Television, Radio, Motion Pictures, Magazines, Newspapers, and Books in the United States*. Vol. 310. New York: Garland Pub, Garland Reference Library of Social Science, 1987.
- Jin, Huimin. *Active Audience: A New Materialistic Interpretation of a Key Concept of Cultural Studies, Volume 41 of Cultural Studies*. Germany: transcript Verlag, 2014.
- Lippmann, Walter. *Public Opinion*. New York: Harcourt, Brace and Co, 1922.
- Livingstone, Sonia. "The changing nature of audience: from the mass audience to the interactive media user." *In Companion to Media Studies. Blackwell companions in cultural studies*, edited by Angharad Valdivia, 337-359. London: Blackwell Publishing, 2003.
- Neuman, Russell W. *Media, Technology, and Society: Theories of Media Evolution*. Ann Arbor, Michigan: Digital Culture Books/University of Michigan Press, 2010.
- Obama, Barack . *Remarks by the President at Hampton University Commencement*. 10 May 2010. https://obamawhitehouse.archives.gov/the-press-office/remarks-president-hampton-university-commencement (accessed September 1, 2016).
- Obama, Barack. *President Obama at Hampton University*. 9 May 2010. https://youtu.be/Hwg636CQnrc (accessed September 10, 2016).
- Rice, R.E. "Artifacts and paradoxes in new media." *New Media and Society* 1, no. 1 (April 1999): 24-32.
- *Share of adult internet users in the United States who use social networking sites from 2005 to 2015*. 10 2015. https://www.statista.com/statistics/273035/share-of-us-adult-internet-users-who-use-social-networking-sites/ (accessed 2016).
- Stevenson, Nick. In Transforming *McLuhan: Cultural, Critical and Postmodern Perspectives*. New York: Peter Lang, 2010.
- *Top Stories of 2010: Haiti Earthquake, Gulf Oil Spill. Pew Research Center*. 21 December 2010. http://www.people-press.org/2010/12/21/top-stories-of-2010-haiti-earthquake-gulf-oil-spill/ (accessed September 1, 2016).
- Tuchman, G. *Making News: a Study in the Construction of Reality*. New York: Free Press, 1978.

BIOGRAPHY

Kareem Collie is the Director of Design and Creativity at the Rick and Susan Sontag Center for Collaborative Creativity (aka The Hive) and Clinical Professor of Visual Communication Design at The Claremont Colleges. His work explores the intersections of Design, Creativity and the Humanities. Kareem is a recent fellow of Stanford University's d.school. He has an MA from NYU and a BFA from Pratt Institute.

Dialectic Volume II, Issue I: Case Study

The Landscape of Community and Participatory Design in Puerto Rico: A Critical Examination of the Effects of Attempting to Facilitate "Listening to Their Voices," ("Escuchando las Voces") the Island's First Exhibition of Community and Participatory Design

MARÍA DE MATER O'NEILL, DDP[1] AND OMAYRA RIVERA CRESPO, PH.D.[2]

1. Rubberband Design Studio, LLP, Santurce, Puerto Rico, USA
2. El colectivo "Taller Creando Sin Encargos" (The group "Creating Without Commissions Studio"), San Juan, Puerto Rico, USA

The exhibition was supported by the Department of Arts, Culture, and Innovation of the Municipality of San Juan, Puerto Rico, under Grant Number 2016-002866. Editorial support for the publication of this article was provided by *Dialectic's* Internal Editing Team, led by Michael R. Gibson, Evelyn Denson, and the late Joan Secrest.

DISCLOSURE STATEMENT: The authors received a minimal honorarium for designing and organizing the exhibition.

SUGGESTED CITATION: O'neill, MM. & Rivera Crespo, O., "The Landscape of Community and Participatory Design in Puerto Rico: A Critical Examination of the Effects of Facilitating the Island's First Exhibition of Community and Participatory Design." *Dialectic,* 2.1 (2018): pgs. 131-168. DOI: http://dx.doi.org/10.3998/dialectic.14932326.0001.306

Abstract

As of this writing in January of 2018, Puerto Rico remains beset by an ongoing financial crisis that has shaken the island economically, socially and politically since late 2005. This situation was made much worse on September 20, 2017, when the island was devastated by Hurricane María, an event that caused this crisis to become a humanitarian one as well. In view of this complex—and socio-economically staggering—situation, Puerto Rican designers are finding that they must reconsider their social, economic and, in some cases, political roles and adapt to the island's new daily realities. This case study explores the findings of an architectural educator and a design researcher who were prompted by the current economic climate to produce a convivial [a] project to assist fellow creatives as they attempted to navigate the ebb and flow of the Puerto Rican economy and its short- and long-term effects on the daily lives of Puerto Rican citizens. This project was planned to meet two goals. The first was to provide a means to explore and experiment with collaborative methodologies. The second was to teach non-designers and practitioners how they might apply these methodologies to provide relief to particular population groups around the island who were experiencing difficult socio-economic and socio-political circumstances. It is the authors' contention that employing the design methodology of co-creation [b] could be an effective means to allow groups of citizens working with designers to tackle day-to-day, community-based, social problems by allowing them to work on locally rooted, transformative projects.

To demonstrate the results of this kind of collaboration, the authors organized the first exhibition documenting the positive outcomes of community and participatory design processes ever held in Puerto Rico: *"Listening to Their Voices"* (*"Escuchando las Voces"*). In 2015 an invitation to submit documentation of works that utilize either or some combination of both community and participatory design was sent to urban planners, artists, designers, and architects across the island. The exhibition organizers (two of whom are authors of this piece) received 15 submissions that documented projects undertaken in various locations around Puerto Rico by individual (or groups of) architects, social scientists, designers or artists. *"Listening to their Voices"* provided an opportunity to share critical information and experiences about these collaborative design approaches with a wider audience. Additionally, it would afford opportunities to survey the processes practitioners formulate and operationalize to create the knowledge and the skills necessary to address the effects of the by then 12-year-long financial crisis on the island's various populations.

*"Listening to Their Voices"*opened in April 2017 and was suspended in September 2017 due to the damage wrought across Puerto Rico by *Hurricane Maria.* Despite this, the authors still felt that sharing the knowledge they were able to construct as they prepared the contents of this exhibition could prove useful. The questions that framed the authors' inquiries regarding how and why participatory and community design could positively affect public policy change in an environment as economically bereft as Puerto Rico have yielded beneficial insights about how these processes could generalize to similar situations worldwide. Despite the problems the authors of *"Listening to Their Voices"* faced due to the hurricane, it is the knowledge they gained during the process of conceptualizing and realizing this exhibition that is of greatest import.

keywords:

community design, participatory design, urban co-planning, Puerto Rico, toolkit, design history

---

a "Convivial" in this context of use conveys the sense of "living-together," or the definition given "conviviality" by Ivan Illich: "I choose the term 'conviviality' to designate the opposite of industrial productivity. I intend it to mean autonomous and creative intercourse among persons, and the intercourse of persons with their environment; and this in contrast with the conditioned response of persons to the demands made upon them by others, and by a man-made environment. I consider conviviality to be individual freedom realized in personal interdependence and, as such, an intrinsic ethical value." (Ilich, I. *Tools for Conviviality.* London, UK/New York, NY, USA: 1973: Marian Boyars, Publishers. Excerpt quoted from Andrea Gibbons, 20 November 2015, Online. Available at: http://writingcities.com/2015/11/20/ivan-illichs-tr-conviviality/ (Accessed February 1, 2018).)

b "Co-creation" in this context is the act of creating or designing with the user by, among other things, exchanging knowledge and experiences, refining ("tweaking") goals, and incorporating perhaps overlooked or somewhat undervalued elements.

The Landscape of Community and Participatory Design in Puerto Rico:

A Critical Examination of the Effects of Attempting to Facilitate "Listening to Their Voices," ("Escuchando las Voces") the Island's First Exhibition of Community and Participatory Design

MARÍA DE MATER O'NEILL, DDP.1 &
OMAYRA RIVERA CRESPO, PH.D.2

Definitions and Descriptions of the Collaborative Methodologies that Guided the Projects Documented in "Listening to Their Voices"

The author acknowledge that many definitions and descriptions of Community and Participatory Design exist in the scholarly literature of design and the social sciences. For the purposes of designing, planning and implementing the *"Listening to Their Voices"* exhibition (and now describing them in this piece), the organizers/authors aligned themselves with what is articulated below. They felt that sharing these understandings would allow the greatest cross-sections of exhibition participants to derive benefit from them:

1. *Community design* (CD): A methodology that focuses on developing contextual projects as a means to improve social and environmental conditions. CD encourages individual and collective participation in the preparation of small-scale projects to revitalize communities and infrastructures. Self-management and cultivating social capital are essential aspects of the comprehensive approaches used to guide the thinking required to facilitate this kind of design method. It is a participatory process in which design work becomes a training experience for citizens involved in project management wherein they are able to learn from their experiences

while exploring the potential positive impact their specific contributions could have on various aspects of their communities.

2. *Participatory design* (PD): A methodology that involves designers engaging in the design process along with a user or group of users of whatever—a space, an experience, an interface—is to be designed; hence, it is also called *Co-Design*. In this context, *participating* means becoming an active contributor to the development and implementation of a given design project. In this way, participants play an essential role in affecting how particular living spaces, systems, and objects are perceived and work in accordance with their own physical and/or emotional needs. Participation is facilitated across a contextual worktable that serves to frame the various factors and conditions that will likely affect the evolution of a given project.[1] This methodology is also fueled by open conversations that allow all of the participants involved in the design and implementation of a given project to learn from each other and to value each other's critical input and feedback.

An Overview of Puerto Rico's Socio-Economic Situation during the Winter of 2017-18

Puerto Rico is a small island about the size of the U.S. state of Connecticut in the northwest Caribbean Sea (Figure 1). It has been a territory of the United States since 1898, and therefore "belongs" to the U.S., but does not have the rights or representation in the U.S. Congress awarded to the fifty states. According to U.S. Census figures from 2015, the island has a population of at least 3.6 million people. Recently, migration from Puerto Rico to the United States has accelerated due to the severe financial crisis that has shaken the island for (as of the publication of this piece) almost 12 years, and, more recently, due to the general slowness of the recovery—economically, technologically and structurally—from the devastation wrought by Hurricane María. Experts estimate that by 2030, the population is expected to have dropped to under 2 million people.[2] According to the 2012 U.S. Census, only 40.5% of Puerto Ricans are participants in the labor force, resulting in a median household income of just U.S. $19,518. "In 2014, the U.S. Census estimated that 58% of Puerto Rico's children live below the federal poverty level—much higher than the overall rate of 22% of children living below the poverty line throughout the United States. Puerto Rico's poverty rate is startlingly higher than that of any U.S. state."[3]

1 Gibson, M.R. & Owens, K.M. "Making meaning happen between 'us' and 'them': strategies for bridging gaps in understanding between researchers who possess design knowledge and those working in disciplines outside design." In The Routledge Companion to Design Research, edited by J. Yee and P. Rodgers, pgs. 386–399. Routledge, NY, NY, USA: 2015.

2 Santos Lozada, A., and Estrada, A.V. "The Population Decline of Puerto Rico: An Application of Prospective Trends in Cohort-Component Projections." Instituto de Estadísticas de Puerto Rico, Série de Documentos de Trabajo, 2015-1 (October 2015): p. 10. Online. Available at: http://www.estadisticas.gobierno.pr/iepr/Sobrenosotros/Seriededocumentosde-investigaci%C3%B3n.aspx (Accessed January 31, 2018).

3 Faccio, B. "Left Behind: Poverty's Toll on the Children of Puerto Rico." Child Trends [blog], 28 March, 2016. Online. Available at: https://www.childtrends.org/left-behind-povertys-toll-on-the-children-of-puerto-rico/ (Accessed January 28, 2018).

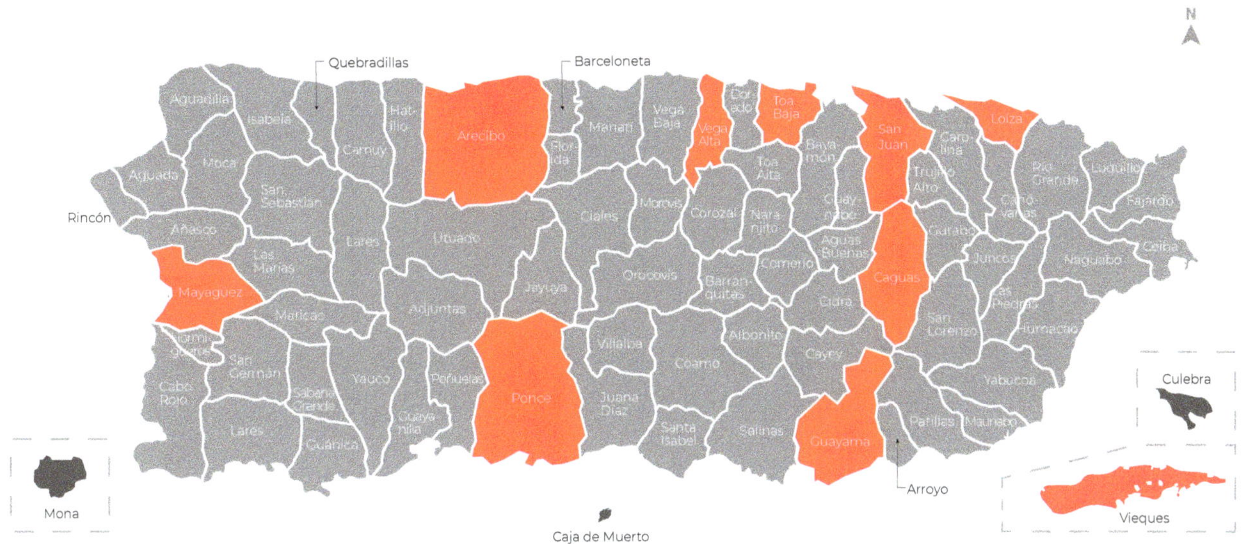

FIGURE 1: Puerto Rico is geographically divided into 78 *municipios*, which are roughly equivalent to American counties. Each *municipio* functions as a governmental entity. Those *municipios* indicated in red on this map indicate areas within which projects that were documented in *"Listening to Their Voices"* transpired.

With these economic factors in mind, two practitioners from the field of architecture (Edwin Quiles and Omayra Rivera) and one with a background in design research (María de Mater O'Neill) decided to come together to create a project that would present and document collaborative design methodologies as one means to address the island's growing social, cultural and economic problems. The goals of this project then extended further to inform the Puerto Rican communities of non-designers and creative practitioners about how they might apply these methodologies, while also demonstrating the positive impact of working collaboratively under the auspices of community and participatory design. More recently, this group has realized that much of what they have learned could be of benefit to populations living in other economically distressed portions of the world.

Understanding the Approaches That Guided the Collaborative Design Methodologies Documented in "Listening to Their Voices"

The authors set out to organize *"Listening to Their Voices"* as it was (and still is) the shared belief of Quiles, Rivera, and O'Neill that co-creation guided by community and participatory design approaches can help guide and fuel social, cultural, and collective change in a setting such as Puerto Rico. The organizers sent out an invitation in 2015 to fellow design practitioners and researchers, urban planners, artists, and architects across the island to submit their documentation of projects that involved or utilized collaborative design methodologies they were currently working on, had worked on in the past, or that were in the planning stages. The aim of the exhibition project was to showcase, explore, and document positive effects and uses of Community and Participatory Design in Puerto Rico, as there is a general lack of local documentation on design culture—and on design in general—from this area of the world. [c] This was not only an opportunity to educate professionals and the public about the processes through which design practitioners create new knowledge and skills: it also was an opportunity to explore the potential positive affect and import of creative collaborative endeavors that had been enacted to address various aspects of the economic crisis on the island.

[c] *The authors discuss this scarcity of documentation on pgs. 151-157.*

This was not only an opportunity to educate professionals and the public about the processes through which design practitioners create new knowledge and skills. It also was an opportunity to explore the potential positive affect and import of creative collaborative endeavors that had been enacted to address various aspects of the economic crisis on the island. The organizers/authors chose not to explore the particular suitability of Community and Participatory Design, as specific types of collaborative design methodologies, as means to guide the projects that comprised *"Listening to Their Voices."* Rather, this choice was made because the essential purpose of the exhibition was to survey *how* these methodologies were implemented in given situations around the island. It should also be noted that the organizers of *"Listening to Their Voices"* had, through their years of experience as designers and design researchers working on the island, accrued significant, personal knowledge of other design practitioners who had been using these types of collaborative methodologies in their work. The fact that the community of urban planners, designers and artists who work this way is relatively small and are not spread across a large geographic area supports collaborative efforts like this in Puerto Rico.

The *"Listening to Their Voices"* traveling exhibition was comprised of 14 sets of interlocking, free-standing corrugated cardboard panels printed with graphics and imagery. These sets of panels (each panel measured ~48"/122 cm x 96"/244 cm; an average of three were used in each display) visually documented the design process and described how each exhibition contributor

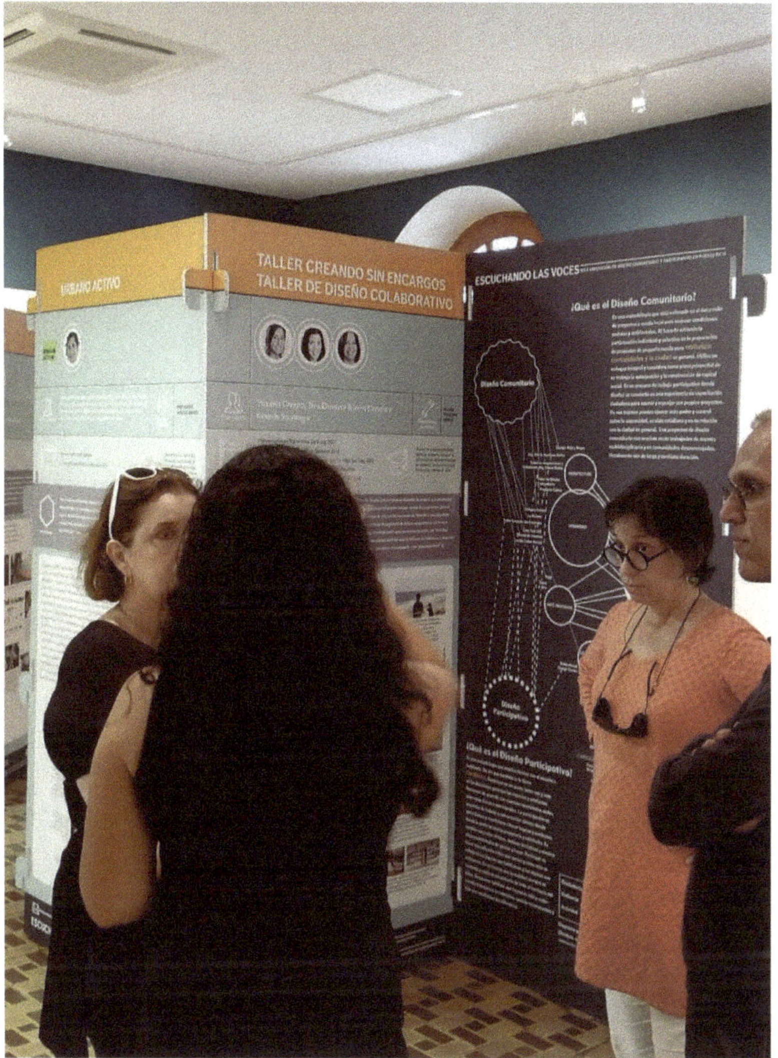

FIGURE 2: Each set of 14, interlocking display panels that comprised the traveling exhibition was designed to make it relatively easy for visitors to *"Listening to Their Voices"* to discern essential information-cum-knowledge about each of the featured Community or Participatory Design projects.

used participatory and/or community-based methods to guide the development of the project they chose to document (see Figure 2). The exhibition was also supported by a published catalogue containing four essays that related to collaboration, and a small "toolkit." This toolkit consisted of 14 illustrated *tactics cards* (referred to henceforth in this piece as *tools*) that contained short descriptions of and guidelines as to how operate Community and Participatory Design tactics as recommended by each of the exhibition participants. The combined intent of the exhibition, the catalogue and the toolkit was to educate Puerto Rican design colleagues and members of diverse communities around the island about the benefits of engaging in and facilitating co-creation by

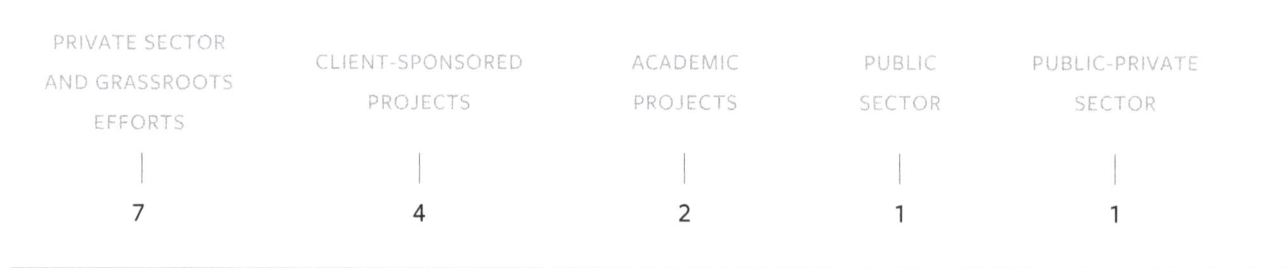

PRIVATE SECTOR AND GRASSROOTS EFFORTS	CLIENT-SPONSORED PROJECTS	ACADEMIC PROJECTS	PUBLIC SECTOR	PUBLIC-PRIVATE SECTOR
7	4	2	1	1

TABLE 1: Group categorizations for *"Listening to their Voices."*

recounting its history and by providing cases studies of successful co-creative projects. *"Listening to Their Voices"* was also supported by lectures, group discussions, a website and a Facebook page.[d]

[d] *Refer to the Project Website and Facebook: escuchandolasvocesblog.wordpress.com, @escuchandolasvoces*

At the time of this writing in the early spring of 2018, *"Listening to Their Voices"* had traveled within Puerto Rico's capital city of San Juan to a fine arts cinema lobby, a school of architecture, the office of a nonprofit foundation, a state-operated art gallery, and a venue supported by a local board of architecture. After the originally planned tour of this exhibition had to be cancelled due to the extensive damage wrought all over the island by Hurricane María, it has continued to travel to design schools and other cultural venues in Puerto Rico outside of San Juan.

Among the 15 individuals and groups that submitted documentation of their work to be included in the exhibition were architects, visual artists, urban planners, socially entrepreneurial sociologists, a choreographer, and a visual-communications designer. The organizers also exhibited collaborative projects that they had personally been involved with. The project submissions that constituted *"Listening to Their Voices"* can be categorized into five groups (table 1).

Several findings and questions arose as the design and implementation of this exhibition progressed. The first two questions were factual/quantitative:

1. What participatory methods, tools, and strategies have been used in design projects in Puerto Rico since the 1960s?
2. Have the Community-based and/or Participatory processes been effective as means to address at least some of the social, cultural, economic or public policy issues that the communities featured in the 15 documented projects wanted to address?

The final two are formative, aimed at gaining insight:

1. Are other creative practitioners (i.e., designers, architects, urban planners) learning from these collaboratively designed, urban planning or artistically rooted community projects, and, if so, how are they developing the communications skills necessary to facilitate effective collaboration with users and user groups?
2. To what extent can these processes be replicated with other projects guided by different sets of parameters?

Much has been written about the ethical obligation to give users a voice in decisions that affect the conceptualization and design of their spaces, and, as an outgrowth of this, how these decisions affect their social interactions and their socio-cultural perceptions of themselves and others.[4] The low rate of citizen participation in local government and community projects in Puerto Rico may stem from a lack of knowledge about (rather than lack of interest in) civic participation in the socio-economic and socio-cultural affairs of a city or town, or of matters of governance, etc. Looking at this from another perspective, designers might consider the possibility that their roles have changed. Therefore, many of them chose to evolve their decision-making processes to take on more active roles in helping various population groups achieve their collective goals. In this way, many designers have moved toward acting as social and cultural change producers and/or facilitators. Because of this evolving and expanding new platform for designers, the facilitators of this planned exhibition sought to challenge participants to not only explore and experiment with the positive impact that collaborative design methods could have within and around a specific community, but also to affect social, cultural and even public policy change with their work.

To give readers a better understanding of the diversity of projects represented in the exhibition, the authors have chosen to showcase the examples seen in table 2.

A Brief, Localized Historical Context

A few years after the creation of architect-based group TEAM 10 (1956)[e] and the participatory design trend taking shape in the Scandinavian countries, in Puerto Rico the *Equipo de Mejoramiento Ambiental* (EMA, *or the "Environmental Improvement Team"*) managed the first community-design project in Puerto

[4] Arnstein, S. R. "A Ladder of Citizen Participation." JAIP, 35.4 (1969): pgs. 216–224; De Carlo, G. "Architecture's Public." In Architecture and Participation, edited by P. B. Jones, D. Petrescu & J. Till, London, UK: Taylor & Francis, 2005 (originally published as "Il pubblico dell'architettura," Parametro, No. 5, 1971); Sanoff, H. Programación y participación en el diseño arquitectónico/Programming and Participation in Architectural Design (bilingual edition). Arquitectonics: Mind, Land & Society series. Barcelona, ES: Ediciones Universidad Politécnica de Catalunya, 2006; Marvel, L. Listen to What They Say: Planning and Community Development in Puerto Rico. Rio Piedras, PR, USA: UPR Press, 2008; Till, J. "The Negotiation of Hope." In Architecture and Participation, edited by P. B. Jones, D. Petrescu & J. Till, London, UK: Taylor & Francis, 2005; Dean, R. "Policy Briefing: There is more than one way to involve the public in policy decisions." Discover Society, 33 (2016).

[e] *The architects who eventually formed Team 10 had been attending meetings of the Congrès Internationaux d'Architecture Moderne (C.I.A.M.) for several years when they began to come together as a group that shared ideas about how modern cities should be planned and designed at the 9th congress in 1953. This small group of (mostly) younger architects made their group "official" (at the 10th C.I.A.M. Congress in 1956). They sought to build a "working-together-technique" (referring to working with the people living in urban environs who would eventually be affected by the decisions of architects) to address many of the issues they felt would affect these populations as cities were modernized. They were primarily concerned with designing and reforming cities so that they would become more effectively organized and efficiently functional and livable for their inhabitants.*

Participant	*Design Realm*	*Project*	*Process*
Rubberband Design Studio	Visual Communication and Industrial Design	Nanoscience Games designed to be facilitated at the Arecibo Observatory in Puerto Rico	A group of 8th-grade students participated, and learned to be proactive in their acquisition of new knowledge; this allowed them to gain a real feeling of ownership of games that they helped design.
Taller de Planificación Social (Social Planning Workshop)	Urban Planning	A Comprehensive Improvement Plan for the community El Gandul in Santurce, Puerto Rico	This endeavor involved establishing community development priorities with input from residents, businesspeople, and social-service providers.
Energía Roja y Negra (Red and Black Energy)	Urban Mobility	Events that invite broad participation of local citizenry in collaboration with the city government of Ponce, Puerto Rico	This project involved educating individuals about urban planning, architecture, and civil rights. This was achieved by allowing locals to help organize cycling trips.

TABLE 2: Examples of of the diversity of projects represented in the exhibition.

Rico (ca. 1964) in the rural barrio of El Cerro, deep in the mountainous region of Puerto Rico in the municipality of Naranjito (reference the map on p. 127).

In Puerto Rico in the 1960s, almost parallel to the creation of academic community-based programs in the United States (which was initiated in part as a reaction to the lack of housing in poor neighborhoods), Edwin Quiles became the first architect to employ Community Design and Participatory Design, incorporating them into the design project for the Tokyo neighborhood on the Martin Peña Channel (in Puerto Rico's capital city of San Juan). This occurred when he worked with the *Volunteers in Service to Puerto Rico* (VESPRA: *Voluntarios en Servicio a Puerto Rico*), a YMCA program—a kind of local Peace Corps—that trained community leaders and university students in community development and assigned them to communities in Puerto Rico and the eastern United States.

At about his same time, *The On-Site Rehabilitation Program of the Puerto Rican Urban Renewal and Housing Corporation* (*Corporación de Renovación Urbana y Vivienda, or* CRUV), later the *Housing Department,* was inaugurated in 1960 with a principle goal of rehabilitating informal settlements across the island where and when possible, rather than subject them to the U.S. federal

1956
TEAM 10 is formed at the 10th Congress of Modern Architecture. The architects who were part of the group were in charge of studying the relationship between people and the spaces they inhabit. The Italian architect Giancarlo De Carlo was one of these architects.

1960s-1970s
Participatory Design originated in the Scandinavian countries and Germany. Workers and their unions were concerned that the introduction of technology design reduced their control over their work situation, planning, and production management. The designers then began to co-create with workers.

1960s
In Puerto Rico, the EMA (Environmental Improvement Team), under the Planning Board, carried out the first project of community design for El Cerro, Naranjito.

1967
In Puerto Rico, architect Edwin Quiles initiated the first project using both community and participatory design in the Tokyo neighborhood on Martín Peña Channel when he worked with VESPRA (Volunteers in Service to Puerto Rico).

1968
In the United States the community design approach started as way to tackle the need for low-income family housing. In 1968 several community design workshops were established in architecture schools, like MIT and Columbia, as a reaction to social inequality and racism.

1969
Italian architect Giancarlo De Carlo established a participatory process of meetings, interviews, and exhibitions for designing Villagio Matteotti houses in Terni, Italy.

1970
Hungarian architect Yona Friedman created a 'machine for inventing apartments' for the Universal Exhibition in Osaka. With this machine, users could choose their housing options. In the middle of this decade Belgian architect Lucien Kroll created software with a database to perform the same function.

1977
Participatory Action Research (PAR) was promoted worldwide by the Colombian sociologist Orlando Fal Borda, when the first PAR world congress was organized, also called Popular Education. Fal Borda postulates that the legacy of the Spanish Conquest in the Americas was the same thing that PAR aimed at: reconnecting with the colonized and their own experiences.

1978
In Puerto Rico, urban planner Lucilla Fuller Marvel, with a team of architects and engineers, directed a community and participatory design project in La Perla. In 2008, it is one of the case studies in her book *Listen to What They Say: Planning and Community Development in Puerto Rico.*

1980s
The term "User-Centered Design" originated in the research laboratories of the University of California, San Diego. The laboratory was then led by psychologist Donald Norman, who popularized the concept in his book *The Psychology Of Everyday Things* (Norman, 1988). It is a process framework (not restricted to interfaces or technologies) in which the needs, wants and limitations of users regarding a product, service or process is given great attention at every stage of the design process.

1985
Lucilla Fuller Marvel engages in participatory planning relocation of new homes for survivors of the landslide in Mameyes, Ponce, Puerto Rico.

1992
First Comprehensive Development Plan for the Cantera Peninsula is implemented to become a pioneering large-scale participatory project.

1997
Following the model of architectural schools of the United States, the first Community Design Workshop is founded at the University of Puerto Rico, Río Piedras Campus.

2001
In Puerto Rico, the *Projecto Enlace Martín Peña* is established. At first it was just a project to dredge the Martín Peña Channel, but then it was realized that it was necessary to work with the community in the whole process of urban design and rehousing.

2002
Artist Chemi Rosado Seijo is selected for the Whitney Museum of American Art Biennial. One of his works was *El Cerro*, where, with the collaboration of the community, 100 houses were painted in shades of green similar to the vegetation of the hillside (el cerro) they were built on.

2005
In Puerto Rico, guidelines for *Sustainable Development of Vieques* are drawn up by the entity Technical and Professional Support for the Development of Vieques, an effort coordinated by Dr. Liliana Cotto Morales, who was responsible for citizen participation, and Edwin Quiles, who was responsible for the participatory design.

Beginning of economic crisis in Puerto Rico **2006**

Beginning of global economic crisis **2008**
Rubberband Design Studio was founded, the first design studio in Puerto Rico to employ design strategies based on resilience and user-centered design.

2009
In Puerto Rico, Beta Local is founded, based on the model of Austrian educator Ivan Illich.

2011
At Beta Local, Dr. María de Mater O'Neill offers a workshop in the Systematization of Experience and incorporates a Participatory Design module. This is the first time that this methodology is recorded as having been used to create a product. Casa Taft 169 founder Marina Moscoso was one of the participants in this workshop. Rubberband, the design studio that O'Neill manages, became finalist in the Iberoamericana Design Biennial, Madrid, Spain (2014) for a research project and participatory design with cancer patients, also done at Beta Local.

2012
Dr. Omayra Rivera Crespo integrates participatory design strategies into her teaching practice. It is the first time that this methodology is recorded in the local teaching of architecture.

2013
Participatory Budget is implemented in the city of San Juan, Puerto Rico, where citizens can propose and decide on the fate of municipal resources.

2015
Casa Taft 169 manages to introduce a bill in the House of Representatives of Puerto Rico that would provide the legal framework for municipalities to establish partnerships with communities to take over abandoned lots. The following year, the bill becomes law.

FIGURE 3: Brief milestones in Community Design and Participatory Design in Puerto Rico and other parts of the world, depicting an emphasis on local practices (O'Neill, 2016).

"urban renewal" (or slum elimination) program. According to urban planner Lucilla Marvel, the emphasis was on urban planning, rather than design, and involved some community participation. [5]

When exhibition co-organizer and co-author O'Neill created the timeline diagram of milestones in community and participatory design (Figure 3), she pointed out that both in the 1960s and from early 2006 on, occurrences of Community Design and Participatory Design across Puerto Rico increased in comparison to the respective previous periods in Puerto Rican history. One of the causes for this intensification might be the extremely rapid socioeconomic transformation that occurred in many parts of the island that was characteristic of the 1960s and the 2000s. At the end of the sixties, the socioeconomic development model used in Puerto Rico began to show signs of exhaustion. [6] In 2006, the current economic crisis began in Puerto Rico, two years *before* the global economic crisis began, and the authors have seen an increase in the instantiation of new community-based grassroots organizations approaching social, cultural and economic matters using these methodologies during this span of time. Locally, in the 1960s and 1970s, participatory initiatives guided by an architecture and urban-planning focus increased across the island, though they declined in the 1980s and 1990s due to a lack of applicable resources. In the arts and in design practices, both of these methodologies reemerged and were applied a decade or more later. For example, in 2002 the artist Chemi Rosado Seijo (assisted by his mother Luisa Seijo Maldonado, a social worker who employed Participatory Action Research) applied this approach to an art intervention in the neighborhood of El Cerro in Naranjito, and in 2008, *Rubberband Design Studio,* where O'Neill is the creative director, began to apply it to product design (where aspects of it informed the creation of their toolkit of resilient thinking for designers). For more examples of how Community Design and Participatory Design were employed to affect social, cultural, economic or public policy change in Puerto Rico, refer to Figure 3.

Three Examples of Public Policy Changes that Occurred in Puerto Rico as a Result of Efforts Rooted in Participatory and Community Design

Participatory and Community design operationalized in the local context in Puerto Rico can be an innovative force. Three urban-focused projects that were documented in the exhibition were undertaken as a means to affect public policy changes:

5 Marvel, L. E-mail to M. M. O'Neill & O. Rivera Crespo, August 21, 2016. Re: adjunto paper de co-creation.

6 Feliciano Ramos, H. "Transformación de una sociedad dependiente: 1940–1994." In Colombia y América Latina después del fin de la historia, Volumen 1, ed. J. Guerrero Barón. Tunja, Boyacá, p. 180. Colombia: Editorial de la Universidad Pedagógica y Tecnológica de Colombia (UPTC), 1997.

1. *The Cantera Península Project* (in San Juan) was initiated in 1990 to ensure the social, economic and cultural development of the Cantera Peninsula community of 10,000 residents who were living in marginal conditions at that time. The community non-profit organization the *Neighborhood Council for the Development of Cantera* was established in 1989 and worked with the *Cantera Peninsula Comprehensive Development Company,* a quasi-public corporation established by Law 20 of July 10, 1992,[f] and a community-based nonprofit, *Apoyo Empresarial para el Desarrollo de la Península,* incorporated in 1992, to draw up a *Plan de Desarrollo Integral de la Península de Cantera* (*Comprehensive Cantera Peninsula Development Plan*). The project was a joint effort that eventually involved four organizational partners. The boards of the public corporation and the nonprofit were comprised of representatives from the community, the government of Puerto Rico and the Municipality of San Juan, and representatives of the private, small business sector. The revitalization of the area (which is currently under way) is based on the *Plan de Desarrollo Integral de la Península de Cantera* (*Comprehensive Cantera Peninsula Development Plan*). The revitalization of the area (currently under way) under the administration of the corporation, implements programs that help guide the development of the infrastructure necessary to support the sustenance of this area's population, together with the on-site, new, low-cost-housing complexes in which many of the residents of the Cantera Peninsula live. This has allowed hundreds of people who formerly lived along the waterways of the peninsula to remain in the vicinity rather than be forced into involuntary displacement.
2. *El Proyecto* ENLACE *del Caño Martín Peña* (*Martín Peña Channel*) and its *Comprehensive Development and Land Use Plan* is also a multi-partner project, involving the *Corporation of the* ENLACE *Project of the Martin Peña Channel, the Community Land Trust* (as established by Law 489 of September 24, 2004[g]), and the organization G-8. G-8 is a non-profit entity that represents the inhabitants of the eight communities that together are comprised of approximately 25,000 people living adjacent to this historically polluted and often debris strewn channel which runs through the center of Puerto Rico's capital city of San Juan. The majority of these people

[f] *The "Law to Create the Cantera Peninsula Comprehensive Development Company."*

[g] *The "Law to create the Caño Martin Peña Comprehensive Development Company."*

want to remain in their neighborhoods and have fought to bring about the dredging of the channel and to delineate a relocation plan that would allow them to move within the same geographic area. They continue to look for funds to support this initiative and to show evidence of how the unhealthy physical state of the Caño Martin Pena causes floods that negatively affect the quality of life and the health of those who live near it. The government initiated the project in 2002, beginning with preparation of a comprehensive plan; the law was enacted two years later and the resulting *Community Land Trust* (*Fideicomiso del Caño Martín Peña*) won the *United Nations Habitat World Award* in 2016. The laws setting up both the *Cantera Peninsula Project* and the ENLACE *Project* require that residents of these communities have seats on the public corporations' boards. Both projects were designed and have been operationalized to facilitate intensive community participation. *The Community Land Trust* protects lots from the negative effects of real estate speculation by ensuring that the land that constitutes the trust belongs to the eight communities that together constitute the G-8, while the houses and other dwellings that occupy the land belong to families or individuals.[h] For a given lot to be sold, the entire community must agree to the parameters specified in the sale agreement.

[h] *The strategically desirable location of this area in the context of the real estate market in and around San Juan makes the action of buying houses and the land they occupy and then selling the two as a combined property much more of an expensive endeavor for would-be speculators seeking to artificially inflate prices in this market.*

3. Puerto Rican House Bill 2583, known colloquially as *Todos somos herederos* (*We are All Heirs*), pushed by *Casa Taft 169* (depicted in Figure 4), is the newest achievement in the realm of a public policy initiatives that have occurred as the result of a participatory or community design undertaking. This bill would allow ownership of properties across the island that have been abandoned or are without heirs to be transferred to the city they exist within, so these can in turn be transferred to community and grassroots organizations who can repurpose them in ways that benefit local populations. The bill became law (Law No. 157) on August 9, 2016. This has the potential to be of great benefit in many areas of Puerto Rico since the number of abandoned properties has risen dramatically due to the ongoing financial crisis that has beset the island, and that has recently been exacerbated by people leaving

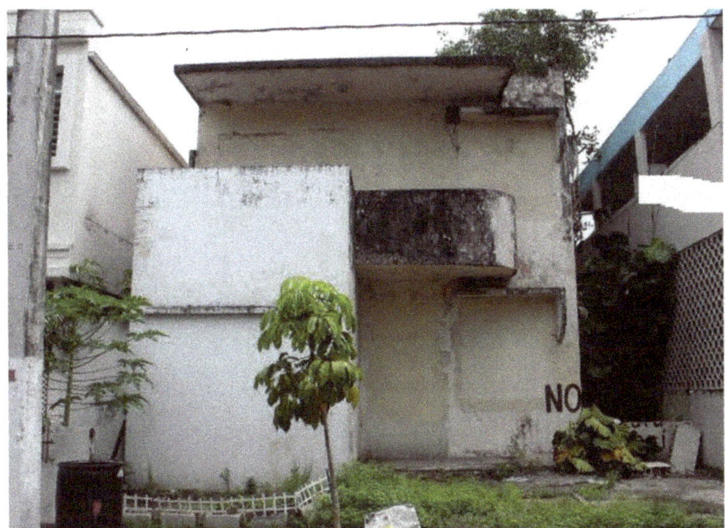

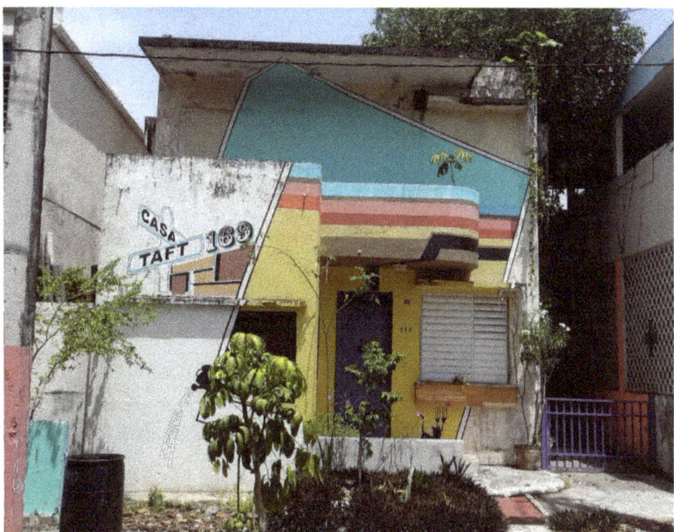

FIGURE 4: The structure Casa Taft 169 before and after its renovation (completed in 2015-16). This photo shows the façade of Casa Taft 169 before the main door to the property, which had been boarded up, was reopened. After decades of complaints by neighbors, the process of declaring the property a public nuisance was begun in 2004, and the structure was totally sealed. (Photo provided by Casa Taft 169.)

the country—and, in so doing, abandoning their properties—due to the lingering effects of Hurricane María.

If Puerto Rican communities can continue to address more of the primary economic and public policy issues that affect the daily lives of their populations in a participatory manner, and the government supports these initiatives, the authors hope that more Community Design and Participatory Design projects will be formulated and operationalized in ways that will yield long-term, positive results, despite the long hard road of economic crisis and Hurricane María recovery efforts that lies ahead.

Assessing the response to engaging in participatory design processes in the local landscape

The *"Listening to Their Voices"* exhibition project has allowed its organizers to survey diverse array of participatory design and urban projects in Puerto Rico that have been undertaken since the beginning of the financial crisis (late 2005/early 2006). O'Neill proposed to identify common design methods and patterns that were utilized or employed as the projects depicted in the exhibition evolved. To obtain data that would shed light on this, a questionnaire was completed by all of the exhibition participants, and semi-structured interviews were conducted between them and O'Neill. The other organizers of *"Listening to Their Voices"* also completed the questionnaires. The data sets that resulted from operating these data gathering activities guided the visual communication strategies that affected the design of both the informational displays and the toolkit cards (the latter evolved to function as a kind of "pocket-pack" of information). O'Neill also mapped each of the respective projects' emphases, methodologies, and locations (Figure 5), while another mapping diagram was completed to depict the types of *tactics* (tools) the various participants preferred to use (Figure 6).

A summative recounting of the findings derived from the questionnaire and semi structured interviews is articulated below.

1. Most of the projects presented were urban-focused, community-design based, and located mostly in Puerto Rico's capital city of San Juan.
2. Public participation tended to occur during the initial stages of design processes (i.e., during exploration of community desires for a given design outcome), although for some projects it was later, when organizers presented prototypes for community consideration. Very few of the projects were iterative, so it is not surprising that participatory design was used less.
3. All participants in *"Listening to Their Voices"* perceived the users they worked with during the evolution of their respective projects as *people,* rather than as subjects of a research study, or clients in a given design project.
4. One participant had an expert mindset (Taller [Workshop] Arq. Elio Martínez Joffre): "he [the architect] brings the expertise…," wrote one respondent to the questionnaire; the remainder of respondents did not consider themselves to be the only expert among the pool of participants. The Architecture Office of Martínez Joffre has completed over twenty years-worth of Community Design projects in Puerto Rico.
5. All participants developed their projects using the User-Centered Design framework, although they may not have been aware of it as they were using it or defined their projects as such. User-Centered Design approaches operationalize "a design process that focuses on [meeting] user needs and requirements."[7]

7 Anon. "What is User Centered Design?," Interaction Design Foundation, 11 October 2013. Online. Available at: https://www.interaction-design.org/literature/topics/user-centered-design/ (Accessed 18 March 2018).

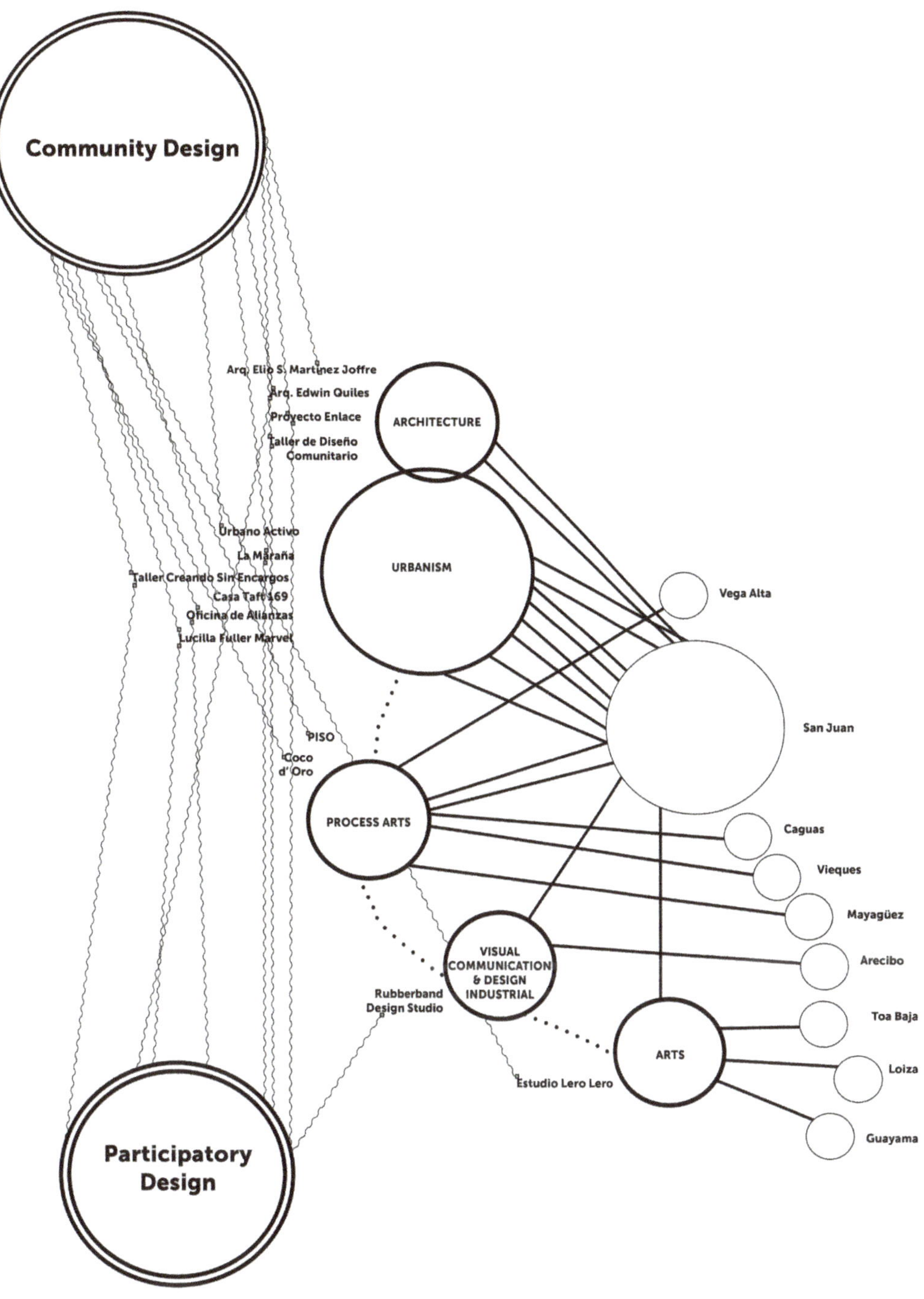

FIGURE 5: A mapping diagram depicting the focus and methodologies of the *"Listening to Their Voices"* projects, based on data gathered from all of the participants in the exhibition. The size of each circle indicates the frequency of occurrence of particular themes, approaches and methods. (O'Neill, 2016)

6. The client-sponsored project by *Rubberband Design Studio* was the only one that operated a contextual inquiry and used cultural probes as part of its methodology.
7. Six participants incorporated design-led research [i] principles: (Taller de Arquitectura y Urbanismo [Architecture and Urbanism

[i] *In design-led research, new knowledge is constructed by engaging in the design process as interactions with a given community or group of users (or an individual) evolve.*

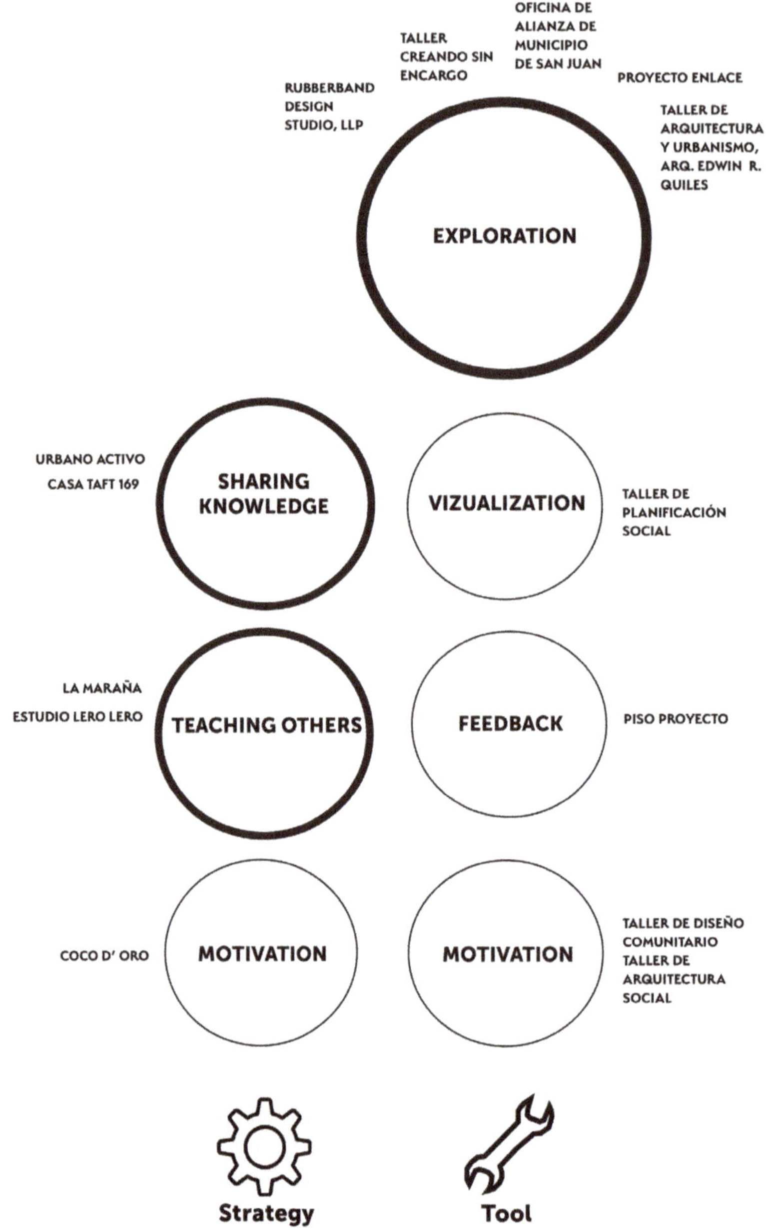

FIGURE 6: This map depicts the types of tools and strategic approaches utilized by the 14 participants in the *"Listening to Their Voices"* exhibition. It is important to note that the categorical depictions of "strategies" and "tools" that appears here guided the eventual creation of the "toolkit" that was comprised of a set of 14 playing card-sized cards that were used to help exhibition participants articulate how they had engaged in the Community or Participatory Design methods that guided the development of their particular projects.

Studio] de Edwin Quiles, Taller de Planificación Social [Social Planning Studio], Proyecto ENLACE [The Link Project], Taller Creando Sin Encargos [Creating Without Commissions Studio], La Maraña [The Tangle], and Oficina de Alianzas [Municipality of San Juan's Alliances] with its Participatory Budgeting Program.

8. Two of the projects profiled in the exhibition were design-led research projects that had been operated by the same participant (*Rubberband Design Studio*).
9. Only five of the participants produced written research reports (the two public sector participants and three of the client-sponsored participants: *Taller de Planificación Social, Rubberband Design Studio, and Taller [Studio] Arq. Edwin Quiles*). Two grassroots organizations are starting to write about their projects and report their findings: *La Maraña* and *Taller Creando Sin Encargos.*

The results of the projects represented in *"Listening to Their Voices"* affect and impact a diverse array of domains. Seven of the participating groups co-created urban projects and design for use in public spaces. (Examples of these include repairing and otherwise "fixing up" recreational facilities, renovating abandoned houses and converting abandoned lots into community parks.) The architectural projects resulted in the creation of low-income housing. One participant, *Rubberband Design Studio,* strengthened opportunities among cancer patients to plan and operate resiliency strategies by allowing them to engage in storytelling, and co-created nanoscience games for middle-school students and teachers by using design-led research and participatory action research to guide development processes. Four exhibition participants concentrated on developing initiatives that strengthened community cohesion.

The exhibition has made visible the history of community and participatory design in the local context. Design students who were either involved in the development of the projects featured in the exhibition or who have seen it gained an increased understanding of how to use participatory-design methodologies, which are not taught locally in the regular curriculum of their design courses.

The exhibition also fostered a generational exchange among practitioners, though it should be noted that there was some confusion among the general public and some design practitioners about the definitions of Community Design and Participatory Design, and about how they are related to and different from each other. To help exhibition attendees better understand this, a "toolkit" comprised of a set of 14 playing card-sized "tactics cards was designed (it was based on the strategies and tools depicted in Figure 6). It proved to be the most successful outreach application operationalized by the *"Listening to Their Voices"* organizers, and also proved to be quite popular among both community members and design practitioners. More information about this toolkit is provided in the next section of this piece.

The documentation of the various activities facilitated by the 15 exhibition participants yielded evidence of two systemic problems that tended to affect the development of their projects. These are discussed in the final, reflective section of this piece.

An Analysis of the Participatory and Community Design Processes, Methods and Working Patterns That Were Operationalized by the Participants in "Listening to Their Voices" to Guide the Development of their Projects

Using the limited resources she had available as preparations necessary to facilitate *"Listening to Their Voices"* evolved, O'Neill sought to increase her understanding of the methods and working patterns employed by the individuals and groups that had produced exhibition content. In particular, she sought to better understand the Participatory Design processes that guided the development of each the 15 featured projects. As a result of this, each set of educational panels included in the exhibition was designed to visually communicate the Community or Participatory Design methods utilized by the individuals or groups that created the projects depicted on them. To support these depictions, a set of illustrated cards were created and shared with exhibition visitors that were designed to help them better understand the various ways that each of the exhibition participants created their projects. This set of cards was designated as "the toolkit."

Some of the participants that created projects featured in *"Listening to Their Voices"* were not aware that they had utilized a design method, as they did not think about or conceptualize the work they undertook in those terms. Some, in fact, stated that they worked "intuitively." When the organizers of the exhibition asked participants to describe the methodologies they engaged in to guide the evolution of their projects in a questionnaire, they became aware that some of them had difficulty fulfilling this request. In this context, many of them confused their understanding of "methodology"—the system of methods they used to guide their actions—with what they described as the visions, missions, and objectives of their respective projects. A similar problem occurred when many participants were asked to define their preferred *tactic* (i.e., tool; see Figure 6) in the questionnaire, they confused tactics with strategies. This problem prompted O'Neill to include a category of strategies in the toolkit.

In the participants' original submissions for inclusion in *"Listening to Their Voices,"* O'Neill was looking for them to provide three essential pieces of information: a description of their preferred tactic for guiding the development of their project (on the tactics cards, these are referred to as "tools"), how they operationalized it, and who constituted their target audience. As her inquiries were more broadly exploratory, O'Neill did not require that individual participants specify a given tactic when they submitted descriptions of their projects to her. Some of the participants described their strategies, rather than their methodologies, for achieving their project objectives. The authors can only speculate that the manner in which many of the groups operated as they engaged in the processes that informed the development of their projects was not at all rigorously systematic. Additionally, their actions depended on the availability of resources and the operation of organizational structures that were often organic. This tended not to be detrimental to the realization of their respective projects, but it is a concerning factor if others around the world should want to replicate these actions. Without clear documentation of processes and methods, learning could be impaired, and the knowledge that could emerge from facilitating this kind of work could be called into question. (The lack of systemic thinking among Puerto Rican creative practitioners might be a tendency they shared, since it was identified in a previous inquiry that examined the administration of local design schools.[8]) Because of these findings, O'Neill decided that the toolkit would be constituted of two types of cards based on the tools and strategies articulated in Figure 6.

Some of the participants whose projects were documented in *"Listening to Their Voices"* worked with specific communities and community groups but not necessarily *for* them. This was true in the sense that their projects were and are community-based, and that they involved and continue to involve members of their given communities in the development of ideas and in encouraging them to provide critical feedback as these evolved, or as they continue to evolve. Other participants did not design *for* the members of a particular community, but constructed the projects they completed *with* a high level of involvement of the members of that community. Despite these differences, these projects are participatory, even if different forms of participation are manifested within their respective structural dynamics.

As the authors wanted to accurately quantify the level of participation inherent in each project, they utilized Sherry Arnstein's model known as the *"Ladder of Citizen Participation"*[j] to do this (this is depicted in Figure 10). Before

[8] O'Neill, M. M. "Views and Reflections on Design Education: Local Voices from Puerto Rico." Foroalfa (2015). Online. Available at: http://foroalfa.org/articulos/views-and-reflections-on-design-education-local-voices-from-puerto-rico (Accessed August 18, 2017).

[j] *Arnstein, S. R. "A Ladder of Citizen Participation." Journal of the American Planning Association, 35.4, 1969, pgs. 216–224. Sherry Arnstein was an American public policy analyst and consultant who worked for and advised the U.S. Department of Housing, Education and Welfare (HUD) from 1964 until 1985. The ideas that she articulated in this paper were and still are referenced as metaphors that can be used to increase understanding about whether or not citizen involvement or participation in a given community initiative is honestly sought and effectively incorporated into its development. When those in power merely create the illusion of involving citizens and other key stakeholders in decision-making processes, only the "bottom rungs" of the ladder—"Manipulation" and "Therapy" (as depicted in Figure 10)—are utilized.*

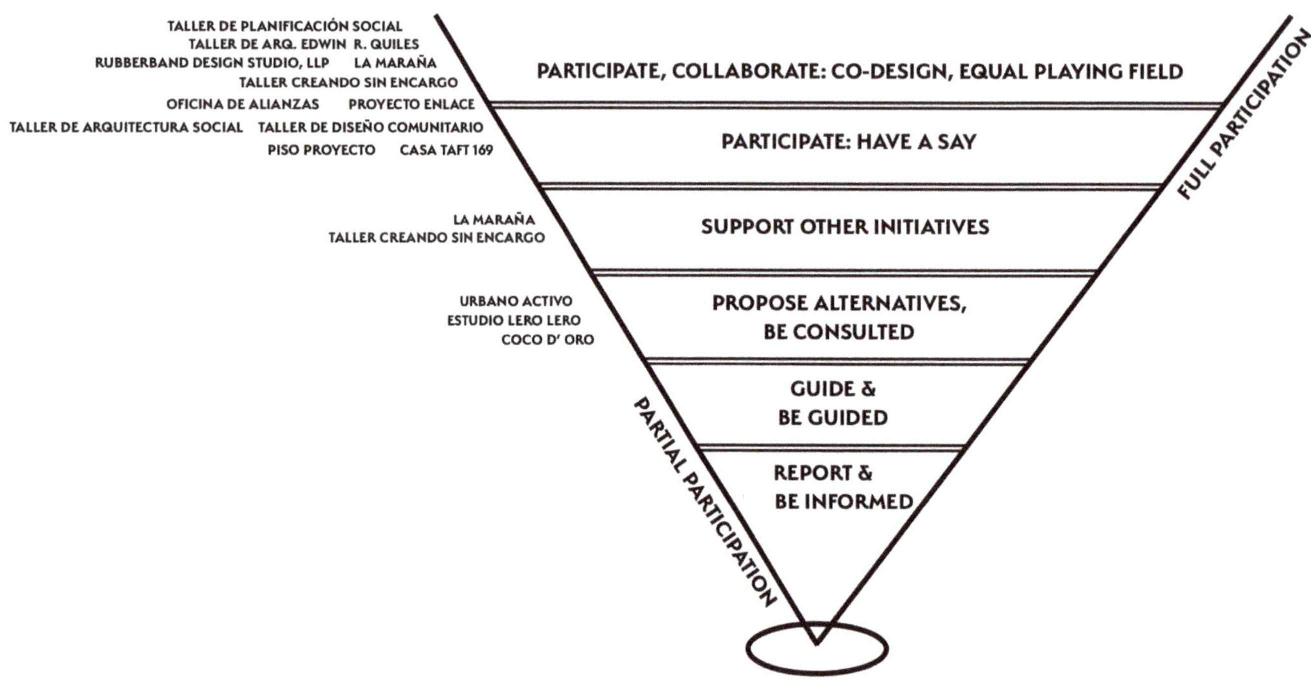

FIGURE 7: *The Six Modes of Participation* (Rivera, O'Neill, 2016). A higher level indicates a more participation on the part of those involved with the development of a given project. The authors could not find a participatory model that applied to all the participants of *"Listening to Their Voices,"* so they created their own.

explaining how this model accounts for how these projects involved different levels of community participation, the authors would like to clarify that, in order to understand local practices in Puerto Rico, O'Neill worked with co-organizer/co-author Rivera to create their own, local, model of participation for the exhibition of the projects that would eventually constitute *"Listening to Their Voices."* Rivera identified six modes of participation among those who submitted projects for inclusion (these are depicted in Figure 7). The authors, like Arnstein, recognized that there are various levels of community participation in the design of each of the projects that were included, but Arnstein's model includes negative categories, like "Manipulation" and "Tokenism," that were not reflected in the work submitted by exhibition participants. The authors created several different mo-dels with which to compare the participation levels in the projects that were included in the exhibition, including the one they created (*"The Six Modes of Participation"*).

For example, designers from the San Juan-based communication design studio *Estudio Lero Lero* (*Lero Lero Studio*) presented an idea that they had conceived prior to the initiation of *"Listening to Their Voices"* to facilitate mural-making by in the Venus Gardens middle school (in San Juan; partially

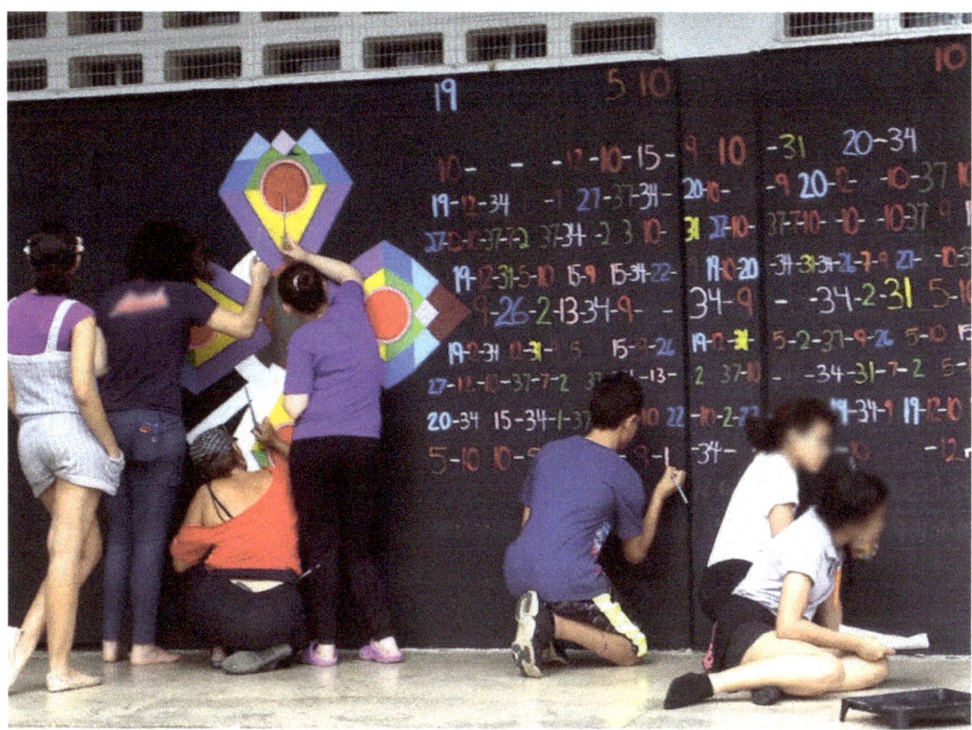

FIGURE 8: Mural "Homage to Puerto Rican Scientist and Educator Ana Roque de Duprey." The mural is part of the *Program of Young STEM Ambassadors* in alliance with Science Puerto Rico and Yale University. It was completed at the Venus Gardens middle school in 2015 and was the first of *Estudio Lero Lero's* murals to receive creative contributions from individuals who possessed different disciplinary backgrounds. Students and teachers who contributed content to this mural had backgrounds in history, science, Spanish, mathematics, and art, and the project was included as part of the school's curriculum. It was designed as an educational tool. (Photo: *Estudio Lero Lero*)

depicted in Figure 8), and out of this idea created and facilitated a workshop during which students and faculty proposed their pictorial ideas (please reference Figure 7, specifically "Level 3: Propose Alternatives: Be Consulted"). According to Daniel Vélez-Climent, the lead designer at *Estudio Lero Lero,* this workshop allowed those middle school students and teachers whose ideas were incorporated into the mural to feel that aspects of themselves were embodied within it; being involved in the development of this project provided them with a great sense of belonging and of empowerment.

El Taller de Diseño Comunitario (*The Community Design Studio; operated by the University of Puerto Rico's School of Architecture as a means for students there to learn to integrate design theory and practice into various communities across the island*) approached the planning and operation of their community-based design initiative differently (Figure 9). They entered into an agreement with members of the Toa Baja community and jointly made a commitment to

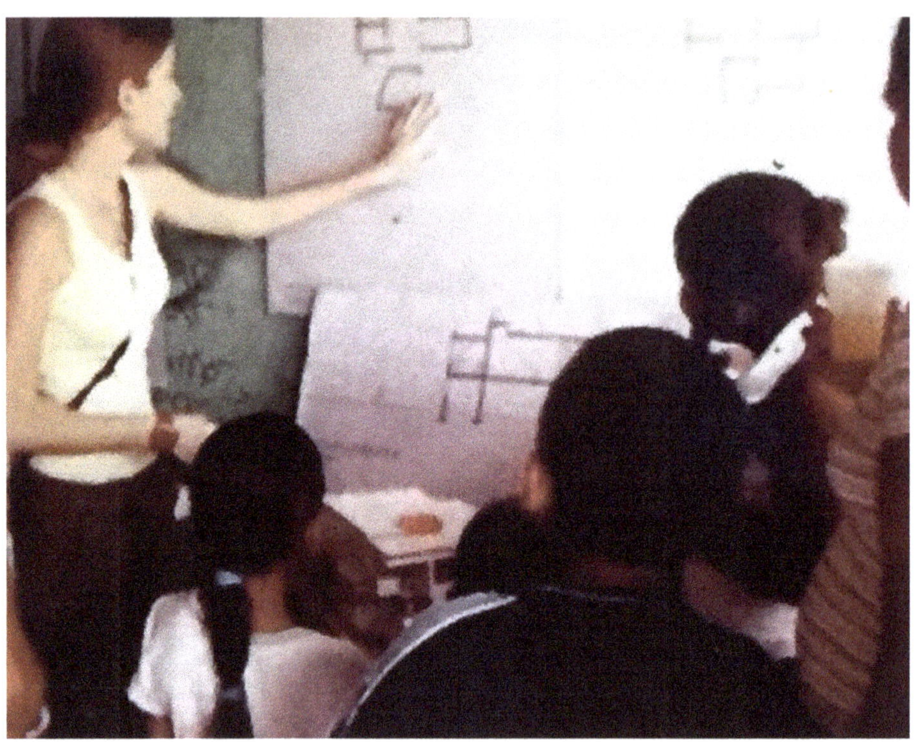

FIGURE 9: A presentation of the design proposals to the girls and boys of *Casa Nueva Esperanza* (*New Hope House*) in the municipio (municipality) of Toa Baja on Puerto Rico's northern coast (2003). This was a way for them to take part in and have a closer understanding of what was being designed for them. (Photo provided by *Taller de Diseño Comunitario*)

improving day-to-day living there, and then established guidelines that facilitated the evolution of an inclusive, participatory design process (please reference Figure 7, specifically "Level 5: Participate: Have a Say"). Although *Taller de Diseño Comunitario* did not establish a collaborative-design methodology, their consultation with residents as the project evolved helped give the people who were involved in it a sense of belonging to a community improvement initiative in which they were essential stakeholders.

In the terms described in the Arnstein model, both *Estudio Lero Lero* and *Taller de Diseño Comunitario*, engaged in levels of community participation that occupy the middle portions of the ladder: "Consultation" and "Partnership" (Figure 10). If the design processes that were operationalized to guide the development of these projects entailed only community *consultation*, this implies that the *participation* of the citizen stakeholders involved in these projects would not have achieved a level of involvement that satisfies the criteria to attain any of the ladder rung positions in the "Citizen Power" portion of the ladder. This is because consultation should almost always be combined with other forms of participation, including but not limited to *co-creation*, *co-decision*

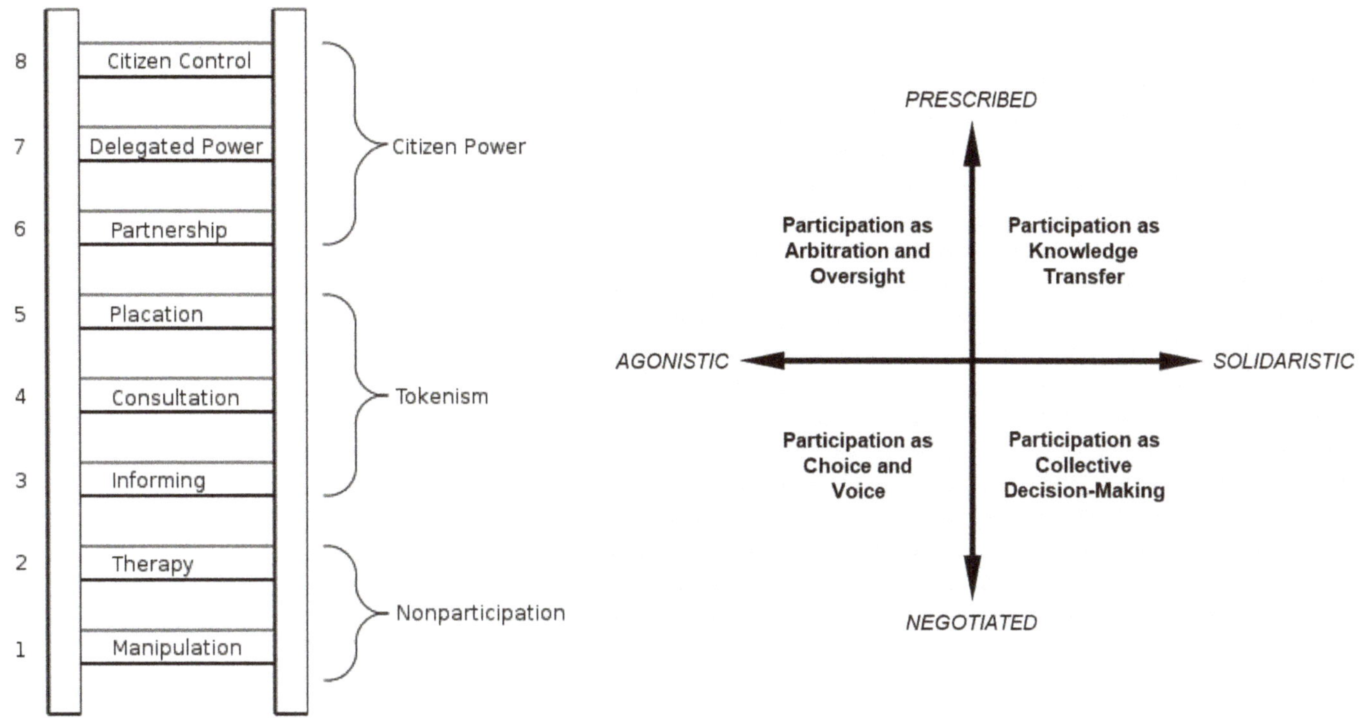

FIGURE 10: (Left) *The Ladder of Citizen Participation* was designed in 1969 by then special assistant to the U.S. Department of Housing, Education and Welfare ("HUD") Sherry Arnstein. She used it to support a set of ideas she promoted in a white paper of the same name that was published the same year in the *Journal of the American Association.* Among other key points that she articulated in this paper, Arnstein argued that some participation initiatives that appeared to involve the participation of citizens from a given community were merely rhetorical (these were described as the bottom rungs of the ladder in the sub-category titled "Nonparticipation").

FIGURE 11: (Right) Four Modes of Participation in Policy Decisions.

and *co-building* (which metaphorically align with the "Citizen Power" portion of the ladder). Using the authors' model of the Six Modes of Participation (Figure 7), *Taller de Diseño Comunitario* facilitated a higher level of user participation as their projects evolved than did *Estudio Lero Lero.* In other cases, participants such as *Rubberband, La Maraña, Taller Creando Sin Encargos, Taller de Arquitectura y Urbanismo de Edwin Quiles,* and *Taller de Planificación Social* employed participation models as a group, in line with both the authors' model (Figure 7, specifically Level 6: "Participate, Collaborate: Co-Design, Equal Playing Field") and the "Citizen Power" portion of Arnstein's ladder.

A third model for gauging and analyzing levels of participation among groups of users or citizens involved in public policy decision-making is that of sociologist Rikki Dean (Figure 11).[9] The Municipality of San Juan's Alliances

9 Dean, R. "Policy Briefing: There is more than one way to involve the public in policy decisions." Discover Society, 1 June 2016. Online. Available at: https://discoversociety.org/category/issue-33/ (Accessed 17 August 2017).

Office practices what Dean calls "participation as collective decision-making." The citizen-participation instrument they have adopted, *The Delegates Committee*, discusses and negotiates the decisions involved in developing projects to be carried out with a "Participatory Budget." This term describes a process that allows community members from a given area not only collaborate in the design for their community, but also allows them to gain experience of having to deal with the constraints imposed by a government budget and set budget priorities through a democratic process of voting (Figure 12).

The exhibition project developed and presented by *Proyecto* ENLACE (*the Link Project*) practiced, again citing Dean, "participation as knowledge transfer." This involves creating channels of communication that can be used by residents of the communities surrounding the trash-strewn, mosquito infested Martín Peña Channel in San Juan so that they can help in making decisions and inform or lobby political leaders. These are government-sponsored projects, and consequently Dean's model is more pertinent in the situations that *Proyecto* ENLACE and the Municipality of San Juan's Alliances Office has attempted to affect, but that was not the case with the other *"Listening to Their Voices"* exhibition participants.

Documenting the Strategies and Tools Used by "Listening to Their Voices" Exhibitors to Facilitate Their Projects: Using the Toolkit to Guide a Hands-On Approach

As was described earlier in this piece, the "toolkit" that was developed by the co-organizers and co-authors of this exhibition to help attendees better understand Community and Participatory Design practices contained Tools and Strategies cards based on the categorical information articulated in Figure 6. The *"Listening to Their Voices"* participant *La Maraña* (*The Tangle*) used "participatory construction" as a strategy to guide the development of their project, and the participant *Piso Proyecto* (*Project Floor*) used the physical presence of the bodies of passing people as a way to help them to think about their body as a tool in the context of an urban environment. Exploration was the exhibition participants' preferred tool (see below), and creating motivation was operationalized as both a tool and a strategy. The following list articulates the patterns of use regarding the exhibition participants' preferred tools (8) and strategies (5):

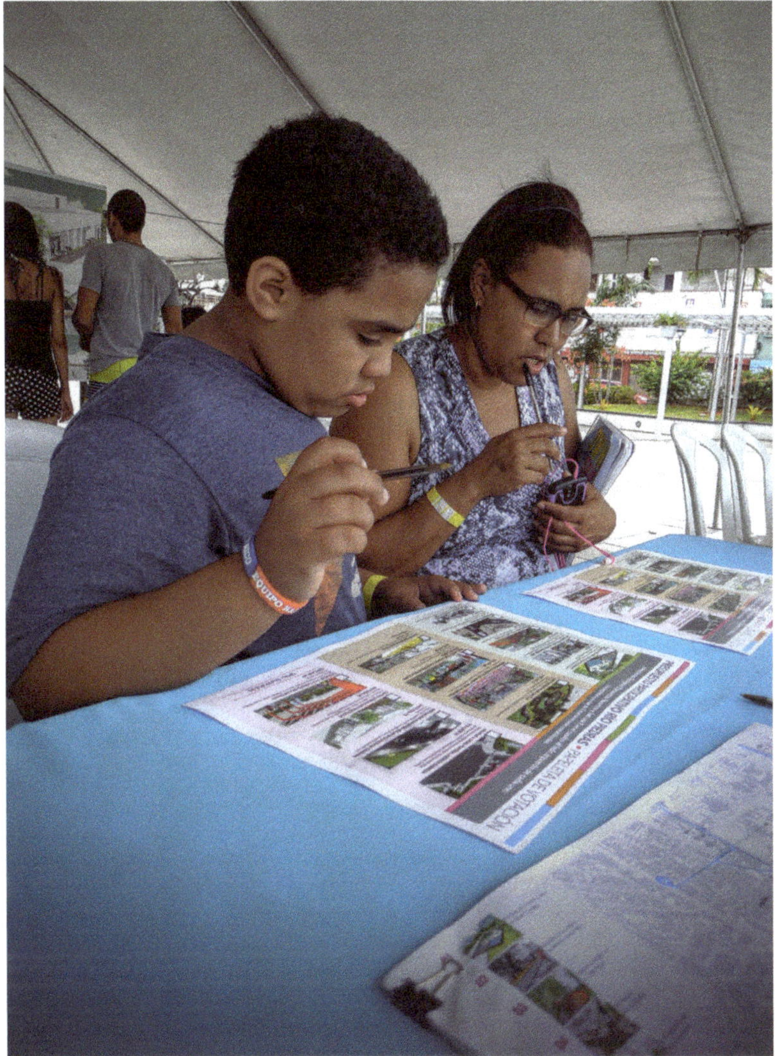

FIGURE 12: Voting process, community-designed projects, *Participatory a Budgeting Program,* Municipality of San Juan's Alliances Office. (Photo provided by Alliance Office)

- Exploration (five tools)—A visual timeline that involves the creation of neighborhood maps, storytelling, making collective photo trips around a specific neighborhood, creating and conversing about portable architectural models, and using input from committees of community representatives.
- Visualization (one tool)—A neighborhood map configured like a jigsaw puzzle on which members of the community could record their requests.
- Feedback (one tool)—Using the body as a physical prop to inform understandings about interactions between people and people and built and natural forms in public urban spaces.

- Motivation (one tool)—A means to reach a collaborative agreement.
- Sharing knowledge (two strategies)—An open-source approach to event-making and sharing a story in local and international forums.
- Teaching others (two strategies)—A workshop themed around construction and the creation of community gardens for public spaces, as well as a workshop that guided the creation of a mural that depicted community issues.
- Motivation (one strategy)—A means to identify a local practice as a collective event (based on oral history).

The tactic of using visual approaches, like jigsaw maps and photography, among others, seemed to be the common pattern among the exhibition's participants. Four of the participants in *"Listening to Their Voices"* used images as part of the toolkits they employed to work with various community members (these *were Taller Creando Sin Encargos* [*Creating Without Commissions Studio*], *Taller de Planificación Social* [*Social Planning Studio*], *Rubberband Design Studio,* and *Taller de Arquitectura y Urbanismo de Edwin Quiles* [*Architecture and Urbanism Studio of Edwin Quiles*]). *Rubberband Design Studio* used illustrated concept cards as a means to help their clients and users tell stories about their experiences living and working in particular situations. *Taller de Planificación Social* used a map constructed out of pieces similar to a jigsaw puzzle. Only one participant, *Proyecto* ENLACE, used an interactive architectural model as its main tool, although the university students involved in *Taller de Diseño Colaborativo* and the architects of the *Oficina de Alianzas* have also used this tool (among others). Using a portable, physical architectural model, potential users can get a better idea of the scale of the project and how each design decision has had an impact on the context within which the project transpired or was placed. *Taller Creando Sin Encargos* and *Taller de Arquitectura y Urbanismo de Edwin Quiles* used photography as an analytical tool, so members of the community could explore new uses for public spaces in their neighborhood (Fig. 11).

These approaches are commonly used in design and architectural practice. Not so common, and therefore more unexpected, was a tactic used by some exhibition *"Listening to Their Voices"* participants: "acting out" as an exploratory approach or to envision future or possible societal interactions (this occurred during the evolution of projects undertaken by the organizations *Piso*

Proyecto [*Floor Project*] and *Urbano Activo* [*Active Urban*]). These approaches may have been intuitively created by their respective project organizers, but each relied on the utilization of immersive practices to exploit knowledge gained from the documentation of both user experiences and the emotional significance regarding human interaction in and around a specific public space. *Piso Proyecto* used a portable wooden dais to facilitate an on-site movement-based performance of the history of specific localities in different places in different cities (for example, forced expropriation in San Juan), and then invited passerby to interact the performers to address community issues. *Urbano Activo* (Figure 14) has facilitated impromptu, open-call community breakfasts in public spaces to involve community members in interactions that help them begin to rethink how the spaces around them and that they inhabit might be used, a strategy that has since been taken up by other organizations.

Final Reflections: Tricky Questions and a New Challenge

In this paper, the authors have identified the participatory methodologies, patterns of use, tactics (tools), and strategies that have been used to guide various types of design and urban projects in Puerto Rico. The primary insights that the authors have gained about these societal-value projects are that many evolved intuitively, and that methodologies were created and are developed further as they emerged from practitioners' tacit knowledge as particular projects evolved. To what extent these processes could be replicated is a tricky question. An important finding of developing and operating *"Listening to Their Voices,"* as a Practice-led Research [k] initiative, reveals a two-pronged challenge. The first is that the majority of the participants in this exhibition do not (and did not) document their work on their respective projects effectively. The second is that very few of them have utilized established internal and external verification procedures to qualify the relative validity of their undertakings, which often involves publishing accounts of their design processes and their outcomes in scholarly venues like *Dialectic*. Addressing both aspects of this challenge becomes inherently complex given the nature of the projects themselves and the lack of resources available to the project organizers and facilitators to undertake these processes effectively.

[k] *Practice-led-research aims to create new knowledge about practice; in this case, the practice of design.*

The importance of documenting and publishing (preferably in rigorously vetted, internationally distributed venues) was and is not widely recognized among the exhibition participants. Projects that have historical precedents, like that developed and operated by the *Taller de Diseño*

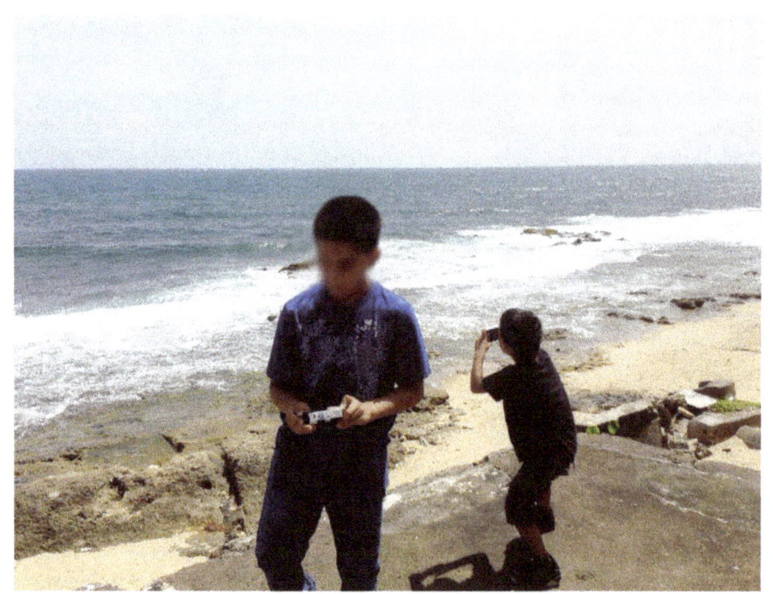

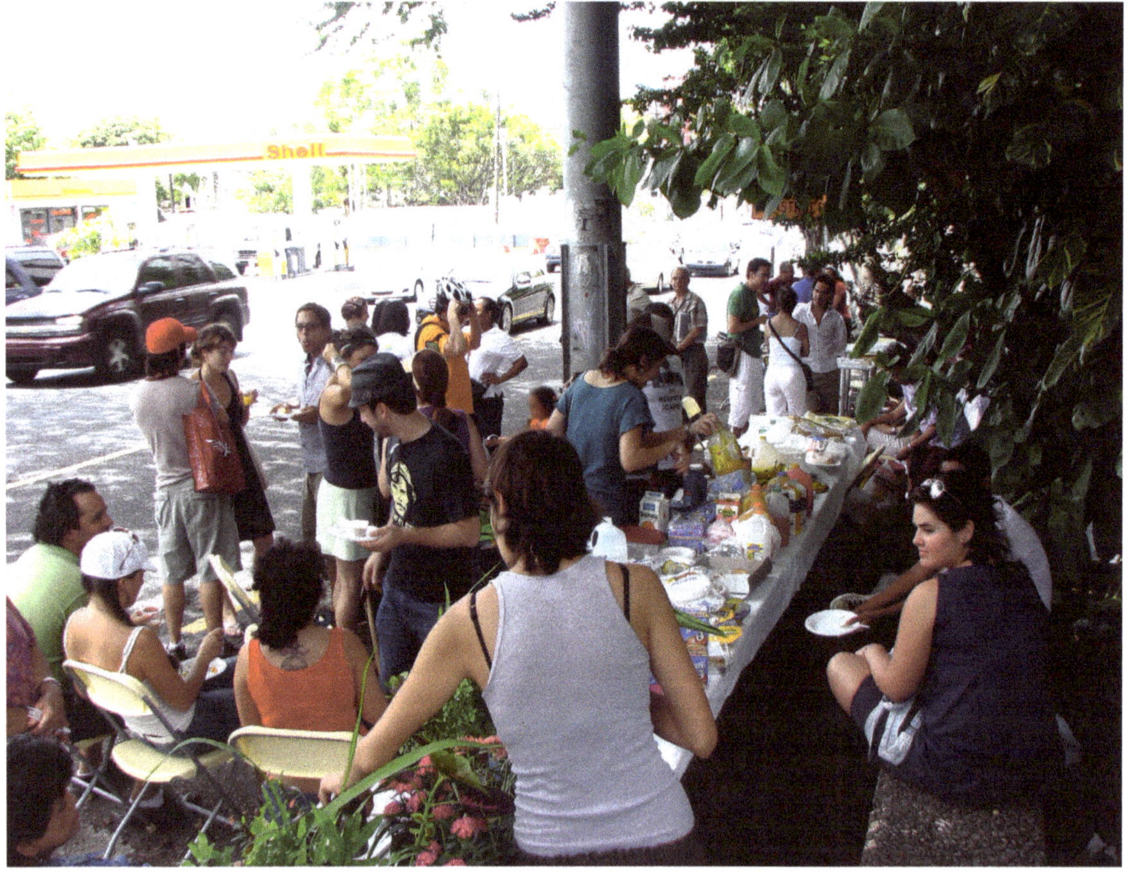

FIGURE 13: (Top) A depiction of a "scavenger hunt" for photos of places in the neighborhood La Perla, in Old San Juan (2003). Single-use cameras were distributed to children in the community with a list of suggestions of places to take pictures of: "your favorite place," "where you and your friends meet or get together," "where you'd like play but aren't allowed to," etc. (Photo provided by Taller Creando sin Encargos)

FIGURE 14: (Bottom) Since 2008, some forty open-call community breakfasts have been held in different cities in Puerto Rico. The public spaces are used for open community debate on issues that affect its various constituencies. Each community member must bring food to the table as a metaphor for bringing ideas to the negotiation table. (Photo provided by Urbano Activo)

Comunitario (*Community Design Studio*) at the University of Puerto Rico's School of Architecture, are often not documented in ways that could positively affect public awareness or action. A previous inquiry determined that at present, local design and architecture schools do not require educators in their employ to publish or to be involved in design research.[10] Indeed, there has been a general lack of documentation of industrial-, graphic-design and community-design projects that have been operationalized by or that have involved contributions from Puerto Rican design educators or their students. There are several reasons for this state of affairs:

- a lack of financial and infrastructure support from both the Puerto Rican *and* American governments and from the educational and professional institutions that are situated on the island to support the instantiation and the maintenance of design process-based and designer archives;
- the transitory/migratory nature of those who practice the design profession, meaning that designers often move from one studio or consulting firm to another, and, as a result of this process, documents, designs, and documentation files are lost or left behind and often later destroyed;
- designers often work on a freelance basis, and do not themselves have the space, time, staff, and—especially—the training and awareness necessary to maintain their archives;
- the lack of almost any academic requirements that encourage or require design students in university programs to document or maintain a history of the decision-making processes that have guided the evolution of their respective projects, coupled with the lack of any training regarding the maintenance of such archival materials (students produce design projects, but are not required to document them or produce essays that describe their design and implementation processes).

This last gap in training means that professionals emerge from design schools being largely unaware of the need for (and) importance of documenting their projects and processes. This may perhaps be the most telling reason of all to explain the "documentation gap."

10 O'Neill, M. M. "Views and Reflections on Design Education: Local Voices from Puerto Rico." Foroalfa (2015). Online. Available at: http://foroalfa.org/articulos/views-and-reflections-on-design-education-local-voices-from-puerto-rico (Accessed August 18, 2017).

Regarding the failure of design academia to foment a culture of documentation and research through design [11,12], Dr. Luz María Rodríguez, an independent design research consultant and architectural historian, says,

> "There is a difference between *doing design* and *generating knowledge in design* [emphasis by the authors of this piece]. In Puerto Rico, the emphasis tends to be on the product, not the process, precisely because it is not the process and, within that, the research, that is rewarded in design courses.... [socio-cultural anthropologist Arjan Appadurai] told me [Dr. Rodríguez] that there is a great deal of talk about research in universities; students are required to "do" research (now even at the undergraduate level), but they aren't taught how. Clearly, this has consequences later, in the way designers approach, frame, execute and assess the effectiveness of their work. For example, there are few designers in Puerto Rico who consciously subscribe to methodologies associated with Design Thinking or Human-Centered Design, which do not [merely] establish methodological maps for the execution of projects . . . the stages they prescribe are, or imply, models or strategies of documentation. . .. When [designers] do not begin with research as a referent, they limit or skip steps, mainly the steps of dissemination and reuse of their findings. [Cross , 2007 [13]] There is a difference between exploration and research. As the RIBA [Royal Institute of British Architects] article titled "What is Architectural Research?" [Till, 2004 [14]] argued, "...whilst architects [designers] may believe that knowledge is there in the building to be appropriated by critics, users or other architects, they [the buildings or the products] very rarely explicitly communicate the knowledge." That requires an interpreter because architects and designers seldom communicate the knowledge contained in their designs in an explicit way. I think this applies to Puerto Rico, too. [15]

The authors want to clarify that this is not the case with Puerto Rican social and community psychologists, who have a prolific history of research, publishing, and systematically documenting their participatory projects. (It should be noted that they generally have university support to formulate and engage in this research.)

11 Frayling, C. (1993). Research in art and design. Royal College of Art Research Papers series, London, UK. Online. Available at: http://researchonline.rca.ac.uk/384/3/frayling_research_in_art_and_design_1993.pdf (Accessed 30 March, 2018).

12 Zimmerman, J., Stolterman, E., & Forlizzi, J. "An analysis and critique of Research through Design: towards a formalization of a research approach," in Proceedings of the 8th ACM Conference on Designing Interactive Systems Conference, 16–20 August, 2010, Aarhus, Denmark, 2010: pgs. 310–319.

13 Cross, N. "From a Design Science to a Design Discipline: Understanding Designerly Ways of Knowing and Thinking," Design Research Now: Essays and Selected Projects (Board of International Research in Design), edited by R. Michel, Basel, SUI: Birkhäuser, 2007, pgs. 41–54.

14 Till, J. Royal Institute of British Architects' Research and Development Committee, "Memorandum: What is Architectural Research?" Architectural Research: Three Myths and One Model (London, UK: RIBA, 2007) Online. Available at: https://jeremytill.s3.amazonaws.com/uploads/post/attachment/34/2007_Three_Myths_and_One_Model.pdf (Accessed 21 November 2017).

15 Rodríguez, L. M. E-mail to M. M. O'Neill, August 19, 2017. "RE: artículo."

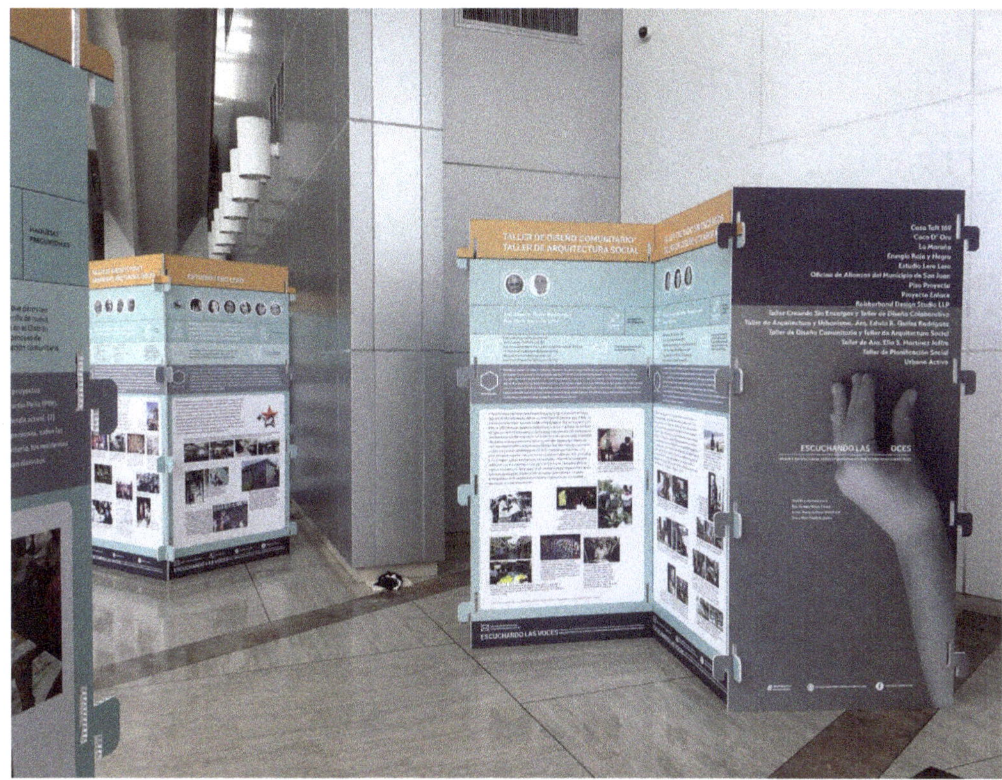

FIGURE 15: The exhibition *"Listening to Their Voices"* at its first venue, the lobby of the *Fine Arts Cinema* in San Juan, Puerto Rico (April 2017).

What is described here is not only true of Puerto Rico, but has also been discussed in the AIGA white paper "The Designer of 2025." AIGA (the American Institute of Graphic Arts) recognized that "there is a shift from asymmetrical, one-directional relationships between users and information to communication strategies built on models of conversation, participation, and community." [16] AIGA and other international design organizations have documented the paradigm changes in design practice that have affected ways of doing research that informs ideation and front-end design results.

Are other creative practitioners learning from the success of these Puerto Rican projects? Are other Puerto Rican practitioners learning new, or at least improved, ways to facilitate user extrapolations and collaborations? These are even harder questions to answer. There are two groups currently making a point of encouraging others to replicate their work: *Casa Taft 169* and *Urbano Activo.* They have reported that other Puerto Rican organizations are beginning to replicate their models—community and artist organizations in the case of *Casa Taft 169* and mostly community organizations in that of *Urbano Activo.* Also, *Rubberband Studios's* cancer project methodology and resources are available online for other groups to replicate, but there is no evidence that (as of

16 American Institute of Graphic Arts. "AIGA Designer 2025: Why design education should pay attention to trends." Design Educators Community (2017). Online. Available at: https://educators.aiga.org/wp-content/uploads/2017/08/DESIGNER-2025-SUMMARY.pdf (Accessed 21 November 2017).

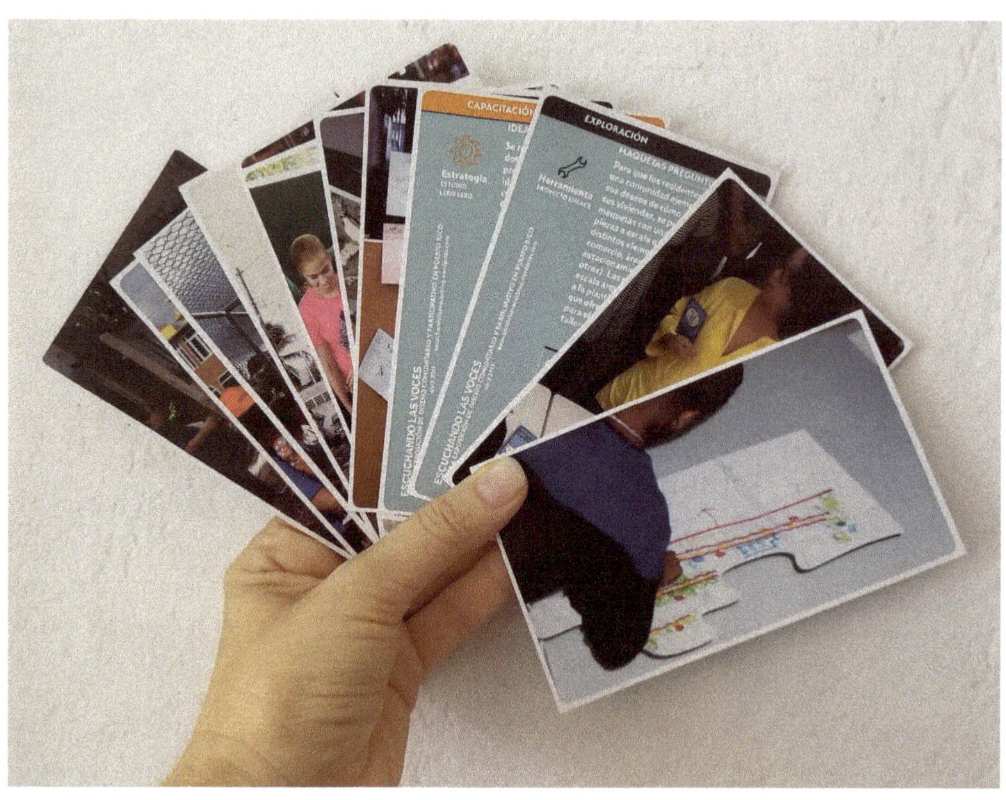

FIGURE 16: The "Toolkit" composed of fourteen cards that articulate the participatory design tactic utilized by each of the participants in the exhibition *"Listening to Their Voices."*

this writing in the spring of 2018) that this has occurred. Lastly, *Taller de Diseño Comunitario* (*The Community Design Studio at the University of Puerto Rico's School of Architecture*) and *Taller de Diseño Colaborativo* (*The Collaborative Design Studio*), which is part of the initiative *Taller Creando Sin Encargos* (*Creating Without Commissions Studio*) operated by the Polytechnic University of Puerto Rico), state that—as an essential aspect of their respective missions—students enrolled in their design programs will learn to design with communities.

Practitioners of projects that have been designed to address difficult problems involving the historical deterioration of Puerto Rico's cities and the complex, societal interrelationships that exist among Puerto Ricans need to incorporate the components of *verification, reflection,* and *documentation* into their approaches and methods. There is no question as to the contributions that the exhibition *"Listening to Their Voices"* participants are making in these vital areas (as depicted in Figures 15 and 16). But what is not documented, sadly, does not exist, because it is invisible, not only locally but also to the international design communities. The primary challenge lies in preventing these contributions from becoming isolated, which would severely limit the scope of change they could affect in and around other communities in the world struggling to address serious natural, financial and public policy challenges. The essential nature of these type of Participatory and Community Design projects provide robust seeds from which positive social, economic and cultural transformation can grow. In these ways, the exhibition *"Listening to Their Voices"* has been an effective means to help designers and their citizen collaborators better comprehend and create new knowledge of and about collaborative design methodologies as they affect and are affected by current design practices and educational approaches.

References

———. *Puerto Rico Unemployment Rate.* Available at http://www.tradingeconomics.com/puerto-rico/unemployment-rate (Accessed July 12, 2016).

American Institute of Graphic Arts. "AIGA Designer 2025: Why design education should pay attention to trends." *Design Educators Community* (2017). Online. Available at: https://educators.aiga.org/wp-content/uploads/2017/08/DESIGNER-2025-SUMMARY.pdf (Accessed November 21, 2017).

Arnstein, S. R. *A Ladder of Citizen Participation.* JAIP, 35.4, 1969.

Cotto Morales, L. "Experiencias en diseño participativo: los múltiples significados de la participación. Un principio de pedagogía urbana." In *Escuchando las voces* (exhibition catalog, 2016): pgs. 23–25.

Cross, N. "From a Design Science to a Design Discipline: Understanding Designerly Ways of Knowing and Thinking," *Design Research Now: Essays and Selected Projects (Board of International Research in Design)*, edited by R. Michel, Basel, SUI: Birkhäuser, 2007, pgs. 41–54.

De Carlo, G. "Architecture's Public." In *Architecture and Participation,* edited by P. B. Jones, D. Petrescu & J. Till, London: Taylor & Francis, 2005 (originally published as "Il pubblico dell'architettura," Parametro, No. 5, 1971).

Dean, R. "Policy Briefing: There is more than one way to involve the public in policy decisions." *Discover Society,* 1 June 2016. Online. Available at: http://discoversociety.org/2016/06/01/policy-briefing-there-is-more-than-one-way-to-involve-the-public-in-policy-decisions/ (Accessed August 19, 2017).

Faccio, B. "Left Behind: Poverty's Toll on the Children of Puerto Rico." *Child Trends,* 28 March 2016. Online. Available at http://www.childtrends.org/left-behind-povertys-toll-on-the-children-of-puerto-rico/ (Accessed August 18, 2017).

Fernández, S, & Bonsiepe, G. *Historia del diseño en América Latina y el Caribe: Industrialización y comunicación visual para la autonomía.* São Paulo: Blücher, 2008.

Frayling, C. (1993). *Research in art and design.* Royal College of Art Research Papers series, 1(1).

Gibson, M.R. & Owens, K.M. "Making meaning happen between 'us' and 'them': strategies for bridging gaps in understanding between researchers who possess design knowledge and those working in disciplines outside design." In *The Routledge Companion to Design Research,* edited by J. Yee and P. Rodgers, pgs. 386–399. Routledge, NY, NY, USA: 2015.

Guerrero Barón, J. *Colombia y América Latina después del fin de la historia,* Volumen 1. Tunja, Boyacá, Colombia: Editorial de la Universidad Pedagógica y Tecnológica de Colombia (UPTC), 1997.

Illich, I. *Tools for Conviviality.* London/NY: Marion Boyers, 1973. Online. Available at http://www.preservenet.com/theory/Illich/IllichTools.html (Accessed July 13, 2016).

Jones, P. B., Petrescu, D., and Till, J. *Architecture and Patricipation.* London: Taylor & Francis, 2005.

Marvel, L. *Listen to What They Say: Planning and Community Development in Puerto Rico.* Rio Piedras: UPR Press, 2008.

————. E-mail to Maria de Mater O'Neill and Omayra Rivera, August 21, 2016. RE: *adjunto paper de co-creation.*

O'Neill, M. M. "Pesquisa sobre la gestión empresarial de Maruja Fuentes Viguié," *iPolimorfo,* San Juan: Polytechnic University of Puerto Rico, 2017, pp. 58–65.

————. "Views and Reflections on Design Education: Local Voices from Puerto Rico." *Foroalfa* (2015). Online. Available at http://foroalfa.org/articulos/views-and-reflections-on-design-education-local-voices-from-puerto-rico (Accessed July 24, 2016)

Quiles, E. E-mail to María de Mater O'Neill, July 14, 2016. RE: *Fwd: coteja esta definición Personal.*

Rigau, J. "MoMA y EMA." *El Nuevo Día* (newspaper), June 2, 2015, Editorial. Online. Available at: http://www.elnuevodia.com/opinion/columnas/

momayema-columna-2054646/ (Accessed July 24, 2016).

———. E-mail to María de Mater O'Neill, July 30, 2016. *RE: Consulta Personal.*

Rivera Crespo, O. *Procesos de Participación: Proyectar, Construir y Habitar la Vivienda Contemporánea.* Barcelona: Editorial Académica Española, 2011.

Sanoff, H. *Programación y participación en el diseño arquitectónico / Programming and Participation in Architectural Design* (bilingual edition). Arquitectonics: Mind, Land & Society series. Barcelona: Ediciones Universidad Politécnica de Catalunya, 2006.

Santos Lozada, A. & Velázquez Estrada, A. "The Population Decline of Puerto Rico: An Application of Prospective Trends in Cohort-component Projections." *Instituto de Estadísticas de Puerto Rico, Série de Documentos de Trabajo,* 2015-1 (October 2015). Online. Available at http://www.estadisticas.pr/iepr/LinkClick.aspx?fileticket=EnVmZKo5nSo%3D (accessed July 13, 2017.)

Till, J. "The Negotiation of Hope." In *Architecture and Participation,* edited by P. B. Jones, D. Petrescu & J. Till, London: Taylor & Francis, 2005.

United States Census Bureau. *Income in Puerto Rico Holds Steady After Recession.* January 30, 2014. Online. Available at: http://www.census.gov/newsroom/press-releases/2014/cb14-17.html (accessed: July 12, 2016).

Zimmerman, J., Forlizzi, J., & Evenson, S. "Research through design as a method for interaction design research in HCI," in *Proceedings of the SIGCHI Conference on Human Factors in Computing Systems,* 28 April–03 May, 2007, San Jose, CA, USA: pgs. 493–502.

Zimmerman, J., Stolterman, E., & Forlizzi, J. "An analysis and critique of Research through Design: towards a formalization of a research approach," in *Proceedings of the 8th ACM Conference on Designing Interactive Systems,* 16–20 August, 2010, Aarhus, Denmark, 2010: pgs. 310–319.

Biographies

Dr. María de Mater O'Neill is the Head Researcher and Creative Director of *Rubberband Design Studio,* LLP and a Fulbright Specialist Roster candidate. She is the recipient of a *Round Four of the Presidential Design's Federal Design Achievement Award for Catalog Design* (United States), and *II Iberoamerican Design Biennal's* BID *Prize for Exhibition Design* (Spain). Her practice-based doctoral research initiative *"Developing Methods of Resilience for Design Practice"* is a design model intended to improve real-time resilience thinking for designers working under a variety of types of economic and socio-cultural stressors. She is member of the Peer Review Collegium of *She Ji—The Journal of Design, Economics, and Innovation,* published by Elsevier in collaboration with Tongji University and Tongji University Press, China, and the *Revista Tecnología & Diseño,* published by Departamento de Procesos y Técnicas de Realización de la UAM-A (México).

Dr. Omayra Rivera Crespo, Ph.D. earned her doctorate from the School of Architecture La Salle in Barcelona. She holds a Master's degree in Architecture from Arizona State University and a Bachelor's degree in Environmental Design from the University of Puerto Rico. She has cultivated experience as an architect and design educator in Boston, Barcelona and Puerto Rico.

She is the author of *Procesos de Participación: Proyectar, Construir y Habitar la Vivienda Contemporánea (Participation Processes: Project, Build and Live in Contemporary Housing, Editorial Académica Española,* 2011), was member of the editorial committee of the magazine *Entorno* and is member of the editorial committee of the magazine *Polimorfo.* She co-founded the collective *"Taller Creando Sin Encargos," (Creating Without Commissions Studio),* founded the *Collaborative Design Studio* in Beta Local and the Polytechnic University of Puerto Rico in San Juan, Puerto Rico, and has worked as Project and Citizen Participation Manager in the Municipality of San Juan. She has also been the Community Art Projects Coordinator at the Puerto Rico Museum of Contemporary Art.

Dialectic Volume II, Issue I: Long Form Case-Study Report

The Design Powers System: Cultivating Design Competencies in Collaborative Endeavors

DENIELLE EMANS[1] AND BASMA HAMDY[2]

1. Virginia Commonwealth University School of the Arts in Qatar, Education City, Doha, Qatar
2. Virginia Commonwealth University School of the Arts in Qatar, Education City, Doha, Qatar

SUGGESTED CITATION: Emans, D., & Hamdy, B. "Design Powers: Cultivating Design Competencies in Collaboration." *Dialectic*, 2.1 (2018): pgs. 171-198. DOI: http://dx.doi.org/10.3998/dialectic.14932326.0001.307

Abstract

This piece begins with the authors' contention that design education must challenge design students to reframe their negative assumptions about teamwork in preparation for collaborations with future colleagues and communities who operate knowledge bases outside of the contexts established for and by designers. Guided by constructive-developmental pedagogy,[a] this case study report recounts a series of undergraduate graphic design courses taught by the authors over a three-year period, along with a secondary analysis of literature on mechanisms of collaboration in both vocational and educational contexts. A constructive-developmental paradigm suggests that undergraduate design students (and undergraduate students from other disciplines) can develop critical thinking and sophisticated problem-solving skills by first constructing a deep, broadly informed understanding of self. The authors propose a model to guide undergraduate design students toward self-discovery based on observable personality traits which they have chosen to refer to as *Design Powers*. By identifying their individual personality traits and creative motivations, young designers can learn to work productively in teams that value meaningful input from diverse personalities.

According to the authors, a *Design Power* is a design personality profile based on what motivates individuals to produce, create, and engage in design. Inspired by American psychologist David Keirsey's idea of the integrated whole,[b] the authors' investigate design personalities by looking at the creative preferences of an emerging designer as a whole, rather than according to independent scales or personality aspects, much like the Myers-Briggs method of personality assessment (also known as the Myers–Briggs Type Indicator).[c] Grouped under four distinct design profiles by the authors—*Tinkerer, Dreamer, Storyteller,* or *Conductor*—the reduction of the personality assessment of given graphic design students to one of these four personality profiles serves to promote self-awareness, rather than diminish, the complexity of individuals.

An outgrowth of this research is the *Design Powers System,* which consists of three learning activities that progressively increase in complexity and structure as they are operationalized at the undergraduate level. These activities celebrate the value of self-discovery in university-level design classrooms and encourage young designers to work in teams comprised of members who possess complementary personality profiles during team-based activities. The findings from the author's three-year study of undergraduate graphic design courses they have taught suggest that groups composed of members who possess varying design acuities (as opposed to teams composed of comparably minded individuals) helps to create and sustain the functionalities of more temporally efficient, conceptually effective, and harmonious teams.

keywords:

Collaboration, Design Education,
Personality Traits, Teamwork

---

a "Constructive-developmental pedagogy is predicated on the idea that effective learning occurs within learning contexts, or developmental conditions, that have been created specifically to allow a given group of students to generate their own ideas and "find their own voices." Excerpted from Baxter Magolda, M.B. *Making Their Own Way: Narratives for Transforming Higher Education to Promote Self-Development.* Sterling, VA, USA: Stylus Publishing, 2004: pgs. 7–12.

b David Keirsey's theory defines four integrated configurations of personality or temperaments. These are: Artisan, Guardian, Idealist, and Rational. He describes temperaments as a "configuration of observable personality traits, such as habits of communication, patterns of action, and sets of characteristic attitudes, values, and talents." For more information on Keirsey's theory, the authors suggest the following reference: Keirsey, D. *Please Understand Me: Temperament,* Character, Intelligence. Del Mar, CA, USA: Prometheus Nemesis Book Company, 1984.

c The Myers-Briggs Type Indicator (MBTI) is a personality inventory that maps four basic dimensions of human personality along a spectrum of extraversion/introversion, sensing/intuition, thinking/feeling, and judging/perceiving. Consisting of a matrix of 16 personality traits determined by these four dimensions, the resulting variations are attributed to judgment and perception. The MBTI uses preferences as a primary indicator of the personality types and is not meant to assess traits, abilities, or character. For more information about the MBTI, the authors suggest the following reference: Briggs Myers, I. *The Myers-Briggs Type Indicator: Manual.* Palo Alto, CA, USA: Consulting Psychologists Press. 1962.

The Design Powers System:

Cultivating Design Competencies in Collaborative Endeavors

DENIELLE EMANS & BASMA HAMDY

Introduction

The nineteenth and early twentieth-century model of design education was primarily guided by the need to satisfy mandates from rapidly upscaling economic and industrial forces. [1] Business plans and entrepreneurial activities attached to design processes celebrated the 'sole creator,' [d] and were structured to undervalue the efforts of team thinking and shared project development . [e] Similarly, educational institutions that taught design at the university level placed great emphasis on "the illusion of original creativity," which involved students learning to generate outcomes to design processes largely in service to an individual organization's economic success and material progress. [2] While the so-called function and intention of the design process has evolved significantly over the course of the last century to teach students to effectively engage in collaborative endeavors that benefit communities, influence public policies or positively alter ways of doing and making, some educators continue to perceive the social, economic and cultural role of the designer as constrained to delivering messages and products. [3]

Recent directions in design practice point toward a more pluralistic discipline characterized by a need to develop more responsive social, environmental, and cultural protocols. [4] *The First Things First* manifesto—originally published by Ken Garland in 1964 [5] and re-published in the 51st issue of *Emigre* as the *First Things First 2000* manifesto in 1999—calls for "a reversal of

1 Findeli, A. "Rethinking design education for the 21st century: Theoretical, methodological, and ethical discussion." Design Issues 17.1 (2001): p. 6.

2 Boekraad, H., and Smiers, J. "The New Academy." European Journal of Arts Education 2.1 (1998): p. 60.

3 Ibid., p. 62.

4 Davis, M. et al. "AIGA Designer 2025: Why Design Education Should Pay Attention to Trends," AIGA Design Educators Community, 22 August, 2017. Online. Available at: https://educators.aiga.org/wp-content/uploads/2017/08/DESIGNER-2025-SUMMARY.pdf (Accessed 4 February 2018).

d *Throughout vocational and academic literature, the terms 'sole creator,' and 'lone genius,' refer to the accepted belief by business and creative leaders that innovation is the product of a single genius rather than the work of a collaborative and diverse group of people.* Sawyer, K. Group Genius: The Creative Power of Collaboration. New York, NY, USA: Basic Books, 2008, p. 5.

e *The authors define 'team-thinking' as a collective cognitive ability to process information and problem-solve complex tasks within a team-based setting. As for the term 'shared project development,' it is the ability to apply methods, skills and knowledge to achieve a set goal.*

priorities in favor of more useful, lasting and democratic forms of communication... a mindshift away from product marketing and toward the exploration and production of a new kind of meaning."[6] In alignment with the first *First Things First 2000* manifesto, this study advocates for the potential of operationalizing design's diverse and broadly informed human resources, and the visual languages that these fuel, to support group productivity (in lieu of a competitive mindset), and promotes the creation of artifacts, systems and experiences that meet real (and sustainable) human needs and goals.

One tranche of design-related research suggests that a collaborative, team-based approach is necessary to guide the development of more economically and environmentally resilient ways of making that extend to public policy and social development.[7] If productivity, project development, and innovation are to be improved, the complexity of working in these environments not only necessitates teamwork, but disciplinary and cultural diversity among team members.[8–12] In light of this, visual communication design education must at least begin to transform its essential practices so that students learn to effectively sustain collaborations with colleagues in disciplines outside design, work with people from communities and cultures beyond their established context, and engage in creative dialogue—rather than compete—with people who have not attended design school.[13,14]

How Competition and Individualism Affect Group Efforts

One day a hare was bragging about how fast he could run. He bragged and bragged about his speed, and even laughed at the tortoise, who was quite slow by comparison (*The Tortoise and the Hare by Aesop*).

In tandem with the need for commercial visual communication design practices to generate economically and environmentally resilient ways of making, moderate to extreme levels of competition among individuals in the workplace can strangle productivity, professional development, and most importantly, team-building.[14] There have recently been several calls from prominent design educators and researchers for visual communication design education to reassess approaches that entail teaching so many students to work in competition-driven learning environments that stress individual achievement over team-based initiatives and projects.[15–17] Despite these

5 Garland, K. "First Things First," The Guardian, 29 November 1963. Online. Available at: http://www.designishistory.com/1960/first-things-first/ (Accessed March 20, 2018).

6 BarnbTook, J. et al. "First Things First Manifesto 2000." AIGA Journal of Graphic Design, 17 (1999): p. 2.

7 Buchanan, R. "Human-centered design: Changing perspectives on design education in the East and West." Design Issues, 20.1 (2004): p. 35.

8 Katzenbach, J. & Smith, D. The Wisdom of Teams. Boston, MA, USA: Harvard Business Review Press, 2015, p. 41.

9 Sawyer, K. Group Genius: The Creative Power of Collaboration. New York, NY, USA: Basic Books, 2008, p. 17.

10 Gratton & Erickson, "Eight Ways to Build Collaborative Teams." Harvard Business Review, (November 2007): 43. Online. Available at: https://hbr.org/2007/11/eight-ways-to-build-collaborative-teams (Accessed May 12, 2017).

11 Ibid., p. 43-44.

12 Buchanan, R. "Human-centered design: Changing perspectives on design education in the East and West." Design Issues, 20.1 (2004): p. 35.

[f] *For a description of this term see note no.4 on 'sole creator' or 'lone genius.'*

13 Gibson, M.R. & Owens, K.M. "Making meaning happen between 'us' and 'them': strategies for bridging gaps in understanding between researchers who possess design knowledge and those working in disciplines outside design." In The Routledge Companion to Design Research, edited by J. Yee and P. Rodgers, pgs. 386–399. Routledge, NY, NY, USA: 2015.

14 Rock, D., Davis, J. & Jones, B. "Kill Your Performance Ratings." Strategy+Business, 8 August, 2014, 76 (2014). Online. Available at: http://www.strategy-business.com/article/00275?gko=c442b (Accessed July 19, 2017).

15 Heller, S. & Talarico, L., "Education Manifesto" in Icograda Design Education Manifesto, Taipei: International Council of Graphic Design Associations, edited by Audrey Bennett & Omar Vulpinari, 11 October 2011: p. 84. Online. Available at: http://www.ico-d.org/database/files/library/IcogradaEducationManifesto_2011.pdf (Accessed May 12, 2017).

16 Hunt, J. "Education Manifesto" in Icograda Design Education Manifesto, Taipei: International Council of Graphic Design Associations, edited by Audrey Bennett & Omar Vulpinari, 11 October 2011: p. 88. Online. Available at: http://www.ico-d.org/database/files/library/IcogradaEducationManifesto_2011.pdf (Accessed May 12, 2017).

17 Friedman, K. "Models of Design: Envisioning a Future Design Education." Visible Language, 46.1/2 (2012): p. 143.

entreaties, contemporary design classrooms the world over nurture cultures of student-versus-student competition as instructors perpetuate the creation of 'portfolio-worthy' projects designed by individual students. These tend to celebrate the assumption of the so-called 'one-size-fits-all designer,' or the 'lone genius' [f] model of designing. The perpetuation of these approaches may be rooted in inherited (but seldom questioned) educational frameworks wherein faculty recycle curricula based on the residing belief that students should be designing to meet the needs and goals of what is (or was) primarily a service economy. Traditional quantitative grading systems also contribute to the perpetuation of competitive spaces in design classrooms, often rewarding the brightest, loudest and most aggressive of students. Much like the hare in Aesop's tale, celebrating the fastest individual rewards the assertion of one facet of an emerging designer's personality, but simultaneously stifles the potential of alternative modes of engagement such as those planned and operationalized by the slow and purposeful tortoise.

David Rock, a leading proponent of combining neuroscience with leadership, describes five domains affecting the human brain during social experience and interaction as part of his neuroscience-based model, SCARF (Status, Certainty, Autonomy, Relatedness and Fairness). In particular, the 'status' factor can contribute to an individual's superiority complex and potential threat response. "Winning a swimming race, a card game or an argument probably feels good because of the perception of increased status and the resulting reward circuitry being activated. The perception of a potential or real reduction in status can generate a strong threat response." [18] Contrary to popular corporate strategies, workplace research suggests that competition is an impediment to development, with performance management systems often failing to motivate or aid the development of employees. These types of performance systems tend to generate a negative neural response and significantly retard efforts among individuals to collaborate by devaluing the role of each individual in a group. [19] Competitive mindsets have also been shown to leave individuals ill-prepared to navigate the complexities of team-based collaboration in these same firms.

Facilitating Effective Collaboration and Teamwork

A Lion used to prowl about a field in which four oxen used to dwell. Many a time he tried to attack them, but whenever he came near they turned their tails to one another, so that no matter which way he approached them, he was met by a set of horns (The Four Oxen and the Lion by Aesop).

In the context of this discourse, *collaboration* describes a situation within which a group of people with complementary skills and bases of knowledge (who make use of various modes and styles of communication) work together toward achieving a common goal. Collaboration and communication strategist Evan Rosen defines collaboration as "[any group of people] working together to create value while sharing virtual or physical space."[20] Bobby Patton and Timothy Downs—researchers on interpersonal and small group communication—similarly define "group-work" as a process involving a small number of individuals, in interdependent roles, utilizing various forms of communication to act as a single unit working towards a collective goal.[21] In their book *The Wisdom of Teams,* Jon Katzenbach and Douglas Smith (both are authorities on organizational culture and leadership in business) describe a 'high-performance' team as a small number of people with complementary skills.[22] Regardless of the terminology, research indicates that group productivity and project development is improved when teams possess complementary skills, diverse communication styles, and *group flow.*[23,24] The idea of group flow grew out of psychological studies of and about why and how collaborative teams—such as writing groups, sports teams and musical ensembles—experience a heightened sense of focus and creativity as they collectively engage in a goal-oriented activity or set of activities in ways that make the individuals in the group less self-conscious.

Keith Sawyer, a Professor of Educational Innovations at the University of North Carolina at Chapel Hill (U.S.) and a leading scientific expert on creativity, innovation and learning, suggests 'improvisation' is the fundamental building block of effective collaboration. In his book, *Group Genius: The Creative Power of Collaboration,* Sawyer emphasizes the importance of brainstorming within organizational hierarchies that encourages free-flowing improvisational approaches and mindsets to guide the process. In this manner, brainstorming enables teams to build from one idea to the next, with shared ideas prompting new insights.[25] Sawyer also argues that group flow plays a significant role in collaborative activities, with peak group performance driven by members who, simultaneously, reach optimal levels of creativity together.[26] A unique and essential component of group flow (or shared creative inspiration) is the necessity to configure teams by members who possess varying

18 Rock, D. "SCARF: A Brain-Based Model." NeuroLeadership, 1.1 (2008): pgs. 46.

19 Rock, D., Davis, J. & Jones, B. "Kill Your Performance Ratings." Strategy+Business, 8 August, 2014, 76 (2014). Online. Available at: http://www.strategy-business.com/article/00275?gko=c442b (Accessed July 19, 2017).

20 Rosen, E. The Culture of Collaboration. San Francisco, CA, USA: Red Ape Publishing, 2007: p. 9.

21 Patton, B.R. & Downs, T.M. Decision-Making Group Interaction: Achieving Quality, 4th Edition. Boston, MA, USA: Pearson, 2002: p. 2.

22 Katzenbach, J. R. & Smith, D.K. The Wisdom of Teams, New York, NY, USA: Harper Business, 2006: p. 41.

23 Sawyer, K. Group Genius. New York, NY, USA: Basic Books, 2017: p. 17.

24 Gratton, L. & Erickson, T.J. "Eight Ways to Build Collaborative Teams." Harvard Business Review, 85.11 (2007): 101-109. Online. Available at: http://morris.lis.ntu.edu.tw/KM2016/wp-content/uploads/KM/W14-1GrattonErickson2007.pdf (Accessed February 9, 2018).

25 Sawyer, K. Group Genius. New York, NY, USA: Basic Books, 2017: p. 17.

26 Ibid., p. 43-44.

communication styles, rather than teams composed of individuals who all communicate in a similar manner.

> *"If everyone functions identically and shares the same habits of communicating, nothing new and unexpected will ever emerge because group members don't need to pay close attention to what the others are doing, and they don't continually have to update their understanding of what is going on."* [27]

Sawyer's view of improvisation and communication challenges traditional opinions about group dynamics wherein teams ideally possess identical communication styles. These dynamics likely arose from organizational communication practices that were commonly operationalized during the industrialization era. During this time period, vertically-oriented hierarchical systems divided roles between disparately ranked members within an organization. [28] This well-established operational modality required focused, parallel communication styles to produce goods in assembly line systems. In other words, individuals within a group would divide the workload by focusing on the same task in analogous paths. Similarly, the modes and methodologies of professional design during the industrialization era also served a trade-based economy based on division of labor and empiricism.

In the post industrialization era, the principles underlying design practice shifted—to one defined in much of the literature as a knowledge-based economy of networked labor and systems thinking. [29] In these cases, teams began to tackle multifaceted challenges with group members of varied skills and intelligences together, rather than dividing the labor. [30] Writing in 2007 in the *Harvard Business Review*, business educators and researchers Lynda Gratton and Tamara Erickson promote the importance of working in diverse business teams to grow ideas together, noting that including people who possess disparate backgrounds and views enable "cross-fertilization that sparks insight and innovation." [31]

By interviewing hundreds of individuals across a range of organizations, business management authors Jon Katzenbach and Douglas Smith associate 'high-performance' teams with a combination of both functional and technical proficiencies, including problem-solving and interpersonal communication. [32] Similar to the four oxen who work together to protect themselves against the lion, high performance teams achieve success when they are equally

27 Ibid., p. 52.

28 Friedman, K. "Models of Design: Envisioning a Future Design Education." Visible Language, 46.1/2 (2012): p. 140-41.

29 Ibid.

30 Katzenbach, J. R. & Smith, D.K. The Wisdom of Teams, New York, NY, USA: Harper Business, 2006: p. 41.

31 Gratton, L. & Erickson, T.J. "Eight Ways to Build Collaborative Teams." Harvard Business Review, 85.11 (2007): 101-109. Online. Available at: http://morris.lis.ntu.edu.tw/KM2016/wp-content/uploads/KM/W14-1GrattonErickson2007.pdf (Accessed February 9, 2018).

32 Katzenbach, J. R. & Smith, D.K. The Wisdom of Teams, New York, NY, USA: Harper Business, 2006: pgs. 47-8.

committed to a common purpose. Katzenbach and Smith go on to say that teams built with complementary skills invest in the personal growth of one another by holding themselves mutually accountable for the success of the group.[33] This kind of group-work encourages team-members to become flexible and responsive to change by establishing trust, defining goals, and building confidence in a project together.[34]

Identifying how Personality Types and Complementary Skills Affect Teamwork

Once upon a time in the Land of Oz, four individuals set out on a strange and dangerous journey. Each of them was lacking something vital to his or her nature, and each wanted to find the great Oz and ask him for help.[35]

Inasmuch as research suggests complementary skills are necessary for effective teamwork, personality types also play a meaningful role in group interactions. Identifying individual preferences can provide insight into worldviews, inspirations, problem-solving approaches, and most importantly, group dynamics. Studies have determined that personality identification is also useful in developing interpersonal growth because it confirms individual value and contribution to the group.[36]

With the ancient study of temperaments tracing as far back as Plato and Hippocrates, recognizing variations among people is by no means a new or groundbreaking concept.[37] Briefly stated, *temperament* accounts for how an individual's combination of mental, physical and emotional characteristics affects their behavior. Several theories of cognitive psychology suggest that the brain is wired to classify and categorize semantically as a way to protect ourselves and make decisions quickly in threat situations. Self-categorization theory suggests that individuals tend to perceive themselves—and others—as belonging to particular groups. Even further, group properties or characteristics tend to shift self-perception from personal to social identity.[38]

Within the psychology community, Carl Jung remains a prominent and influential figure due to his extensive research in the area of analytical psychology. His theory of psychological types, developed in 1921, was guided by the notion that humans experience four mental functions: *sensation, intuition, feeling,* and *thinking.* In 1962, Katharine Briggs, and her daughter Isabel Briggs Myers, adapted his theory to produce the Myers-Briggs Type Indicator (MBTI).

33 Ibid., p. 41.

34 Ibid., p. 12.

35 Keirsey, D. Please Understand Me: Temperament, Character, Intelligence. Del Mar, CA, USA: Prometheus Nemesis Book Company, 1984: p. 17.

36 Richardson, R.C. & DeVaney, T.A. "Personality Instrument to Increase Collaboration." Educational Research and Reviews, 3.4 (2008): pgs. 121–127.

37 Ibid., p. 123.

38 Turner, J., Oakes, P., Haslam, S., & McGarty, C. "Self and Collective: Cognition and Social Context." Personality and Social Psychology Bulletin, 20.5 (1994): pgs. 454-463.

In the following years, the MBTI was further modified by various psychologists and continues to serve as a primary indicator of personality variation.

The MBTI involves identifying four basic dimensions of human personality along a spectrum of extraversion/introversion, sensing/intuition, thinking/feeling, and judging/perceiving. Consisting of a matrix of 16 personality traits, determined by these four dimensions, the resulting variations are attributed to judgment and perception.[39] Over the past decade, the MBTI was used by approximately 80% of Fortune 500 companies as a scientific measure to ensure employees were placed in the correct roles or to help teams work together.[40] Furthermore, the authors of the book, *Do What You Are* argue that millennials will achieve greater job satisfaction if they can identify a profession that will accommodate their MBTI personality preferences.[41]

In *Please Understand Me II,* David Keirsey discusses the recurrence of the number four when looking at personality patterns in humans. Heavily influenced by Myers' indicators, Keirsey poetically relates the recurring number four in personality traits to the classic children's book *The Wizard of Oz,* highlighting how these distinct differences have been identified in people for thousands of years.[42] Consequently, his theory, which is inspired and influenced by ancient and historical theories of temperaments, also outlines four configurations. Keirsey defines temperament as a "configuration of observable personality traits, such as habits of communication, patterns of action, and sets of characteristic attitudes, values, and talents." Building on Plato's description of personality types, Keirsey defines the four integrated configurations of personality, or temperaments as *Artisan, Guardian, Idealist,* and *Rational.* He relates his perspective to that of "organismic wholism," wherein personality traits develop through differentiation, similar to cells in the body.[43] If varying personality traits begin with an integrated whole, then the need to identify variations in humans is a logical starting point to produce a harmonious group.

The authors of this piece propose that contemporary design education programs can benefit from this line of research in psychology to help students identify their individual personality traits and prepare them to work productively in teams that value personality diversity. The conventional teaching approach, one that measures students as identical contenders in an assessment race, contradicts major studies in both psychology and collaboration that emphasize the importance of diversity within business teams. Furthermore, research demonstrates how multifaceted challenges are often solved by teams who possess varied skills and intelligences.

39 Tieger, P., Barron, B., & Tieger, K. Do What You Are: Discover the Perfect Career for You Through the Secrets of Personality Type. New York, NY, USA: Little, Brown and Company, 2014: pgs. 12-13.

40 Winterhalter, B. "ISTJ? ENFP? Careers Hinge on a Dubious Personality Test." The Boston Globe, 31 August 2014. Online. Available at: http://www.bostonglobe.com/opinion/2014/08/30/istj-enfp-careers-hinge-dubious-personality-test/8ptUGXhu6DndFdjCngcxSN/story.html (Accessed January 19, 2017).

41 Tieger, P., Barron, B., & Tieger, K. Do What You Are: Discover the Perfect Career for You Through the Secrets of Personality Type. New York, NY, USA: Little, Brown and Company, 2014: p. 5.

42 Keirsey, D. Please Understand Me: Temperament, Character, Intelligence. Del Mar, CA, USA: Prometheus Nemesis Book Company, 1984: pgs. 17–18.

43 Ibid: p. 31.

Examining the Research Opportunity in the Design Powers System and the Methodology that Guided its Development

Recent scholarship from design suggests the need for emerging designers, design educators and scholars to learn to work more effectively in teams. The capacity to learn how to think and work empathetically as part of a collaborative working group is particularly meaningful as initiatives such as design for good, design for democracy, and design for social change continue to gain traction. In his handbook *An Introduction to Wicked Problems*, Jon Kolko explains that an essential aspect of beginning to address social or cultural problems involves learning to work collaboratively across disciplines.[44] More recently, the team of authors who created the future-focused missive The AIGA Designer of 2025 offered that, "...systems today...are built on models of conversation in which power is shared and content develops collaboratively and organically."[45] Opining from these perspectives, it is essential to equip emerging designers with the skills and bases of knowledge necessary to help them communicate and collaborate with colleagues in disciplines outside design.

Numerous studies explore the benefits and applications of collaboration in design classrooms;[46–47] however, few studies articulate effective procedural approaches to facilitate acuity-based team creation.[g] Additionally, little research exists on the relationships between collaboration and identifying personality traits in the context of design education. This gap in research suggests an opportunity to contribute to the scholarly literature in and around this area by working with design students to ascertain which of their skill-based competencies might most effectively fuel collaborative methodologies in and outside design classrooms, as well as prepare them for engaging in the coordination of complex projects that respond to socially or culturally specific problems.

Traditional approaches and processes of teamwork fall short of fully addressing the *dynamic nature of design*[49] and *wicked problems*[h] in which there are a wide variety of complexities that make definitive and objective outcomes to design processes impossible to achieve. Building self-awareness coupled with respect for perspectives different from one's own is necessary if design students are to effectively engage with people from communities and cultures outside of their established contexts of work or understandings, especially if these people have not attended design school. This involves developing the capacity of a designer to be emotionally open enough to move outside of his-or-her psychological comfort zone to at least partially embrace logical and conceptual ambiguity as situations demand.

44 Kolko, J. Wicked Problems: Problems Worth Solving: A Handbook & A Call to Action. Austin, TX, USA: ac4d, 2012.

45 Armstrong, H., Blume, M., Chochinov, A., Davis, M., Dubberly, H., Kincaid, K., Lee, J., Irwin, T., Pangaro, P., Stillion, D., Yap, M. "The Designer of 2025: Why Design Education Should Pay Attention to Trends." AIGA, 22 August, 2017. Online. Available at: https://educators.aiga.org/wp-content/uploads/2017/08/DESIGNER-2025-SUMMARY.pdf (Accessed March 10, 2018).

46 Peeters et al., "Design Behavior Questionnaire for Multidisciplinary Teams." Design Studies, 28.6 (2007): pgs. 623–643.

[g] *Acuity-based team creation is defined by the authors as a process involving the identification of dominant skill-based acuities in order to create diverse, yet, synergetic teams.*

[h] *Wicked problems are complicated social or cultural issues that cannot be completely described or solved in traditional linear methods because each problem is a symptom of another problem. There are a number of reasons why wicked problems are difficult to solve, including large economic burdens, incomplete or contradictory knowledge, and the involvement of numerous people and opinions in the social challenge. For more information about Wicked Problems, the authors suggest the following reference:* Kolko, J. Wicked Problems: Problems Worth Solving: A Handbook & A Call to Action. Austin, TX, USA: ac4d, 2012, and Buchanan, R. "Wicked Problems in Design Thinking." Design Issues, 8.2 (1992): pgs.: 5–21.

Like the four main characters in the *Wizard of Oz* using their combined powers to complete their journey, this study supports the notion that diversified design teams fuel high levels of innovation and invention. Building on Keirsey's idea of the integrated whole and the Myers-Briggs [Personality] Type Indicator (MBTI), along with theories of collaboration proposed by Katzenbach and Smith, Rosen, Sawyer and Patton,[50–53] a preliminary model for team-based collaboration was developed for use in an undergraduate learning environment that could operationalize both the value of the individual talent—or power—of a given design student as well as his-or-her membership in a diversely populated team.

Over a period of three consecutive years (2014–2017), the *Design Powers System* was tested in four separate undergraduate graphic design classrooms consisting of an average of 20 students residing in Qatar. During this time, these design students participated in a series of activities and observations that challenged them to focus on *self-reflection* and *self-identification* to determine their dominant design profiles—Conductor, Storyteller, Tinkerer, or Dreamer (see Figure 2). These varied activities aimed to empower students to make meaningful contributions to group projects and celebrate their unique roles as integral contributors to design teams. Faculty observations and individual discussions were a necessary aspect of the data gathering and analysis process that informed this research, and helped inform the testing and evaluation of the *Design Powers System* and, ultimately, contextualize the resulting student feedback.

To manage and refine the collaborative processes, the two design faculty who facilitated this testing administered written assessment forms and engaged students in providing verbal feedback through open-ended discussions. Data was collected both during and after student immersions in learning experiences that were affected by the *Design Powers System*. Specifically, individual feedback was collected from each student using an anonymous short-answer questionnaire that functioned as a written assessment of each student's ability to achieve certain learning outcomes. The goal of the survey was to position the student's role within the collaborative team and to examine to what degree it confirmed or contradicted her/his identified competency.

A Contextualized Description of the Four Dominant Design Profiles

This research identifies four *design dualities* (see Figure 1), presented as continuums, that are inspired by the Meyer Briggs [Personality] Type Indicator's four

47 Dong, Kleinsmann & Deken, "Investigating Design Cognition." Design Studies, 34.1 (2013): pgs. 1–33.

48 Van Leeuwen, van Gassel & den Otter, "Teaching Collaborative Design." In Proceedings of the International Workshop on Construction Information Technology in Education, 7 September 2004 Istanbul, Turkey, 2004: pgs. 1–9.

49 Armstrong, H., Blume, M., Chochinov, A., Davis, M., Dubberly, H., Kincaid, K., Lee, J., Irwin, T., Pangaro, P., Stillion, D., Yap, M. "The Designer of 2025: Why Design Education Should Pay Attention to Trends." AIGA, 22 August, 2017. Online. Available at: https://educators.aiga.org/wp-content/uploads/2017/08/DESIGNER-2025-SUMMARY.pdf (Accessed February 4, 2018).

50 Katzenbach, J., & Smith, D. The Wisdom of Teams: Creating the High-Performance Organization. New Boston, MA, USA: Harvard Business Review Press, 2015.

51 Rosen, E. The Culture of Collaboration: Maximizing Time, Talent and Tools to Create Value in the Global Economy. San Francisco, CA, USA: Red Ape Publishing, 2007.

52 Sawyer, K. Group Genius: The Creative Power of Collaboration. New York, NY, USA: Basic Books, 2008.

53 Patton, B.R. & Downs, T.M. Decision-Making Group Interaction: Achieving Quality, 4th Edition. Boston, MA, USA: Pearson, 2002: p. 2.

REASON — INTUITION	EMPATHY — PRAGMATISM
Reason-based designers focus on facts to make objective decisions. They are practical, detail-oriented and excellent at detecting flaws in various project components. They build on real-life experiences and dislike speculation or information that is not verified. They prefer controlled work environments and enjoy following step-by-step instructions to learn new skills. **Intuition-based designers** do not accept the status quo and often think about alternative directions and possibilities. They tend to be imaginative and discover opportunities for improvement by establishing new design trends and patterns. They normally prefer to 'feel-out' new territory and tend to avoid step-by-step instructions to learn new skills.	**Empathetic designers** are diplomatic and tactful individuals. They are highly considerate of how people feel and give more weight to principles over professional success. They are emotional, compassionate and care deeply about how people see them. They are sensitive and promote harmony in the world around them. When dealing with people, they find it difficult to be brutally honest and can sometimes be too idealistic. **Pragmatic designers** tend to be analytical, and rely on facts and experience to make decisions. They are quick to shut down ideas that seem illogical, far-fetched or unrealistic and prefer to carefully plan and structure projects. Designers who are more pragmatic tend to approach design decisions from a detached standpoint using logic and reason to come to a conclusion. When collaborating with others, they prefer to be honest rather than tactful or diplomatic.
CONCRETE — ABSTRACT	**INTERNAL — EXTERNAL**
Concrete designers have a strict work-ethic and like to adhere to rules and established codes. They are excellent at organization, planning, and will always have multiple backup plans. Designers who are more concrete are excellent at making sure a project is completed to the highest standard. They sometimes miss seeing new or unexpected opportunities because they are too focused on the task at hand. **Abstract designers** are excellent at discovering new and unexpected connections through improvisation. They are spontaneous, flexible and do not conform to traditions, habits or societal norms. Designers who are more abstract can be impulsive, rebelling against their teachers, supervisors or managers. They sometimes miss deadlines or may forget to complete tasks if they are too focused on open-ended possibilities.	**Internal designers** are thought-oriented and more sensitive to external stimulation. They prefer to isolate themselves in order to be more productive. Internal designers can get overwhelmed by an excess of sights and sounds and would rather not take the lead in social situations such as public speaking or presentations. Their preference is to have less frequent, but more meaningful interactions with those around them. **External designers** are action-oriented and seek energy from their environment and the people around them. They become energized with frequent interaction and often take the lead during presentations or group situations. They prefer to engage in many different activities and feel most productive when expressing themselves. Their preference is to connect horizontally, creating a social network with all team-members.

FIGURE 1: This table depicts the four "design dualities," from which the dominant design traits depicted in Figure 2 are derived.

basic dimensions and the observable skilled-actions described by Keirsey. The four design dualities were extracted by the authors after extensive observation, discussion, and daily work with the undergraduate design students from Qatar. These dualities can be considered as building blocks that determine how a creative individual might operate in a collaborative group setting. If one trait becomes dominant on a given continuum, it can help to determine that design student's patterns of action, communication style, attitudes, and values as he-or-she engages in a specific design challenge. In this manner, the dominant design profile for that individual can be identified. Figure 1 articulates in-depth descriptions of the four design dualities: *reason/intuition, empathy/pragmatism, concrete/abstract* and *internal/external.*

The four design dualities described here produce four dominant traits of character, or *design profiles*. Mapping these dualities onto the *Design Powers Wheel* demonstrates how a given student designer's personality traits can be

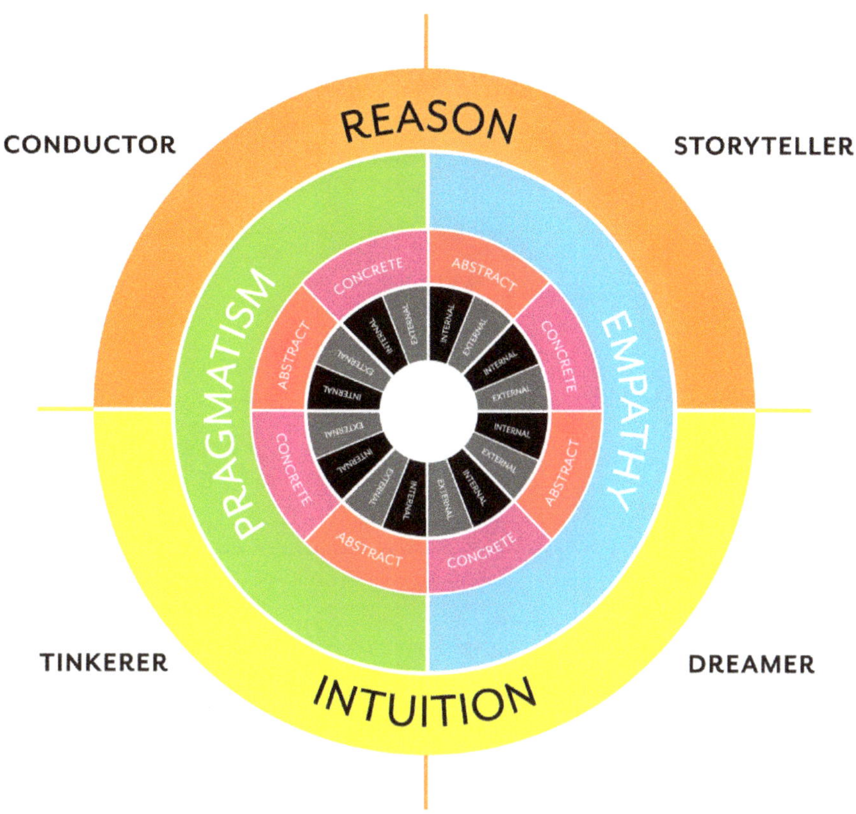

FIGURE 2: *The Design Powers Wheel,* which depicts how different personality traits exhibited by given design students are affected by their possession of or identification with particular, sometimes overlapping, values and competencies. These traits are integrated around portions of the circumference of the wheel—grouped into oppositional pairs called "dualities—to create four dominant design profiles.

integrated to produce the four dominant profiles (depicted in figure 2). The *Design Powers Wheel* was adapted primarily from the *Myers-Briggs Type Indicator Model*, the *Insights Discovery Model* [i], and the *Tilt Leadership Model* [i] to visually demonstrate how the spectrum of creative motivations relate to personality traits, behavioral patterns, strength-based assessments and other qualities. The *Design Powers Wheel* illustrates that designers may possess aspects of two competencies that lie along the same spectrum, but self-identify with one competency over the other (by choosing the one that best maps to their social, economic or cultural values and creative motivations). For example, a designer who identifies as *empathetic* may also be *pragmatic* at times, but still chooses to see *empathy* as a dominant value in their profile.

When presented in a design classroom, the four dominant design profiles are often best introduced by a faculty member who is conducting a

[i] *The Insights Discovery System builds on the work of Swiss psychologist C.G. Jung's attitude preferences (extraversion and introversion) and rational functions (thinking and feeling). From this foundation, a wheel diagram is used to help individuals identify areas for personal growth, along with organizational strengths and weaknesses when the data is collated with others' profiles. For more information on the Insights Discovery System, the authors suggest the following reference:* "Comparison of Insights Discovery System to Myers-Briggs Type Indicator." pgs. 1-5. Online. Available at: http://www.inside-inspiration.com.au/factsheets/insights-discovery-and-mbti-comparison.pdf (Accessed May 12, 2017).

[i] *The Tilt Leadership Model is a scientifically validated development tool created by Pam Boney to guide leaders in the assessment of character-based strengths to increase business productivity and innovation. For more information on the Tilt Leadership Model the authors suggest the following reference:* Boney, P. True Tilt: An Uncommon Quest. Bloomington, IN, USA: Author House, 2010.

Conductors are skilled leaders adept at problem solving. They possess strong organizational skills and enjoy managing discreet details throughout the design process. Similar to an orchestra conductor, these designers are skilled at encouraging teams to work harmoniously together by creating environments that support innovation and creativity. With strong management skills, Conductors are driven by the excitement of guiding a group through a project's deliberate and strategic growth. They are detail-oriented and diligent, possessing a mastery of skills in communication, pragmatism, and assessment.	**Storytellers** are articulate orators adept at the visualization and articulation of outcomes. With empathetic and observational abilities, they can express design challenges, processes, and outcomes through compelling narratives. When others struggle to find the right words, Storytellers can say the right thing and strike the right tone. Storytellers have an instinctive ability to describe, understand, and elaborate on the experiences of others. They can help express ideas to clients or team members and facilitate trust-building and communication. Storytellers acknowledge the value of debate and discussion, but ultimately believe that realistic ideas are what matter most.
Tinkerers are natural risk-takers energized by new possibilities and eager to tackle the unknown. They are anxious to uncover new approaches and want to make ideas become a physical reality. With an eager sense of determination, they find confidence in mastering a new skill and naturally see how things work. Tinkerers possess high technical mastery in both digital and hands-on applications with a focus on the tangible. Tinkerers are motivated to invent solutions and turn ideas into action by diving into the making process allowing mistakes to happen, and delighting in the results.	**Dreamers** enjoy the possibility of the unknown and consider the future as an opportunity to stretch the boundaries of design ingenuity. With imaginations full of new possibilities, Dreamers are visionaries who fluently generate concepts with little pragmatic consideration. Dreamers are ethical idealists striving to reach new heights through visions of a better product, intervention, or idea. They are hindered by real world restrictions and guided by emotional depth. They understand the importance of connecting with people and have a natural intuition for reading people's emotions.

FIGURE 3: The four dominant design profiles that result from allowing design students to operate the wheels that comprise the *Design Powers System* are described briefly here.

collaborative design project. This process involves asking students to choose one side of each duality (reason *versus* intuition; pragmatism *versus* empathy; etc.). The visual representation of the two sides of the wheel (reason/intuition and empathy/pragmatism) and the oppositional concepts embedded around the two inner circles of the wheel (concrete/abstract; external/internal) exist to highlight the importance of integrating each of the paired qualities into a given student's personal design process. This means that this particular student should not, for example, discount the importance of empathy, even when he-or-she prefers to engage in a more pragmatic approach to a specific design challenge. Additionally, the visibility of these creative motivations—as two sides of one wheel and equally distributed portions of two inner wheels—suggests the potential for an expansion of an individual student's personal growth by making him-or-her aware of qualities they might want to emphasize, hone, or improve in the future. For instance, if a student generally prefers to follow *intuition* as he-or-she engages in his-or-her design work, there may be an opportunity to follow *reason* as a way to expand their creative thinking in a forthcoming project.

The primary goal of this activity is for each student in the design classroom to self-identify with one of the four design profiles—*Tinkerer, Dreamer, Storyteller,* or *Conductor*—(Figure 3) to facilitate the composition of balanced design teams. The following example illustrates this self-identification process and demonstrates how a particular individual can engage with the *Design Powers System.*

> *Hypothetical student "Mary" chooses the personality trait 'reason' over 'intuition' on the Design Powers Wheel, as she is practical, detail-oriented and excellent at detecting flaws. She identifies with the personality trait 'empathy' over 'pragmatism' since she is emotional, compassionate and cares deeply about how people perceive her. She is 'abstract' rather than 'concrete' because she is spontaneous, flexible and does not always conform to traditions, habits or societal norms. Finally, she is an 'external' person because she is action-oriented and seeks energy from her environment and people. Based on the summation of these traits, as they are operationalized across the wheels that comprise the Design Powers System, Mary is categorized as a Storyteller.*

Building on multiple trait-based theories, such as Carl Jung's *Personality Types,* the *Myers-Briggs Type Indicator Model,* and *Keirsey's Temperament Theory*—the four dominant design profiles represent four integrated configurations of design personality. These four configurations are distinct portraits of preferred creative motivations that cling together to create a "whole" depiction of an individual design student. The poetic titles of the four design profiles (*Tinkerer, Dreamer, Storyteller,* and *Conductor*) were created to capture the imaginations of students and promote the idea that each profile is crucial to the social dimension of the group. They are exaggerated representations of particular design-based traits, and are by no means intended to limit or define individual acuities or to prevent members from utilizing their other skills and bases of knowledge.

Ideally, the four dominant profiles are distributed across an equal number of team members, resulting in groups of four design students each. In alignment with the research in psychology and theories of collaboration described earlier in this piece, this approach intends to support the value of identifying individual strengths as part of building team synergy to produce more temporally efficient and conceptually effective design projects. By allocating distinct responsibilities to each group member of a given design team, the model stimulates shared ownership for project outcomes and addresses (and helps prevent) skill-duplication or redundancy between team-members as a means to increase the working efficiency of the entire group. Clarity of purpose enables each student to focus on a particular goal, with discrete competencies often dominating different stages of the design process. For example, in the initial stages of the project, the *Dreamer* will likely play a significant role in brainstorming ideas whereas, towards the end of the project, the *Storyteller* may direct the presentation of the final work.

A Contextualized Description of the 16 Design Powers that Result from Operating the Design Powers System

In addition to the four overarching dominant design profiles (*Conductor, Storyteller, Tinkerer, Dreamer*), the *Design Powers System* supports a detailed description of an individual design student's unique Design Power. Two main dualities—reason/intuition and empathy/pragmatism—serve as the core components of an individual student's design profile, and the two additional dualities of abstract/concrete and internal/external determine additional variations within the overarching profiles. This yields a total of 16 possibilities described as *design powers* (these are depicted in Figure 4). In other words, by operating the *Design Powers System* on behalf of a particular design student to pinpoint a unique cluster of skills, talents, values, and attitudes, as well as communication and interaction methods, a unique *design power* can be identified. Examining each of the 16 powers can provide insight into some individual design student's strengths, as well as more specific clues about how he-or-she might perform in a group.

Four possible *design powers* exist under each of the four distinct design profiles (these are also depicted in Figure 4), and while these might share similar core dualities, they differ with regard to how they describe attitudes toward the outside world. For example, a *Wizard, Analyst, Developer* and *Director* all fall under the design profile of *Conductor* because their core dualities ('reason' and 'pragmatism') describe them as practical, detail oriented, analytical and logical. However, a *Director* is external and concrete, and therefore, may be

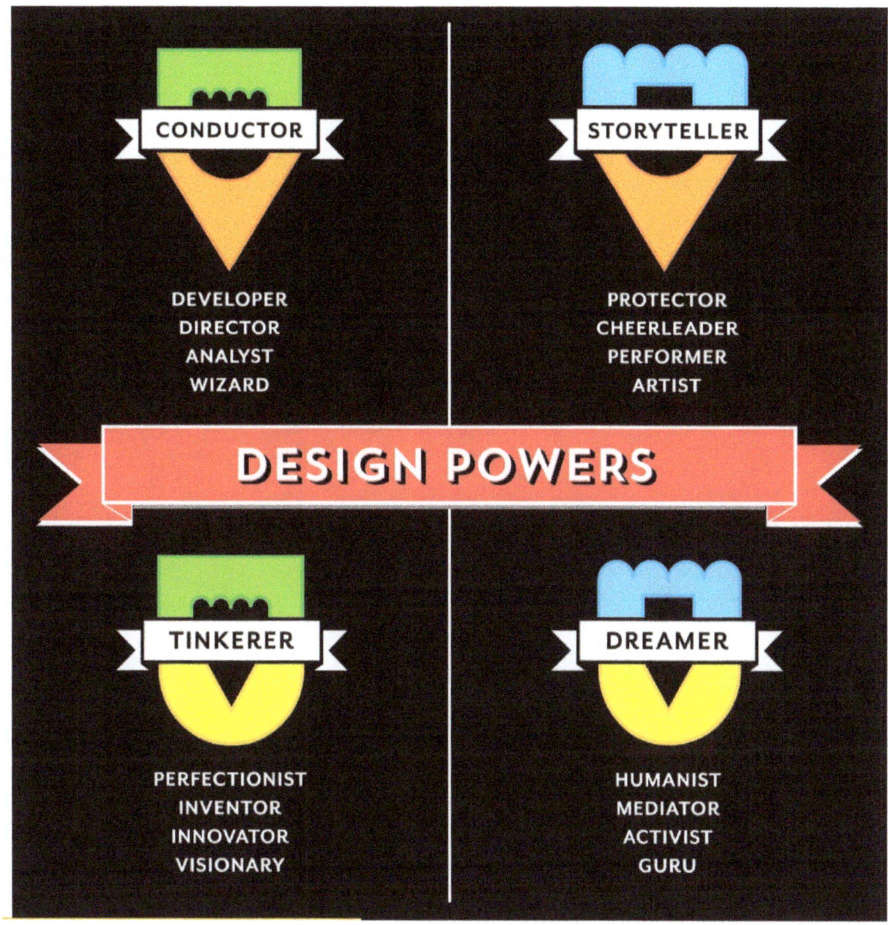

FIGURE 4: Each of the four dominant design profiles—*Conductor, Storyteller, Tinkerer,* and *Dreamer*—correlates with a group of four distinct *design powers.*

more suited to fulfill a role as an art director or a manager, while a *Wizard* is internal and abstract and may prefer to work as a programmer or developer.

While a detailed description of all 16 of these variations is beyond the scope of this paper, the following section provides an overview of the various classroom-based activities used to determine the four dominant design profiles and the 16 *design powers* that correlate with them.

A Description of the Operation of the Design Powers System

The operation of the *Design Powers System* constitutes three activities that progressively increase in complexity and structure. Each of these is centered on the identification of an individual design student's personality traits. By revealing a configuration of creative preferences, the three activities offer design faculty multiple entry points to help students build self-awareness and work in groups. Using one, or all, of the activities outlined below is an opportunity to help students take ownership of their unique combination of creative

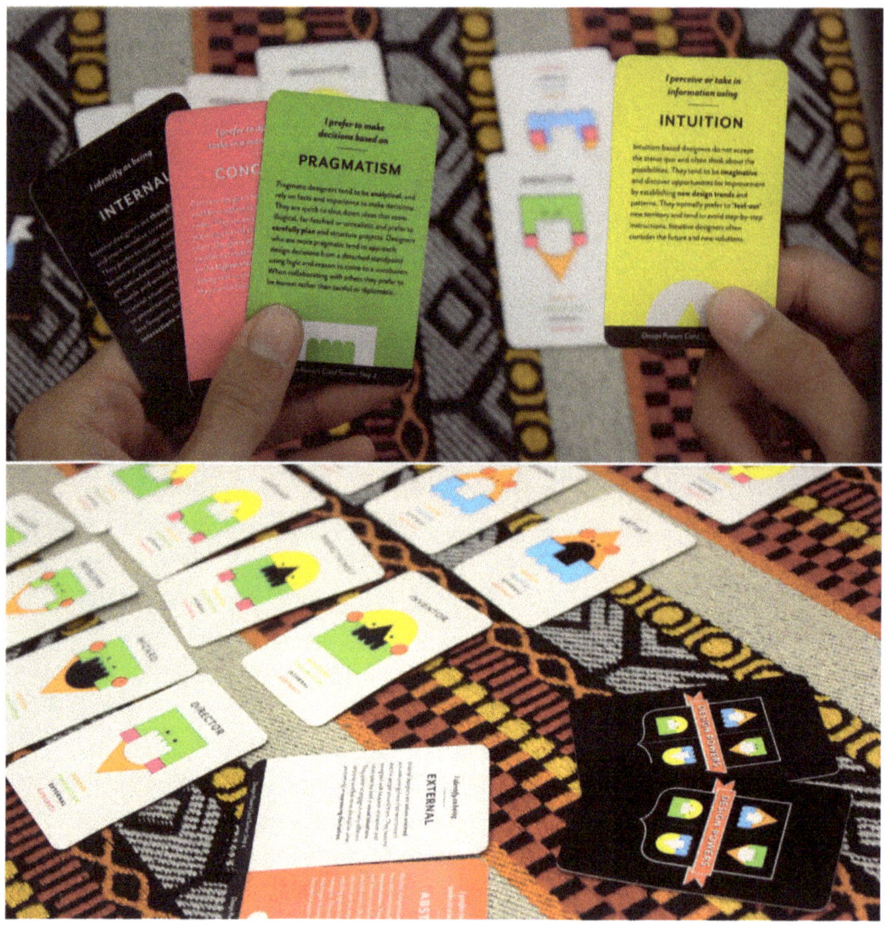

FIGURE 3: Operating the Design Powers Card Sorter affords individual student designers an opportunity to engage in a concrete, interactive activity with a specific goal. Doing this helps them work through the process of utilizing the four sets of design dualities to identify the specific design power from the group of 16 that is most applicable to them.

motivations to promote self-discovery and the accrual of a higher level of personal insight. These activities are often integrated into the preliminary phases of a collaborative project to familiarize the team with each member's acuities before they begin their design process together.

Activity One: Utilizing Discussion to Facilitate Self Identification

The first, and perhaps most simple of the three activities entails each student self-identifying with one of the four dominant design profiles: *Conductor, Storyteller, Tinkerer and Dreamer* (depicted in Figure 4). The activity is structured to extract, through conversation, observable dominant design preferences in individual design students. By introducing each of the four profiles through discussion, the in-class activity highlights how each dominant profile shapes an individual's role within a given group. As they engage in this activity, students discover where they fit on the design dualities continuum and participate in small group discussions about how their dominant traits align with their personal proclivities. While the four dominant profiles are not meant to serve as comprehensive, all-encompassing descriptions of a given design student's self-perception, they should resonate with him-or-her.

Activity Two: Operating the Design Powers Card-Sorters

The next evolution of the design profiles and *design powers* identification process is to utilize the *Design Powers Card-Sorter* as a fun and effective way to engage design students in identifying and realizing their uniquely personal means for engaging in design decision-making processes. The card deck that the authors created to operate the *Design Powers Card-Sorter* offers an interactive method to physically sort through the different design dualities inherent in the *Design Powers Wheel* using an "either-or" scenario (Figure 5). The cards are designed to help students make a choice between the design dualities that occupy each end of the spectrum, with each 'player' placing their choice "face up." This card sorting activity eventually reveals one of the 16 *Design Powers.* By identifying their personal proclivities (based on how a given individual design student prefers generally to think and act), the designer uncovers his-or-her unique power, such as *Cheerleader.* The card deck is sorted in the following order:

Step 1: Reason or Intuition
Step 2: Empathy or Pragmatism
Step 3: Concrete or Abstract
Step 4: Internal or External

Activity Three: Operating the Design Powers Questionnaire

The final, and more detailed activity of the *Design Powers System* is the *Design Powers Questionnaire.* This is a comprehensive method of analysis developed by the authors to help student designers identify their individual *Design Power,* from the group of 16. Much like questionnaires developed to assess personality by Myers-Briggs and Keirsey, this method of personality identification helps students discover their unique design preferences and motivations.

Administered as part of a classroom-based activity, design students choose their level of agreement or disagreement, on a 5-point Likert scale, in response to statements that capture the intensity of their attitudes towards various design-related scenarios. When administering the questionnaire, faculty should encourage design students not to provide any "neutral" answers and, instead provide their most typical response or feeling to the situation posed in the prompt or question (see the bulleted items in the "Sample Statements" section below). The questionnaire utilizes a series of statements measuring the four design dualities (*reason/intuition, empathy/pragmatism, concrete/abstract, internal/external*) that result in one of 16 design powers. The final score is calculated based on the following range: 1=disagree, 2=slightly disagree, 3=neutral, 4=slightly agree and 5=agree.

Sample statements include:

- *You are obsessive about checking Rotten Tomatoes for ratings before you see a movie.*
- *Your friend fell and broke her leg, and the first thing you ask is "How?" rather than "Are you OK?"*
- *You think that everyone's views should be respected regardless of whether they are supported by facts.*
- *You like to read and follow instructions before trying to put a new piece of furniture together.*

Faculty Observations and Student Reflections about Operating the Design Powers System to Affect Group Design Work

In the experience of the authors, group design work is sometimes viewed by graphic design students as an exceptional task that is unfair to some members of the team. In these instances, students take issue with what they define as an unequal distribution of the workload, varying levels of commitment by team-members, and biased assessment by faculty. In the anonymous surveys administered by the two faculty at the onset of this study, some students expressed hesitation about engaging in teamwork, noting that their previous experiences with team-based projects felt unproductive. One student also noted that she took the backseat during group projects due to predominating personality dynamics that she felt oppressed her ability to express her views. In light of these concerns, the *Design Powers System* was developed and tested in a range of graphic design courses over a three-year period, involving approximately 80 students located at Virginia Commonwealth University School of the Arts in Qatar. The cumulative findings indicate that facilitating acuity-based group creation as a team-building activity has the potential to improve communication among student design teams, bring students together around commonly identified, project-centric goals, and increase productivity.

The two faculty who formulated and operated this study observed that without the *Design Powers System* activities to guide group formation and operation, students were naturally drawn to their peers who possessed similar competencies, rather than to those who possessed competencies and skills that were complementary to their own. The system's emphasis on diversity helped prevent skill-duplication and allowed for a more balanced distribution of strengths within the group. Because the *Design Powers System* prioritized group decision-making, each student contributed equally to overall design decisions, but, at the same time, participated in the project according to their particular creative preferences. Students learned to depend on each other in more-or-less equal degrees as they realized how individual behaviors exhibited by some, directly and indirectly, influenced others. For instance, at the beginning of the project, the *Dreamer* and *Tinkerer* often guide out-of-the-box thinking and playful generation of creative ideas.

Moreover, the identification of a specific role for each individual helped students to better navigate areas of discord and potential conflict by recognizing when a team-member was acting in alignment with his-or-her design profile. For instance, one student felt that her occupation of leadership roles (during previous group projects) unfairly forced her to push along classmates. However, identifying as a *Conductor* helped her build confidence in her leadership qualities, while her team-members became more aware of and gained more understanding about the purpose of her management role. At the same time, this explicit role enabled another team-member to not feel "slighted" by the leadership power dynamic that sometimes manifests in this personality.

Leading the process was both challenging and rewarding, with both of the faculty members who designed and led the study needing to remain sensitive to student perceptions that one of the four distinct design profiles was potentially more, or less, valuable than another. Other challenges included students' attempts to resist, or control, the process. In one case, students self-identified with a false *Design Power* to create a group composed of friends, with clashing strong personalities and ambitious goals that culminated in conflict. The challenges of group dynamics increased when language barriers created communication obstacles, with an opportunity for cultural exchange ending in perceptions of isolation and frustration for one team-member. But beyond a few isolated incidents that resulted in some negative perceptions of collaboration, the two faculty members observed how the correct identification of a *Design Power* could serve as a powerful tool to guide teamwork. When introduced at the initial stages of a project, it proved to be a fun and engaging activity that boosted students' confidence and sense of purpose in terms of their design work in collaborative teams.

Limitations Inherent in the Structure of this Research

The *Design Powers System* is intended for use within a collaborative design framework and, despite promising findings, the study is limited in some key ways. First, the collaborative component of the study restricted teams to an equal distribution of design profiles and team-members. Future research will investigate the expansion of groups as part of a strategy to support projects that require greater use of a single competency. For instance, two *Tinkerers* might discover or invent the means to overcome a technical hurdle through extensive, experimental making, while two *Dreamers* might increase the number of 'big ideas' needed to address and effectively resolve a given design challenge. Two-person teams embedded within groups of five or six students might serve as mini-think tanks, helping to spur shared creativity.

Another limitation to the study was its locale. The research was conducted and tested within a single University in one region in one Middle Eastern country and occurred within a conventional graphic design curriculum. To be accurately assessed, the methodology utilized to facilitate the *Design Powers System* will eventually need to be operated and assessed in multiple classroom environments, across diverse types of curricula, and within a varied array of institutions of higher learning. While the *Design Powers System* addresses the development and refinement of personal creative preferences, bases of knowledge and skills needed for successful collaboration; contextual and geographic differences could produce unanticipated effects or result in unexpected successes or failures of the model. As is the case with many types of qualitatively guided approaches to design research, achieving a high level of external validity is not possible, but it should also be understood that this could be an impediment to implementation.

The next phase of this research will address the original study's limitations by calling for design educators to participate in user-testing and patterning in different types of university-level design education settings to evaluate the efficacy of the methodology across a wider spectrum of design learning environments. The integration of a measurement method as this next phase is operationalized could also help faculty assess particular collaborative components, operational dynamics, and relative strengths and weaknesses that may develop as a result of the interactions within a team (or as a result of contextual factors surrounding the team) that could affect its functionality. These include but are not limited to the social, economic and technological environments within which a given team operates.

Finally, the *Design Powers Questionnaire* should not be used to analyze, evaluate or comment on the personality-based weaknesses and strengths of individual design students. Instead, the aim of utilizing this instrument is to learn from the psychological approaches and the theories of collaboration described in this discourse to produce an accessible and useful tool for use in design environments in a variety of educational contexts. Moreover, utilizing the analogue format of the *Design Powers System* as a worksheet or card-deck has the potential to skew results, enabling participants to identify a given role for themselves or others by manipulating the process. Future versions of the *Design Powers System* could benefit by being operationalized through digital mediums to produce randomized ordering and to provide immediate feedback to designers without biasing key aspects of its use.

Future Directions and Implications for Further Development and Testing of the Design Powers System

Conceived to dispel the myth of the one-size-fits-all designer, the *Design Powers System* celebrates the value of both individual talent and diverse team-membership. Recognizing how personality (and the traits and temperaments that affect it) shape interactions between collaborators has practical implications for the facilitation of design education at the undergraduate and graduate level. The approach can serve as a guide for design educators to identify student acuities and to facilitate collaboration between different types of learners in design classrooms. Research attests to the capability of small groups, comprised of individuals who possess blended complementary skills, to effectively tackle complex projects. Guiding students to discover their strengths by de-emphasizing competition can also improve the overall productivity and effectiveness of teams. Accordingly, individuality and difference should not be viewed as sources of contention, but instead, celebrated as necessary for group success.

Encouraging emerging designers to better understand themselves and their design process through the assessment of design-based preferences offers the potential for team-members, including those who are working across disciplinary boundaries, to see design as a richly informed, deeply probative discipline with multiple facets for affecting change. The act of naming the diverse and extensive characteristics designers possess could bridge the persistent divide between the public's understanding of design and the capacity of designers to contribute to all aspects of a project's ideation, development, and resolution. Moreover, recognizing the diverse capacity of designers to contribute their ways of working and thinking across a wider variety of modes and mediums could expand preconceived notions about design research and processes. In other words, it could help dispel the myopic assumption that design is simply a service profession, associated with the digital execution of files. This may also help sensitize those outside of design, to recognize the contributions designers could make to socially and critically relevant projects that require inter-and-even-transdisciplinary collaboration. These implications support a complex, collaborative, and nuanced view of the design discipline that aims to fulfill more responsive social, environmental, and cultural purposes.

References

Barnbrook, J. et al. "First Things First Manifesto 2000." *AIGA Journal of Graphic Design*, 17 (1999): p. 2.

Baxter Magolda, M.B. *Making Their Own Way: Narratives for Transforming Higher Education to Promote Self-Development.* Sterling, VA, USA: Stylus Publishing, 2004: pgs. 7–12.

Boekraad, H., and J. Smiers. "The New Academy." European Journal of Arts Education 2, no. 1 (1998): pgs. 60–65.

Boney, P. *True Tilt: An Uncommon Quest.* Bloomington, IN, USA: Author House, 2010.

Buchanan, R. "Human-centered design: Changing perspectives on design education in the East and West." *Design Issues*, 20. 1 (2004): pgs. 30–39.

Buchanan, R. "Wicked Problems in Design Thinking." *Design Issues*, 8.2 (1992): pgs. 5–21.

"Comparison of Insights Discovery System to Myers-Briggs Type Indicator." pgs. 1–5. Online. Available at: http://www.inside-inspiration.com.au/

factsheets/insights-discovery-and-mbti-comparison.pdf (Accessed May 12, 2017).

Davis, M. et al. "AIGA Designer 2025: Why Design Education Should Pay Attention to Trends," *AIGA Design Educators Community,* 22 August, 2017. Online. Available at: https://educators.aiga.org/wp-content/uploads/2017/08/DESIGNER-2025-SUMMARY.pdf (Accessed February 4, 2018).

Dong, A., Kleinsmann, M., & Deken, F. "Investigating Design Cognition in the Construction and Enactment of Team Mental Models." *Design Studies,* 34.1 (2013): pgs. 1–33.

Douglas, M. "A History of Grid and Group Cultural Theory." University of Toronto, Toronto, Canada, 2007. Online. Available at: http://projects.chass.utoronto.ca/semiotics/cyber/douglas1.pdf (Accessed May 12, 2017).

Findeli, Alain., "Rethinking design education for the 21st century: Theoretical, methodological, and ethical discussion." *Design Issues* 17.1 (2001): pgs. 5–17.

Friedman, K. "Models of Design: Envisioning a Future Design Education." *Visible Language,* 46.5 (2012): pgs. 132–153.

Gibson, M.R. & Owens, K.M. "Making meaning happen between 'us' and 'them': strategies for bridging gaps in understanding between researchers who possess design knowledge and those working in disciplines outside design." In *The Routledge Companion to Design Research,* edited by J. Yee and P. Rodgers, pgs. 386–399. Routledge, NY, NY, USA: 2015.

Gratton, L., & Erickson, T.J. "Eight Ways to Build Collaborative Teams." *Harvard Business Review,* November 2007. Online. Available at: https://hbr.org/2007/11/eight-ways-to-build-collaborative-teams (Accessed May 12, 2017).

Heller, S., & Talarico, L. "An Education Manifesto for Icograda" in *Icograda Design Education Manifesto 2011,* Taipei: International Council of Graphic Design Associations, edited by A.G Bennett & O.

Vulpinari, 2011: pgs. 82–85. Online. Available at: http://www.ico-d.org/database/files/library/IcogradaEducationManifesto_2011.pdf (Accessed May 12, 2017).

Hunt, J. "Icograda Design Education Manifesto" in *Icograda Design Education Manifesto 2011,* Taipei: International Council of Graphic Design

Associations, edited by A.G Bennett & O. Vulpinari, 2011: 86-89. Available at: http://www.ico-d.org/database/files/library/IcogradaEducationManifesto_2011.pdf (Accessed May 12, 2017).

Katzenbach, J., & Smith, D. *The Wisdom of Teams: Creating the High-Performance Organization.* New Boston, MA, USA: Harvard Business Review Press, 2015.

Keirsey, D. *Please Understand Me II: Temperament, Character, Intelligence.* Del Mar, CA, USA: Prometheus Nemesis Book Company, 1998.

Kolko, J. *Wicked Problems: Problems Worth Solving: A Handbook & A Call to Action.* Austin, TX, USA: ac4d, 2012.

Patton, B., & Downs, T. *Decision-Making Group Interaction: Achieving Quality,* 4th Edition. Boston, MA, USA: Pearson, 2002.

Peeters, M., van Tuijl, H., Reymen, I., & Rutte, C. "The Development of a Design Behavior Questionnaire for Multidisciplinary Teams." *Design Studies,* 28.6 (2007): pgs. 623–643.

Richardson, R., & DeVaney, T. "The Development and Validation of a Personality Instrument to Increase Collaboration." *Educational Research and Reviews,* 3.4 (2008): pgs. 121–127.

Rock, D. "SCARF: A Brain-Based Model for Collaborating with and Influencing Others." *NeuroLeadership Journal,* 1.1 (2008): pgs. 44–52.

Rock, D., Davis, J., & Jones, B. "Kill Your Performance Ratings." *Strategy+Business,* 8 August, 2014. Autumn 2014, Issue 76. Online. Available at: http://www.strategy-business.com/article/00275?gko=c442b (Accessed July 19, 2017).

Rosen, E. *The Culture of Collaboration: Maximizing Time, Talent and Tools to Create Value in the Global Economy.* San Francisco, CA, USA: Red Ape Publishing, 2007.

Sawyer, K. *Group Genius: The Creative Power of Collaboration.* New York, NY, USA: Basic Books, 2008.

Tieger, P., Barron, B., & Tieger, K. *Do What You Are: Discover the Perfect Career for You Through the Secrets of Personality Type.* New York, NY, USA: Little, Brown and Company, 2014.

"The Tilt Leadership Model: Conscious Leadership to Create Innovative Performance." *Brainard Consulting,* 2010: pgs. 1-16. Online. Available at: http://www.brainardconsulting.com/wp-content/uploads/2010/02/The-Tilt-Leadership-Model4.pdf (Accessed May 12, 2017).

Turner, J., Oakes, P., Haslam, S., & McGarty, C. "Self and Collective: Cognition and Social Context." *Personality and Social Psychology Bulletin,* 20.5 (1994): pgs. 454–463.

Van Leeuwen, J., van Gassel, F. & den Otter, A. "Teaching Collaborative Design." In *Proceedings of the International Workshop on Construction Information Technology in Education,* 7 September 2004 Istanbul, Turkey, 2004: pgs. 1–9.

Winterhalter, B. "ISTJ? ENFP? Careers Hinge on a Dubious Personality Test." *The Boston Globe,* 31 August 2014. Online. Available at: http://www.bostonglobe.com/opinion/2014/08/30/istj-enfp-careers-hinge-dubious-personality-test/8ptUGXhu6DndFdjCngcxSN/story.html (Accessed January 19, 2017).

Biographies

Denielle Emans, an Associate Professor at Virginia Commonwealth University School of the Arts in Qatar, has spent 14 years navigating a diverse career path between research and design in higher education and practice. She is passionate about bringing social innovation and intercultural communication together to fuel creative action. Professor Emans' principal area of concentration involves investigating and analyzing participatory and collaborative design methods, with attention to the inclusion of diverse voices as part of the planning and operationalization of the design process. She is currently a Ph.D. Candidate at the Centre for Communication and Social Change at the University of Queensland in Brisbane, Australia. She holds a Master's degree in Graphic Design from North Carolina State University's School of Design and a Bachelor of Arts in Communications from the University of North Carolina, Chapel Hill. (*djemans@vcu.edu*)

Basma Hamdy is a research-based designer, author and educator producing work that explores historical, political and social issues. Her book *Walls of Freedom: Street Art of the Egyptian Revolution,* written in collaboration with Don Karl, was published in March 2014 (Berlin, Germany: From Here to Fame Publishing). She is currently working on her second book *Khatt: Egypt's Calligraphic Landscape* (London, UK: Saqi Books; to be published in October 2018). Professor Hamdy earned an MFA from the Maryland Institute College of Art and is

a Ph.D. candidate at PhDArts: Leiden University and The Royal Academy of Art (KABK), The Netherlands. She has taught at the University level for over 14 years and is currently an Associate Professor of Graphic Design at Virginia Commonwealth University School of the Arts in Qatar.
(*bwhamdy@vcu.edu*)

Dialectic Volume II, Issue I: Research Paper

Energetic Alpha: Co-Designing a Tool that Encourages Three- to Six-Year-Olds to Develop Handwriting Skills

AOIFE MOONEY,[1] MARIANNE MARTENS,[2] AND GRETCHEN RINNERT[3]

1. School of Visual Communication Design, Kent State University, OH, USA
2. School of Information, Kent State University, OH, USA
3. School of Visual Communication Design, Kent State University, OH, USA

SUGGESTED CITATION: Mooney, A., Martens, M., & Rinnert, G. "Designing Energetic Alpha: A Research-Based App to Support the Teaching and Practice of Letter-Writing." *Dialectic,* 2.1 (2018): pgs. 201-238. DOI: http://dx.doi.org/10.3998/dialectic.14932326.0001.308

Abstract

The bedrock of our communication remains rooted in our alphabet—the ultimate confluence of concept, sound, and image in a systematic code. This paper documents the research and prototype design of an iPad app—*Energetic Alpha*—in the service of teaching three- to six-year-old children to write. Examining the decision-making processes that guided the development of this interdisciplinary project highlights opportunities and challenges for designing interactive and flexible technology for a young audience. The authors discuss the approaches and decision-making strategies and methods that shaped their research and design decision-making processes as they developed this app.

Energetic Alpha is neither intended as a prescriptive tool nor as a replacement for classroom tasks. Instead, it can supplement classroom exercises and practice materials and enhance a three- to six-year-old child's confidence and familiarity with letter writing, letter sounds and the alphabet. In this article, the authors trace the trajectory of their interdisciplinary project's goals and design process and reflect on key insights and pivotal decisions that shaped their thinking as the project progressed. They also highlight opportunities and challenges that they observed in this area of study that may constitute worthy pathways for future research, with particular regard to designing interactivity and typography for children in and across new media formats.

keywords:

Children, Co-Design, Digital Media, Handwriting,
Interaction, Interface Design, Type Design

Energetic Alpha:

Co-Designing a Tool that Encourages Three- to Six-Year-Olds to Develop Handwriting Skills

AOIFE MOONEY, MARIANNE MARTENS, & GRETCHEN RINNERT

Introduction and Context

"The important thing is to know and to teach that handwriting, not the computer, is a root of democracy and rational thought." [1]

In elementary-level curricula across the U.S. and Europe, there have been attempts to shift the focus from teaching cursive to teaching typing. [2] One such attempt in the U.S. came in the form of the

2010 Common Core State Standards. [3] These academic standards, which were adopted by forty-two states, stipulate what children are required to know at the end of each grade and emphasize the teaching of typing skills over handwriting. According to the standards, students should "...'demonstrate sufficient command of keyboarding skills' by fourth grade but they were required to teach students 'basic features of print' only in kindergarten and first grade. Cursive was left out entirely." This new curricular change indicated that in the states adopting the Common Core State Standards, public schools would reduce the overall time for teaching handwriting to two years, essentially limiting instruction to basic print (unconnected) letterforms and curtailing the teaching of cursive (joined) handwriting." [4]

The main argument in favor of diminishing the role of cursive handwriting asserts that the ubiquity of digital media and the requirement for

1 Baudin, F. "Education in the Making and Shaping of Written Words," in Computers and Typography, edited by Rosemary Sassoon. Oxford, UK: Intellect, 1993, p. 127.

2 Ujifusa, A. "Resistance to the Common Core Mounts," Education Week, 28 April, 2014. Online. Available at: http://www.drmichelson.org/web_documents/resistance_to_the_common_core_mounts_-_education_week.pdf. (Accessed February 4, 2018).

3 "About the Standards," Common Core State Standards Initiative. Online. Available at:http://www.corestandards.org/about-the-standards/ (Accessed February 27, 2018).

4 Trubek, A. "Opinion | Handwriting Just Doesn't Matter," New York Times, 20 August, 2016. Online. Available at: https://www.nytimes.com/2016/08/21/opinion/handwriting-just-doesnt-matter.html (Accessed February 28, 2018).

printed or screen-based typographic presentation of content makes the ability to write well in cursive redundant.[5] This trend can be seen internationally as well: in 2014, Finnish schools replaced teaching cursive with teaching typing.[6] *It is the position of the authors that this overall reduction in time spent on learning handwriting erodes the connection between concept and form that is fundamental to the acquisition of this language learning code.*[7]

Although this elementary-level teaching trend directly affects the teaching of cursive rather than its precursor, 'print' handwriting, the authors contend that such policy decisions by legislative bodies governing children's education constitute a shift toward demoting the acquisition of fine-motor and cognitive skills in favor of acquiring digital literacies and competencies. The authors believe these decisions highlight an underlying bias, which demonstrates a willingness to jettison long-practiced, fine-motor skills that are associated with children's cognitive development. Instead, we believe that the digital environment and new media can serve as possible teaching tools to support and enhance the teaching of manual writing skills.

As people learn to write, they learn to sort and recognize myriad of nuanced shape variations of individual letters (and the phonemes they signify) in whatever alphabet they are attempting to learn. This process allows them to learn to identify letterforms by a range of characteristics. They assimilate the structures and the differentiating features of each letter to make a mental model of the concept (rather than the concretely defined shape) of an 'a'. Reading and writing serve in equal measures to shape and reinforce the various methods children use to make meaning,[8,9] and then to interpret and ultimately codify their perceptions of the world.

Following a summit convened in 2012 titled *Handwriting in the 21st Century?*,[10] the United States Board of Education published a policy update that countered the trend toward teaching typing in lieu of teaching cursive handwriting,[11] citing a body of research amassed over the course of the previous 15 years. The research upon which this policy update was based articulated the benefits of teaching cursive as a means to help children develop cognitive abilities, literacy, brain development, memory, and self-expression, as well as benefits that children with disabilities accrue if they learn to write by hand. Research described in 2013 by *The New York Times* and *The Washington Post* on the longer-term educational benefits of teaching cursive also directly questioned this trend and suggested that being deprived of the cognitive skills developed

5 Kysilko, D. "The Handwriting Debate," National Association of the State Boards of Education Policy Update 19.7 (2012). Online. Available at: https://www.hw21summit.com/media/zb/hw21/H2989_NASBE_PolicyUpdate_TheHandwritingDebate.pdf (Accessed February 1, 2018).

6 Must, M. "Schools Will Start Teaching Typing Instead of Longhand," Helsinki Times, 20 November, 2014. Online. Available at: http://www.helsinkitimes.fi/finland/finland-news/domestic/12767-schools-will-start-teaching-typing-instead-of-longhand-2.html (Accessed January 28, 2018).

7 Berninger V., et al., "Early Development of Language by Hand: Composing, Reading, Listening, and Speaking Connections; Three Letter-Writing Modes; and Fast Mapping in Spelling," Developmental Neuropsychology 29.1 (2006), pgs. 61–92.

8 McLuhan, M. The Gutenberg Galaxy: The Making of Typographic Man. Toronto, CA: University of Toronto Press, 2011.

9 Wolf, M. Proust and the Squid. New York, NY, USA: Harper, 2008.

10 Saperstein Associates. "Handwriting in the 21st Century? An Educational Summit." White Paper. Columbus, Ohio: Saperstein Associates, 2012. Online. Available at: www.hw21summit.com/media/zb/hw21/H2948_HW_Summit_White_Paper_eVersion.pdf (Accessed March 5, 2018).

by learning to write in cursive can negatively affect a student's learning experiences as they progress through the American K–12 education system. [12,13]

In the United States, learning to read and write are prioritized as a means to teach young children to communicate over learning to do this by painting, drawing, and reading visuals. The United States' educational curriculum from kindergarten through twelfth grade does not typically prepare most individuals with the skills necessary to create or read visually communicative or expressive work. [14] The authors hypothesize that, as a result of this, the ability of many American children to effectively progress their educational experiences from concrete learning (using images and visuals) to abstract learning (using symbols, letters and numbers) is significantly inhibited. This, combined with the increasing prevalence of digital media (and pressure to teach K–12 students to use it) in many American elementary, middle and high school classrooms, as well as at home, led the authors to identify a need and an opportunity to *support and extend* the teaching of traditional hand skills, such as print handwriting, in these learning environments. To test this premise, they chose to design, implement, test, and then develop a touch pad application that could help introduce 'print' (unconnected) handwriting to three- to six-year-old children in a small scale, applied design research project.

Typically, the teaching of cursive, or letters that are physically joined together by connecting strokes, follows the teaching of print handwriting. Print letterforms are the foundational forms for handwriting in the Latin script and are formed as individual units that do not formally connect. The essential forms that constitute print handwriting are simpler than those of cursive and are built out of simple strokes consisting of straight lines, diagonals and circular movements for letters like 'c' or 'o.' Cursive handwriting extends these print stroke behaviors to make the letters connect. This form of handwriting is more complex because it requires the child to consider and then effectively execute not just the strokes that build the identifiable parts of a given letterform, but also the correct position from which to make connections to the next one. Additionally, the child must learn new, alternate forms for the letters they have previously learned to write in their unconnected context, such as the lowercase 'f' or 'r,' which differ in form in each of these handwriting models.

Learning print handwriting initiates the process whereby children learn to write in school and/or with their parents, and the authors felt that, due to this fact, it should also be the starting point for this applied design research project. To test our hypothesis with as few variables as possible, we designed

11 Kysilko, D. "The Handwriting Debate." National Association of the State Boards of Education Policy Update 19.7 (September 2012). Online. Available at: https://www.hw21summit.com/media/zb/hw21/H2989_NASBE_PolicyUpdate_TheHandwritingDebate.pdf (Accessed November 7, 2017).

12 Shapiro, T. R., "Cursive handwriting is disappearing from public schools." Washington Post. Online. Available at: https://www.washingtonpost.com/local/education/cursive-handwriting-disappearing-from-public-schools/2013/04/04/215862e0-7d23-11e2-a044-676856536b40_story.html?utm_term=.3ed9342e706b (Accessed November 7, 2017).

13 Asherson, S. B., "The Benefits of Cursive Go Beyond Writing," The New York Times, 30 April, 2013. Online. Available at: https://www.nytimes.com/roomfordebate/2013/04/30/should-schools-require-children-to-learn-cursive/the-benefits-of-cursive-go-beyond-writing (Accessed November 7, 2017).

14 Kress, G. R. and van Leeuwen, T. Reading Images: The Grammar of Visual Design. New York, NY, USA: Routledge, 1996.

an app to help preschool age students (between 3- and 6-years-old in the U.S.) become more familiar with hand-formed letters, and to help them recognize words in this print handwriting model. We did not conduct investigations regarding how the affordances of this learning tool might affect the children's construction of more complex cursive script due to time and resource limitations. It is also our intent to address this area of research and development in a future project.

By following a *goal-directed design process*, as described by Cooper, Reimann & Cronin in their seminal book on interaction design titled *About Face, The Essentials of Interaction Design*, we acknowledged that a designer or a design team must learn *why* their users might engage in a given experience to accomplish a particular goal or reach a specific aspiration. Ascertaining this would also require us to understand what types of experiences they find appealing and rewarding. [15] We know that young children are entertained and engaged by iPad applications and touchpad interfaces. [16] Our goal was to create an app that was educational and that would support the playful exercise of letter-writing and the synthesis of visual and verbal language skills. The user group for this applied design research endeavor was comprised of preliterate learners, as well as their educators, caregivers, and parents. For the purpose of this research, we defined 'preliterate' children as young (roughly 3- to 6-years-of-age), non-readers who have not yet assimilated any type of writing code and who are gaining early familiarity with the shapes and behavior of the alphabet in representing sounds, or phonemes, and combining them into meaningful units (words and simple sentences).

To facilitate the development and testing of our ideas, we designed an iPad app called *Energetic Alpha*, which is a learning tool that uses interaction and motion to engage preliterate children in handwriting practice. It was the result of a collaborative research project undertaken between three university-level educators specializing in different areas, including: typeface design and typography, children's literature and new media formats, and motion and interaction design. Our team also included an iOS developer who coded and produced the interface and back-end functionality of the app, a photographer who was part of the motion design team and documented our co-design process in still images and video, and a doctoral student who assisted with field notes.

Creating Technology that Supports Traditional Handwriting Practice

15 Cooper, A, Reimann R. & Cronin D., About Face 3 The Essentials of Interaction Design, Indianapolis, IN, USA: Wiley Publishing, Inc., 2007: p. 25.

16 Rosin, H. "The Touch-Screen Generation," The Atlantic, 15 March 2013. Online. Available at: https://www.theatlantic.com/magazine/archive/2013/04/the-touch-screen-generation/309250/ (Accessed April 18, 2018).

"The instructions of the teacher consist then merely in a hint, a touch—enough to give a start to the child. The rest develops itself." —Maria Montessori, Ph.D. [17]

Our first step involved a critical examination of existing apps designed to teach children the alphabet as well as those that instruct children in basic skills such as recognizing shapes, numbers and colors. We found that many apps designed for early learners are difficult for children to use, do not hold children's attention, or have little to no educational value. In contrast, traditional writing worksheets and booklets offer educational value and practice space but they lack engagement and motivational features that digital technology is able to provide in the form of rewards, music, entertainment and participatory play. Our team decided to create an iPad application to encourage children to practice traditional handwriting. Children are enamored and encouraged in digital environments, specifically those with touch pad interfaces. The immediacy of the feedback paired with colorful graphics and sound create the perfect platform to capture their attention. Subsequently, we reviewed the scholarly literature as described next.

Review of the Literature

The literature review that framed and supported this applied design research project is categorically divided into these four areas: 1) *handwriting in context;* 2) *a review of issues related to designing typography for children;* 3) *educational research;* and 4) *an evaluation of extant children's apps.* These topics subsequently support the formulation of our research methodology, which is described later in this piece.

Handwriting in Context

Handwriting has significant value and impact on the development of student writing skills. "If children cannot form letters—or cannot form them with reasonable legibility and speed—they cannot translate the language in their minds into written text. Struggling with handwriting can lead to a self-fulfilling prophecy in which students avoid writing, and see themselves as not being able to write, and fall further and further behind their peers." [18]

In their comprehensive scholarly survey of handwriting research conducted between 1980 and 1994, Graham and Weintraub outline the findings of a multitude of studies on pre-school and school-aged children describing how

17 Montessori, M. Montessori's Own Handbook. New York, NY, USA: Schocken Books Inc., 1965: p. 59.

18 Graham, S., "Want to Improve Children's Writing? Don't Neglect Their Handwriting," American Educator, 76.1 (2010): pgs. 49–55. Online. Available at http://www.aft.org/sites/default/files/periodicals/graham.pdf. (Accessed March 5, 2018).

they responded to prompts to write or draw by doing so interchangeably because they perceive the practices to be interwoven.[a,19] In an increasingly networked and digitally mediated world, digital devices are a part of a workflow of activities—including standardized testing—that occurs in most classrooms in the United States and other Group of 20 (G20) nations. Twenty-first century education of children ages 3 to 18 in these areas of the world is facilitated by an abundance of graphically packaged inputs.[20] As Graham describes, the mechanical act of writing develops cognitive abilities that allow us to give form to ideas confluent with our thoughts and to interpret the visual forms of letters derived from a broad range of sources, which leads to visual fluency with the alphabet. In the parts of the world that have regular access to the internet and therefore where there is a plethora of digital media, it is easy to overlook the role handwriting plays in the development of cognition or to view manual skills like cursive handwriting as being outdated. In developing Energetic Alpha, we aimed to use the affordances of digital media as a tool to enhance, rather than subordinate, the role of the manual handwriting practice.

[a] *Graham and Weintraub summarized their findings on the confluence of writing and drawing among these groups of children as follows: "Thus, as often as not, these students' compositions combined writing and drawing in unconventional ways. They also frequently interchanged the terms drawing and writing, particularly writing for drawing, when describing the composing act. This did not appear to be a consequence of being unable to distinguish writing from drawing, but probably represented overlapping definitions for the processes involved in the two acts (e.g., creating objects for others)".*

A Brief Overview of Issues Related to Designing Typography for Children

British graphic designer, author and Pentagram co-founder Alan Fletcher once described typography as "the alphabet in a straightjacket."[21] By this he meant that the typographic forms of the alphabet are more systematized and rational than those produced by the hand. Typefaces are systems of shapes with repetition and modularity inherently built into the design of the letters. This differs from letters created by even the most systematic of writers whose nuance is influenced by the pressure and movement of their hands and fingers. When Gutenberg placed cast, metal letters of the Latin alphabet onto moveable metal plates, he established a process for rationalizing and systematizing the shapes and spaces within and between letters and the 'lines' of words created from them. These conventions for arranging letter and word shapes and the spaces between them continues to affect design decision-making to this day. Typographic letterforms and numerals are distinct from handwritten symbols in the sense that they use repeating, identical symbols to produce a body of text, and are without the idiosyncrasies, errors, and variation derived from the inherently manual practice of handwriting commonly seen in written text. The authors survey of typography and typographic systems intended to facilitate children's reading and writing revealed that there is a limited range of typefaces

19 Graham, S. & Weintraub, N. "A Review of Handwriting Research: Progress and Prospects from 1980–1994." Educational Psychology Review, 8.1 (1996): pgs. 7–87.

20 Chetty, K., Josle, J., Gcora, N., Aneja U., & Vidisha, M. "Bridging the Digital Divide: Skills for the New Age," G20 Insights, 13 October, 2017. Online. Available at: https:// http://www.g20-insights.org/policy_briefs/bridging-digital-divide-skills-new-age/ (Accessed April 19, 2018).

21 Fletcher, A. Beware Wet Paint. New York, NY, USA: Phaidon Press, 2004.

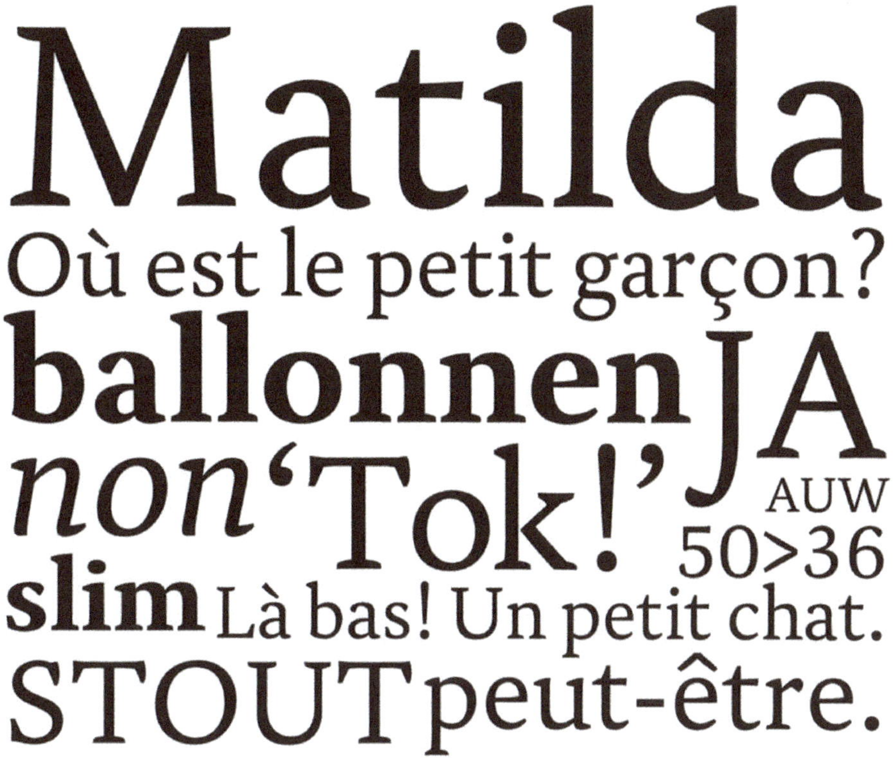

Matilda
Où est le petit garçon?
ballonnen JA
non 'Tok!' AUW
50>36
slim Là bas! Un petit chat.
STOUT peut-être.

FIGURE 1: *Matilda,* designed by Ann Bessemans in 2014, is an example of a typeface explicitly designed for children. Online. Available at: https://typography.guru/journal/legibility-children/ (accessed March 12, 2018).

suggested for use in these contexts for an audience of (mostly) three- to six-year-old children. When presented in typographic form, the configurations of individual letters and words are governed not only by the archetype they describe, but also by typographic conventions.

The appearance of individual letters also vary according to the genre of the type into which the typeface might fit. For example, the multiple forms of a sans serif 'a,' whether it be a glyphic sans, a humanist sans or a geometric sans, all deviate from and constitute a refinement of the natural form of the letter as created by the movement of a hand. The underlying modularity of any typeface, in which the letters are governed not just by the archetype, but by system-wide shape behaviors, indicates that there is a "...split between the constructed and the organic"[22] forms of the letters.

To better understand the context of typography for children, the authors surveyed typefaces explicitly designed for children, as well as research projects that described the considerations involved in designing typographic systems, layouts, and typefaces for them. A common result, or outcome, of these research projects was often a typeface. These typefaces were also used

22 Carter, M. "Theories of Letterform Construction (Part 1)." Printing History, 13-14.1/2 (1991-1992): p.1.

ABCDEFGHIJKLMNOPQRSTUVWXYZ
abcdefghijklmnopqrstuvwxyz

The quick brown fox jumps over the lazy dog.

FIGURE 2: *Fabula* was created by a design team led by Sue Walker. The *Kidstype Project,* based at the University of Reading, UK, and more formally titled *"The Typographic Design for Children"* aimed to "find out how typography can help children's reading." Online. Available at: http://kidstype.org/?q=node/49 (accessed March 5, 2018).

to showcase the research project's findings and to illustrate the embodiment of what the author considered to be "best practices" in typefaces designed for young children. These vary from examples like serif offerings such as *Matilda,* "a research-based font for improving reading" (Figure 1), which emerged from Ann Besseman's *Readsearch* legibility project, [b] to the sans serif pencil forms of the *Fabula* typeface (Figure 2), which resulted from the *KidsType* [c] project that was formulated and operated at the University of Reading in the United Kingdom.

Typographic researcher and designer Juliet Shen's *Early Bird* typeface (Figure 3) was developed for Oxford University Press in 2005 [d] and shares formal similarities with traditional, uncomplicated sans serif typefaces like Paul Renner's *Futura* (often used in children's texts) and Eric Gill's *Gill Sans Infant* (Figure 4) [23] in its use of basic geometric forms and simple in-strokes and out-strokes. [e] Another example of. Typeface designed for use by young readers is the *Heinemann Special* collection of types (Figure 5), which were also produced in consultation with "children, literacy advisors, teachers of special needs/dyslexia, and primary school teachers," and were tested over a period of 8 years. [f] Similarly, the *Twinkl* fonts (Figure 6) were developed for educational use and in consultation with teachers. [24] The *Twinkl* Handwriting Font is one of the few families found by the authors that was designed specifically to facilitate the process of learning to write among young children. It was developed in the UK in 2016 "with teachers and industry experts, the *Twinkl* Handwriting Font is aligned with the National Curriculum guidelines to aid the development of handwriting for children of all age groups." [25]

[b] *The Readsearch Project, based in Hasselt University in Holland, is a research group focused on so called 'reading research', and, according to their website, "explores borders of legibility for several target groups' including but not limited to 'dyslectic readers, beginning readers, readers with visual impairment,' " and others.* Bessemans, A. "Matilda: A Research-Based Font for Improving Reading." Filmed 17 May 2013. TYPO Talks Berlin, Germany, 46:20. Online. Available at: https://www.typotalks.com/videos/matilda-a-reasearch-based-font-for-improving-reading-2/ (Accessed November 7, 2017). Matilda was designed by Ann Bessemans in 2014. Online. Available at: https://typography.guru/journal/legibility-children/ (Accessed March 5, 2018).

[c] *The Kidstype Project, based at the University of Reading, UK, and more formally titled "The Typographic Design for Children," aimed to "find out how typography can help children's reading."* Walker, S. "Kidstype." 2005. Online. Available at: http://kidstype.org/ (Accessed March 5, 2017).

[d] *Earlybird was designed by Juliet Shen in 2005. Earlybird was developed for use by Oxford University Press in primary level publications and is not commercially available for purchase.* Shen, J. "Typography and Graphic Design." Juliet Shen (blog). Online. Available at: http://www.julietshen.com/typography-and-graphic-design (Accessed July 24, 2017).

23 Gill, E. "Gill Sans Infant" typeface family, designed by Eric Gill between 1928–30 and published by Monotype. Online. Available at: https://www.fonts.com/font/monotype/gill-sans-infant (Accessed March 5, 2018).

Earlybird Regular, *Italic*, **Bold** and ***Bold Italic*** ©Juliet Shen 2007

There was an old woman who lived in a shoe.
She had so many children she didn't know what to do;
She gave them some broth without any bread;
Then whipped them all soundly and sent them to bed.

012
345
678
910
6÷3=2
½ ¼ ¾

&&

Shall we read together at 2 o'clock?

Let's play ball at recess!

ABCDEFGHIJKLMN
OPQRSTUVWXYZ
ÀÅÉÎÕabcdefghijklm
nopqrstuvwxyzàåéîõ
&1234567890($£.,!?)

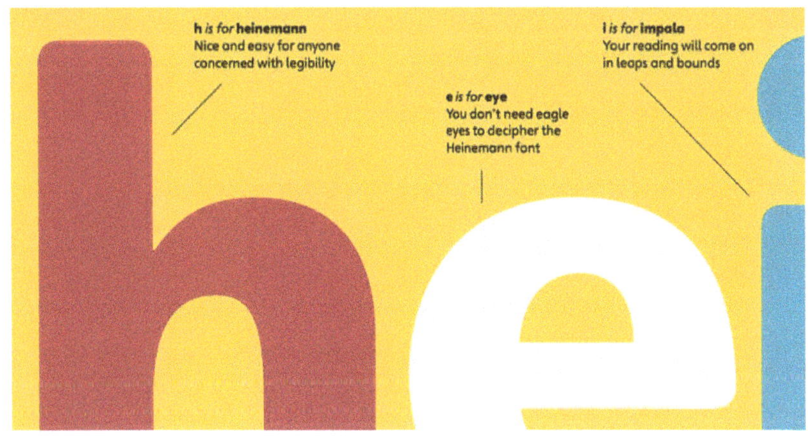

Twinkl Font

Be kind to yourself, you're doing wonderfully.

The quick brown fox jumps over the lazy dog.

AaBbCcDdEeFfGgHhIiJjKkLlMmNnOoPpQqRrSsTt
UuVvWwXxYyZz0123456789

Available in 3 weights

Bold	**Be kind to yourself, you're doing wonderfully.**
Regular	Be kind to yourself, you're doing wonderfully.
Thin	Be kind to yourself, you're doing wonderfully.

TOP TO BOTTOM:

FIGURE 3: Juliet Shen designed the *Earlybird* typeface family on behalf of Oxford University Press. It was designed to be used in their primary level publications.

FIGURE 4: British type designer Eric Gill designed Gill Sans Schoolbook, now known as Gill Sans Infant, in 1931 with the intent to have it be used in language teaching, children's books and school texts.

FIGURE 5: The *Heinemann Collection* was designed by the in-house design team at Heinemann Publishing Company, 2008. http://www.myfonts.com/fonts/fw-heinemann/heinemann/ (accessed March 5, 2018).

FIGURE 6: The *Twinkl* Handwriting Font was designed by Twinkl in 2016. http://www.twinkl.com/twinkl-font (accessed July 24, 2017).

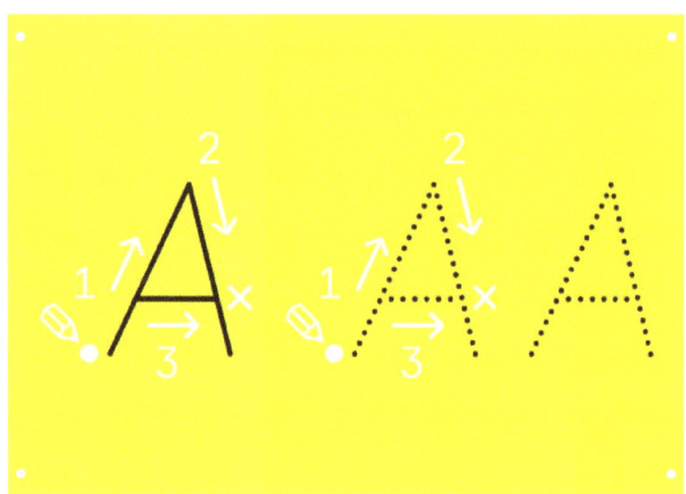

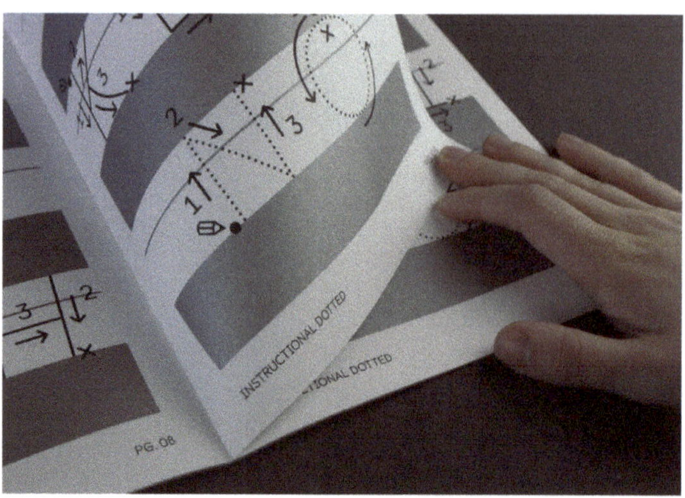

FIGURE 7: The *Castledown Instructional Typeface Family* was designed for use among young children learning to write and read at the *Castledown Primary School* in the United Kingdom. The typeface comes with three levels of instructional cues that direct students how to write letters in the proper stroke order. https://www.colophon-foundry.org/typefaces/castledown/ (accessed March 12, 2018).

The scholarly literature regarding the design and implementation of these typefaces suggests that the majority of the studies and research processes that informed their designs centered on improving the *reading* experience of the early reader, rather than explicitly developing typographic forms and systems that could function as means to bridge the gaps between learning to write and read handwriting and learning to read typography. Notable exceptions include the recent *Castledown Instructional* family published in 2014 by *Colophon* in the UK (Figure 7),[g] which is directed toward the teaching of handwriting, and the long-established *Sassoon Primary* family (Figure 8).[h] Both of these include what is called an 'instructional' style where the letter-writing movements are made explicit. First designed and published in 1985 by Rosemary Sassoon, Sassoon Primary is perhaps the most versatile and extensively researched example of a typeface that, although it was developed to facilitate reading among early readers, is comprised of shapes and styles across the full family that cater to teaching both reading *and* writing. This includes the 'instructional' style, which functions to indicate the order in which the strokes should be formed as well as the movements required to create them.

Sassoon Primary also includes a 'semi-serif' style, which presumably was designed with the aim of familiarizing children with typographic forms and helping them transition from rendering letterforms manually to reading them typographically. The technology that facilitates type design and usage has evolved considerably since the development of *Sassoon Primary* in 1985, and

[e] *The terms 'in-stroke' and 'out-stroke' describe shapes formed in the manual formation of letterforms. Sans serif typefaces often show no indication of this letter formation characteristic, shedding the manual or 'organic' influence in favor of adhering to the typeface system. An in-stroke is the shape formed by a stroke that begins a letterform, such as a slight curl in the top left of an n, following the behavior of the pen. An out-stroke is the shape formed by a stroke that exits a letterform, or completes it, such as that in the lowercase 'a' of Gill Sans Infant, shown here.*

[f] *The Heinemann Special Fonts collection was designed were designed in 2008 by the in-house design team of Heinemann educational publishing "to reate a highly legible font family for reading books and literacy products."* We and the Color, "Heinemann Special Fonts Collection." Online. Available at: https://weandthecolor.com/heinemann-special-fonts-colection/29643 (Accessed March 5, 2018).

Teachers at last now have
a typeface that links the teaching of reading and the teaching of handwriting

Standard letterforms in Infant fonts have the looped k and q with exit stroke, essential preparation for later joining of letterforms

ÆŒABCDEFGHIJKLMNOPQRSTUVWXYZ&

æœabcdeffifighiijklmnopqrstuvwxyzß

1234567890£$ƒ¢¥%*¶·

.,:;!?'"""„()[]/-–—_«»‹›|\+=÷±'"°@©®™

ÅÄÁÀÂÇËÉÈÊÏÍÌÎÑÖÓÒÔÕØÜÚÙÛŸ

åäáàâãçëéèêïíìîñöóòôõøüúùûÿ

Alternative letterforms in Infant fonts for educators

G I J & b f k q t t ß 1 4 7 9

A large type size, such as 250 point, can be used for 'finger tracking' exercises. Starting points for letters can be indicated in colour and arrows added to show the direction of strokes. The letterforms can be reproduced larger and in outline for tracking exercises.

Letters up to A4 size can be printed to make a frieze for the wall. All this can easily be done on a computer enabling parents and teachers to develop their own professional-looking handwriting material to suit their chosen policy, either alphabetically or in stroke related families as above.

The larger dots show starting points. Where there is only one large dot, the fingers or pen don't leave the page until the letter is finished...

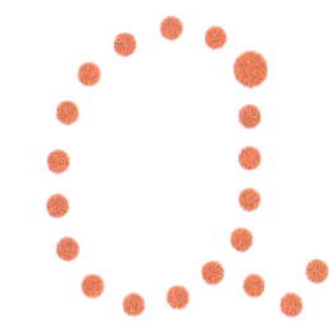

FIGURE 8: The *Sassoon 'Infant' Type Specimen* was designed for and with children. During their study, Sassoon and Williams found that children prefer slight slants, sans serif typefaces, exit strokes, and enhanced ascenders and descenders. Source: *Why Sassoon? Sassoon & Williams,* 1985-2015 http://www.sassoonfont.co.uk/fonts/sas/WhySassoon1.3.pdf (accessed July 24, 2017).

[g] *Colophon Type Foundry. "Castledown Instructional Family." 2012–2014. Online. Available at: http://www.colophon-foundry.org/typefaces/castledown/ (Accessed July 24, 2017). The Castledown Instructional Family is one part of a larger family of typefaces developed between 2012 and 2014 by The Entente and later released by the Colophon Type Foundry for use within the Castledown Primary School, in Hastings, UK. The whole family is designed with young children learning to write as well as to read in mind, but the instructional set of typefaces includes prompts for the children designed to help them negotiate the tasks inherent in forming individual letterforms. This functionality is built into the design of the typeface, which includes small scale icons and drawings within the font itself, using Open Type features to turn the styles on and off—a good example of type design being used in service of this important area, and one that is made more important in the context of writing applications designed for touch-screen use, where the adaptability of digital fonts must be effectively harnessed.*

[h] *The Sassoon Primary Typeface family was originally designed in 1985 and was intended to meet the needs of young children who were learning to both read and to write.* Sassoon, R. & Williams, A. "Why Sassoon?" Online. Available at: http://www.sassoonfont.co.uk/fonts/sas/WhySassoon1.3.pdf (Accessed July 24, 2017).

this has helped speed up the design and production of typefaces. Additionally, these technological developments, which include the introduction of innovations such as the *Open Type* format for intricately scaling computer fonts by the *Microsoft Corporation*, have facilitated the development of typefaces that can include a much higher level of formal variability. This includes but is not limited to facilitating the deployment of alternate characters that support end-user customization, depending on the context within which they are used. However, the innovative research and useful tools that were formulated and operated during the design processes that yielded the design of *Sassoon Primary* have not been expanded upon in ways that (as of this writing in the spring of 2018) would allow for a wide variety of alterations in early writing and reading classrooms.

An Overview of How the Authors' Educational Research Informed the Design of Energetic Alpha

While there are a wide variety of apps intended to teach and entertain young children on offer in the App Store of the Android and iOS platforms, there are limited resources for evaluating them. Librarian Claudia Haines has designed an app evaluation rubric,[26] which consists of eleven questions and focuses on both user experience and content. Using Haines' rubric for guidance and taking inspiration from educational theorist Maria Montessori, who advocated for young learners to have parameters rather than prescriptions to guide their approaches to solving learning problems,[i] we created a typographic and iconographic interface that supports young users and encourages haptic learning. We employed Cooper's principles for harmonious interactions,[j] and combined these with the basic elements of gameplay (i.e., interactivity, choice, feedback, rules, and rewards)[27] to create a gender-neutral context of use for the interface we designed that conveys authority and stability to parents while engaging children with play. We supported these approaches by deploying a bright color palette across our systems of interface components. Montessori's pedagogical philosophies of sequential and multisensory experience also influenced our research approaches and interaction design strategies, as we hoped these would allow children to "develop prelinguistic and preliteracy skills [...] for the development of symbolic language spoken and written."[28]

This multi-sensory experience was reflected in our design decision early on to expand the functionality of the app from a more entertainment-based focus (video watching only), to requiring the young children who comprised our user groups to interact with the various letters and numerals presented within our interface design by tracing them on the screen. In this way, we created a learning tool that relied on facilitating actual gameplay rather than one that relied on facilitating a gamification-based approach (Deterding et al. define "gamification" as "the use of game design elements in non-game contexts;" gamification also implies that competition between players or participants, often abetted by scoring, is a key aspect of the experience).[29] According to Nicholson, educational contexts can be gamified by adding "points, levels, and achievements."[30] However, Nicholson describes a downside to gamification as users shift their focus away from playful elements of game-like qualities and onto extrinsic values such as earning points and increasing scores. We wanted to ensure that *Energetic Alpha* offered children a haptic and visually guided learning experience on a digital platform that necessitated hand movements that would mimic those involved when writing on a paper substrate. This was also done as a means to ensure that they would develop cognitive abilities similar to those necessary to write effectively on paper. According to Tekinbas, "The promise of game-based learning lies in the premise that the technology provides an efficient and effective tool with which to replace a points-based extrinsic motivation system with a contextualized hands-on learning experience."[31]

The design and functionality of the *Energetic Alpha* interface playfully challenges a child to learn to create the series of marks (or strokes) necessary

[i] *In Dr. Montessori's Own Handbook, she describes the duty of a teacher as that of facilitator, who encourages self-reliance and independent problem solving. Developing parameters for identifying and framing problems is emphasized over mandating prescriptions for "solving" them.*

[j] *The design followed the principles Cooper et al describe for designing harmonious interactions: "1. Follow users' mental models. 2. Less is more. 3. Enable users to direct; don't force them to discuss. 4. Keep tools close at hand. 5. Provide modeless feedback. 6. Design for the probable; provide for the possible. 7. Provide comparisons. 8. Provide direct manipulation and graphical input. 9. Reflect object and application status. 10. Avoid unnecessary reporting. 11. Avoid blank slates. 12. Differentiate between command and configuration. 13. Provide choices. 14. Hide the ejector seat levers. 15. Optimize for responsiveness; accommodate latency."* Cooper, A, Reimann R. & Cronin D., About Face 3: The Essentials of Interaction Design, Indianapolis, IN, USA: Wiley Publishing, Inc., 2007; p. 203.

24 Twinkl Handwriting Font. Online. Available at: http://www.twinkl.com/twinkl-font (Accessed July 24, 2017).

25 Ibid.

26 Claudia Haines, Evaluating Apps and New Media for Young Children: A Rubric, (2015). Online. Available at https://nevershushed.files.wordpress.com/2015/01/evaluatingappsandnewmediaforyoungchildrenarubric1.pdf. (Accessed March 28, 2018).

27 Salen, K. and Zimmerman, E., Rules of Play: Game Design Fundamentals. Cambridge, MA, USA: MIT Press, 2004.

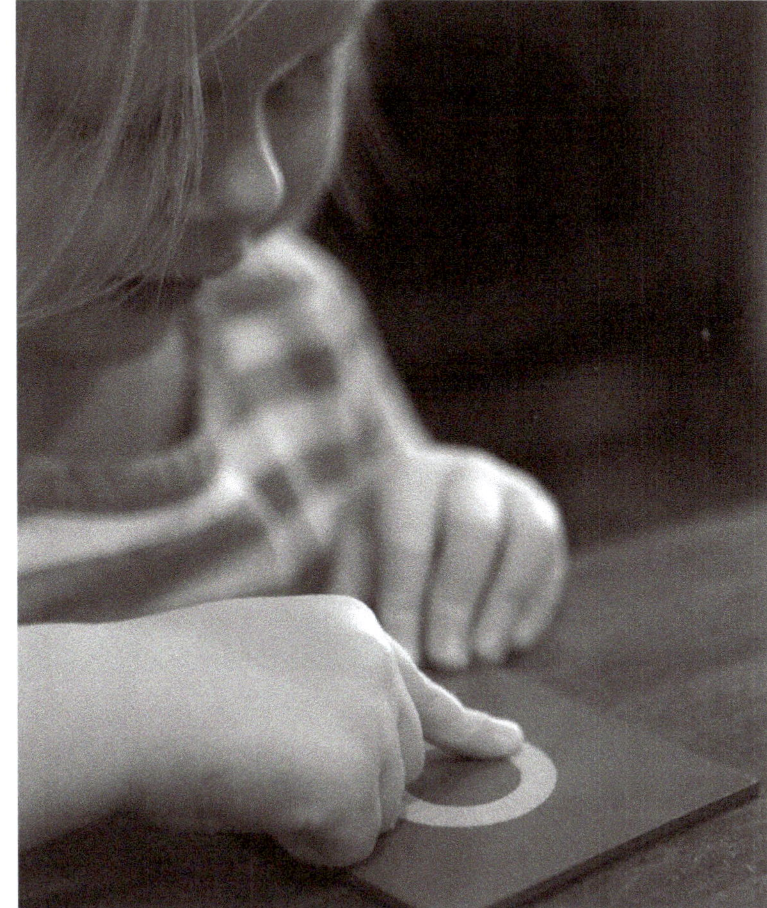

FIGURE 9: This young child is engaging in the Montessori teaching method of "sandpaper letters" to use tactile, auditory and vision senses to familiarize herself with how individual letters are formed and sound. This method is often operationalized as a "pre-reading" exercise. Source: Rinnert, G., 2018.

28 Richardson, S. E. "The Montessori Preschool: Preparation for Writing and Reading." Annals of Dyslexia 47 (1997); p. 255. Online. Available at http://www.jstor.org/stable/23768103. (Accessed May 5, 2017).

29 Deterding, S., Khaled, R., Nacke, L. E., and Dixon, D. "Gamification: Toward a Definition" in Proceedings of the CHI Conference, Vancouver, BC, Canada, May 2011. Online. Available at: http://gamification-research.org/wp-content/uploads/2011/04/02-Deterding-Khaled-Nacke-Dixon.pdf (Accessed March 5, 2018).

30 Nicholson, S. "A user-centered theoretical framework for meaningful gamification." Paper presented at Games+Learning+Society 8.0, Madison, WI (2012). Online. Available at: http://becauseplaymatters.com/pubs/ (Accessed October 30, 2017).

31 Tekinbas, K. S. "Getting in the Game." In Mindshift Guide to Digital Games and Learning, edited by J. Shapiro, p. 9. New York, NY, USA: The Joan Ganz Cooney Center, 2014. Online. Available at: https://a.s.kqed.net/pdf/news/MindShift-GuidetoDigitalGamesandLearning.pdf (Accessed October 30, 2017).

to write a given letter correctly. Doing this unlocks the playing of an animation that visually and verbally articulates a verb that begins with the corresponding letter ("a = appear," "m = melt," and "s = slither"). The child sees the visual demonstration and then hears the narrator say: "B is for Build." In the context of this research project, our goal was to embed the tasks of recognition, shape-composition, reading, experiencing, and hearing as interrelated and mutually reinforcing while providing a multisensory (auditory, visual, and tactile) experience for each child user. This "tracing-while-hearing" approach differs from the traditional 'copying' approach found in the teaching of handwriting. It more closely aligns with the combination of haptic, auditory and visual processes that children utilize when they work with Montessori's 'sand-letters' (Figure 9), where children follow the shape of a given sandpaper form with their fingertip and receive haptic feedback from the friction created by the sandpaper texture as they do this. This approach is also advocated by the popular learn-to-read website, Reading Rockets, which encourages the child to create sweeping movements with the whole arm rather than just the hand to encourage conceptual learning of the letter's structure. [32]

By requiring manual handwriting skills to be practiced in the digital learning environment facilitated by *Energetic Alpha*, we aimed to harness the affordances available within it to provide more engaging, multi-sensory writing exercise options to early learners. We also hypothesized that this might expand the possibilities for how writing might be taught most effectively and help us critically interrogate current practices. There are multiple approaches for teaching children to write letterforms by dissecting them into ordered strokes. To align with common educational practice, we chose to take a hybrid approach to stroke order prompts, combining the *Handwriting Without Tears* (HWT) [33] and the Zaner-Bloser [34] models. HWT has been established in the U.S. since 1977 and Zaner-Bloser since 1888 and both are widely used.

A Critical Evaluation of the Extant Array of Children's Teaching and Learning Apps

The team reviewed Apple's App Store for learning-to-write alphabet apps during the initial research phase by using Claudia Haines' rubric for assessing the quality of apps designed primarily for use by children. [35] We found that, despite receiving positive reviews from a wide variety of mostly non-academic, not critically educated or trained assessors, many of the existing apps were poorly designed in terms of how their combinations of typography and imagery were configured. They often ignored basic, two-dimensional design principles (among them: establishing contrasting relationships between key formal elements, using negative spaces effectively, and achieving balance and emphasis effectively). Many of them also tended to flout many essential User Interface (UI) conventions, such as using common UI elements consistently, strategically using color and texture, and using typography to create hierarchy and clarity. More specifically, problematic design issues among these apps included a lack of negative space (i.e., the available "screen real estate" was overcrowded), poor visual spacing among letterforms, or color palettes that vibrated. Often, animations and interactions were devoid of contextual meaning, and instead of supporting learning among their child users and audiences, served instead as distractions to the task at hand. Other apps lacked or omitted the types of crucial feedback scenarios and error prevention that young users often need to ensure that the goals of a particular learning scenario are met. These types of

32 Spear-Swerling, L. "The Importance of Teaching Handwriting." Reading Rockets, 22 August, 2006. Online. Available at http://www.readingrockets.org/. (Accessed March 12, 2018).

33 Authors(s) unknown. "Handwriting Without Tears." Research Review, 27 January 2015. Online. Available at: https://www.lwtears.com/files/HWT%20Research%20Review.pdf (Accessed March 5, 2018).

34 Authors(s) unknown. "Pre-kindergarten Handwriting." Zaner-Bloser website. Online. Available at: https://www.zaner-bloser.com/products/index.php?product=handwriting (Accessed March 5, 2018).

35 Haines, C. "Evaluating Apps and New Media for Young Children: A Rubric." Online. Available at: https://nevershushed.files.wordpress.com/2015/01/evaluatingappsandnewmediaforyoungchildrenarubric1.pdf) (Accessed July 24, 2017).

36 Wickremasinghe, M. "The Movable Alphabet App." Mobile Montessori. Online. Available at: http://www.mobilemontessori.org (Accessed March 7, 2018).

UI-based problems often cause children (and adults) to get stuck in so-called interface loops, which inhibit or prevent their ability to move forward or progress in skill-level within a portion of a given app. As these negative experiences continue, frustration levels rise, particularly among children.

Looking specifically at apps that use the *Montessori Method* [k] as the foundation of their interaction, we reviewed Mobile Montessori's *The Movable Alphabet App,* [36] and Montessorium's *Intro to Letters.* [37] Mobile Montessori's *The Movable Alphabet App* was specifically designed to support the development of writing in younger children. However, unlike the tracing functionality that is designed as an inherent functional feature in *Energetic Alpha*, *The Movable Alphabet App* does not utilize interactive movements that directly connect form and movement.

An app that does share our approach is Montessorium's *Intro to Letters,* [38] which operates like a touch-screen version of sandpaper letters and uses the sound of chalk on a blackboard to imitate the feedback a child receives during a manual handwriting experience. In evaluating *Intro to Letters* specifically, we found that while it incorporated in-app recording features, letter pairings, and audio playback, rewards for completing a task did not exist, and children had no additional motivation to move forward in the application or to continue playing. Additionally, the app's navigation is confusing to both children and parents. In *Intro to Letters*, the rewards for the child's accuracy in tracing are limited to audial feedback and linear progression to the next part of the application. In this sense, *Energetic Alpha* expands the possibilities of the medium by incorporating ideas of practice, play, and exploration throughout the interface and the animations, and empowers users rather than prescribing tasks. By focusing on the properties of movement, touch, and free-form learning of the Montessori school, *Energetic Alpha* highlights opportunities for interactive app and typeface design to function in ways that meet the essential needs of its early childhood learners. The knowledge the authors gleaned from their abbreviated review of literature and their assessment of extant early writing facilitation apps led us to articulate and explore the set of research questions that are described in the next section of this piece.

The Research Questions that Guided Our Methods for Designing Energetic Alpha

We sought to find out how a game-based learning tool could exercise letter writing skills for young children while encouraging "meaningful play." [l] By

[k] *The Montesssori Method" allows an individual three- to six-year-old child to make personal choices relative to what he/she is interested in learning about or from within a given learning environment with the supportive guidance of a teacher. Lessons and materials are adapted to what are referred to as "sensitive periods, or windows of opportunity" along a given child's learning trajectory. Learning through sensory-motor activities and working in situations with materials that allow them to develop their cognitive powers through direct experience—seeing, hearing, touching, tasting, smelling, moving—allows children to both self-construct and absorb knowledge.*

[l] *We define both games and meaningful play using Salen and Zimmerman's definition from their book Rules of Play. They define a game as, "a system in which players engage in artificial conflict, defined by rules, that result in quantifiable outcome." They define meaningful play as something that, "in a game, emerges from the relationship between player action and system outcome; it is the process by which a player takes action within the designed system of a game and the system responds to the action. The meaning of an action resides in the relationship between action and outcome."* Salen, K. and Zimmerman, E. Rules of Play: Game Design Fundamentals. Cambridge, MA, USA: MIT Press, (2004). Unit 1 Summary, pgs. 28–115.

[37] Montessorium. Online. Available at: https://montessorium.com/ (Accessed July 27, 2017).

[38] Ibid.

incorporating something pre-literate children enjoy using (touch-pad interfaces) and connecting it to something they need to learn, we wanted to know if we could effectively engage children to participate in a tedious but required learning activity using an entertaining screen interface. This led us to formulate the following questions.

1) What does the context of direct interaction with a letterform through touch-screen tracing tell us about the relationships between the typographic and handwritten forms of given letters in teaching preliterate children to write and read? What unmet need does this reveal among the current offerings of typefaces available for children's reading?
2) By reflecting on the relationship between the typographically and manually rendered forms of letters, how could our work inform the development of new typefaces intended to help pre-literate children learn to write and read?
3) Specifically, what specific aspects of a given typeface make it easy or difficult for children to recognize and recreate letterforms and words in written form, i.e., what formal typographic characteristics are most crucial to rendering typographic elements—like letters—in a digital environment in ways that would be most helpful to children attempting to learn to write and read? (Such characteristics could include but are not limited to typographic weight, utilizing serif or sans-serif typefaces, employing in-strokes and out-strokes, employing single-story vs. two-story forms of specific letters, and relative contrast between the stroke weights of particular typefaces.

The next section describes the methods we used to address our research questions.

An Analytical Description of our Research Methods

After reviewing the contemporary offerings of typefaces designed for children (outlined in the section *"A Brief Overview of Issues Related to Designing Typography for Children"* earlier in this piece), we chose to use a typeface to use during the facilitation of our initial pilot study that possessed some of the formal characteristics of type designs that are often advocated for use in children's

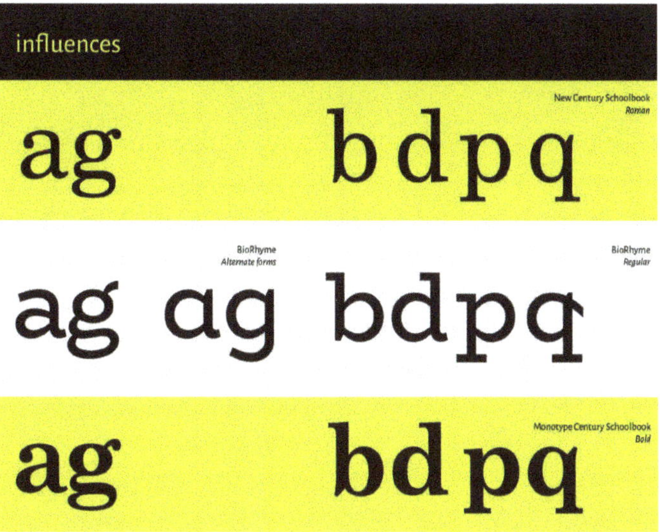

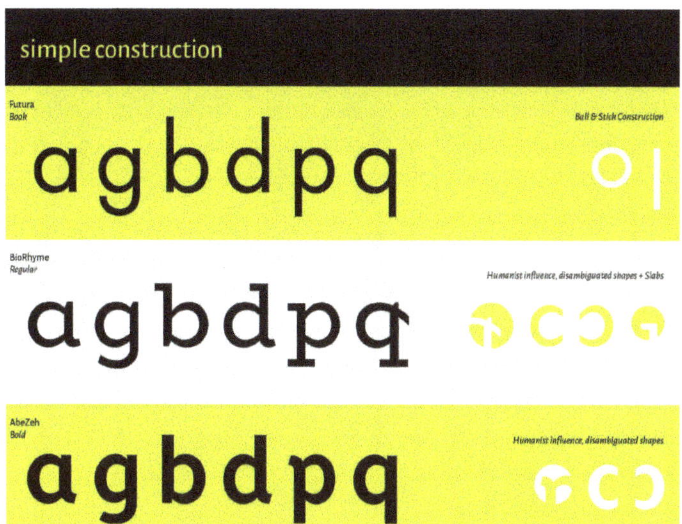

FIGURES 10A: (Left) This illustration depicts how the design of the typeface *Bio-Rhyme* has been influenced by *Century Schoolbook*.Source: Mooney, A. 2016.

FIGURES 10B: The *BioRhyme* typeface as compared to *Futura* and the final typeface choice for implementation in *Energetic Alpha—AbeZeh*. Source: Mooney, A. 2016.

texts. *BioRhyme*, a typeface created by co-author Aoife Mooney, was influenced by the warmth and didactic feel of Morris Fuller Benton's *Century Schoolbook* (Figure 10a). Century Schoolbook was developed to incorporate the results of research [m] into the typographic needs of children and was used extensively in the first half of the twentieth century in texts set for children who were learning to read. *BioRhyme* also echoes the 'simplified' construction of Paul Renner's *Futura* (Figure 10b), which is often used for the 'ball-and-stick' construction advocated and discussed by practitioners and teachers writing about the teaching of handwriting in the early part of the twentieth century. [39] It is a monolinear family of typefaces imbued with generous apertures, large counters, and straightforward and uncomplicated letter structures.

Compared to the typographic shapes found in reading material intended for consumption by adults, letterform structures that are used to teach children to *write* are (generally) simplified in terms of their formal characteristics. Letters such as "a" and "g" are typically depicted as single-story forms in contexts where they might be encountered by young children learning to write, as well as in situations that involve attempts at early reading. Typefaces designed or adapted for children will often feature exit strokes and alternate type characters and more cursive variants of forms for letters like the "k" and "e." *BioRhyme* also incorporated these formal features (Figure 11), which sought to reflect the action of the hand in creating a pen stroke. [40]

[m] *In his 1919 design of the typeface Century Schoolbook, Morris Fuller Benton incorporated what had been reported as "best practices for the design of letterforms intended for young for children" that had been advocated by the British Association for the Advancement of Science in a report they issued in 1913 that was based on research conducted by faculty at Clark University.*

39 Walker, S. "Letterforms for Handwriting and Reading: Print Script and Sans Serifs in Early Twentieth-century England." In Typography Papers, 7 (2007): pgs. 81–114.

40 Sassoon, R. "Through the Eyes of a Child–Perception and Type Design," in Computers and Typography, edited by R. Sassoon. Oxford, UK: Intellect, 1993.

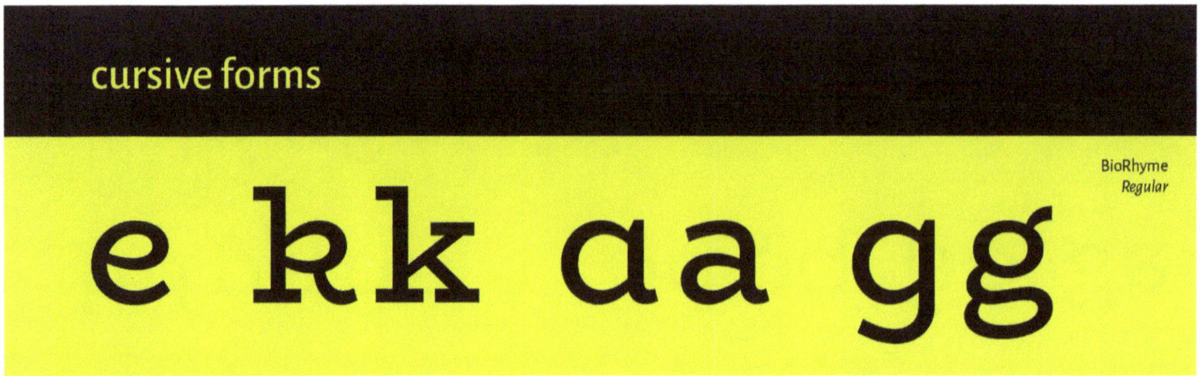

cursive forms

e kk aa gg

BioRhyme
Regular

FIGURE 11: *BioRhyme:* Examples of cursive and alternate forms of BioRhyme characters. Source: Mooney, A. 2016.

Having established the initial look, feel, and basic interactivity of our app, we involved a total of 20 members of our target audience and user group—young children—as co-designers in the process as described in the User Studies detailed in the next section of this piece.

The Effects of User Studies on Design Decision-Making in the Development of Energetic Alpha

Scholarly work by Druin [41] and Sanders [42] on co-design and co-creation [n] informs our study. Dr. Druin is the founder of the International *Children's Digital Library* at the University of Maryland, which was designed in part by allowing children to make creative contributions to the decision-making processes that informed its development. Dr. Sanders is an Associate Professor at The Ohio State University and the founder of *Make Tools.* Her writings on co-design techniques, tools, and methods provided much of the foundational literature for participatory design and co-design strategies. As we designed *Energetic Alpha,* we operationalized co-creative methods that included pre-literate children (20 in all) as our design processed progressed to create an end-product that supports their needs. By incorporating feedback from children in the user studies that guided the development of our prototypes, we were able to develop and design a much more useful and usable set of interactive experiences for them. This strategy facilitated both user testing and user designing. We incorporated storyboard sketching focused on ideation of possible reward animations. Children were also asked to help design the sounds for the app by providing comments on chimes and buzzer sounds for user feedback and by helping to choose music for the app.

[n] *John Chisholm of Design for Europe describes co-design as approach to creative practice that grew out of the participatory design techniques that originated in Scandinavia in the 1970s. It is an approach to designing that relies on processes that, "... enable a wide range of people [including those who have not been to design school] to make a creative contribution to the design process... A key tenet of co-design is that users, as 'experts' of their own experience, become central to the design process."* Excerpted from Chisholm, J. "What is Co-Design," Design for Europe, 8 September 2016. Online. Available at: http://designforeurope.eu/what-co-design (Accessed April 28, 2018).

41 Druin, A. "What Children Can Teach Us: Developing Digital Libraries for Children with Children." The Library Quarterly, 75.1 (2005): pgs. 20-41.

42 Sanders, E. "Co-creation and the new landscapes of design." CoDesign: International Journal of CoCreation in Design and the Arts, 4.1 (2008): pgs. 5-18.

We gained valuable input from these activities as we engaged in the iterative processes that guided the development of the app. Overall, we operated a total of four user studies including a pilot study. The pilot study allowed us to test the design of our initial typeface, *BioRhyme*, and its overall readability among pre-literate and newly literate children. The first iterative studies allowed us to test the technical functionality of the app, provide error prevention and correction, and observe the overall response from children. Initially, as the children tested the app, it crashed repeatedly within a single testing session. Because of this, the app had to be completely recoded and rebuilt by our developer. The second iterative study incorporated co-design methods by engaging children in designing the rewards and sounds that were associated with the completion of particular tasks. This allowed us to imagine what a child would want to see and engage with while practicing their writing of individual letters. It also allowed us to test the functionality of the interface and the animation as a reward structure. Finally, we tested the app with pre-school and kindergarten teachers at Kent State University's *Child Development Center.* Their feedback helped us make design adjustments within the app, which will be addressed in future research.

The user studies we conducted with children each followed a similar structure: 1) participants were given semi-structured interviews (questions are available in Appendix A); 2) participants were asked to provide feedback by sketching out design ideas and improvements on iPad shaped paper; and 3) participants had an opportunity for free play with the app. Ethnographic field notes [43] were taken during each study, which allowed us to capture other activity that was occurring in the room during testing, such as how parents were interacting with their children (or not), and descriptions of what other children (such as younger siblings) were doing during the study, which might have distracted the test subjects.

The initial study sought to test the viability of several aspects and elements that were incorporated into the design of the app our approach to designing it. These included using a serif typeface in specific sizes, and critically examining details of the interactive behaviors that the child might experience during a usage experience. Additionally, we assessed the overall user experience and understandability of the app with our child subjects, and incorporated children's input as co-designers. Our approaches were rooted in the principles of user-centered design in that feedback from our young participants was allowed to influence the design of *Energetic Alpha.*

43 Emerson, R.M., Fretz, R. I., & Shaw, L. L., Writing Ethnographic Fieldnotes, Second Edition. Chicago, IL, USA: University of Chicago Press, 2011.

44 Montessori, M. Dr. Montessori's Own Handbook. New York, NY, USA: Schocken Books, Inc., 1965, p. 109.

Study	*Particpant*	*Description*
Visual Communication and Industrial Design	Two children ages 7 and 10	1) Free play with app 2) Interviews 3) Children made suggestions for improvements to the app on iPad shaped paper 4) The researchers facilitated a follow-up interview to gather children's suggestions 5) Many of the ideas gathered were incorporated into the app's design.
Co-Design Session 1	Four children ages 4-6; and six children ages 7-11	1) Free play with app 2) Conducted one-on-one interviews 3) Children made suggestions for improvements to the app on "app" shaped paper 4) The researchers facilitated a follow-up interview to gather children's suggestions 5) Many of the ideas gathered were incorporated into the app's design
Co-Design Session II	Five children aged 4-6; and nine aged 7-11	1) Children completed Task Booklets 2) Children made suggestions for improvements on iPad shaped paper
Teacher Study	Two pre-kindergarten teachers and one kindergarten teacher at Kent State's Child Development Center	Interviewed teachers in a focus group within a small school conference room. No children were present. 1) Discussed general writing curriculum in schools, and their personal strategies 2) Introduced Energetic Alpha and allowed free play with app 3) Received feedback and suggestions on how the app could be improved.

TABLE 1: Description of user studies.

For the second user study, we developed a two-part task booklet. The first part was designed to capture the children's initial feelings about using the app while giving the authors (and app co-creators) a way of assessing how its functionalities affected the children's overall user experience. To accomplish

Overview of Tasks

Pg	Letters	Sound	Animations	Studying
5	E			Testing Trace Hints and Navigation
5	L/l			
6	J/j			
7	Co-Design Activity #1, Animation A: Storyboarding			
8	Q/q	X		Testing Trace Hints and Navigation
8	W/w	X		
9	Y/y	X		
10	Co-Design Activity #2, Sound			
11	A Stop Motion	X	X	Facial Responses Questions about Preferences
11	D Video	X	X	
12	M, B or G Time Lapse	X	X	
12	K, P, C, S or X Vector	X	X	
13	F, H Hand drawn	X	X	
14	Co-Design Activity #3, Animation Comparison			
15	Follow Questions			
16	Type Study			

contents

PAGES	LETTER	STUDYING
2-3	p	impact of removal of instroke on recognizability and construction
4-5	p	does the instroke help with recognition of letter and construction?
6-9	p	does the instroke help the child identify the letter amongst other letters?
10-13	p	Does the instroke aid in disambiguation of the p/bdq? Does the in stroke add extra similarities or reduce similarities perceived?
17/19	l	does the outstroke/tail help with recognition of letter and construction? (distribute separately)
20-23	l	does the outstroke/tail help with recognition of letter and construction?
24-27	l	does the outstroke/tail help the child identify the letter amongst other letters?
30-31	G	does the child find the simplified form easier to trace/identify?
32-35	A/k	does the child find the contrasted form easier to trace?
36-37	d	Handwriting Without Tears derived worksheet testing screen and hand tracing

FIGURES 12: Task Booklets: these guided the co-design activities and user testing sessions. Source: Mooney A., Martens, M. and Rinnert, G., 2017.

this, we assigned the children specific tasks and had them respond by using a child-friendly Likert scale.

The second part of the booklet allowed us to explore how manipulating a typographic variable such as contrast—the variation between the thick and thin parts of the letter and the distribution of weight along a curve—might be used as an indicator of stroke order within an individual character (Figure 12). We also explored how the scale of the presentation of a given letterform on screen and on paper affected the children's successful reproduction of letters (Figures 13 & 14) with reference to Montessori's three periods of procedure for the education of the senses: 1) recognition of identities; 2) recognition of contrasts and; 3) discrimination of objects very similar to each other. [44]

From a typographic perspective, the second part of this study examined the role of monolinearity and low contrast as a means to 'simplify' forms [°] in a Type Study (Figure 14). The insights gleaned from this last round

[°] *This reflected Edward Johnston's advocacy of utilizing the broad nib pen to teach children to construct the elemental strokes of letterforms and explored whether the weight distribution of strokes rendered by the broad nib pen might have helped children understand the importance of rendering strokes in a particular order, through the implied gesture it indicates, and without need for prompts.* Excerpted from Johnston, E. Writing & Illuminating, & Lettering, London, UK: John Hogg, 1917; pgs. 70–98.

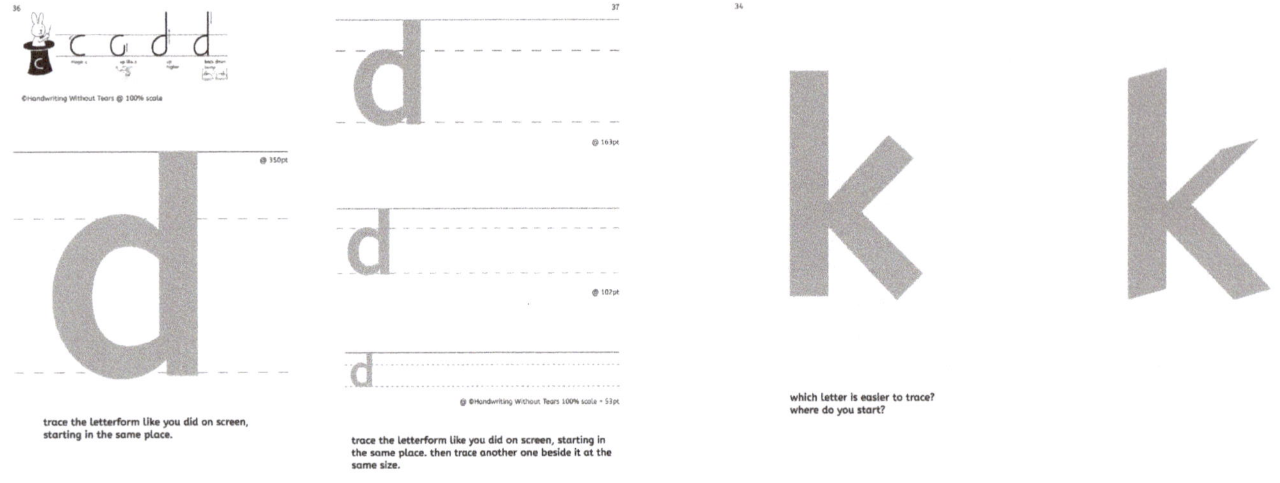

FIGURES 13: (Left) Testing the relevance of scale and screen/hardcopy on trace, *Energetic Alpha Task Booklet,* Type Study. Source: Mooney A., Martens, M. and Rinnert, G., 2017.
FIGURES 14: Testing role of contrast as an indicator of stroke order. Source: Mooney A., Martens, M. and Rinnert, G., 2017.

of testing revealed pathways for the development of interactive apps as a tool for research.

Findings

Assessment: Co-Design Session I, April 30th 2016

The first user study testing session with an early iteration of the app included 10 participants ranging between 4- and 10-years-old. Preliterate and preschool aged children between the ages of 3-6 are the target age range of the app. Children aged 7-11 were recruited to serve as "co-designers" because we expected this group to provide more concrete feedback and reflection. We watched the children interact with the interface, alphabet, and animations on the screen; we photographed and recorded video; and we interviewed our participants and their guardians to gain insights into the children's experiences with digital technology and using *Energetic Alpha* (Figure 15).

Our initial user testing session yielded two key findings. We observed that the younger children, those aged between 4- and 6-years-old had difficulty both tracing and identifying letters with serifs. They tended to see the forms as abstract and unrelated to the letters they knew. Despite our efforts to add design elements to serif letterforms that we thought might help their recognition processes, we learned that we needed to choose less formally complex

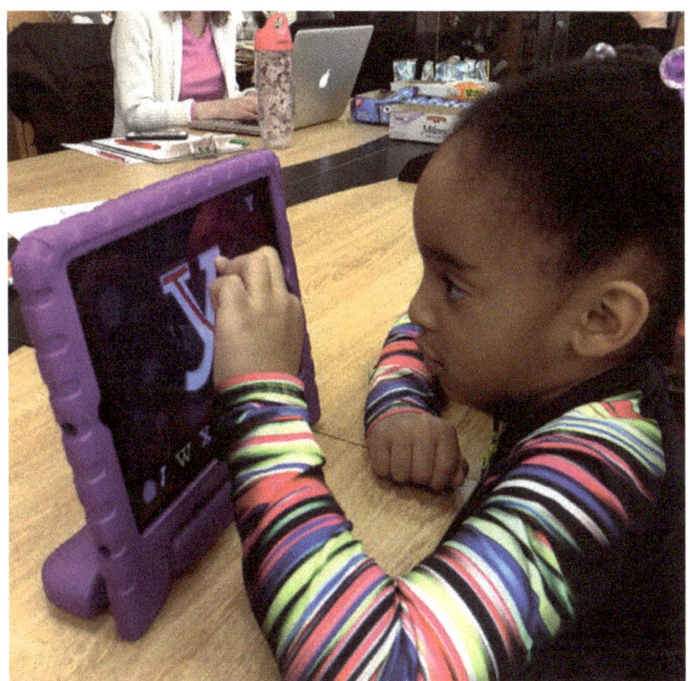

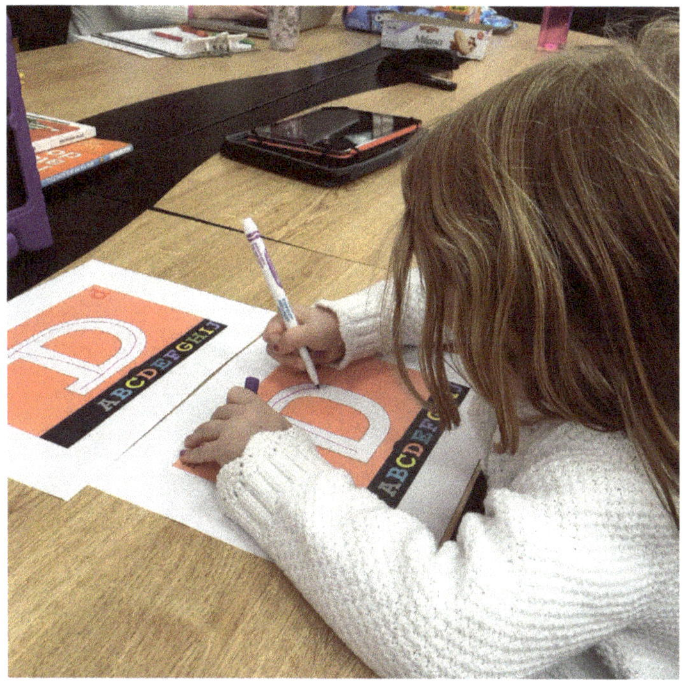

FIGURES 15: User Testing Documentation showing children tracing over early iterations using *BioRhyme* on an *iPad* and on paper (left) and tracing over different typefaces (right). Source: Rinnert, G. 2016.

typefaces. One boy was shown two letters (one with serifs and one without) and was asked if they were the same letter. He replied, "no" and explained, "this one has lumpies on the top and standees on the bottom." When asked which one was in his name, he indicated the sans serif letter but not the serif form of the same letter, which he did not recognize.[45] Based on children's initial feedback, we learned that, as a slab typeface, *BioRhyme* was confusing to the children of our study. Our attempt to employ a slab serif in conjunction with a trace feature to reflect the relationship between typographic and manual forms was embedding too many complexities in the task of tracing and was inappropriate for 3- to 6-year-old children learning to write.

Working with the children to test various aspects of *Energetic Alpha's* functionalities revealed a second key finding. We learned that its trace function was overly sensitive, which made unlocking animations extremely difficult for our child users. This led to us lowering the haptic tolerance levels that facilitated this function (failing to do this would have caused the children's general interest levels to wane). Finally, we identified the need for letter writing feedback. When children wrote a letter in the wrong order or incorrectly, they needed an immediate response from the system to help them self-correct. In

45 Andersen, C. "Energetic Alpha Field Notes." April 30, 2016.

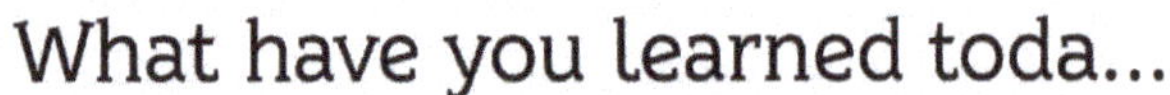

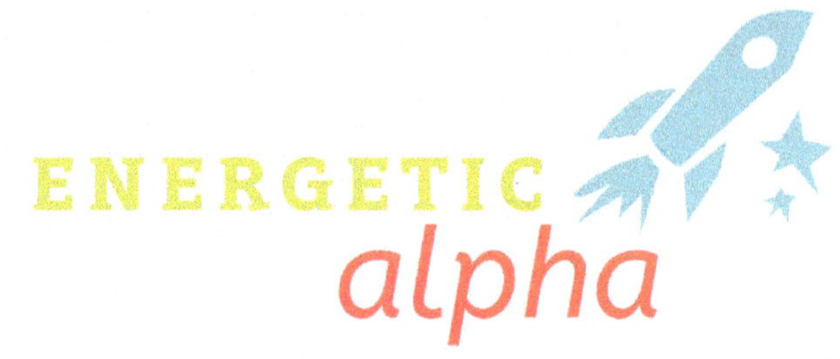

FIGURES 16: *AbeZeh Slab Weights:* https://bboxtype.com/typefaces/ABeZeh/#!layout=editor (accessed March 8, 2018).
FIGURES 17: *Energetic Alpha* Logo Source: Mooney A. and Rinnert, G. 2016.

response, we created animated trace hints that act as prompts to help a child get started, initiate engagement, and self-correct writing errors.

In our study, a typeface was used to guide handwriting practice and the relationship between the two types of letterforms (typographic and handwritten) had to be a close one. For a letterform to be the skeleton, or *frame,* to effectively facilitate handwriting practice, we determined that had to find a typeface that closely aligned with the 'print' [P] or 'manuscript' convention taught in schools. We envisioned that allowing the app to foster this practice would allow children to see the connection between the two different (but related) forms.

Selecting a new typeface family for use across the interface design of Energetic Alpha

To better implement the trace function of the app and incorporate feedback from the first user testing session, the authors and co-creators decided to implement Anja Meiner's *AbeZeh* typeface family (Figure 16) across the interface prior to facilitating the second user testing session.

This typeface, which is described as 'the friendly learning typeface family,' [46] was designed "to cross the rather unexplored typographical area of children's and school books." [47] In choosing *AbeZeh,* we implemented a typeface choice that aligned more closely to the 'print'? [q] or 'manuscript' convention taught in schools in the U.S. without leaving the realm of typographic form altogether (we did this to retain the focus on the relationship between typographic and the manual letterforms). The design features of *AbeZeh* fused

[P] *In an article she published in 2007 and in a book she published in 2013 (see below), Professor Sue Walker of the Department of Typography and Graphic Communication at University of Reading discusses the origins of the teaching of 'print' or 'manuscript' handwriting in the UK and attributes the origins of this approach to calligrapher and type designer, Edward Johnston. Johnston looked to the Roman form of the letters as a guide to teaching handwriting and the teaching of simplified, essential forms, broken down into strokes. This idea was adopted by the teaching profession in the early 20th century and many teachers created their own versions of this simplified 'print' script.* Walker, S. "Letterforms for Handwriting and Reading: Print Script and Sans Serifs in Early Twentieth-century England." Typography Papers, 7 (2007): pgs. 81–114. Walker, S. Book Design for Children's Reading–Typography, Pictures, Print. London, UK: St. Bride Foundation, 2013.

46 Meiners, A. 'AbeZeh'. Online. Available at: https://carrois.com/typefaces/AbeZeh/#!layout=specimen (Accessed March 5, 2018)

atmosphere and convention effectively to meet our goals, as it includes a slab serif counterpart (Figure 16) and an icon set, which allowed us to expand our options for the design of the *Energetic Alpha* interface. This was something that was important to us in creating and an integrated visual language to function as an immersive environment (Figure 17).

From this typeface, we derived a set of forms to guide hand tracing based on our research and reflections about the relationship between the typographic and manual forms. We reversed our research approach from that of observing the child's interaction with typographic letterforms to the speculative design of traceable 'manual'-looking letterforms, which we could test with the children using the app. Ultimately, this was a much more successful approach. In adapting the typeface for our 'scribable' purposes, the relationship between manual and typographic letterforms became clear.

After licensing the weights required, we contacted the designer, Anja Meiners, for advice and for her permission to alter some of the forms. We wanted to allow for the possibility of removing or attaching in-strokes and out-strokes to some of the letterforms to: 1) test the impact of these visual cues on shape recognition and traceability; 2) be able to customize letterforms for testing purposes; and 3) create an altered version of the typeface that could be overlaid on top of the standard forms in our design to indicate the skeleton structure of each letterform, which is what we called a 'trace-weight' of the typeface (Figure 20).

The 'trace-weight' design is based on the lightest existing weight of the *AbeZeh* typeface, which was altered to lay over the heavier weight of the typeface within the app interface. The use of the trace-weight ultimately appears in the "animation hint" (Figure 19). As a child uses the app, a red pulsing dot on each letterform shows the child where to start. When the child encounters a letter they cannot write, they can select the "help button," which is identified by a question mark at the bottom right hand corner of the screen. This button triggers an animation that plays over the top letter shape and includes two components: first, a graphic of a child's hand moving in the proper stroke order, and then (and underneath) the trace weight of the letter fading in one stroke at a time. When the animation ends, the child can replicate the hint animation or play it again if more assistance is needed. If the child pauses on a screen without action, this also triggers the animation hint. This strategy allows the child to be independent in their play and capable of self-correction when encountering handwriting errors. The trace-weight functions as a

47 bBox Type Foundry. 'AbeZeh Type Specimen'. Online. Available at: https://bboxtype.com/typefaces/ABeZeh/#!layout=specimen. (Accessed March 12, 2018).

q *In an article she published in 2007 and in a book she published in 2013 (see below), Professor Sue Walker of the Department of Typography and Graphic Communication at University of Reading discusses the origins of the teaching of 'print' or 'manuscript' handwriting in the UK and attributes the origins of this approach to calligrapher and type designer, Edward Johnston. Johnston looked to the Roman form of the letters as a guide to teaching handwriting and the teaching of simplified, essential forms, broken down into strokes. This idea was adopted by the teaching profession in the early 20th century and many teachers created their own versions of this simplified 'print' script.* Walker, S. "Letterforms for Handwriting and Reading: Print Script and Sans Serifs in Early Twentieth-century England." Typography Papers, 7 (2007): pgs. 81–114. Walker, S. Book Design for Children's Reading—Typography, Pictures, Print. London, UK: St. Bride Foundation, 2013.

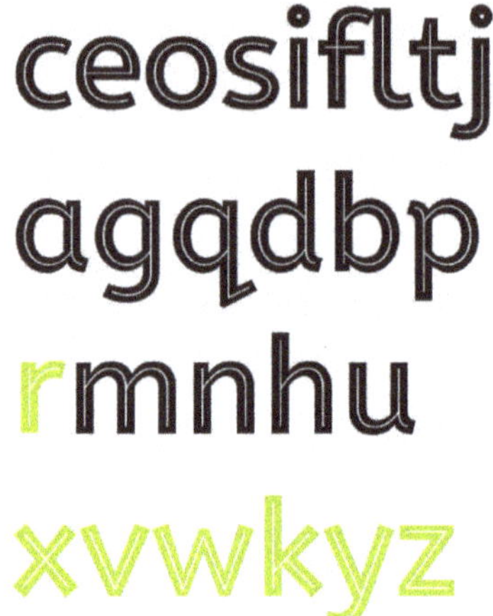

FIGURE 18: Alterations to weights of Abezeh to provide 'trace-weight' letterforms (where the lightest weight would sit on top of the heavier weight with adaptations to the shapes to make them center in the strokes and mimic the stroke behaviors of the hand) and in- and out-strokes on both weights. Source: Mooney, A. 2016.

skeleton letterform that visually represents the perfect letter mark (Figure 20) and provides a guide for the child user to mimic. The stroke order prompts we used are based on the combined approaches of the *Handwriting Without Tears*[48] and *Zaner-Bloser*[49] stroke order guides. This shows the child where to start each letterform and how many strokes were required (Figure 20).

Assessment: Co-Design Session II, February 17, 2017

In February 2017, after incorporating feedback from the initial study into the full prototype featuring a new typeface and updated interactivity, we tested *Energetic Alpha* with 13 participants between the ages of 5- and 11-years-old. The testing sessions lasted 30 to 40 minutes, and all were conducted with a guardian present as per our university's Institutional Review Board mandates. In the first part, the children provided concrete feedback on: 1) whether the interface was functioning properly, i.e., if they were able to navigate through the interface without getting stuck; and 2) were they able to complete a full navigation loop by reproducing the letterforms and subsequently getting the reward of unlocking videos.

In the second part of the study, children were tasked with sketching their ideal rewards on storyboards. In the third part, we tested sounds with the

48 Author(s) unknown. Handwriting Without Tears K-5. "Research Review." Online. Available at: https://www.lwtears.com/files/HWT%20Research%20Review.pdf (Accessed March 5, 2018).

49 Authors(s) unknown. "Pre-kindergarten Handwriting." Zaner-Bloser website. Online. Available at: https://www.zaner-bloser.com/products/index.php?product=handwriting (Accessed March 5, 2018).

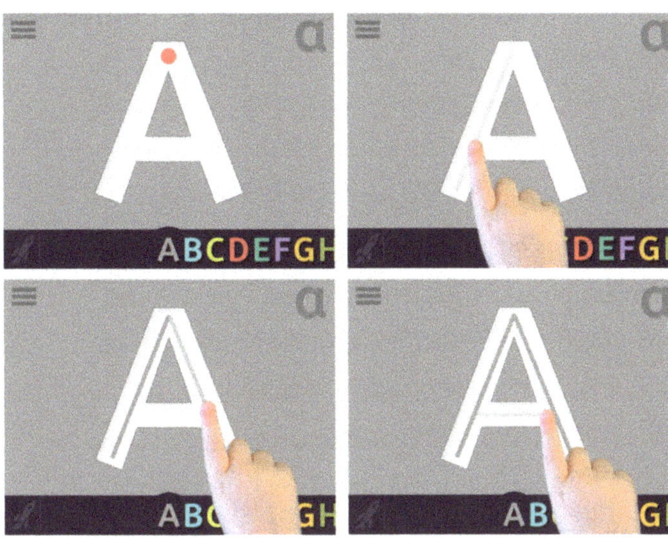

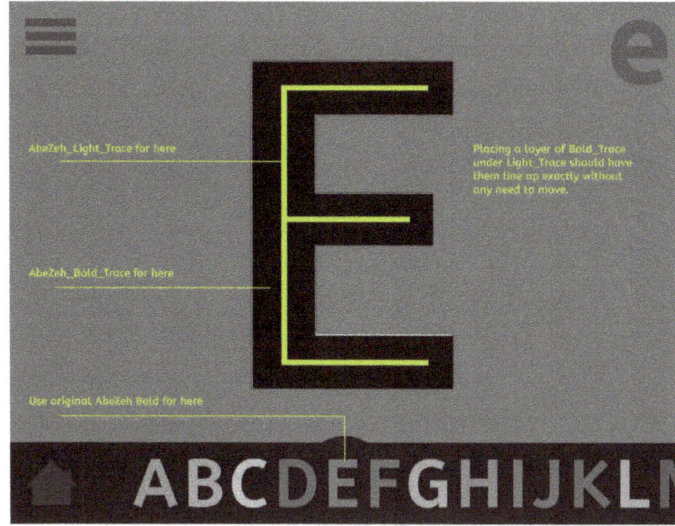

FIGURES 19: Animation stills from the trace hint sequence that shows proper stroke order for the letter "A," 2018.Source: Rinnert, G. 2018.
FIGURES 20: Trace adaptations when interfacing with instructions for use in design and development. These images were created as a guide for *Energetic Alpha's* iOS developer. Source: Mooney, A. 2016.

children and got feedback on which sounds they found appealing and which ones were annoying. In the final activity, the children compared animations to see if they preferred a specific style (vector/stop-motion/time lapse)—or if there was one they did not like. Overall, the children were receptive to and engaged with all of the activities.

We received concrete feedback that our new and revised typeface functioned well in the interface. Children recognized the letters and confusion was eliminated. The decision to add both trace hint animations and visual cues (for example, a glowing red dot that indicated where children were to begin) helped them use the app in the way it was intended.

In this second user study, participants gave us positive feedback on improvements to the interface and the new typeface. In our *Task Booklet's Type Study* section, we gathered information about the impact of using typefaces that exhibit more contrast between the thick and thin parts of the letters and their effect on the child's ability to recognize and trace a given letter, which we will explore in future research. Initial findings from our small study suggest that using contrast could help children more easily recognize the way the shape is constructed and thus make writing more accessible. This runs counter to the general trend in typeface design for children, which has produced primarily low-contrast sans serif typefaces.

Limitations and Future Research

Once we were entrenched in the full development process, our team had to deal with technology from a critical design perspective as well as from a product-development position. Not all of our big goals were possible. We sought to rigorously follow Haines' rubric [50] for quality app design, but one particular criteria could not be met with our app's goals (i.e., structure) and the current iOS development recommendations that state that apps should be under 4 GB in size. [51] Haines recommends that apps be "free of links to social media and the internet." [52] *Energetic Alpha* contains 26 animations that are between 10 seconds and 3 minutes in length. To comply with iOS guidelines, we designed the app to work with Internet videos that download on an as-needed basis. The app can function without Internet connectivity, but to have the full app experience it works best connected to the Internet. Finally, the study should be repeated with the finished app.

Conclusions

In developing *Energetic Alpha*, the authors set out to investigate the possibilities for enhancing letter-writing practice in a digital environment by creating a game-based learning tool in which a child traces directly over a letterform on an iPad screen to unlock an animated reward. Data we collected from our child co-designers in interviews and task booklets as described herein allowed us to reflect on: 1) the possibilities of the screen as an interactive learning tool for teaching handwriting; 2) the relationship between typography and handwriting, and in particular, its potential to highlight a means for typography to more closely align with or support pedagogical strategies that improve handwriting; 3) the potential for type designers to create forms specifically for use in the context of the kind of direct interaction found in the trace function in *Energetic Alpha*; and finally, 4) it demonstrated the success of the animations to encourage a young audience to playfully engage with letter-writing practice.

In developing *Energetic Alpha*, we investigated how a game-based learning tool could engage children with meaningful play in which children are excited and motivated to play with an app that serves as a pedagogical tool to increase their familiarity with the alphabet and handwriting. In the process, we collected input from children, teachers, and parents, and observed children using the app to trace letters and enjoying the animated rewards from their work.

The app supports preliterate learners by providing a context that allows them to directly correlate given letterforms to their typographical

50 Claudia Haines, Evaluating Apps and New Media for Young Children: A Rubric, (2015). Available at https://nevershushed.files.wordpress.com/2015/01/evaluatingappsandnewmediaforyoungchildrenarubric1.pdf. (Accessed February 27, 2018).

51 Apple Help Library, help.apple.com/itunes-connect/developer/#/dev611e0a21f. (Accessed March 6, 2018)

52 Claudia Haines, Evaluating Apps and New Media for Young Children: A Rubric, (2015). Available at https://nevershushed.files.wordpress.com/2015/01/evaluatingappsandnewmediaforyoungchildrenarubric1.pdf. (Accessed February 28, 2018).

counterparts and extends this experience by augmenting it with sound and animation. In the heuristic and iterative processes that guided our development of this app, we observed the limitations of typographic letterforms to depict handwritten letterforms for use in the context of children learning to recognize the constituent parts of letters. This was particularly noticeable when children attempted to directly trace over them as a means to gain familiarity with their essential forms. In our secondary research, we examined letterforms and typographic systems designed for children in our age group, and this allowed us to reflect on the relative dearth of typefaces designed expressly for the purposes of teaching children to write as a distinct task from learning to read.

Our research questions allowed us to explore the potential for new media to support established pedagogical strategies like those espoused by Maria Montessori,[53] and highlighted the continued relevance and immediate possibilities for further typographic and psychological research in this area.

Based on our observations of the children interacting with *Energetic Alpha*, and the feedback we received from our study participants, we believe that touch screens can serve as a tool for helping early writers practice handwriting. Our study demonstrated the capacity of digital media to support traditional methods of handwriting instruction, as well as to extend these methods. By using digital tools as an alternative approach to encouraging play and motivating learning, apps such as *Energetic Alpha* can facilitate interactions that are entirely led and paced by the child. In our user-centered design study, children had leadership roles as co-designers. Their feedback informed our decisions about typeface, sound and design within the app.

With this in mind, we believe that the disciplines of typography and typeface design have significant roles to play in the development of interactive tools for children engaging directly with letterforms as they learn to write. Expression, tone and context must be considered as judiciously for typography intended to be read and traced or mimicked by children as it is for reading-literate adults, and so far, the range of typefaces designed to facilitate children's digital writing and reading experiences does not reflect this. If not solely for the benefit of the child, typography that facilitates a wider visual range of expression and contexts can also provide more opportunities for creating learning tools and environments that are varied and expressive. In the United States, schools have used sans serif versions of teaching letterforms that do not incorporate in-strokes and out-strokes. Our research shows that while slab typefaces like *BioRhyme* were confusing to the young children of our study, in-strokes

53
Montessori, Dr. Montessori's Own Handbook, p. 26.

and out-strokes were helpful for the children to disambiguate letterforms from each other and also to find the starting point of a stroke. This confirms suggestions made by Rosemary Sassoon and evidenced in her Sassoon typeface family, included in the *A Brief Overview of Issues Related to Designing Typography for Children* section, above.

We intend to continue to refine and test *Energetic Alpha* by conducting larger studies with parents, librarians and media mentors, and children. Future research will expand upon questions opened by these initial inquiries and, in particular, might compare how learning to write in a purely manual environment (i.e., using conventional writing tools like pencils and paper) and learning to write in a digitally facilitated environment (like a touchscreen) changes students' learning processes.

References

Asher, Asha V. "Handwriting Instruction in Elementary Schools." *American Journal of Occupational Therapy,* 60 (2006): pgs. 461–471.

Asherson, S. B., "The Benefits of Cursive Go Beyond Writing," *The New York Times,* 30 April, 2013. Online. Available at: https://www.nytimes.com/roomfordebate/2013/04/30/should-schools-require-children-to-learn-cursive/the-benefits-of-cursive-go-beyond-writing (Accessed November 7, 2017).

Baudin, F. "Education in the Making and Shaping of Written Words." In *Computers and Typography,* edited by R. Sassoon, Oxford, UK: Intellect, 1993: pgs. 102–128.

Berninger, V., et al. "Early Development of Language by Hand: Composing, Reading, Listening, and Speaking Connections; Three Letter-Writing Modes; and Fast Mapping in Spelling." *Developmental Neuropsychology,* 21.1 (2006): pgs. 61–92.

Bessemans, A. "Legibility Research: Type Design for Children with Low Vision." *Typography. Guru,* 1 October, 2013. Online. Available at: https://typography.guru/journal/legibility-children/ (Accessed November 7, 2017).

Bessemans, A. "Matilda: A Research-Based Font for Improving Reading." Filmed 17 May 2013. TYPO Talks Berlin, 46:20. Online. Available at: https://www.typotalks.com/videos/

matilda-a-reasearch-based-font-for-improving-reading-2/ (Accessed November 7, 2017).

Carter, M. "Theories of Letterform Construction (Part 1)." *Printing History,* 13–14.1/2 (1991–1992): p. 1.

Chetty, K., Josle, J., Gcora, N., Aneja U., & Vidisha, M. "Bridging the Digital Divide: Skills for the New Age," *G20 Insights,* 13 October, 2017. Online. Available at: https:// http://www.g20-insights.org/policy_briefs/bridging-digital-divide-skills-new-age/ (Accessed April 19, 2018).

Chisholm, J. "What is Co-Design?," *Design for Europe,* 8 September 2016. Online. Available at: http://designforeurope.eu/what-co-design (Accessed April 28, 2018).

Dehaene, S. *Reading in the Brain.* London, UK: Penguin, 2010.

Deterding, S., Khaled, R., Nacke, L. E., & Dixon, D. "Gamification: Toward a Definition" in *Proceedings of the CHI Conference,* 7–12 May 2011, Vancouver, BC, Canada. Online. Available at: http://gamification-research.org/wp-content/uploads/2011/04/02-Deterding-Khaled-Nacke-Dixon.pdf (Accessed October 30, 2017).

Downton, P. *Design Research.* Melbourne, VIC, AU: RMIT University Press, 2003: p. 17.

Druin, A. "What Children Can Teach Us: Developing Digital Libraries for Children with Children." *The Library Quarterly,* 75.1 (2005): pgs. 20–41.

Entente, The. "Castledown Typeface." *Colophon Type Foundry.* 2014. Online. Available at: https://www.colophon-foundry.org/typefaces/castledown/ (Accessed July 24, 2017).

Fletcher, A. *Beware Wet Paint.* New York, NY, USA: Phaidon Press, 2004.

George, B., George, J. & Nassner, A. George. *Montessori LetterWork.* New York, NY, USA: Abrams Appleseed, 2012.

Graham, S. "Want to Improve Children's Writing? Don't Neglect Their Handwriting." *American Educator,* 76. 1 (Winter 2009-2010): pgs. 49–55, Online. Available at: http://www.aft.org/sites/default/files/periodicals/graham.pdf (Accessed November 7, 2017).

Graham, S., & Weintraub, N. "A Review of Handwriting Research: Progress and Prospects from 1980–1994." *Educational Psychology Review* 8.1 (1996): pgs. 7–87.

Haines, C. "Evaluating Apps and New Media for Young Children: A Rubric." *Never Shushed* (blog). 2016. Online. Available at: https://nevershushed.

files.wordpress.com/2015/01/evaluatingappsandnewmediaforyoungchildrenarubric1.pdf (Accessed November 7, 2017).

Haines, C. & Campbell, C. *Becoming a Media Mentor: A Guide for Working with Children and Families.* Chicago, IL, USA: The Association for Library Service to Children, a Division of the American Library Association, 2016.

Kress, G. R., & van Leeuwen, T. *Reading Images: The Grammar of Visual Design.* New York, NY, USA: Routledge, 1996.

Kysilko, D. "The Handwriting Debate." *National Association of the State Boards of Education Policy Update* 19.7 (September 2012). Online. Available at: https://www.hw21summit.com/media/zb/hw21/H2989_NASBE_PolicyUpdate_TheHandwritingDebate.pdf (Accessed November 7, 2017).

Learning Without Tears. "About Us." Online. Available at: https://www.lwtears.com/about-learning-without-tears (Accessed November 7, 2017).

McCloud, S. *Understanding Comics.* New York, NY, USA: William Morrow, 1994.

McLuhan, M. *The Gutenberg Galaxy: The Making of Typographic Man.* Toronto, ON, CA: University of Toronto Press, 2011.

Meiners, A. "AbeZeh Specimen." *Carrois Apostrophe GbR.* 2016. Online. Available at: https://carrois.com/typefaces/ABeZeh/#!layout=specimen (Accessed November 7, 2017).

Meiners, A. "About." *Carrois Apostrophe GbR.* 2016. Online. Available at: https://carrois.com/about/AnjaMeiners (Accessed July 24, 2017).

Monotype, Fonts.com. "Gill Sans Infant." Online. Available at: https://www.fonts.com/font/monotype/gill-sans/infant. (Accessed July 24, 2017).

Montessori, M. Dr. *Montessori's Own Handbook.* New York, NY, USA: Schoeken Books, Inc., 1965.

Mobile Montessori. Online. Available at: http://www.mobilemontessori.org/ (Accessed July 24, 2017).

Montessorium. Online. Available at: https://montessorium.com/ (Accessed July 24, 2017).

Must, M. "Schools Will Start Teaching Typing Instead of Longhand." *Helsinki Times.* 20 November 2014. Online. Available at http://www.helsinkitimes.fi/finland/finland-news/domestic/12767-schools-will-start-teaching-typing-instead-of-longhand-2.html (Accessed July 24, 2017).

Nicholson, S. "A user-centered theoretical framework for meaningful gamification." *Paper presented at Games+Learning+Society* 8.0, Madison, WI (2012). Online. Available at: http://becauseplaymatters.com/pubs/

(Accessed October 30, 2017).

Noordzij, G. *The Stroke Theory of Writing.* Translated by Peter Enneson. London, UK: Hyphen, 2005.

Petzold, D. "Heinemann Special Fonts Collection." *We and the Color.* Released by MyFonts 2008. Online. Available at: http://weandthecolor.com/heinemann-special-fonts-colection/29643 (Accessed July 24, 2017).

Richardson, S. O. "The Montessori Preschool: Preparation for Writing and Reading." *Annals of Dyslexia* 47 (1997): pgs. 241-256. Online. Available at: http://www.jstor.org/stable/23768103 (Accessed July 24, 2017).

Rinnert, G., Mooney, A. & Martens, M. "Energetic Alpha: A Design Continuum Created Through Collaboration." In *The Theory and Practice of Motion Design: Critical Perspectives and Professional Practice,* edited by Brian Stone and Leah Wahlin. NY, NY, USA: Routledge, an imprint of the Taylor Francis Group. Expected publication date: Summer/Fall 2018.

Sanders, E. "Co-creation and the new landscapes of design." *CoDesign: International Journal of CoCreation in Design and the Arts* 4.1 (2008): pgs. 5–18.

Salen, K. & Zimmerman, E. *Rules of Play: Game Design Fundamentals.* Cambridge, MA: MIT Press, 2004.

Saperstein Associates. "Handwriting in the 21st Century? Research Shows Why Handwriting Belongs in Today's Classroom." Summary of research presented at Handwriting in the 21st Century? An Educational Summit. Columbus, OH, USA: Sapersten Associates. 2012. Online. Available at: www.hw21summit.com/media/zb/hw21/H2948_HW_Summit_White_Paper_eVersion.pdf (Accessed July 24, 2017).

Sassoon, R., ed. "Through the Eyes of a Child—Perception and Type Design." In *Computers and Typography,* edited by R. Sassoon. Oxford, UK: Intellect, 1993.

Sassoon, R. & Williams, A. "Why Sassoon?" Last modified 2015. Online. Available at: http://www.sassoonfont.co.uk/fonts/sas/WhySassoon1.3.pdf (Accessed July 24, 2017).

Shen, J. "Typography and Graphic Design." *Juliet Shen* (blog). Last modified 2017. Online. Available at: http://www.julietshen.com/typography-and-graphic-design (Accessed July 24, 2017).

Shapiro, T. R., "Cursive handwriting is disappearing from public schools." *Washington Post.* Online. Available at: https://www.washingtonpost.com/local/education/cursive-handwriting-disappearing-from-public-schools/2013/04/04/215862e0-7d23-11e2-a044-676856536b40_story.

html?utm_term=.3ed9342e706b (Accessed November 7, 2017).

Sousanis, N. *Unflattening.* Cambridge, MA, USA: Harvard University Press, 2015.

Spear-Swerling, L. "The Importance of Teaching Handwriting." *Reading Rockets.* 2006. Online. Available at: http://www.readingrockets.org/article/importance-teaching-handwriting (Accessed July 24, 2017).

Steven, R. "Colophon Releases Castledown Type Family." *Creative Review.* 26 March 2014. Online. Available at: https://www.creativereview.co.uk/colophon-releases-castledown-type-family/ (Accessed July 24, 2017).

Striver, I. "Typography for Children." *Monotype.* Online. Available at: https://www.fonts.com/content/learning/fyti/situational-typography/typography-for-children (Accessed July 24, 2017).

Tekinbas, K. S. "Getting in the Game." In *Mindshift Guide to Digital Games and Learning,* edited by J. Shapiro, p. 9. New York, NY: The Joan Ganz Cooney Center, 2014. Available at: https://a.s.kqed.net/pdf/news/MindShift-GuidetoDigitalGamesandLearning.pdf (Accessed October 30, 2017).

Trubek, A. (2016, August 20). "Opinion | Handwriting Just Doesn't Matter." *The New York Times.* Available at: https://www.nytimes.com/2016/08/21/opinion/handwriting-just-doesnt-matter.html (Accessed October 26, 2017).

Twinkl Font. Online. Available at: http://www.twinkl.com/twinkl-font (Accessed July 24, 2017).

Ujifusa, A. "Resistance to the Common Core Mounts." *Education Week.* 21 April 2014. Online. Available at: http://www.drmichelson.org/web_documents/resistance_to_the_common_core_mounts_-_education_week.pdf (Accessed July 24, 2017).

Walker, S, & Reynolds, L. "Serifs, Sans Serifs and Infant Characters in Children's Reading Books." *Information Design Journal+Document Design* 11.2-3 (2003): pgs. 106–122.

Walker, S. "Letterforms for Handwriting and Reading: Print Script and Sans Serifs in Early Twentieth-century England." *Typography Papers,* 7 (2007): pgs. 81–114.

Walker, S. *Book Design for Children's Reading—Typography, Pictures, Print.* London, UK: St. Bride Foundation, 2013.

Wolf, M. *Proust and the Squid.* New York, NY, USA: Harper, 2008.

Zaner-Bloser. Authors(s) unknown. "Pre-kindergarten Handwriting." *Zaner-Bloser* website. Online. Available at: https://www.zaner-bloser.com/

products/index.php?product=handwriting (Accessed March 5, 2018).
Zapf, H. *About Alphabets: Some Marginal Notes on Type Design.* Cambridge, MA, USA: MIT Press, 1970.

Biographies

Aoife Mooney is an Assistant Professor in the School of Visual Communication Design at Kent State University in Kent, Ohio, USA, where she teaches classes in Typography, Graphic Design, Identity and Typeface Design. She holds an MA in Typeface Design from the University of Reading (UK), and is a practicing typeface designer, having previously worked in-house for Hoefler & Co. and as a freelance designer with Frere-Jones Type and Google. Her research interests are centered around critically examining the practice and theory of this discipline, including the broader cultural contexts and implications of typeface design and its relationship to other design disciplines. She is a member of the International Society of Typographic Designers, and is the North American Coordinator for their annual Student Assessment Scheme. (*amooney2@kent.edu*)

Marianne Martens is Assistant Professor at Kent State University's School of Information in Kent, Ohio, USA, where she teaches classes including Materials and Services for the School Age Child, Youth Literature in the Digital Realm, Art and Story: The Study of Picturebook Art, and International Children's Literature and Librarianship. Her interdisciplinary research, grounded in Library & Information Science and Media Studies, converges at the intersection of books and technology in new literary formats--from picture book apps to multiplatform books. Martens has an extensive background in children's publishing, has translated over 100 picture books into English, is co-chair of the Association for Library Service to Children's Task Force on Evolving the Carnegie Award, a member of ALSC's Children and Technology Committee, and serves on the Littlelit Advisory Board. You can read more about her work at mariannemartens.org. (*mmarten3@kent.edu*)

Gretchen Rinnert is an Associate Professor in the School of Visual Communication Design at Kent State University in Kent, Ohio, USA. She teaches interactive media and motion design. She is a graduate of North Carolina State

University's College of Design. As a researcher, her work focuses on the intersection of design and education, classroom participation, and tools that aid in understanding and comprehension. She continues to research participatory culture by investigating learning spaces, digital tools, online video, and time-based media. You can visit her portfolio at www.flyingtype.com. *(grinnert@kent.edu)*

The typographic structure of *Dialectic* employs typefaces from four different families: Fira (Sans and Mono), Freight, Idealista, and Noe Display.

Fira Sans was introduced in 2013 as Feura Sans, and was designed by Erik Spiekermann, Ralph du Carrois, Anja Meiners and Botio Nik-toltchev of Carrois Type Design. Fira Sans and Fira Mono (the latter was designed as a monospaced variant of the former) are based on Speikermann's typeface designs for the FF Meta family of typefaces, which originated in the 1980s. Fira is classified as a humanist, sans-serif typeface family.

The Freight family of typefaces—"Big," "Display," "Sans," and "Text—was designed by Joshua Darden in the early 2000s and is comprised of over 100 styles. The Freight families are currently licensed through Darden Studio, and, with the exception of the "Sans" variants, may be classified as a display, serif typefaces.

The Idealista family was designed by Tomáš Brousil and released in 2010. It is comprised of ten style variations and five weights. It may be classified as a geometric, sans serif typeface, and is available from MyFonts.com.

The Noe Display family was designed by Lauri Toikka in 2013 and is available through the Schick Toikka digital foundry. It is comprised of four Roman and four italic variants, ranging in weight from "regular" to "black." It may be classified as a display serif typeface, and shares some formal characteristics (sharp, angled serifs, high contrast between thick and thin strokes) with the Noe Text family.

www.ingramcontent.com/pod-product-compliance
Lightning Source LLC
Chambersburg PA
CBHW041133280526
45792CB00014B/2409
* 9 7 8 1 6 0 7 8 5 5 1 0 1 *